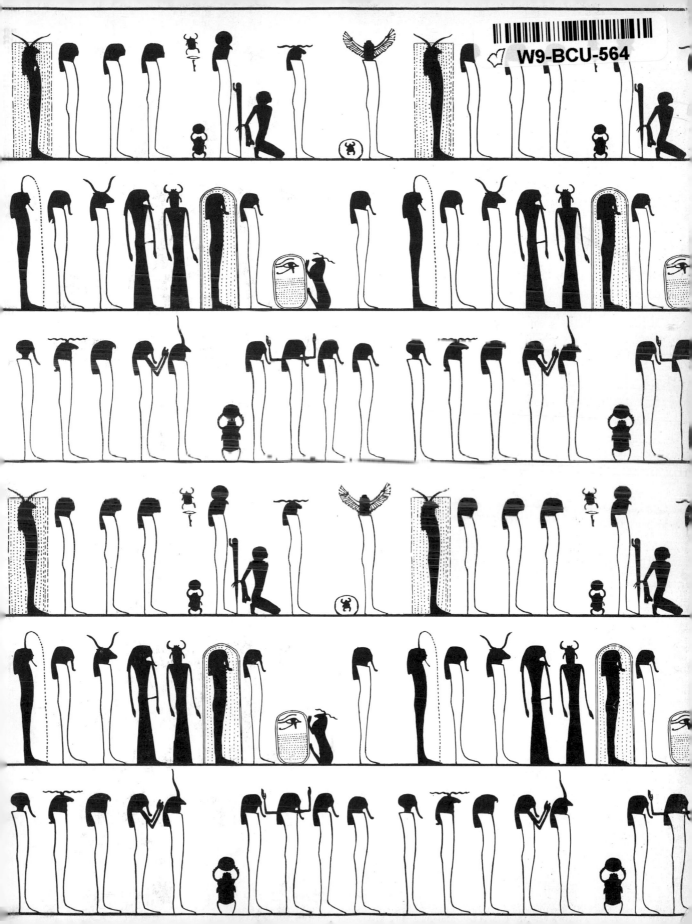

VALLEY OF THE KINGS

The sultan had a slave who was called 'Umdat al-daula', and this slave was the Amir of the Mutalibis and extremely rich and wealthy. Mutalibi is what they call those who search for treasures and buried hoards in the pits of Egypt. People come from all the West and the lands of Egypt and Syria, and each of them toils hard and spends much money in the pits and stony places of Egypt. To many it has happened that they have found hoards and treasures, and many have incurred expenses and found nothing. For they say that the wealth of Pharaoh is buried in these places.

Nasir Khusrau, *Safarnama*, 441 AH
(A.D. 1049–50)

To have seen the Tombs of Thebes is to have seen the Egyptians as they lived and moved before the eyes of Moses—is to have seen the utmost display of funereal grandeur which has ever possessed the human mind. To have seen the royal tombs is more than this—it is to have seen the whole religion of Egypt unfolded as it appeared to the greatest powers of Egypt, at the most solemn moments of their lives.

Dean Stanley, *Sinai and Palestine*, 1856

VALLEY
OF THE
KINGS

JOHN ROMER

HENRY HOLT AND COMPANY
NEW YORK

Library of Congress Catalog Card Number: 88-45752
ISBN 0-8050-0993-0

Henry Holt books are available at special discounts
for bulk purchases for sales promotions, premiums,
fund raising, or educational use. Special editions
or book excerpts can also be created to specification.

 For details contact:

 Special Sales Director
 Henry Holt and Company, Inc.
 115 West 18th Street
 New York, New York   10011

Designed by Trevor Vincent
Printed in Portugal
10 9 8 7 6 5 4 3 2 1

Contents

List of Color Plates

Preface

Valley of the Kings contains two interlinked stories: the first is the history of the travellers and scholars who studied and excavated the royal tombs of the Valley; the second is that of the tombs themselves and the motives and methods of the people who made them. It is a continuous narrative from ancient times until the present day, a narrative that moves at different speeds through successive phases of the Valley's history.

The principals in this drama were an unusual mixture of men, most of whom were as sure of their history and expertise as they were physically tough enough to withstand the rigours of desert life and excavation. For some it was a job of work – a part of the service that their Empires demanded of its sons; for others it became a lifelong fascination. Their work in the Valley resulted in a dazzling succession of discoveries that uncovered the tombs of almost the entire line of kings of the Egyptian New Kingdom period. In the heyday of those excavations, before World War I, at least one royal tomb was discovered every year.

My own interest in the Valley began in 1966 when, as a student fresh from the Royal College of Art in London, I worked on an expedition, drawing the great wall reliefs and paintings in the temples and tombs of ancient Thebes. The Valley and its huge tombs appealed to me from my first visit. Several people who have worked at the site have remarked that there is something very particular in the air of the place: it is as if the rock-bound tombs radiate a strong presence of an incomprehensible and distant past. While I worked in the royal tombs I began to notice the tell-tale signs of slow deterioration in them, and I became aware of the ominous and constant threat of severe damage or even total destruction that is posed by the threat of flooding and associated rock slides in the Valley. With one or two exceptions tombs of the Valley are little known, either by specialists or by the general public. During the past fifty years one third of them have been reburied in the loose debris of the Valley floor, six royal tombs require major excavation to free them from flood debris, and ten

more require major restoration and protective installations.

In 1977, with public interest in Egypt high, and the travelling exhibition of treasures from Tutankhamen's tomb spotlighting the Valley of the Kings, I resigned from my regular archeological work to establish an expedition that would be concerned exclusively with the documentation and conservation of the royal tombs of Thebes. During its first two years, detailed studies of the geology and hydrology of the Valley were made along with aspects of site planning that are essential for the better protection and exhibition of the tombs in this era of mass tourism. Archeological work began inside the tomb of Rameses XI – the last royal tomb to have been excavated in the Valley. Apart from some fine restoration by the Egyptian Antiquities Service in its upper sections, this tomb had been completely neglected since ancient times. In 1979, with the help of a group of friends, the Theban Foundation was established in Berkeley, California with the aim of continuing this programme, which until that time had been conducted under the auspices of The Brooklyn Museum and financed by the Coca-Cola Company of Atlanta, Georgia.

Virtually the entire history of the Valley and its exploration is contained in this book; very few accounts of the early travellers have been omitted and those only when they had nothing original to say. All the records of the archeologists known to have worked in the Valley have been consulted – a process that has entailed a search through personal papers, diaries, annotated publications and even the gleaning of information from fragmentary maps and photographs excavated by our expedition from the ruins of the Valley's old expedition house.

However, like most history books, *Valley of the Kings* stands heavily upon the shoulders of its predecessors. One work in particular, *The Royal Necropoleis of Thebes* by Elizabeth Thomas, not only introduced me to the intricacies of Valley scholarship but has remained an indispensable guide and bibliography in all my subsequent researches. Miss Thomas has long encouraged those interested in the archeology of the Valley, a subject which she virtually invented, and I hope that she will enjoy this book and find new things to interest her in its pages. Over the years, some of the manuscripts of Valley archeologists have become valuable companions in my work, and Miss Helen Murray and Miss Fiona Strachan of the Griffith Institute at the Ashmolean Museum, Oxford have allowed me continual access to those that are in their charge. Their particular help in the preparation of many of the illustrations is greatly appreciated.

It took me several years to write this book, and for taking care of that which I should have done, yet left undone, during much of that time, I am especially grateful to: my Berkeley friends, Linda Rhodes and Sarita Waite, who attended to the bulk of the paperwork of the Foundation; to Louis and Norah Romer, my parents, who helped me in innumerable ways; and to Caradoc King, literary agent, whose criticisms and advice are those of a good friend. Without the aid of Beth Romer, my wife, this book, quite simply, could not have been finished. She has argued over the text, typed the manuscript, sketched the maps and plans, translated texts and corrected proofs – often while living out of a suitcase in three different continents.

The production of this book was a stimulating experience and its appearance is the result of many expert hands; Trevor Vincent, designer; Constance and Brian Dear, who drew the maps and plans for publication: Derrick Witty, who photographed many of the books and documents that illustrate the text, and my endlessly patient and careful editor, Peter Coxhead.

The dates of the reigns of the ancient kings were taken from the tables of the second edition of the *Cambridge Ancient History*, and ancient political history was drawn largely from sources listed in the Select Bibliography. I have deliberately refrained from discussing some of the unresolved problems of New Kingdom chronology although the Valley and its tombs certainly contain much unknown or unrecognized material that will help to resolve some of these dilemmas in the future. I have attempted to render ancient names in a straightforward manner; nothing but confusion would be served by adopting some of the variants recently suggested which, in many cases, are still the subjects of dispute. It is in this context that I have spelt the name of Tutankhamen in the manner adopted by the discoverer of the tomb. Valley scholars may notice that some of the epigraphers who have worked in the Valley during the last sixty years, such as Paul Bucher and Félix Guilmant, have not been included. This is because their work was not archeological nor did it add anything to the sum of the main story of this book. Neither have I included pictures of the celebrated objects from Tutankhamen's tomb; so much material of equal interest remains unknown and even unpublished, and it is on this that I have concentrated.

The term 'Valley' that is used throughout the book describes the central (eastern) branch of the Valley of the Kings. Short passages of translation that appear in the text are from the publications of Černý, Gardiner and Piankoff – their exact sources may be found in the Select Bibliography. With one exception, all the plans have been drawn in the same scale but they should not be regarded as archeologically accurate – they were compiled from a combination of earlier surveys and my own observations. The entrance to the tombs is usually by means of a staircase; the royal sarcophagus, typically at the deepest point in the tomb, is indicated in the plans by a black rectangle.

JOHN ROMER
Aiola, Tuscany

Part I

THE ANCIENT SETTING

1

Egyptian Landscape

Inevitably, there is no better way to start a description of a part of Egypt than to begin with its relationship to the River Nile. For, without the Nile Egypt could not exist; it has shaped the land, created the environment and made it habitable. In Egypt the river enters one's sensibilities, becomes the point of reference for all things, it is the yardstick of the country, its beginning and its end.

Running north from Ethiopia, the Nile cuts the North African Desert in two. The Western Desert runs towards Libya and the Sahara, the Eastern across ranges of mountains until it sweeps down to the Red Sea coastline. Ancient Egypt's southern border at Aswan was determined by the huge granite outcrops that the river passed over at that point before entering its final phase, as it runs slow and wide through the majestic valley of Upper Egypt. Just north of modern Cairo this valley ends and the river fans out into a huge deltaic region, a fertile equilateral triangle of flatlands composed of the black Ethiopian silt—a product of the melting snows of the Ethiopian mountains—which, over the millennia, the river has carried from its homeland and deposited during its annual flood. The delta is well cultivated, as are the lands along the river in Upper Egypt, from its Cairene apex to its Mediterranean baseline. Satellite photographs show the powerful water carrying the silt far into the salt waters of the sea. In Upper Egypt the Nile has made the land a sort of thin linear oasis of easily irrigated silt. The form of Egypt as an inhabitable country has always been shaped by the great river rather than by rulers, geographers or political treaties. Today the High Dam at Aswan has virtually levelled the river's height throughout the course of the year; the annual inundation of the land is no more; the sharpness of the effect of the river upon the land has been considerably blunted.

In Upper Egypt the Nile Valley is, typically, about five miles wide. The steep cliffs that limit it are not the great mountain ranges they appear, but the edges of the desert plateaux. The Nile Valley provides a calm and fertile environment, well sheltered from the strong desert winds. Its endlessly repeated natural

forms of river and cliff were, for the ancient Egyptian, the entire world. Outside the area of the riverside bands of fertile black silt, nothing grows; and without irrigation by means of canals and trenches, the crops die. There are no seasonal rains here, although sometimes unexpectedly, torrents of water from a flash flood, which has run across the dusty surface of the dry, high desert after a storm, will pour down into the Nile Valley cutting small subsidiary valleys with the force of its flow, destroying everything it touches.

Outside the valley of the Nile there is little but sand and rock, no greenery, sparse animal life. For the ancient Egyptians this desert was a region of great danger and complete emptiness, visited only for the wide variety of beautiful hard stones that could be quarried there, and for the occasional adventurous trip to a foreign land. For the ancient Egyptians, conditioned to the special environment of Egypt, all the world outside their homeland was chaotic and formless. The Nile Valley on the other hand, lay on the points of the compass; the river, governed by its high banks and the endless lines of cliffs beyond, flowed almost due north and the sun crossed it daily, rising behind one great screen of cliffs and setting behind another. Herodotus, a traveller and historian of the ancient Greek period, called Egypt 'The Temple of the World'. He too was affected by the country where the rhythms of nature are daily run from east to west with the sun and annually from south to north with the inundating river. These two events, both seen by the ancient Egyptians as examples of a mystical birth, a life-giving force, were dramatized and set into a theology—the stories concerning Horus, Lord of Heaven, and Osiris, who caused the crops to grow after the waters of the flood had covered the land. Both deities were identified in the person of the king. The physical world thus contained a cosmic order that was a clear geometric spiritual reality.

Journeying by boat or road through the Nile Valley is a strangely two dimensional experience in horizontal bands of colour; the blue river below the black bank, the green cultivation under ochre cliffs and the whole beneath a bright blue sky that burns the unwary and dazzles the walker. It is impossible to get lost in the Nile Valley—one may always look for the river and that sequence of colours and textures to be exactly orientated by them. All the places in this land are either up stream or down stream, north or south, journeying in other directions leads only to the desert, with the exception of some passes to the Red Sea or to a desert oasis. The sunlight in the Nile Valley is very clear and strong, shrinking all distance until the elements of the landscape stand one on top of another, making distance difficult to judge. The cliffs and buildings shimmer in the layers of hot air that build up around them as the stone heats in the sun. It is a very particular environment, one of profound beauty and incredible contrast. Crops that grow greener than the plants of other lands, or, at least, have their greenness more illuminated here than in foggier countries, grow next to warm soft lifeless sand. One may stand with one foot in green damp fertile silt and the other in the desert's preservative aridity, the driest place on earth, where the ancient Egyptians buried their dead.

Such a strongly defined environment obviously had a deep effect upon the ancient Egyptian architects and artists. When trapped in the cases of museums, the fragments of Egypt that are displayed there often look over-refined, obsessive in detail and lacking in an overall unity. But in Egypt, those same forms standing in the sun, or lit in the darkness of a tomb by the torch of a visitor, are perfectly suited; in that country it is the transplanted gothic forms of Cairene Anglicanism that crumble in the Egyptian sunlight. The amazing mixture of exuberant vegetation amid absolute desert sterility, the strong vertical lines of the cliffs and the horizontals of the cultivation allow only a particular architecture and design to be engendered, and the Egyptians evolved a style in both that was subtle in its employment of form and gentle with the landscape that held it. The ancient Egyptians recognized particular areas in their land which conformed to the requirements of their gods and the architects placed the monuments with a care that made the whole land sing. Like the purpose of the rituals in the temples that they designed, the architects joined heaven and earth and man to god by placing him in special relationship in the land and the sky. The ancient practice of siting buildings in alignment to particular stars, the study of which is still in its infancy in Egypt, is but one rather prosaic aspect of this. Visiting the sites of the towns and temples of ancient Egypt one continually meets different environments, new moods created by parti-

cular placements and differences of scale and design. It is always worthwhile to visit a fresh site in the Nile Valley, however destroyed or bereft of monuments it may be, simply to admire this exquisite sense of appositeness with which the ancient architects sited their buildings, and, given the narrow vocabulary of form they chose to employ, the extraordinary range of design they managed to encompass.

This subtle feeling for the land that gave them life led the ancient Egyptians to site the tombs of the kings and nobles away from the green cultivation where things grew damp and rotten, into the warm dry cliffs of the west Nile Valley or the strip of desert that runs between the cliffs and the cultivated area of silt. This environment is so dry that everything is desiccated and preserved. It is an area, therefore, where time is effectively stopped, there is no decay, things lie sterile in the sun. On a winter's day it is possible, by these cliffs, to push your hands into the sand and feel the warmth of the sun trapped within. The corridors of the tombs that tunnel deep into the cliffs remain at a constant temperature all year round, varying only one from another if the tomb doors are differently located, in sun or shadow. Yet the objects and bodies brought here from the fertile areas are changed by desiccation. Wood becomes feather light, cloth brittle, the pigment of the ancient blue paint turns green in millennia-slow reactions with the gases of the air; and mummies, when the natron of the ancient embalmers has not dissolved all their fats, obtain a sweet smell of rancidity. Yet the desert is so gentle in its preservation of things that, as one chemist has observed, if the ancient Egyptians had just placed their dead in the sand, as they had done in the remote ages before nationhood, the corpses would have been better preserved than by all the efforts of the embalmers. However, it is important to add that these tradesmen were not just technicians of the flesh, but an important part of a long ritual of passing the dead person from one stage of existence to another.

Scratch upon a rock on these cliffs or deserts of the Nile Valley and the mark is left forever; it is a timeless place. Some of the cliffs of Thebes have drawings and writings on them that chronicle all the time that man has passed in the Nile Valley, from the beautiful drawings of ostriches and elephants by Stone Age men—animals long since vanished from the Egyptian Nile—to the careful records of the ancient Egyptian scribes on tours of inspection of the tombs, and modern archeologists who document the ancient records. The only physical difference in the condition of these three types of mark is the relative amount of rich ochre patination that the wind has deposited upon the limestone in which they were cut. This patination of golden clay dust is the colour of suntan; it gives the Nile cliffs their distinctive hues so beloved of European watercolourists from Edward Lear to Paul Klee.

For nearly a thousand years, from 2060 until 1085 BC the city of Thebes, which Homer dubbed 'hundred-gated' to distinguish it from the 'seven-gated' Thebes of Greece, had more temples, palaces and tombs built in and around it than any other place on earth. To this day archeological remains stretch for miles along the banks of the river and into the desert beyond. There are, indeed, hundreds of temples at Thebes, ranging from the largest single temple in the world, that of Amun Re, king of the Theban pantheon of gods, to numerous small box-like buildings that stand in the precincts of the temples of the principal gods. The temples that were the houses of the gods were built upon the east bank of the river, while upon the west side, running along the desert edge for almost two miles, were constructed the temples of the cults of the dead kings and the chapels of their ministers and courtiers. They contain some of the finest reliefs and paintings ever made by the ancient Egyptians. The Valley of the Kings lies behind these lines of temples and tomb chapels, separated from them by an immense ridge of cliffs which run parallel to the river like a high wall.

Today it is difficult to give a ready practical explanation of why the location of Thebes was chosen for the site of a major city. In the Nile Valley there are few significant material advantages in one location over another. Although frequently claimed to be of unique beauty, the Theban Hills can be matched by other locations in the land, with one significant exception, and that is the size of the western cliffs. The entire area of the west bank at Thebes has a most human scale, and it is an unusually variegated area of desert landscape dominated by a two-mile long prominence of cliffs, some 600 feet high, that form an extraordinary backcloth for the temples on the east bank. On the west the area in front of these cliffs provided an easily accessible series of small valleys, clefts and plains which are now sprinkled with tombs and temples. In the rest of Egypt it is difficult to discover such an area of variety; it is as if all the landforms found within the Upper Egyptian landscape had come together in one place, an area so small that it may easily be walked over in an afternoon, yet so

various that the huge temples are hidden from sight of each other. The site is so interlaced with ancient paths and the ritual ways to the temples that no one person could really claim to have seen all of the monuments that they encompass.

Stretched around the temples and actually penetrating the chambers of some of the tombs is a series of houses which form the community called Gurna. It is an extraordinary extended village of loosely joined dwellings and stables, half the inhabitants still living off the land in a manner similar to their ancient predecessors—though more changed in lifestyle in the past twenty-five years than in the previous two thousand—and half are members of that curious international race that live off the needs and whims of tourists and travellers; here they supply the visitor with everything from antiquities, both real and recent, to cab rides, cola and fresh local oranges and bananas. The *Gurnawis*, as these people are called, have also provided for over two hundred years the basic workforces of the numerous archeological expeditions that have worked in the area. Some of the older *Gurnawis* were the first men to see some of the most famous Egyptian objects as they appeared in the dirt during excavation. It is strange to hear a man tell of finding an object and then suddenly realize that what he describes as being taken from the dust is now carefully floodlit in a climate-controlled museum case. The *Gurnawis* are not, in the main part, the descendants of the ancient artists and workers who once inhabited this area, but derive from a Beduin tribe that settled in the area some hundreds of years ago. But be that as it may, the *Gurnawis* know the monuments well, and some of the most famous discoveries of archeology have been made by these people who, with an amazing mixture of shrewdness, cunning, dignity and sociability, leave an indelible mark upon all those who come into contact with them.

In the very centre of the Theban Hills is a huge semicircle of cliffs where the rock rises sheer to its full height straight from the floor of the Nile Valley. The celebrated temples of Deir el Bahari fit into this great desert bay which, by day, is always burning bright and hot, the semicircle of cliffs providing a vast focusing reflector for the heat of the sun. For a brief period in the last century the spot held the world's temperature record. Since the mid-1960s a Polish expedition has worked there, piecing together sections of the limestone temples that have been smashed and displaced over the centuries, both by man and by the cliffs above, sections of which have split off and dropped into the courtyards and terraces of the temple below. Standing on top of these cliffs, looking down at the intricate view which holds the width of Egypt in one movement of the eye, one might imagine that these temples and stone blocks laid neatly in rows awaiting re-emplacement in the destroyed walls are like the remnants of some ancient aircraft disaster, twisted and smashed fragments exquisitely worked, that once joined perfectly together into a complex machine with a very specific purpose. In previous ages people regarded Thebes as so remote from the centres of civilization that they could legitimately tear down the monuments and plunder these tombs and temples for fragments of their art. This process has filled museums and, unfortunately, is still stocking private collections; but today scholars are putting back together the remains of the buildings in the place where they were made.

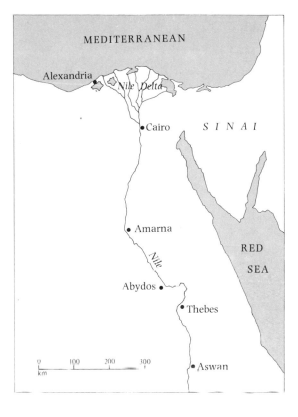

General map of Egypt and a simplified sketch map of the Theban area showing its more important archeological and geographical features. The small rectangle encloses the area of the Valley of the Kings that is used in the maps elsewhere in the book

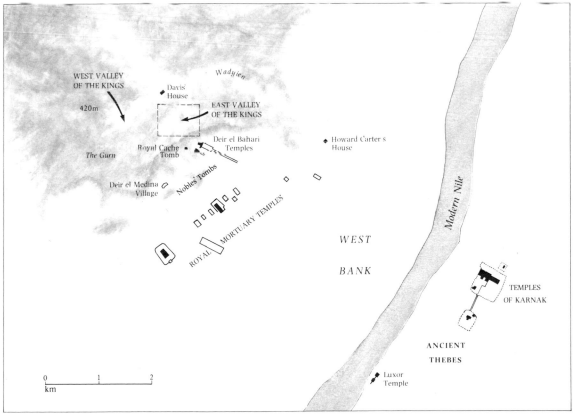

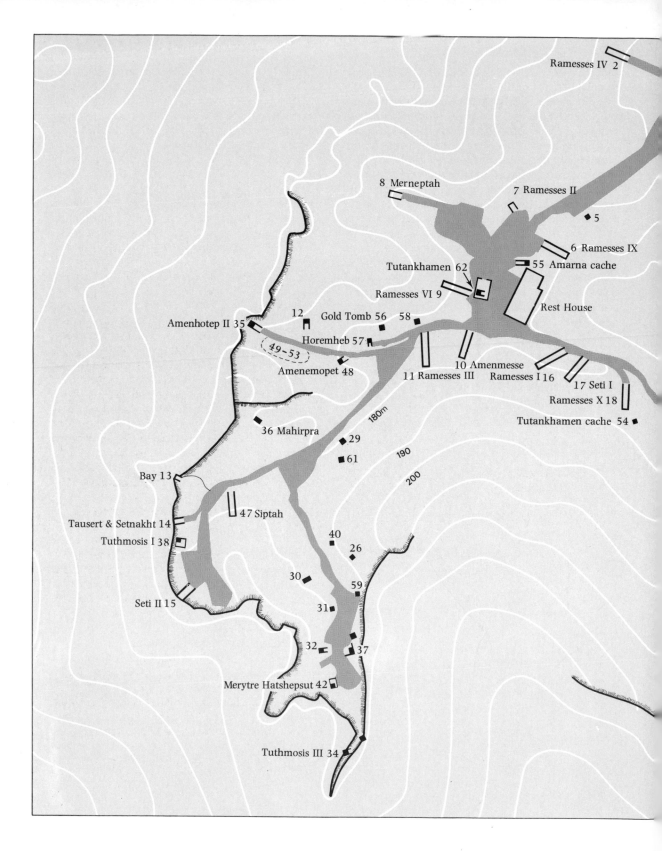

Ramesses IV 2

8 Merneptah

7 Ramesses II

5

6 Ramesses IX

Tutankhamen 62

55 Amarna cache

Ramesses VI 9

Rest House

12 Gold Tomb 56 58

Amenhotep II 35

Horemheb 57

49-53

10 Amenmesse

Amenemopet 48

Ramesses I 16

11 Ramesses III

17 Seti I

Ramesses X 18

Tutankhamen cache 54

36 Mahirpra

180m

29

61

190

Bay 13

200

47 Siptah

40

Tausert & Setnakht 14

26

Tuthmosis I 38

30

59

Seti II 15

31

32 37

Merytre Hatshepsut 42

Tuthmosis III 34

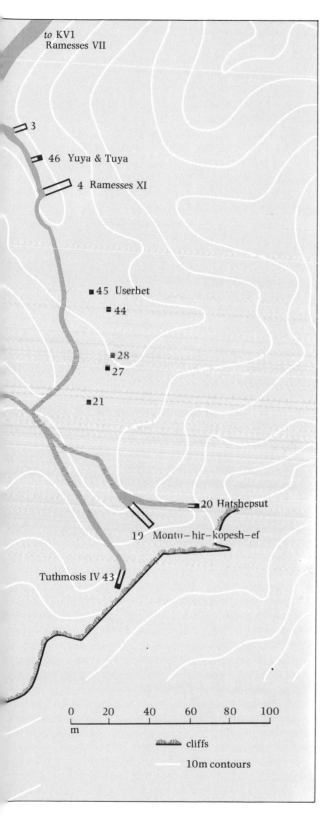

to KV1
Ramesses VII

3

46 Yuya & Tuya

4 Ramesses XI

45 Userhet

44

28

27

21

20 Hatshepsut

19 Montu–hir–kopesh–ef

Tuthmosis IV 43

| 0 | 20 | 40 | 60 | 80 | 100 |

m

cliffs

10m contours

The Valley of the Kings

Behind this screen of cliffs at Deir el Bahari lies the Valley of the Kings, the head of a long desert wadi called by the *Gurnawis* the *Wadi Biban el Moluk* (the Valley of the Gates of the Kings). The wadi was made during a wetter age than the present, when flood waters ran off the Theban Hills down to the Nile Valley with such force and regularity that a displacement in the limestone cliffs was eventually eroded into a valley, the Valley of the Kings. It is similar to many thousands of such wadis that are now quite dry, occasionally containing the waters of a flash flood, that cause any seeds lying in the sand of the valley floor to germinate, subsequently providing the surreal vision of flowering plants and green succulents flourishing in the centre of a desert. Cracked patterns in the mud and the dried stems of plants that these rare floods leave behind them, give the impression that water still flows regularly down these wadis, that they are still in the process of being cut. Great boulders, some of many tons, are strewn over the wadi floors, banks of sand and loose stones are washed down and gouge out lumps from the base of the cliffs. But this jetsam stands on the deposits of very much older erosions, when the Sahara had been a green veldtland, and ostriches and elephants were stalked by Stone Age hunters. These were the men who used the flints, which are dusted all over the hills and screes of the area, for their tools and weapons. They have left so many piles of fine flint chippings, that one can easily imagine the hills ringing with sharp noises while the hunters made their spears and slaughtering implements. These flints have become coloured by their exposure to the elements, as if varnished with a fine Vandyke brown, the usual pallid grey of flint only appearing if the stone has been broken or buried in the water-borne debris that covers the wadi floors. This rich brown colour is so well known to specialists that they can tell whether a flint originated in Upper Egypt solely on the basis of this acquired colour.

The great long wadi, of which the Valley of the Kings is part, drained down behind the Deir el Bahari cliff terrace and emptied at the northern end of the Theban Hills. The entire wadi is called, in Arabic, *Wadyein*—Two wadis—for the Valley has two separate heads. Archeologists have named these endings the East Valley and the West Valley; both hold the tombs of kings, but the East Valley alone holds the title *Wadi Biban el Moluk*, along with the majority of the tombs. The West Valley, however, is the grander. It goes up sharply to enormous cliffs from a golden valley floor, the ancient footpath getting narrower and narrower until it stops at the bottom of a steep cliff where there was once a waterfall. Unlike its eastern partner, the valley is quite silent, apart from the swish of the wings of swifts, which fly low to catch the insects that hover between the line of sun and shade. Rarely, a pair of ravens can be seen flying to a high nest in the mountains above; sometimes crows and hawks stop in the valley. Bats hang hidden in small cracks in the cliffs, leaving tell-tale black stains on the rock and guano at their bases. They chatter and squeak if disturbed, and fly blindly off into the bright light. Sometimes a white fox flashes along one of the small paths that the animal has worn on its route down to the cultivation and villages to hunt for food. That, too, is where the bats head at night, for there is little in the wadis for them to eat. Strangely, the sloughed skins of cobras, and live scorpions can also be found in these remote places that give the impression of holding no life at all. These animals are so perfectly discreet that one feels totally alone in the golden amphitheatre of rock, with a brilliant blue sky above and the tombs of kings at one's feet.

The East Valley is quite different in character—the tourists are noisy, the landscape softer. Above it a high smooth-sloped peak, shaped like a pyramid, slopes down into a vast depression capable of holding huge volumes of water which, in the past, drained gently away through cracks in the limestone to the valley below. In this valley there are softer erosion patterns, not like the tearing and gouging in the West Valley, so that although the landscape bears the scars of the great forces that have acted upon it, the action has been slower and gentler. In this process, water cut an amphitheatre of rock, even more complete than the half circle of cliffs at Deir el Bahari, although here the cliffs are not more than 150 feet high. With a walkway around this cliff edge and a very narrow entrance to the Valley's head—now enlarged to take a modern road but visible in old photographs—the entire area, actually more than forty acres in extent, must have been easy to patrol. In common with other small valleys, noise is easily transmitted from side to side—another important factor of security; even the sound of walking feet can be clearly heard there, let alone the chipping of a robber's chisel. To the east on the top of the Valley cliff, there is a gentle slope up to the spectacular edge of the very much higher cliffs that overlook the temples of Deir el Bahari. To the west a well-constructed ancient path leads to the head of the West Valley. All around its floor in the central area that now holds the rest house, and at the base of its cliffs are the tombs of the kings and some of their exalted queens and courtiers.

2

Royal Tombs

Unlike Western civilization, which has been fractured from the beliefs of its most ancient past, the ancient Egyptians stood firmly with their feet in the clay of their own beginnings. They worshipped the same gods as their prehistoric ancestors and, indeed, most of them shared the same daily existence. Throughout their long history the most basic and distinctive elements of ancient Egyptian culture were upheld and emphasized by the arts and religion. The permanent abiding values, the divine order, manifested itself in society in the concept of nationhood, the invention of which was, for the ancient Egyptians, the mainspring of their culture. It was continuously celebrated in their monuments and arts from the beginning to the end of their history; an unchanging order as consistent as the rhythmic patterns of nature or the gods themselves.

Ancient Egypt was one of the most self-possessed and carefully maintained societies the world has ever seen. Its extraordinary continuity of culture which, nevertheless encouraged the creation of artistic masterpieces at almost every period of its history, was not the dull product of an innate conservatism, but the result of an energetic preservation of custom and style. The culture was an iconography, scrupulously maintained and carefully developed: the reasons why the ancient Egyptians cut and decorated the royal tombs in the Valley of the Kings derived from the customs of periods in their history long before the Valley was ever considered for use as a royal burial ground.

To judge from the manner in which they recorded the passing of their time, a simple linear dating system such as the modern calendar, would have been of very small significance for them: they lived inside a continuum, but for us, looking in at them from the outside, it is difficult to appreciate the span of their history or the development of their arts and architecture in any other way. Between the reign of Menes, first king of the first dynasty of Egypt and the Byzantine Emperor Justinian, in whose reign the last temples of the ancient Egyptian gods were finally closed, is a span of nearly four thousand years. It encompasses whole empires, thirty dynasties of kings, virtually endless generations of simple agrarians. Traditionally, this history is divided into three principal 'Kingdoms'—periods of national unity. These three Kingdoms are called, in order of their antiquity, the Old, the Middle and the New. Between them, they lasted for more than twelve hundred years. The Kingdoms were preceded by an archaic period—the time between the end of village and town culture of Egypt and the establishment of the mature ancient Egyptian state, about 2686 BC—and were followed by the Late Period, a 700-year span of smaller dynasties, myriad small divisions and foreign invasions, the Macedonian Ptolomaic Dynasty and, eventually, absorption into the Roman Empire.

The three principal Kingdoms were further separated from each other by two ages of national disunity, of about 200 years each, when the political control in the land shrank from a national level to that of separate towns and districts. The three Kingdoms were the illustrious periods in which the great works of architecture and art were made, whereas the intermediate periods, generally times of hardship and uncertainty, seem to have inspired a particularly introspective literature of almost existentialist intensity and an art of a provincial caste. This convenient sequence of the three Kingdoms, of order and chaos repeated three times, is a simple formula for historical outline but it tends to shrink the appreciation of the vast spans of time that were involved. The sense of historical intricacy, of lifetimes expended, of generations succeeding each other, is easily lost. This process is aided by the relatively thin information that we possess concerning most of the history of ancient Egypt, a lack made more poignant by the relative abundance of surviving evidence of a personal and intimate nature: ancient flowers, food, furniture, clothing, even, in mummies, the corpses of the people themselves. All the daily impedimenta, in fact, of a nation that held such different concepts of vice and virtue to those of the West and who spoke a language whose very sounds have quite disappeared from the peoples of the earth.

A simple chart may quickly demonstrate the vast spans of time through which the history of ancient Egypt passed. The royal dynasties are employed as subdivisions of the larger periods; the Valley of the Kings was used for the burial of the royal dead during the New Kingdom, that is the Eighteenth, Nineteenth and Twentieth Dynasties.

Period	elapsed time (in years)	approximate dates (BC)	royal dynasties
Archaic	414	3100–2686	I & II
Old Kingdom	505	2686–2181	III–VI
First Intermediate	190	2181–1991	VI–XI
Middle Kingdom	205	1991–1786	XII
Second Intermediate	219	1786–1567	XIII–XVII
New Kingdom	485	1570–1085	XVIII–XX
Third Intermediate or Late Period	743	1085–342	XXI–XXX

This system of the royal dynasties was first ordered by an Egyptian priest of the Classical period called Manetho who, used the ancient hieroglyphic sources that were still accessible to him, and his basic scheme is still in use. Modern study has shown that certain key dynasties are of far greater historical importance than others, while some, such as the ephemeral Fifteenth Dynasty for example, seem to have been little more than a literary device employed to indicate a rapid succession of kings during a politically disturbed period of history. In the New Kingdom, however, Manetho's dynastic divisions have proved to be far more than that, representing real turning points in history. They embody changes in family dynasties of the rulers and also enable us to group products of art and literature into meaningful divisions.

The kings who ruled over ancient Egypt were descended from dynasties of gods who, before the foundation of the Kingdoms, had formulated the principles by which society existed. The order of Egyptian society had emerged from a many-layered primeval world of multifarious mythical events. In these stories it was, ultimately, the king who was the upholder of truth, the vindicator of wrongs, the successful litigant and the defeater of wicked enemies; he was fused with the identities of many of the god-participants. Neither was this the simple political propaganda of a nervous ruling class. There were no cults of regal individuality and in all of the history of Pharaonic rule barely more than a handful of personalities can be discerned. In the tombs in the Valley of the Kings it is impossible to distinguish any one of the kings as an individual, neither is there a single description that tells of the life of a king, of his great deeds or acts of state. Even the texts and pictures in the temples describing military campaigns have a strongly repetitious air about them and record, in the main, the inevitable glories of Egypt and the offices of state rather than the deeds of men. This principle is emphasized in other temple scenes which show figures of the kings making ritual offerings to figures of themselves as kings! but despite this political anonymity the kings held divinity in their being. Their very shadows were powerful. The royal progress through Egypt was a part of the cosmic progress, and their boats and chariots were receptacles for the journeys of the sun. The king was vital to ancient Egypt, an essential element in the maintenance of the position of society in the order of creation. It was a state system that stretched far beyond any modern conceptions of nationhood. To the modern popular imagination the huge monuments of ancient Egypt may represent the forced labours of slaves and of nations in chains, but to the Egyptians these temples and tombs were a vital part of this union between the people, the state and the gods. They were also a clear proof of the powerful unifying force of a stable monarchy.

What a crisis then, when the King, this essential element of cosmic order died! With order and rhythm as the primary values of society, such a solitary disordered event was dangerous; incomprehensible. So, in death, the king could not cease to be, could not be annihilated, but had to be maintained and nourished by a specialized cult. Part of this cult was the realization, in the most literal manner possible, of the passage of the king from his earthly death to rebirth as a divine being and these were the central purposes of the ceremonies and rituals that surrounded his death and burial. The royal tombs are so consistent and precise in their form, their decoration and contents made with such intense care and skill that one may quickly appreciate that they embodied the most specific ritual functions and these seem to hover, almost imminent, in the tombs still. The tombs are far more than grandiose burial crypts filled with riches, and such lazy explanations as the whims of kings or the mechanical requirements of a conservative tradition do not begin to grasp the motivations for these burials or explain the continuous rigorous effort that was expended upon them for millennia after millennia.

The ancient Egyptians had many different versions of the after-life and provided the king with a multitude of destinies that would follow his death, but through all these stories and scenes, rituals and ceremonies that accompanied the cult of the dead king, are certain constant preoccupations. The death of the king was seen as the beginning of a journey of resurrection, the establishment of the king with the gods with whom he would unite to become a powerful part of the endless cycle of birth and rebirth, the cosmic and agricultural rhythms of Egypt. The dead king was carefully prepared for this difficult journey to the gods; a journey that took many forms.

How much of all this was understood by the priests and the other participants in the offices of burial is impossible to know; it was never formulated in coherent abstract conceptions but the priests certainly understood that the precise and correct establishment of the king in his tomb was a vital national activity; that the death of the king was a national trauma through which the state with the aid of ritual must pass to recover its previous order. Even before the new king could be crowned, he had to confirm his right to succession by ensuring the proper installation of his predecessor in his tomb and, thereby, in the other world. The royal tombs and their contents were part of the technology of a culture that, in common with many religious societies, did not distinguish between liturgy, ritual and the science and politics of everyday life. It is not inappropriate to regard the hieroglyphs and the scenes on the tomb walls as the printed circuits of these ritual systems and the precious amulets that were bound up into the wrappings of the royal dead as the silicon chips of the Bronze Age.

The enormous quantity of funerary goods that have survived from ancient Egypt are evidence of the affection the ancient people had for their dead; they emphasize how strongly they held to their beliefs and how unafraid of death and the dead they were. The dead king's continuing existence, aided by the food, domestic goods and ritual paraphernalia that filled his tomb was a source of potent energy for the nation and the land. The kings were animate in death, and contained in their tombs were the powers of germination and fertility, of resurrection and the constancy of the world order. But all this could only be achieved if the rituals of the royal burial had been performed in the correct way, everything done as it had been prescribed at the beginning. This included the making and decorating of the tomb and the fine craftsmanship of the artists, whose labours were directly responsible for the successful installation of the dead king with the gods.

Time has mellowed the tombs, blunted the hard edges of the ritual functionalism that was the impetus

of their creation. But they remain strange monuments; so apart from our usual experiences it is surprising that any part of them still communicates with us. Yet they do, and the royal tombs of Egypt attract more visitors every year. Perhaps this is because of the freshness of the ancient aesthetic experience for us, one so extremely particular and profoundly different from our own. The ancient Egyptians inhabited a world with a very different variety of colours and textures from those of the present day. There were, of course, no bright machine-made objects, all possessions being manufactured by the human hand; a flat surface, for example, represented hard work and concentration. It was something to be attained; something almost alive. As well as this there were also very different qualities of life and of almost every aspect of daily existence. Despite this gulf there are still those physical experiences which are shared by all humanity; and they are the qualities that enable us to share with the ancient people part of a response to their works of art and architecture.

The ancient Egyptians cared more for the proper burial of their kings than any other nation that has existed. Royal tombs and their accompanying monuments were the first works of architecture ever made by the ancient Egyptians. One royal tomb, the Step Pyramid complex, was the first group of buildings in the world to be built of stone blocks. Within sixty years of that archaic masterpiece, in an incredible explosion of energy, the nation was engaged in the construction of the largest of its pyramids—also to hold the burial of a king. Between these early monuments and the later royal tombs of the Valley of the Kings there are strong links, strong common themes, which it is important to establish.

The first royal tombs of Egypt, built during the Archaic Period, dominated the ridge of the desert escarpment that overlooked the Nile Valley at Memphis, the first capital of Egypt, now close to modern Cairo. Memphis was built on the silt of the Nile Valley and was constructed largely of mud bricks made from this alluvium, as were the royal tombs on the desert plateau above. Originally no more than about twenty feet high, these large, solid, rectangular structures built on the skyline of the cliffs could be seen for miles across the valley. The dead kings in their tombs were literally 'upon their horizon', and the immediate descendants of these archaic tombs, the pyramids, followed this conception and were given names such as the 'Horizon of the King'. They, too, completely dominated the skyline in an extra-ordinary manner as many of them still do. Thus, when the king died it was said that he had 'gone to his horizon' which, with the royal tombs situated upon the western bank of the Nile, was also an identification of the king with the setting sun.

It has been suggested that during the royal funerary rite at Thebes, when the king was taken for burial, that the coffins and the royal mummy were carried in procession from the mortuary temple in the Nile Valley, over the ridge at the top of the Theban cliffs and straight down into the tomb in the Valley of the Kings behind the western horizon, like the setting sun itself. In this way the route of the funeral procession was joined to the daily path of the sun. During the funeral the king entered his horizon and withdrew, united with the sun, into the evening Underworld. In ancient times, the corridors of the royal tombs were called 'the corridors of the sun's path' and the death of one king and the accession of his successor is sometimes represented in similar terms.

> King Tuthmosis III went up to heaven;
> He was united with the sundisk;
> The body of the god joined him who had made him.
> When the next morning dawned
> The sun disk shone forth,
> The sky became bright,
> King Amenhotep II was installed on the throne of
>   his father.

The playing-out of these events in the form of the journey to burial would certainly have been planned to coincide with an appropriate moment in the astronomical calendar. Indeed, the entire ceremony of burial was a part of the theological exercise designed to create order out of the potentially disastrous event that had befallen the nation on the death of its king; and the nucleus of the ritual and at the heart of the monument, was the mummy of the dead king. The silhouettes of the archaic royal tombs and the pyramids that held the royal dead high on the Nile cliffs were images of immense power and security for the Egyptians. The colossal effort required to erect these buildings had welded the nation together and given it order and identity. Today they remain, quite literally, the embodiment of the state which made them.

The pyramids were the architectural descendants of the huge archaic royal tombs that had been built on the Memphis skyline. Indeed, the first pyramid ever made, the Step Pyramid, is near these earlier tombs and actually contains an example of the earlier tomb-type embedded in its lower courses. Set back as it is from the skyline which was then crowded with earlier royal tombs, the added height of a pyramid was a necessary addition to the older style of monument if the royal tomb was still to be visible from the Nile Valley below. During the course of the Old and Middle Kingdoms over seventy more pyramids were built, stretching in a line along the edge of the valley around Memphis for more than eighty miles. The later pyramids were frequently much smaller but the attendant buildings were greatly elaborated. Inside, their enormous bulks contained merely simple progressions of corridors and chambers, one of which housed the royal sarcophagus.

The temple of the cult of the dead king, usually situated at the foot of the pyramid upon its eastern side, was connected by a long enclosed causeway which ran to another temple by the banks of the Nile. The body of the king was brought to this lower temple by boat, then taken up the causeway to the cult temple before the entombment in the pyramid itself. This journey from the Nile to the sarcophagus was an important part of the religious drama of the burial, a journey that took place through a series of carefully controlled architectural environments, which changed theatrically from the darkness of the temple interiors and the spare natural lighting in the causeways to the sunlit courtyards of the temples in front of the pyramids. From these dazzling courtyards of the pyramid cult temples, the royal mummies were taken inside the pyramids through small, relatively insignificant entrances usually situated at the foot of the pyramids' northern faces.

The comparatively small dimensions of the corridors and chambers inside the pyramids would have effectively prohibited any ritual activity involving more than the smallest group of participants. Indeed, the corridors in even the grandest of the pyramids are so small that visitors must bend down to descend into the interior chambers. Of necessity the great stone sarcophagi of the kings were left in the burial chambers during the course of the pyramid's construction and even the introduction of the royal mummy and his coffins into the burial chamber must have proved an awkward exercise.

Thus although the engineering of these strange passages and chambers inside the pyramids is often very impressive and demonstrates massive skill and incredible human effort, in the end we may see that these burial chamber systems served but one principal purpose: that of access to the burial chamber in the centre of the pyramid where, after an intimate ceremonial of interment, the king was left to lie in his sarcophagus for all eternity.

The Old Kingdom pharaohs rested safe in the belief of eternal inviolability in their tombs and they may well have lain for several hundred years before tomb robbers disturbed and plundered their burials. The Middle Kingdom monarchs, less certain of their eventual fate, had their pyramids designed with interiors that contained architectural tricks: corridors with blind ends, doors to the burial chamber situated at unexpected angles in the approach corridor, all designed to fool intruders. These pyramids were further integrated into the huge complexes of accompanying temple buildings, which were provided with elaborate arrangements, financed by the revenues from huge estates, to continue the cult of the king throughout all eternity. Nevertheless, with the exception of some pyramids that have been flooded following a rise in the water table of the Nile Valley, all of them were robbed.

The Old Kingdom pyramids, too, had contained architectural arrangements designed to protect the burial chamber from intruders but these, constantly duplicated in each successive pyramid, can hardly be regarded as realistic security devices. Their origins may be still seen in the remains of the Archaic tombs, where the large stone slabs, which completely blocked the corridor to the burial chamber, have an air of practical purpose about them. With that attitude so very typical in the designs of later royal tombs in the Valley of the Kings, once such an element had been introduced into the royal tomb plan it was never discarded. Thus, although the primitive stone portculli of the Archaic Period tombs were retained and enormously enlarged in the interiors of the later pyramids, they were easily circumvented by thieves who, being well aware of these traditional hazards, merely quarried through the softer stones in which the granite blocks were embedded. Only a very few tombs, made late in Egypt's history, ever fulfilled Hollywood's dream of cunning and deadly hydraulic devices that operated with sand.

The corridors and burial chambers of many pyramids were inscribed with lengthy hieroglyphic inscriptions known as the Pyramid Texts. They deal with themes of the ritual and resurrection and are the oldest surviving body of religious writing in the world. However, like so many other writings—a single edition of a modern newspaper, for example—they assume familiarity with a larger body of knowledge that is not presented in the texts themselves. The only way in which they can be interpreted is by reference to more explicit texts of the later religious literature. Fascinating attempts have been made to fit the Pyramid Texts to the rituals that took place in the pyramids at the time of the royal interment but these proposals still lack verification. Unfortunately, from the periods before the New Kingdom, there is very little surviving information about any of the ceremonials connected with a royal burial.

At New Kingdom Thebes the burial chambers of the king and the temple of the royal cult were physically separated. The tomb was set in the desert landscape of the Theban Hills, the temples left in the Nile Valley. An impressive row of these mortuary temples was built along the edge of the cultivation on the west bank of the Nile. With almost every reign they were enlarged and, eventually, they became the centres of administrative complexes that housed the government. These temple towns physically demonstrated the Egyptian conception of religion, government and the kingship as parts of a unified whole.

At their heart, these majestic temples of New Kingdom Thebes were designed in much the same way as their predecessors in the pyramid complexes. However, the role of the lower temple beside the Nile was reduced to that of a landing stage and the stone causeway, which ran up to the mortuary temple, was changed in later New Kingdom times to a canal system that led to a dock by the front of the main temples and was, perhaps, more suited to the landscape of the area. These Theban mortuary temples must have provided a splendid scene. Rows of long, low, whitewashed buildings covered with brightly coloured reliefs surrounded by massive mud-brick enclosure walls over which appeared the tall temple flagpoles capped with gold that flashed in the sunlight, each with long pennants flying. Across the river on the east bank, the series of vast temples which housed the great gods of the Theban Pantheon also sheltered the smaller shrines of other Egyptian gods whose temples at Thebes served to establish their occupants at the religious heart of the nation. The great temple of Amun Re, King of the Gods, at Karnak is the largest temple enclosure and the most massive religious edifice ever built.

A vital part of the great ritual calendar of Thebes was the huge feast-day processions when the figures of the gods were taken from their temples to visit the houses of other gods. These movements of the gods were a central element of the religion, great popular festivals that still have their equivalents in some of the rituals of Christianity. Both the funeral of the king and the rituals of the royal mortuary cult were inte-

grated into this ceremonial calendar. At appointed times, each temple in which the cult of the dead was being celebrated was visited by the King of the Gods, Amun Re, whose statue was brought across the river from the sanctuary in his temple at Karnak. In the darkness of the most sacred central chambers of the mortuary temples, the god of Karnak would meet the god of the dead king. At the rear of these temples, as there had also been in the pyramid temples, there was a huge sculpture of a stone door and through it the spirit of the dead king could pass regularly from the Underworld of his tomb. Through the medium of this false door the royal spirit received the daily offerings of food and drink which, after the royal presence had extracted the elements essential for his spiritual survival, were later distributed between the

priests and the other staff of the cult. In return for this intangible offering the dead king spread throughout the land, his revitalizing powers that he had fought for in the Underworld, and the offices of the cult brought order and restraint to the administration of the nation.

The actual tombs of the New Kingdom Pharoahs, situated mostly in the Valley of the Kings, were the

A composite photograph of the upper corridors in the tomb of Ramesses IX that, by stretching the real width of the corridor, enables the decorations of both its walls to be seen in the same picture

23

equivalent of the burial chamber systems inside the earlier pyramids. They were cut into cliffs below the skyline of the Theban mountains, the splendid natural range that stands across the Nile opposite Thebes, replacing the dominating shapes of the pyramids of earlier periods. It has sometimes been claimed that the mountain peak of the Gurn (The Peak) high above the Valley was imagined by the ancients to be a natural pyramid and that the tombs in the Valley were simply quarried into these cliffs to make the corridors and burial chamber reflect those of the pyramids. Little attempt was ever made, however, to enter this 'pyramid' at its correct ritual location on the north face. This mountain was identified as a holy place of quite a different type from the pyramids of earlier times. Neither do the royal tombs of the Valley appear to have any special relationship with their mortuary temples over the ridge of cliffs in the Nile Valley below. Although it is sometimes said that the royal tombs were located upon the main axes of the huge temples, most of them are miles out of any such alignments. However, the selection of the Valley for the royal tombs and the way in which these monuments were set into its landscape is the work of artists attuned to very different processes than those of today. The Egyptians dwelt in a sacred landscape inhabited by the gods and, like Delphi in Greece, Carnac in Brittany and other ancient religious landscapes, the Valley of the Kings was made as a theatre for the gods, a carefully selected and controlled setting for great cosmic dramas. The Valley, however, was not made for the worship or habitation of the gods but for the secret hidden dramas of royal death and resurrection.

The royal tomb and its burial chamber system of New Kingdom Thebes was dramatically changed from those in the pyramids of the earlier kingdoms. Fresh theological concepts had complicated the fate of the royal dead and extended the earlier conception of the royal destiny. New religious texts were composed and drawn upon the walls of the tombs. The dramatic, if somewhat utilitarian arrangement of the interior of the pyramids was transformed by a brilliant series of architectural designs that were constantly refined and enlarged in each succeeding tomb. The spare vertical rows of elegant blue hieroglyphs, which had been the sole decorations of the burial chamber systems in the pyramids, were superceded by elaborately detailed wall texts and pictorial scenes of great beauty and visual complexity. The corridors and rooms were enlarged in size and eventually became

a succession of vast halls and corridors without equal in the rock-cut architecture of Egypt. Hidden in their desert valley beneath the horizon of the Theban cliffs, the royal tombs are a five-hundred-year-long series of refined architectural environments decorated and designed with great skill and high intelligence. With their basic designs and decorations repeated over and over again, the tombs are as alike as Byzantine icons, yet individually each possesses its own characteristic qualities and distinctive atmosphere.

The men who made these tombs were working in a continuous tradition of more than 2,000 years and were extraordinarily detached from what we would normally regard as the processes of artistic creation. They pursued their task of making a suitable burial place for the kings with great economy and precision; yet, despite the rigid and functional nature of their work they made beautiful environments which are still effective today. Their style was the product of the strict and powerful system of a most individual society, but it permitted the architects and artists to select an alternative design with a degree of accuracy seldom possible in modern works of art and architecture.

The Theban royal tomb is a succession of rock-cut passages carefully ordered by a series of doors, which lead down into the largest chamber where the royal sarcophagus lies, deep in the limestone cliffs. During the five hundred years in which they were planned and excavated the tomb designs underwent many drastic changes but the basic order of their rooms and corridors was never altered. By a process of accretion, new elements were added, but very little was discarded. At the same time, the architects strove to simplify and unify the different parts of the tomb and weld them into one dramatic architectural concept. One of the basic principles of ancient Egyptian art, that of never truly abandoning any of its forms but continually perfecting and refining them in subsequent designs, is shown to its maximum advantage in these royal tombs. This is one of their fascinations.

They form a closed sequence of designs all made for exactly the same purpose and provide a unique opportunity to study a group of ancient architects at work on the same problems over a long period of time. The architects who designed these royal tombs were subject to three sometimes opposing criteria— a situation which constantly demanded the most thoughtful responses and provided each of the monuments with its own loveliness. First, the original features of the earlier tombs, considered to be part of the essential identity of a royal tomb, were always retained. Second, there was a strong impulse to achieve regularity and geometric symmetry in the tomb plans, a constant process of aesthetic development. The third factor was the necessity to assimilate new features into the designs for both ritual and practical purposes, such as the change-over from sealing the tombs with rough stone walls to wooden doors. This required extra sills and door jambs in the tomb and the repositioning of reliefs so that the new doors would not cover them when they were opened. This change was a part of the programme of general tomb enlargement and it is likely that the increase in door size and tomb accessibility was the result of changing ritual requirements at the tomb. It is these three imperatives of design which give the tombs of the Valley their particular beauty, a faultlessly designed lineage that gives an uncanny sense of interrelationship, sublime order and unerring correctness.

It is always as well to bear in mind that there was never any sort of inevitability in the gradual development of these tomb designs. They were the work of living people and the slowly changing designs in the royal tombs show a keen intelligence and extraordinarily consistent approach that is apparent only in the work of the finest architects. If their designs appear to us to alter one after another in an almost living, natural way, slowly developing like a plant from shoot to flower, this is simply the manner of artists so close and so attuned to the slow rhythms and forms of agrarian life that there came to be a profound consistency among them.

Oswald Spengler, a man more in sympathy with the past than he was with his own times, brilliantly described the aesthetic results of the formal ambitions of the ancient architects in a text which is particularly appropriate to the tombs of the Valley:

The dominance of the horizontal, the vertical and the right angle, and the avoidance of all foreshortening, support the two dimensional principle and serve to insulate the strong experience of depth which coincides with the way and the grave at the end.
It is an art that admits of no deviation for the relief of the tense soul. Is this not an expression in the noblest language that it is possible to conceive of, what all our space theories would like to put into words?

The near five-hundred-year timespan of the New Kingdom witnessed the rise and decline of the ancient Egyptian empire in the Near East. Some of the kings of the period were great soldier-monarchs who built the wealth of the nation from their conquests and maintained the splendours of huge international courts. It was the most hectic period of Egypt's long history, when historical or linear time, in the form of treaties, battles or diplomatic encounters, intruded into the eternal cyclic patterns of the older Egyptian way of life. In the royal tombs, however, it is quite impossible, as has already been stressed, to distinguish the tombs of the famous kings from those of their less distinguished counterparts although there is some connection between the finished state of a tomb and the length of reign of the king for whom it was made. The relative lengths of reigns may also be largely responsible for the relative fame of the monarchs as well, for a long reign would see the completion of more building projects, statues and other inscribed memorials of the reign.

For their own purposes of record keeping, the ancient Egyptians used the year dates of the reign of the incumbent king, which is still a most practical rule-of-thumb in determining what might be expected of any particular royal building programme in the Valley of the Kings. Ramesses I, for example, was buried in a drastically curtailed and hastily finished tomb, number 16, because he died before the tomb had been completely quarried. On the other hand, the tombs of Seti I and Ramesses II are finished in both their plans and their decoration, reflecting the long reigns of these two most celebrated kings. This ancient system of the king's year dates may not, however, be trusted to produce an accurate cumulative chronology, for the numerous kings that were later considered to have been illegitimate occupants of the throne were all struck off the royal registers and the overall framework of elapsed time, which the modern historian has tried so carefully to discover, was completely inaccurate.

XVIIIth DYNASTY: 1570 BC–1320 BC

King	Years of Rule	Modern Tomb Number in the Valley
Amosis	24	none known
Amenhotep I	30	none known
Tuthmosis I	13	38, made by his grandson?
Tuthmosis II	8	none known
Hatshepsut	21	20
Tuthmosis III	54	34
Amenhotep II	25	35
Tuthmosis IV	8	43
Amenhotep III	38	22
Akhenaten	17	buried away from Thebes
Smenkare	3	55
Tutankhamen	9	62
Ay	4	23
Horemheb	28	57

The Eighteenth Dynasty is one of the best documented periods of ancient Egyptian history; so much is known about it that it is often possible to subdivide individual reigns and assign different artistic styles for each subdivision. It was a dynasty composed principally of a succession of monarchs of one family. The beginning of the dynasty saw the establishment of the New Kingdom, as the kings fought for and slowly won control over the country of Egypt, and made Thebes its capital. The Egyptian empire was won shortly after the reunification of the land, and the enormous wealth that it brought to Egypt, and especially Thebes, is reflected in the refinement and sophistication of the arts of the reign of Amenhotep III, called 'The Magnificent'. Following the disturbed reign of the heretical King Akhenaten and the young Tutankhamen, the bloodline finished. The end of the dynasty saw the reign of a high priest, and a general. This later period is one of religious strife and it found a reflection of an unusual kind in the tombs of the Valley of the Kings. The general, Horemheb, named his chief minister to succeed him to the throne, and this elderly man became the first king called Ramesses and the initiator of the Nineteenth Dynasty.

XIXth DYNASTY: 1320 BC–1200 BC

King	Years of Rule	Modern Tomb Number in the Valley
Ramesses I	2	16
Seti I	14	17
Ramesses II	67	7
Merneptah	13	8
Amenmesse	5	10
Seti II	6	15
Siptah	9	47

This dynasty, of approximately 120 years span, is dominated by the near seventy-year reign of Ramesses II, called 'The Great'. Both his reign and his father's saw remarkable achievements in architecture and decoration, and this period had a profound effect upon the design of the tombs in the Valley.

The kings of this dynasty fought many large wars, first to hold the Empire, then to protect Egypt herself. The end of the dynasty was politically disturbed; even the order of the succession has been the subject of recent debate.

XXth DYNASTY 1200 BC–1085 BC

King	Years of Rule	Modern Tomb Number in the Valley
Setnakht	2	14
Ramesses III	32	11
Ramesses IV	6	2
Ramesses V	4	9
Ramesses VI	8	9 (shared with previous king)
Ramesses VII	1	1
Ramesses VIII	7	none known
Ramesses IX	19	6
Ramesses X	8	18
Ramesses XI	28	4

This last dynasty of the New Kingdom is usually identified as one of dissolution, 'the decay of empire'. Among earlier historians, descriptions of the period prompted many moralistic observations of the *sic transit gloria mundi* variety. In truth, the period is still obscure, but even at the end of the dynasty, after the reigns of many ill-documented kings called Ramesses, Egypt was still a relatively rich and powerful state when compared with the rest of the Middle East, although nothing like the great imperial power it had been in the earlier part of the New Kingdom. Following the end of the dynasty, the court moved to the Nile Delta and Thebes was no longer the capital of the land. Without their Valley tombs the very existence of some of these Ramesside kings would be in doubt. Yet these tombs are among the largest and most magnificent of the Valley.

Opposite: the Nile and its west bank at Luxor (above). The Valley of the Kings lies behind the high screen of cliffs that faces the river. Below, desert wadis at western Thebes. The Valley is in the shadow of the mountain peak—the Gurn—at the top right of the photograph

Overleaf: a general view of the west side of the Valley. The doorways of many of the royal tombs are visible, from Ramesses VII's on the extreme right to Amenhotep II's in the shade of the cliffs at the end of the white path on the left

Facing p. 27: above, the entrance to the tomb of Ramesses VII (tomb number 1). Two wall paintings (below) in the burial chamber of the tomb of Ramesses I. The King enters the presence of the gods

Part II

TRAVELLERS AND ADVENTURERS

3

Pilgrims, Conquerors and Travellers

During the long reign of Ramesses XI, the last ruler of the New Kingdom, Egypt was divided and ruled in two separate halves, north and south. In the south, Thebes retained its role as the principal centre of the state religion, although most of the Ramesside kings now lived in sumptuous palace-cities in the delta. When Ramesses XI eventually died, Prince Smendes, who had administered the north of the country, became king and although he confirmed the southern ruler, the High Priest Pinejem I, in his position at Thebes many of the offices of the state and the site of the royal burial ground were transferred to the north. Thus the Valley of the Kings was abandoned as the royal cemetery of Egypt at the same time as the New Kingdom came to its end and although it never lost its significance as a holy place, during the next thousand years its identity changed from that of the sacred burial ground of kings to a holy place where man and god might communicate.

The last tomb to be cut in the Valley was made for Ramesses XI, but it was never finished and the king was never buried in it. The documentation and clearing of this neglected tomb was the first project of the archeological section of our expedition to the Valley during 1978–9 and in it we found unexpected evidence from almost every period of the Valley's long history following the fall of the New Kingdom. Mixed with the chippings of the ancient quarrymen, which still lay over the tomb's rooms and corridors, were scraps of antiquities and litter that dated back over three thousand years. Both ancient and modern tourists had scratched and scribbled on the flat soft plaster surfaces of the tomb walls. We found writings of ancient Egyptians, Christian hermits, early travellers and pioneer egyptologists as well as the soldiers of the armies of ancient Rome, Napoleon and the British Empire. We also discovered the last hieroglyphic inscription to have been written in the Valley, a text of Pinejem that restored a part of the original decoration of the tomb, painted in the name of Ramesses XI, that had collapsed shortly after the tomb had been made.

The southern line of priest kings, of which Pinejem

was the third, had taken great care of the royal burials in the Valley, many of which had suffered damage at the hands of robbers. Some of the royal tombs had already been broken into by this time, the rich burial equipment had been plundered and many of the royal mummies were mauled and broken in the search for valuable amulets and jewellery. Many of the royal dead had been carefully re-wrapped in fresh linens by a series of re-burial commissions that were established by the northern rulers and overseen by the southern priest-kings. Temporarily, the royal mummies were gathered together in communal burials placed in a few of the Valley tombs and later they were split into two main groups, one being deposited in a well-hidden Valley tomb and the other in a small tomb of a queen that had been especially enlarged to hold its new tenants. These two caches of kings lay undisturbed for nearly three thousand years before both were discovered during the last century.

Once the Valley of the Kings was no longer used to hold the royal dead, the desert village that had housed the community of tomb workers was no longer supplied and provisioned from the royal estates and the community moved away. Similarly, the guards, workmen and artists who had once inhabited the Valley all left. Emptied of their kings and ransacked for their treasures the great tombs in the deserted Valley lay open and unattended. Some of them were soon covered over, lost under the rubble of the debris that sweeps down from the slopes above the Valley in times of rain and flood. Small tombs were easily jammed shut again, but the large tombs —those of the delta-dwelling Ramesside kings which had never been walled up or covered over—lay wide open in the sun, their huge doorways brightly decorated and prominent at the foot of the cliffs. Some of these empty tombs were used to hold the modest burials of later ancient Egyptian families, some burial parties even taking over the huge open sarcophagi of the departed kings to house their dead. Others left their encoffined mummies in the side chambers of the great tombs, which they carefully cleared out and swept clean, and some burials took place in the small tombs originally cut for ancient nobles who had been buried close by their kings in the Valley.

During the work in the tomb of Ramesses XI our expedition discovered rough texts scratched into the wall plaster which showed that the tomb had been regarded by later ancient Egyptians as a kind of shrine. These inscriptions, written in demotic Egyptian (a partially hieroglyphic-derived script developed during the last phases of Egyptian history) are a type of *ex voto*, a name left in a holy presence by a pilgrim. They show that there had taken place a most basic change in the identity of the Valley, from that of a closed cemetery to an open place filled with ancient wonders.

In the middle of the 1st century BC, Thebes was visited by the Greek writer Diodorus Siculus, who recorded a conversation with some temple priests who talked of the royal tombs of the Valley of the Kings. Despite the suspicion that, like so many later travellers in Egypt, Diodorus may have incorporated the experiences of others into his *General History* this short account, a spy hole into the ancient world, is the first surviving record of the Valley in literature since the ancient workmen left:

The priests said that in their records they find forty seven tombs of kings, but down to the time of Ptolemy, son of Lagos, they say only seventeen remained, most of which had been destroyed by the time that we visited those regions.

Another writer, the Roman Strabo, visited Upper Egypt about seventy years later with his friend Aelius Gallus, who had been appointed Governor of Egypt by the Emperor Augustus. The two of them travelled up the Nile Valley and found at Thebes that:

Above the Memnonium, in caves, are the tombs of Kings, which are stone hewn, are about forty in number, are marvellously constructed, and a spectacle worth seeing.

Although Strabo partly repeats the information of Diodorus, the enthusiasm with which he describes the royal tombs was surely either gained at first hand or from the direct report of another traveller.

Strabo's 'Memnonium' is, in fact, the beautiful mortuary temple of Ramesses II that still stands in the plain of Western Thebes. Some classical writers identified this ruin as Memnon's tomb, but the most popular location for the burial place of this mythical warrior was the Valley of the Kings. There, the tombs were called Syrinxs or 'shepherd pipes' probably because their deep corridors were all of different lengths and seemed like gigantic Pan pipes. The tomb believed to have been Memnon's was that of Ramesses VI, a spacious and richly coloured monu-

Until the beginning of the present century the road to the Valley of the Kings had changed little from ancient times. This old photograph shows the ancient track to the Valley as it left the plain to start its gentle climb up the Wadyien to the Valley

ment that lay in the centre of the Valley. Perhaps the sound of the title used by many Egyptian kings, *Mery Amun* (beloved of Amun) had suggested the name Memnon to an inquisitive Greek while he questioned the local priests about the monuments.

The ancient visitors to the Valley celebrated their journey in graffiti of which more than 2,000 have been recorded. They are found in eleven of the royal tombs and their dates span virtually the entire period of Roman rule in Egypt, the last recording a visit to the tombs during the 6th century AD by a certain Count Orion who, his graffito informs us, had been appointed Governor of Upper Egypt by the most holy Christian Emperor, Justinian.

These graffiti are usually scratched on the surface plaster of the tomb walls with a sharp point that skips lightly over the solid sculptured reliefs and the careful brushmarks of the ancient Egyptian artists. Most of them are so unobtrusive that they are unnoticed by modern visitors, though in some of the tombs, such as Memnon's, which contains more than a thousand of them, they crowd over the walls shimmering like the chatter of a group of tourists. The comments they contain are usually fulsome. Some say that they marvelled at the tombs, that they are huge, a revelation; there are even short poems and literary quotations. To this lonely Valley came writers and poets, soldiers and administrators, historians and philosophers. Their inscriptions are a real microcosm of the late Classical world.

The tombs visited by these ancient people were those that had always stood open. They were the largest in the Valley, those of the kings of the late-Nineteenth and Twentieth Dynasties. Whereas the entrances to the earlier royal tombs had been rough cut and at the bottom of flights of irregular steps, these later tombs have the spaciousness of processional ways and are similar in size and decoration to the ceremonial doorways of temples and palaces. They had originally been shut off from the world by sets of tall thin double-leafed cedar doors. In some of the tombs, fragments of the plaster used to seal these into position still adheres, preserving an exact casting of their thickness. The holes drilled into the rock lintels to hold the doors are surprisingly small and such flimsy doors as they would have supported could have provided little direct security for the rich contents of the royal tombs.

In fact, the security of the burials had been guaranteed not by their architectural arrangements but by the constant presence in the Valley of large numbers of tomb workers, officials and necropolis guards.

When this community was disbanded after the court moved to the delta its last task had probably been to collect all the royal mummies and rebury them in secret locations, having previously stripped the tombs of all their valuables.

The Count Orion, who inscribed his name in the Valley in AD 537, had been a Byzantine, a citizen of the Eastern Empire of Christ. At that time, Thebes was the scene of a profound religious experiment which, during the previous two centuries had seen the birth of Christian monasticism, monasteries and hermitages. Among the lonely desert cliffs above the Nile Valley the hermits led the simplest of lives. They rejected material possessions, suffered appalling hardships and left a body of writings remarkable for their faith and humility. In their desert solitudes many of them founded strange forms of Christianity that are once again attracting interest. The old Egyptian values of a balanced and somewhat hedonistic existence were replaced by a harsh aestheticism. Mind and will, and the combating of sin became central issues, the ancient virtues of good government and a highly ritualized public life were ignored. Hair shirts and self-flagellation were common in the monastic communities, while handweaving sharp palm fibre into coarse rope was considered suitable employment. Yet, in their own severe way great stress was placed on kindly spiritual values, and this, in a predominantly cruel and bad-tempered society.

At the time of the official establishment of Christianity in Egypt the ancient monuments had been heavily attacked and it is therefore extraordinary that the small Christian community which lived in some of the royal tombs in the Valley for more than two hundred years did the tombs no harm. Judging from their graffiti, many of the trips of the earlier pagan visitors to the tombs were akin to pilgrimages, a visit to the Underworld itself, an environment inhabited by gods but not one in which they were worshipped. Similar beliefs may account for the interest and care shown by the Christians in the tombs; the ancients had inadvertently bequeathed them a powerful vision of hell, a most vital institution in the violent bestiary of the religion of those days.

The small Valley community, in common with Christian pilgrims, expressed their faith in inscriptions that they wrote in the open tombs. The majority of these are simple prayers and other religious sentiments; others are straightforward records of names and events in peoples lives; most are written on the tombs' walls in a straggly hand with a poor brush and in the dull natural pigments of red earth:

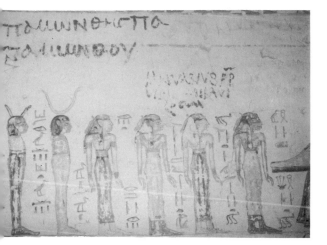

*Coptic graffiti drawn among the ancient decorations in the
tomb of Ramesses VI*

*I beseech thee, Jesus Christ, my Lord, suffer me not
to follow after my desire; let not my thoughts have
domination over me: let me not die in my sins, but
accept thy servant for good.*

In the rear of tomb number 3, made originally for
a prince of Ramesses III, an elaborate chapel was
built with a tiled floor and locally made, rather
wobbly columns of the Corinthian order, cut from
the sandstone fragments of an ancient temple.
Around the mouth of a nearby tomb, that of Ramesses
IV, the remains of another, simpler church and several
households were uncovered and cleared away as
excavators dug through the debris in the search for
royal tombs beneath. Papyrus letters, small stones
and pieces of pottery with letters and prayers written
upon them, cooking vessels, bread ovens and grana-
ries, water pots, shells of the strange nut from the
plant *Balinites*, which produces hallucinations when
it is eaten, fodder for animals, beehives, honeycombs,
and chicken bones formed the remains of this small
colony of Christians that lived in the ancient Underworld.

These austere Valley dwellers wore the dull
browns and purples of coarse peasant clothing. On
feast days they ate the strong garlic and Nile fish
dishes of the period but on the whole they saw little
meat or other luxuries on the table. Today we would
hardly recognize the services that these early Christians held in their small tomb-churches with their
different attitudes of prayer and long recitals of plain
liturgical rhythmic chanting accompanied with

drums, sistra and small cymbals. All this time the
great tombs, with their bright pagan images, stood
open and defenceless against anything and anybody.
If it was the clever siting of many of the tombs that
saved them from their destruction by flooding, it was
surely the piety of the sentiments perceived in the
ancient paintings that saved them from attack by
the hermit priests and from being damaged in the idle
moments of the donkey boys who brought provisions
to the Valley.

During our work in the tomb of Ramesses XI we
found several simple constructions that had been
built by the Christians who had used the tomb as a
stable and a kitchen. We found fragments of a large
variety of cultivated plants, many of which were
mixed with the great heaps of golden straw that still
lay in a collapsed dry stone manger at the rear of the
upper corridor. Also in this straw was a mite (a tiny
Byzantine coin) and some fragments of the fine pottery of the period, skilfully painted in bold lines of
cream and black on red ware. Nearby there was a
broken cooking pot, the rough palm-fibre string with
which it had been suspended over a fire still passing
through its handle. A small thin-shelled hen's egg
filled with ancient maggots formed the remaining
debris of the household. The burial chamber at the
end of the tomb had been walled off and its deep shaft
had been used for rubbish and the corpses of many
unwanted puppies, huddled together and starved to
death.

At that time the economy of Egypt was on a down-
hill path. By the time of the Arab invasion of Egypt
in AD 639 the government was unable to offer any
effective opposition although the sheer size and wealth
of the nation was still more than a match for the small
Arab force, had it been effectively organized. But the
Emperor in Constantinople was ill and the Governor
of Upper Egypt, 'The renowned general and consul,
the most magnificent patrician of the Empire, Theo-
dosius', simply collected the taxes and left for Alexandria where, in the September of 642, the Imperial
fleet sailed away leaving Egypt forever. The delighted
Arab general Amr Ibn-al-As wrote to the Calif Omar
in Mecca that he had taken the huge defenceless city
of Alexandria and that all Egypt was his.

The powerful Christian church of Egypt came under
considerable pressure to convert to the new faith.
Some of the monasteries were taxed so heavily that
they were forced to close, while those that resisted
were put to the sword. The small hermitic groups,
such as the one in the Valley that had been supported
by the monasteries, died out. About one hundred

years after the Arab conquest, the Valley of the Kings was again deserted—the last fragile links with ancient Egypt finally broken.

The new rulers of Egypt brought a different, fluid vision of history to the land. The ancient Egyptians were regarded, if at all, as a remote race who had lived in the land long before. Large numbers of Egyptians converted to the new faith and the country was heavily settled by tribes of Beduin who came to the great river to cultivate its rich silt. At Thebes, large numbers of Ababda tribesmen, crossing from Arabia over long periods of time, settled in villages by the ancient tombs and temples. These desert people counted their descent from Abdullah Ibn-al-Zubain of the Quraysh tribe, to which General Amr Ibn-al-As had belonged. In the first accounts of Thebes since Classical times, medieval Arab travellers wrote more about the large local potteries and of the donkey and camel markets than of the ruined monuments that littered the small towns. In Europe too, the Valley of the Kings and, indeed, Thebes itself, had disappeared from the geographies and lived, like Troy and Mycenae, only as a part of the fabulous legends of Classical manuscripts.

Many of the contemporary commentaries on the Classical authors bemoaned the fate of the great city whose magnificence was described in dozens of texts from the Bible to Homer. 'What beauties might we not find if we could reach the royal city' declared the learned Boussuet in his discourse written for the education of the future French king, Louis XV. But although the ancient city was visited by a succession of European travellers during the 17th century none of them recognized the vast ruins as those of 'hundred-gated' Thebes. Two missionary Jesuits, Fathers Protias and François measured and counted the ruins so carefully that it is still possible to recognize many of the monuments of Thebes from their descriptions, and yet the essential connection was missed. They also visited the Valley of the Kings, 'the place of mummies called the Biban el Melouc'. The Arab name means 'The doorways of the Kings' but although the true purpose of the Valley had been retained in this name, the connection was still not made.

Then, in 1707, another Jesuit, Father Claude Sicard, was sent from a previous post in Syria to manage the mission at Cairo. On the orders of the Dauphin he was to make records and plans of the monuments of Egypt and, with the zest typical of his order, he ventured further up the Nile than any other European had done and lived to tell his tale. Sicard was the first European to record descriptions of the monuments of Aswan and Philae and he also recognized, amid the small towns and villages that were built by the dusty mounds of ruined temples and tombs that were situated on a bend in the Nile, the remains of ancient Thebes. No educated person travelled without the Classical texts for authority and guidance and Sicard carried both Strabo and Diodorus with him and both texts confirmed his identification of Thebes and its monuments. In the course of several trips to Thebes Sicard compiled careful records of the monuments and made a remarkable series of maps and plans. He also identified the Valley of the Kings and his account of the royal tombs, the first in more than one thousand years, begins:

These sepulchres of Thebes are tunnelled into the rock and are of astonishing depth. Halls, rooms, all are painted from top to bottom. The variety of colours, which are almost as fresh as the day they were finished, gives an admirable effect. There are as many hieroglyphs as there are animals and objects represented, which makes us suppose that we have there the story of the lives, virtues, acts, combats and victories of the princes who are buried there, but it is impossible for us to decipher them at present.

In the Valley Sicard counted ten open tombs, which were undoubtedly the same group that had been inscribed by the visitors of the Classical period. In 1716 he published an account of his journeys in the form of a letter to the Comte de Toulouse and in the following year a missionary journal in Paris printed a memoir of one of his trips. Some of the material gathered by Sicard, including a few maps, was placed by him in the Bibliothèque Nationale, where they were consulted by many of the cartographers of the day. It is a great misfortune that the large part of Sicard's papers were lost after his death in Cairo, during the plague of 1726; a mournful ending for the man who had rediscovered the city of Thebes.

The next account of the Valley was published in 1743 by Richard Pococke in his *Description of the East*. Pococke, an English clergyman, who later became a bishop, had sailed right through Egypt and spent a lot of time in the Valley making drawings and maps of the tombs. A later traveller, William Hamilton, recorded a graffito of Pococke's that he found on the wall of a Theban tomb during his visit in 1803—'Richard Pococke Anglus, September 16 1739'. Unfortunately its position was not noted and it is now lost. Pococke's account of the Valley provides us with the first modern description of its landscape:

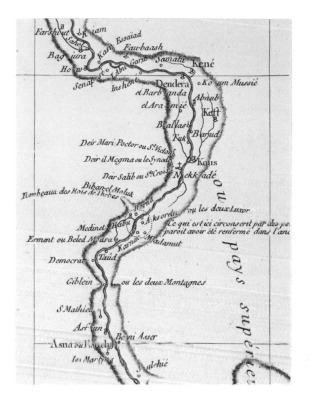

A detail from one of the first maps to include the Valley of the Kings. Published by the French cartographer d'Anville in Paris, this edition was prepared for the French Government commission that accompanied the Napoleonic army in 1798

We came to a part [of the path] that is wider, being a round opening, like an amphitheatre, and ascended by a narrow steep passage about ten feet high, which seems to have been broken down through the rock. By this passage we came to the Biban el Meluke. There are signs of about eighteen tombs, if I made no mistake. However, it is to be remarked that Diodorus says seventeen of them only remained until the time of the Ptolomies; and I found the entrance to about that number, now there are only nine that can be entered into. The hills on each side are high steep rocks, and the whole place is covered with rough stones that seem to have rolled from them, the grottoes are cut into the rock in a most beautiful manner in long rooms or galleries under the mountain, which are of a close white freestone that cuts like chalk, and is as smooth as the finest stucco work, some of them painted, being as fresh as if they were but just finished.

It is an honest description and seldom have the later writings on the Valley conveyed their information in such a clear way. But Pococke's manuscripts and his book, which despite its great price was very popular with his contemporaries, contains some mysteries. Later archeologists have puzzled over the positions of some of the tombs shown on his plans: are some of them tombs that have been covered over and lost since Pococke's time? Now, most of the tombs have been identified but this first map of the Valley has become, in part, a sort of treasure map.

Pococke's drawing of the Valley—the oldest that is known. Many of the tomb entrances shown may be readily identified but others, perhaps incorrectly drawn by him, have since caused much speculation among archeologists. The lower half of the drawing accurately illustrates Pococke's written description of the ancient entrance to the Valley

The Sepulchres of the Kings of Thebes. To the Honourable William Herbert.

After Sicard and Pococke, travellers to the Valley carried these accounts of discovery with them to aid their investigations, but their journeys were still dangerous for all that. James Bruce, the Scottish explorer, visited the Valley in 1768 on his way to Ethiopia during his search for the Nile:

> It is a solitary place; and my guides, either from a natural impatience and distaste that these people have at such employments, or that their fears of the banditti that live in the caverns of the mountains were real, importuned me to return to the boat, even before I had begun my search, or got into the mountains where are the many large apartments of which I was in quest.
>
> Within one of these sepulchres, on a panel, were [painted] several musical instruments strewed upon the ground, chiefly of the hautboy kind, with a

One of the harpists from the tomb of Ramesses III as published by Bruce. His original sketch, now long lost, has been greatly elaborated by the plate engraver who, unused to the ancient Egyptian manner, interpreted it in the contemporary neo-classical taste

mouthpiece of reed . . . In three following panels were painted, in fresco, three harps, which merited the utmost attention . . . As the first harp seemed to be the most perfect, and least spoiled, I immediately attached myself to this, and desired my clerk to take upon him the charge of the second. In this way, by sketching exactly, and loosely, I hoped to have made myself master of all the paintings in that cave, perhaps, to have extended my researches to others, though, in the sequel, I found myself miserably deceived. Upon seeing the preparations I was making to proceed farther in my researches, my conductors lost all sort of subordination. With great clamour and marks of discontent, they dashed their torches against the largest harp, and made the best of their way out of the cave, leaving me and my people in the dark; and all the way as they went, they made dreadful denunciations of tragical events that were immediately to follow upon their departure from the cave. There was no possibility of doing more. Very much vexed, I mounted my horse to return to the boat. The road lay through a very narrow valley, and a number of large stones were rolled down upon me. Finding, by the impatience of the horse, that several of these stones had come near him, I levelled my gun as near as possible, by the ear, and fired one barrel among them. A moment's silence ensued, and then a loud howl, which seemed to have come from thirty or forty persons. I took my servant's blunderbuss and discharged it where I heard the howl, and a violent confusion of tongues followed, but no more stones.

> Fearing further hostilities, we cast off our rope that fastened us, and let ourselves over to the other side. About twelve at night a gentle breeze began to blow, which wafted us up to Luxor, where there was a governor, for whom I had letters.
>
> We were well received by the governor, who, having made him a small present, furnished us with provisions, and, among several other articles, some brown sugar; and as we had seen limes and lemons in great perfection at Thebes, we were resolved to refresh ourselves with some punch, in remembrance of Old England.

The drawing, which Bruce made in the tomb, appeared as a plate in his five-volume account of his travels, published in 1790. It was the first picture of a scene in the royal tombs to be published and it caught the imagination of many; it was as if the Old Testament musicians had been seen anew. The tomb in which Bruce had made his drawing, that of Ramesses III,

A section of the Wadyien *about half a kilometre from the entrance to the Valley. Another old photograph of the ancient track to the Valley that is now covered with asphalt and flanked with lamp posts and roadsigns*

became known as 'Bruce's Tomb', and the painted harpists were among the most celebrated sights in the Valley. It shows harpists playing before some of the ancient gods –an unusual representation in Egyptian art of an act of worship by music. Curiously, the scene which so excited Bruce and his successors is quite different from the usual tomb decoration in the Valley

in that it was painted in one of a number of small side chambers to the main tomb; these are equally atypical.

Most of the other travellers who visited the Valley during the last years of the 18th century were content to describe what Pococke and Bruce had seen before them. One traveller who stands out from the rest, however, is another Englishman, 'Will Geo. Browne 1792' as he wrote his name in a graffito in another of the small side chambers in Bruce's Tomb. Browne's description is written in a lucid and straightforward style that rings true even when it differs from other descriptions of the time:

35

An engraving from a photograph, made one hundred years after Bruce's visit, showing the doors of some of the sidechambers in the tomb of Ramesses III. At that time the tomb was still half-choked with rocks and debris brought down by periodic flash floods

Several of these sepulchres have been described by Pococke with sufficient minuteness; he has even given plans of them. But in conversation with persons at Assiut and in other parts of Egypt, I was always informed that they had not been discovered till within the last thirty years, when a son of Sheik Mamam, a very powerful chief of the Arabs, who governed all of the South of Egypt from Achmimi to Nubia, caused four of them to be opened, in expectation of finding treasure.

They had probably been rifled in very ancient times; but how the memory of them should have been lost remains to be explained. One of those I visited exactly answers Dr. Pococke's description; but the other three appear materially different from any of his plans. It is therefore possible that some of those which he saw have been gradually closed up by the sand, and that the son of Mamam had discovered others.

They are cut into the free-stone rock, in appearance upon one general plan, though differing in parts. First a passage of some length; then a chamber; a continuation of the first passage turns abruptly to the right, where is the large sepulchral chamber, with a sarcophagus of red granite in the midst.

In the second part of the passage of the largest are several cells or recesses on both sides. In these appear the chief paintings, representing the mysteries, which as well as the hieroglyphics covering all the walls are very fresh. I particularly observed the two harpers described by Bruce; but his engraved figures seem to be from memory.

In this text, Browne, not usually given to extravagant description, gives us information not found elsewhere. One unusual observation is that of the shape of a 'typical' royal tomb, for there are very few that have a sharp right turn in them, and only one of these, that of Ramesses II, is known to have been open in Browne's day. But if the story of the excavations in the Valley by the Sheik's son is accurate, it may indeed be possible that Browne did visit two such tombs, for another example of this type of tomb was discovered lying open in the West Valley within ten years of Browne's visit. It is possible, therefore, that Browne visited this tomb—the results of the 'Turkish excavations'—and if true, it is a unique account of what must have been a most interesting operation: the first archeological exploration of the Valley of the Kings!

4

The Emperor's Engineers

The work that first enabled Europe to share some of the visual delights of ancient Egypt and the Valley of the Kings was the magnificent '*Description de l'Égypte, ou Recueil des Observations et des Recherches qui ont été faites en Égypte', publié par les ordres de sa Majesté l'Empereur Napoleon le Grand, à Paris de l'Imprimerie Imperiale*. This book, even grander than its title, represented the labour of a commission of a hundred men of science and arts who had worked in Egypt for nearly three years. Its effect upon European taste was substantial; it laid bare the Egypt described by the solitary travellers of the previous half century in plates of great skill and artistry. In size, too, it represented grandeur, for the work was published in twenty-one unwieldy leather-bound folios that weighed close to forty pounds each. These elephantine books were accompanied by a smaller-sized set of commentary volumes that fill well over a yard of bookshelf. Between them, they represented the single successful outcome of Napoleon's excursion to Egypt.

Conceived in the Emperor's most Alexandrian of moods, Napoleon's plan, with British interests ever at the front of his mind, was to take Egypt as the first stage of the invasion of the East as far as India, where he had engaged in an alliance with some dissatisfied Indian princes who welcomed the chance to throw the British out of their country and were prepared to fight. The grand design collapsed, however, when Nelson sank the French fleet off Alexandria, in the 'Battle of the Nile', thus isolating the expeditionary force from Europe and causing Napoleon to lose interest in his grandiose plan. He soon abandoned the Army of the Orient for the richer political pastures of Europe, but the three-year occupation of Cairo by the French army, which he left behind, had a profound cultural effect upon Egypt that has lasted until the present day. The enormous public interest that the campaign generated, which was nobly served in the publication of the *Description* that began in 1809, brought European awareness of Egypt and its antiquities to a new height. Despite the fact that the band of scholars who accompanied the army on the campaign were used for military as well as cultural purposes during their stay in the East, one receives the curious impression from the *Description* that here was the General of the armies of France on a grand tour. What other reason could sensibly see Napoleon in Bethlehem? Though far more brutal in his methods than even the most chauvinistic tourist, Napoleon appears like an English lord taking the tour, accompanied by his bodyguard, his doctor and his artists!

Following the defeat of the Mameluke army, who had controlled Egypt at that time, Napoleon settled with his troops in Cairo. To 'help Egypt towards the Light' the Institut National d'Égypte was quickly established, and housed in a villa of one of the deposed Mamelukes. It had four divisions of scholarship: 1. *Mathématiques*, 2. *Physique*, 3. *Litterature et Arts* and 4. *Économie politique*. The members of this Institut were recruited from the hundred-strong body of scholars brought, by order of Napoleon, with the army from France—the Commission of Arts and Sciences.

At that time basic information about Egypt was limited to the few books containing the observations of travellers in the country. Straight away the Commission started to survey and study the area around Cairo, the population, the architecture of all periods, and the flora and fauna, with a thoroughness of attention to which no area in the East had previously been subjected. In the buildings of the Institut, scientific experiments were conducted in the presence of interested Cairenes who could also have their portraits painted by one of the Institut artists whose *atelier* had been established nearby. If Napoleon's handling of the military campaigns in Egypt and Syria was cruel and ill-considered, the purpose and function of the Institut and the Commission was a marvellous, daring, intellectual idea. Napoleon meant the French presence to be felt in Egypt, in preparation for the long occupation that was never to be. The *Description* was put into the plans of the Institut at the very beginning of the Egyptian adventure, to be made for the people and scholars of France and paid for from public funds. Three years later, and after many trials and tribulations, and the death of thirty-four of their colleagues, the scholars of the Commission returned to France with its precious collections of plans and manuscripts.

In practice the Commission had the traditional strengths and weaknesses of all committees. While it possessed the abilities to cover far more territory than any one person could, in times of stress or danger the relationships between the individual members of the Commission, and between them and the army, became highly acrimonious and their work suffered. Nevertheless, the *Description* was a pure triumph of the system. Though it contains the work of many different people, no one man, no one discipline, no small clique of people, may be said to have exercised ultimate intellectual authority over the whole work—unless one acknowledges the pervading inspiration of Napoleon himself, who gave birth to the project and whose continuing attentions saw that it reached a satisfactory conclusion. Despite the fact that the campaign could well have been a bad memory for the Emperor and one which he did not want memorialized, the Commission produced the first volumes of the *Description* within eight years of its return to France.

Following his occupation of Cairo, Napoleon dispatched an army in pursuit of some of the Mameluke nobles who had fled to Upper Egypt. This force, commanded by General Desaix leading four brigades, drove right through Upper Egypt eventually forcing

Desaix and Belliard watching Denon working on a drawing of the facade of Denderah temple, close to Thebes

the retreating enemy beyond the first cataract of the Nile at Aswan. With Desaix rode Baron Vivant Denon, a most remarkable man who later, in the post of Director General of the Museums of France, helped to found the collections of the Louvre. A friend of Madame de Pompadour and Louis XV he embarked upon a diplomatic career during which, it has been suggested, he became the lover of at least three European queens. Denon was out of France when the revolution broke and his properties were confiscated in his absence, but later he returned and at the *salon* of Josephine he was introduced to and befriended by Napoleon, who invited him to Egypt with his 'Army of the Orient'. Although a member of the Institut, Denon was not a part of the Commission but travelled widely with the army, drawing everything that caught his eye with a fine, bold, Rembrantesque line. During the ride into Upper Egypt he describes the French Army breaking into an 'ecstacy of admiration', clapping their hands and shouting aloud as they sighted the monuments of Thebes. 'The complete possession of Egypt was achieved, we occupied the ancient metropolis'. From the many memoirs of the Napoleonic incursion into Upper Egypt one gains the impression that it was partly conducted in a spirit of amazement and revelation. The expedition was not, after all, the solitary wanderings of men who spent their lives with the unusual and exotic, but a relatively well-equipped army of many hundreds of men, where conversation and companionship allowed a flow of impressions and comparisons among the participants.

Upon reaching Thebes, Desaix rested his army in a camp on the east bank of the river. Here, according to the poet Barthèlemy, they relaxed:

> Desaix, now far from the fields of Mars
> commends the exploits of the army to the
> engraving tool,
> and the same hand that belabours Mamelukes,
> during a day's respite, captures monuments
> in wonderful works to witness his remarkable journey.

From this encampment, near the temples of Karnak, Denon travelled across the Nile to western Thebes, Gurna and the Tombs of the Kings. His account of his journey to the Valley is so evocative that it is worth quoting at length. It is full of the adventures of a party of young bored army officers, in the bright blue, white and gold uniforms of the French Army, riding past the ruined temples of the Kings in the company of this compelling antiquarian, now over fifty and grown a little portly but as energetic as ever.

Keeping before the troop, who had, however gained on me, I hastened to the two colossal statues, and took a full view of them with the effect of the sunrise, at the same hour as strangers used to report hither to hear the musical sounds from the colossus of Memnon. I then proceeded to the solitary place called the Memnonium. Whilst I was thus absorbed in observation, my companions forgot to call me, then perceiving the detachment half a league ahead of me, I galloped up to rejoin them. The troops were tired and I found them debating whether they should not give up the expedition to the tombs. For my own part, vexed as I was, I said not a word, and I profited more by my silence than I should probably have done by giving loose to my feelings, for we at length resumed our journey without any further discussion. We first passed through the villages of Gurna, the ancient Necropolis, and in approaching their subterranean habitations, we were for the third time saluted by the incorrigible inhabitants by a volley of musketry. This was the only place which held out against our government. Strong in their sepulchral retreats, they came out like spectres only to alarm men; culpable by many other crimes they concealed their remorse and fortified their disobedience in the obscurity of their excavations, which are so numerous as of themselves to attest the immense population of ancient Thebes.

It was across these humbler tombs that the kings were carried two leagues from the palace, into the silent valley that was to become for the future their peaceful and lasting abode; this valley to the north-west of Thebes becomes insensibly narrower, and flanked as it is with perpendicular rocks, whole ages have been able to produce only very slight alterations of its ancient form. Towards the extremity, the opening between the rock even now offers scarcely space enough to pass by the tombs, so that the sumptuous processions which no doubt accompanied the ceremony of royal interment must have produced a striking contrast with the frowning asperity of these wild rocks; if however they went by this road, it was probably only for the purpose of obtaining a longer space, in which to roll the full tide of funereal pomp, for the valley, even from its commencement tending towards the south, the spots where the [private] tombs are, cannot be a great distance from the Memnonium.

In the second paragraph Denon describes the ancient entrance to the Valley of the Kings that has now been destroyed to allow the tarmacadam road to carry automobiles and buses right into the heart of the Valley. This natural gate, so easily guarded in ancient times, must have provided the early travellers with a very different experience from today's. On their arrival at the Valley they would have passed through a steep narrow crack in the rock terrace and climbed some fifteen feet up to the floor of the centre of the Valley. Another member of the Commission, Costaz, commenting upon the narrow entrance, the only way one could obtain access to the Valley by the long road from the plain of Thebes, suggested that it had been cut through the rock terrace by the ancient Egyptians to allow access to the tombs above, isolated in the solitary basin in the cliffs. Later commentators on the Valley have little to say about the ancient entrance and it was slowly enlarged, without record, until the final breaking through of the modern road in the 1950s. Denon continues his account:

It was not until after marching three quarters of an hour in this desert Valley, that in the middle of the rocks we observed all at once, some openings parallel to the ground: these openings at first displayed no other architectural ornaments than a door in a simple square frame, with a flattened oval in the centre of the upper part, on which are inscribed in hieroglyphics a beetle, the figure of a man with a hawk's head [here Denon forgets, it is a ram-headed sun god that appears over the doors of the tombs] and beyond the circle, two figures on their knees in the act of adoration.

Apart from confusing this sun god with hawk-headed Horus, Denon gives a good description of the outer doorways of the tombs that were open in the Valley. The two kneeling women sitting either side of the oval—which is really a circle, but Denon was standing on the ground beneath and perspective must have flattened it for him—are Isis and Nepthys, two sister goddesses who were the chief mythic mourners at ancient Egyptian funerals. The circle is the sun, centred over the outside door directly above the 'passages of the sun's path', the corridors of the tomb. Inside the red sun, the figures of the sun god and the beetle represent the rebirth of the king. Here the sun god symbolizes the flesh of the king's corpse, the scarab beetle the mysterious regenerative force that aided resurrection. On some of the tomb doors the sun disk is drawn appearing between two hills at the time of daybreak. These hills are the hieroglyph for 'the horizon over which the sun rises' and it is this dawning sun, the revived king, that the two sister goddesses worship. In some of these scenes they

The first known photograph of the Valley of the Kings, published by the Englishman Francis Frith in 1860, shows the rock screen that hid the small natural entrance to the Valley

A drawing of one of the best examples of the scene placed over the entrances of the later royal tombs in the Valley. Before World War 1 the scene was almost completely destroyed by flood water

are joined by two figures of the king himself, all worshipping together the mysterious reappearance of the day, and of order in the land of Egypt.

The representation of the beetle that appears in the sun drawn above the tomb doors is of *Scarabeus sacer*, which lays its eggs in a ball of dung some two inches across; this it subsequently pushes around with its rear legs with great determination, looking for a suitable crevice in which to deposit it. Inside the ball, the larvae feed on the dung—until they eventually break through the ball to freedom. This was regarded by the ancient Egyptians as a most mysterious process of self-generation: the young beetles appearing from a ball of dung after they had been helped only by a single scarab beetle. In a grand analogy, it was a beetle that was seen to be rolling the sun itself over the eastern horizon, as the climax to the self-generative processes that had taken place during the night. The beetle itself became a symbol for the change of state from death to rebirth, which was of primary interest to the ancient theologians, who described it in some of the long texts of the royal tombs in extraordinary detail. The beetle also became one of the most popular symbols of ancient Egypt and small scarab seals were made in millions, a tradition that continues to this day. It seems too, that parts of the mysterious functions of this beetle have never been lost since ancient times; early in the present century the village women of Thebes ate these horny black insects which were supposed to aid their fertility, and many properties similar to the ancient symbolisms are attributed to *Scarabeus sacer* in the writings of the mediaeval alchemists.

Denon continued:

As soon as the threshold of the first gate is passed, we discover long galleries twelve feet wide and twenty in length cased with stucco sculptured and painted: the arching of an elegant elliptical figure [across a vault] is covered with innumerable hieroglyphics, disposed with so much taste, that not withstanding the similar grotesqueness of the forms, and the total absence of tones or aerial perspective, the ceiling makes an agreeable whole, and a rich and harmonious association of colours.

Denon and the officers continued their inspection of the tombs, 'preceded by torches' but the officers were impatient to return to camp and he was only allowed a short time in each of the six tombs he visited and, 'even this was not granted with the best possible grace'. Denon, amazed by the works of art that surrounded him and which, as he says, would have taken weeks to study completely, still did not possess the key to the language; only the artists' skills could tell him of the quality and care of the monuments. So he went from tomb to tomb decorated 'with a taste that might decorate our most splendid salons' until the time came to leave.

The trumpet had already sounded to horse when I discovered some little chambers, on the walls of which were represented all kinds of arms, such as panoplies, coats of mail, tiger skins, bows, arrows, quivers, pikes, javelins, sabres, casques and whips. [In common with many other travellers he had come across the small chambers in Bruce's tomb and, he too, compares the splendours of pharoahs court with the accoutrements of his own time.] How was it possible to leave such precious curiosities without taking a drawing of them? How to return without having a sketch to show? I earnestly demanded a quarter of an hour's grace: I was allowed twenty minutes; one person lighted me, while another held a taper to every object that I pointed out to him, and I completed my task prescribed with spirit and correctness.

Denon had spent three hours in the tombs and was hurried away back to camp where he observed: 'nobody had anything to do. I found on this occasion, as on all others, that a visit to Thebes was like the attack of a fever; it was a kind of crisis which left behind an impression of indescribable impatience, enthusiasm, irritation and fatigue.' A sentiment that many others have since shared!

Having left Egypt in 1799 with Napoleon, Denon was able to steal a march on the *Description*, to which he later contributed, by publishing his own account of the Egyptian adventure which was widely read. This hefty portfolio of engravings with a written account, was the first set of drawings of the Egyptian scene by an accomplished professional hand that Europe had seen and it was these pictures more than any others that started the craze that brought Egyptian styles into the European decorative arts.

A small body of scholars was sent by the Commission to follow the army of General Desaix into Upper Egypt. They were lead by Girard, of the First Section of the Institut and Chief Engineer of Roads and Bridges. The group, consisting of three mining engineers, four bridge and road builders, and a lone sculptor, left Cairo for Assuit in Upper Egypt on 18 March 1799 with the munitions and supply barges that were being dispatched to Desaix's army and arrived at Thebes ten days later. Two of the group stand out from the rest in their extraordinary devotion to the study of the monuments—Prosper Jollois and Baron Edouard de Villiers du Terrage. When they left Cairo they were aged 23 and 29 respectively. Eventually these young men were to have as great an influence over both the Commission and the *Description* as any of their august contemporaries. As soon as they came into contact with the great temples of Upper Egypt they were completely overwhelmed by them and spent all their time carefully measuring and drawing the architecture. Both Jollois and de Villiers were engineers, and it was their training in accurate scientific draughting which supplied the model for the style and method of their work upon the monuments. During their research they had many arguments with poor Girard who was more concerned with the physical properties of the Nile than with the ancient tombs and temples. In the accounts of these heated exchanges, one of which took place in the embarrassed presence of General Desaix himself, one may detect all the impatience and ardour of people who are hindered in their work by those whom they feel neither care nor understand it.

Jollois and de Villiers were the first to survey the Valley using cartographic principles. Their map in the *Description* shows sixteen tombs, eleven of which were open; two more than Pococke, their predecessor, was able to locate. In late August 1799 they made a spectacular discovery:

A detail from the enormous map of the Valley prepared by Jollois and de Villiers for the Description. *A plan of Amenhotep III's tomb, which they discovered lying open in the West Valley, is shown set into the surrounding landscape. The tomb's corridors are about three metres wide*

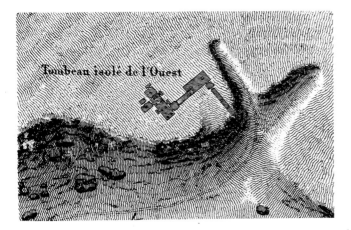

Tombeau isolé de l'Ouest

It was in the course of our researches in the Valley of the Kings that crossing the ridges on the west side, we were led, Jollois and I, into a secondary valley where we found a tomb which had not been noticed by any of the travellers who had preceded us. As much as the care which we had put into looking into all the grottoes which can be found in this portion of the Lybian Hills, it was chance that made us discover it.

The tomb is still difficult to locate today and the two energetic engineers must have been examining the landscape very carefully. But were they really the first travellers to visit the tomb? The tomb they found was that of Amenhotep III, situated in the West Valley away from the majority of the royal monuments. It is typical of the Eighteenth Dynasty, designed to be covered over after the royal burial, its entrance hidden. The area of the tomb is particularly vulnerable to flash flooding and the accompanying slurries of wet debris would almost certainly have kept the entrance blocked despite any forced opening of the tomb by robbers in ancient times. Yet it is unlikely that the two Frenchmen did more than walk in the door of the open tomb, since they had a limited time at Thebes and there were thousands of locations in the Theban Hills more suggestive for a little tentative digging than this lonely spot. The matter is a little strange, especially if we bear in mind the earlier description of the shape of a 'typical' royal tomb by Browne: 'First a passage of some length; then a chamber; a continuation of the first passage turns abruptly to the right.' Possibly Browne had already visited Amenhotep III's tomb in the West Valley. Inside the tomb, the two Frenchmen found 'considerable portions of the plaster were detached from the wall in a manner in which it was possible to carry away, but we found that their fragility rendered their transport impossible.' Water damage of wall plaster is what they describe, and it is certainly still visible. Certainly many of the Valley's tombs were damaged by water within a few years of their rediscovery, due to the fact that the huge wells in the tombs, which trapped the incoming flood waters, were used as rubbish tips for the encumbering debris as it was cleared from the lower corridors and chambers. So it may be that Jollois and de Villiers were visiting the site of an earlier clearance, perhaps the 'Turkish' excavations that Browne described. Indeed, the fact that Browne's description of the 'typical' tomb and the excavations of the sheik's son both come from his account of the Valley suggests a single

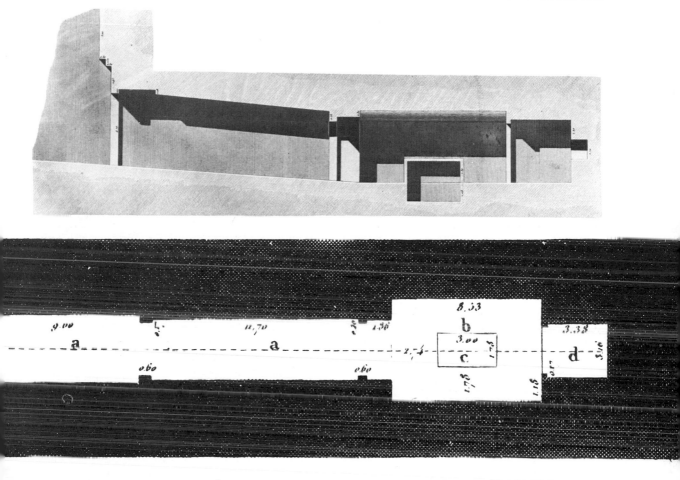

The plan and elevation of the tomb of Ramesses VII from the Description. Following the field work of Jollois and de Villiers, the engravers who made the plates for the Description employed the elegant conventions used in the engineering drawings of the day. Unfortunately, the beauty of these plans belies their many inaccuracies

source, and that Browne had an informant with some knowledge of the Valley and its then recent history.

On the same day that Girard's party left Cairo for Upper Egypt the director of the Commission, Monge, appointed two further commissions to study in Upper Egypt. The scholars were having a thin time in Cairo: the population had become antagonistic toward the occupying army and during Napoleon's brief incursion into Syria many of the members of the Commission had seen their fellows die in the vicious short campaign. Monge showed an almost complete ignorance of Upper Egypt and its whereabouts in conversation with his fellow Institut members but he was persuaded to allow two parties of twenty men each to embark upon trips up the Nile as far as Aswan and Philae. One of these groups of scholars was to examine the hieroglyphic inscriptions in an attempt to decipher the ancient writings which had not been read for over a thousand years. Upon their arrival at Thebes the two groups met the members of Girard's commission

who had been living in and studying the monuments on both sides of the river. The methods and conventions established by Jollois and de Villiers were adopted by the rest of the commission in their maps and drawings and all the scholars mingled together in their tasks and travels, some venturing as far as the Red Sea. But the perilous state of the French-occupying forces in Cairo and Alexandria interrupted these idylls in the south; Commissioner Monge had already left the country with Napoleon's personal party and on 6 September 1799 the scholars reluctantly returned to Cairo so as not to be cut off from the French Army.

After protracted negotiations with the British, who now controlled the situation in Egypt after landing a force near Alexandria, it was agreed that the scholars should be allowed to leave Egypt with their papers, but that any large antiquities gathered by the army or the Commission should be surrendered to the British force. Eventually the scholars reached France with their papers in 1801, when schemes were initiated by Monge and others to set up an editorial board and engravers to produce and publish the data. The homeward journey was a terrible mixture of administrative incompetence and personal animosities. In 1825 the French government, at the suggestion of the publishing committee, presented a special set of the *Description* to Sir Sydney Smith who, as commander of the British naval blockade of the French force, aided the passage of the scholars and their precious papers back to France aboard the freighter *l'Oiseau*. Stripped of virtually all their collections the true memorial to their labours would be the *Description* itself—only a very few antiquities from the Valley of the Kings ever reached France.

Considering its resources and attitudes it is most surprising that the French expedition collected so few large antiquities in the course of its investigations. Apparently, this was not the intention of all the members of the Commission for, according to the poet Barthèlemy:

Perhaps one day, struck by so much glory
Incredulous sons will disbelieve our story
But the marbles of the Nile conquered by these feats
True witnesses, will lift their voices.

In fact only eighteen pieces of stone were surrendered to the British forces at the departure of the French army, and these now lift their voices in the British Museum. Little else reached France with the soldiers and scholars except the precious papers of the Commission.

In the tomb of Amenhotep III de Villiers had found four small funerary figurines of the king and these did reach France but are still in the possession of his family. A small head in hard green schist that was also found in the tomb by the engineers is now in the Musée de Louvre. In the *Description* are pictures of these objects, but today it is difficult to recognize them, for they are drawn with scant understanding of the ancient and, at that time, little-known style. Nevertheless, it is easy to recognize the names of many kings in the engravings of the *Description*, for although no one could yet read the ancient texts, the artists made their copies with more care and accuracy

A funerary figure of Amenhotep III found by the French in that king's tomb. The small alabaster head of the king was also found in the tomb and is a rather more beautiful object than the drawing of the uncomprehending engraver would imply. It is presently in a collection in New York

than any previous examples. Among the objects Denon had taken from the royal tombs were some figures of deities in light-coloured wood that sound from his description to be similar to the figures of gods that have been uncovered by later archeologists in the Valley. The small foot of a mummy, also discovered by Denon, may have been that of a royal child, many such burials being placed in the royal tombs. After commenting upon its small size, Denon wrote, rather gallantly:

It was no doubt the foot of a young woman, a princess, a lovely creature, the perfect form of which had never been cramped by the absurdity of fashion.

Many of the men of the Napoleonic expedition left graffiti in the temples and tombs of Upper Egypt. Philae, the ultimate destination of the army and the parties of scholars on their Nile trips, contains the longest and most famous text giving measurements of the latitude and longitude of the major monuments they had visited, and the exact length of the metre unit. Even the laconic Girard left his name with a 'year 7' (of the Republic) in one of the temples that the indignant de Villiers accused him of sleeping in longer than studying. The sculptor who accompanied Jollois and de Villiers seems to have carved his fine epigrammatic surname, Castex, over half the monuments of Egypt; it seems that he was employed by Desaix's army as its monumental mason. The Valley, too, had many records of his passage. Later, he carved, doubtless with great delight, the famous lengthy inscriptions at Philae with the names of many soldiers and commission members. One might well imagine the burly red-headed fellow, arriving chisel in hand to spend a day chipping stealthily at the monuments. Unlike the numerous anonymous 'Kilroys' of today, these scholars are a most individual part of the Valley history and it is pleasant to read the names of the Girard expedition members in the royal tombs, as well as those of two botanists and their military friends who were part of the two Monge commissions. In one of the small side chambers in the tomb of Ramesses III, next to one containing Bruce's harpers, and in that of Ramesses IV—the first tomb that the visitor sees when approaching the centre of the Valley—are the names of all the scholars who worked at the site: Jollois, de Villiers, Costaz, who wrote the memoir of the Valley for the *Description*, and their friends. Prominent among the names is that of General Belliard, who commanded one of the four brigades of Desaix's army to Upper Egypt. Belliard later had the unenviable task of treating with the British to allow the 13,000 men under his command to leave the citadel of Cairo where they were trapped. He accomplished the task with honour and efficiency. At that time Desaix, who had left Egypt with Napoleon, had been dead a year, shot with a musket ball at the battle of Marengo, which he had

Apart from the graffiti left by members of the Napoleonic expedition on the walls of the royal tombs, the sole record of their visits in the Valley of the Kings is two scraps of paper that were excavated in the tomb of Ramesses XI during the work of our expedition in 1979. They had been screwed up, lighted and thrown down a dark deep shaft, presumably so that the scholars could see what lay at its bottom. On one of the pieces was a list of ordinance, unfortunately incomplete; the other, shown here, is an order to the quartermasters for a release of a ration of bread. The signatory of the order, with his lavish capital 'D' could, conceivably, have been Desaix himself. As in the graffiti that they left, the dates of the expedition are recorded by the years and months of the Revolutionary calendar

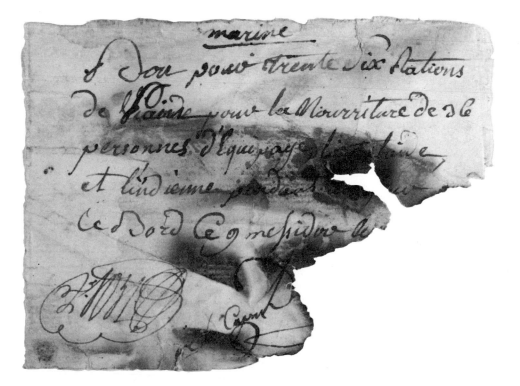

won for the French army. The brilliant young general, appointed commander of the projected army of occupation of England, would be sorely missed by Napoleon; in Egypt he had been known as the 'Just Sultan'.

Despite the limited time that the officers of the Commission had at their disposal and the uncertain conditions under which they worked, the members had produced marvellous results. Jollois himself became the last of three secretaries appointed to see the great volumes through the press. When the work of engraving and printing was completed in 1822, Napoleon was on Elba, and the books had been thirteen years in production. Today they are among the great books of the world and if we look into the magnificent frontispiece we may see, drawn upon a tablet leaning against a colossal statue at the left of the picture, a reproduction of the harpists that James Bruce had so inaccurately drawn some thirty years before the arrival of the Commission in the Valley, and which had added such a potent image to Europe's scanty vision of Ancient Egypt.

Time moved slowly in the realms of discovery during the 18th century. The map that Napoleon took with him to conquer Egypt had been made by d'Anville in 1766. The cartographer had been extremely careful in his choice of source material, comparing the accounts of the classical scholars with those of modern travellers that were available to him. Poor James Bruce was mortified to find upon his return from his journeys to the source of the Blue Nile that his discoveries had been pre-empted by the d'Anville map, which had employed the information of two Portuguese travellers who had visited the area more than one hundred and fifty years before. Such good information on Upper Egypt was difficult to come by. Napoleon sent Desaix and his army up the Nile with d'Anville's map which, as its chief authority on the region, utilized the fifty-year old manuscripts of Jesuit missionary, Father Claude Sicard. By the time that Napoleon's army had embarked from Egypt for Europe under the eyes of the British, Egypt's situation in the world had changed for ever. The country had been mapped, both its cultivated land and the two major cities of Cairo and Alexandria. Its flora and fauna had been classified and described, as had virtually all aspects of its culture and monuments. All this information appeared in both pictures and text in the volumes of the *Description*.

5

Lord Elgin's Agent and the English Squires

In the wake of the British Expeditionary Force that expelled the Napoleonic army from Egypt, a small party of officers and diplomats travelled through Upper Egypt visiting most of the sites that had held the camps of the army of General Desaix and the expeditions of the Commission the previous year. Led by William Hamilton, the party visited the major monuments of the Nile Valley and at the same time, made diplomatic contact with the factions that were alternatively fleeing and fighting in the power vacuum created by the French withdrawal. Hamilton was a professional diplomat and sometime antiquary, secretary to the British Ambassador in Istanbul, Lord Elgin. It was Hamilton who organized the removal and chipping of the splendid marble reliefs from the Parthenon of Athens that have since borne his master's name. Hamilton explored all over Egypt, and was also involved in the negotiations with the French concerning the antiquities that the Commission had gathered and which, as a part of the treaty concluded between the two armies, were to be surrendered to the victorious British force. Having a field liaison between the British Expeditionary Force and the French in such matters would have been of great interest to the British Government, especially considering the rapacious activities of Napoleon in other countries that had suffered conquest by him.

By far the most significant antiquity collected by the French, and handed over to the British army only after much heated debate, was a broken basalt slab inscribed with a text repeated in three scripts, one in Ptolomaic Greek and two in the ancient Egyptian. Of little consequence in the burden of its message, and coming from a town of little ancient importance, the stone was valuable only in that it held a key to the ancient writings which had so far eluded decipherment. With the ancient language accessible, the ancient Egyptians and their culture would be revealed and brought to life. Most of the surviving monuments were covered with hieroglyphics and they would be thus transformed into an open book. However, such

intellectual possibilities were far from the minds of the British and French soldiers as they bickered over the ownership of the stone in a house in Alexandria. Already the inscription had been inked and impressions sent to scholars in Europe for study. Casts had also been taken from the stone and these too were circulating. Ownership of the stone was, therefore, simply a matter of which nation should take the precious plunder. Already the importance of the slab was apparent to the officers of both armies who were concerned with the fate of the trophy. When Champollion deciphered the ancient hieroglyphic scripts in September 1822, the information gleaned from this trilingual stone from Rosetta was one of the crucial keys to the first dramatic moments of understanding.

At the time when the Rosetta stone was wrested from the French by Hamilton and his compatriots, this revelation was still a generation away, and Champollion was but eleven years old. The study of ancient Egypt was in the lull before the great waves of scientific interest would engulf the monuments and make them give up so many of their long lost secrets and messages. Hamilton's accounts of his journey in Egypt represent, probably for the last time, the efforts of a lone, informed but hieroglyphically illiterate traveller describing in general the monuments of Egypt as best he could and which, because of the scarcity of such accounts, could still be of interest to the scholar as well as the layman. For although there would be a huge increase in published accounts of travellers in Egypt and the Valley of the Kings over the next years they would be of little value to scholarship, on the whole simply reiterating what earlier tourists had seen before them—often, indeed, plagiarizing whole passages from the earlier accounts.

Hamilton's trip to the Valley in the last years of its innocence followed only months after the last visits of the French. As others before him, and as his successors would certainly do again, Hamilton begins the account of his trip with a faithful description of the long ride up the *Wadyein* to the tombs of the kings:

After travelling about one mile and a half among the mountains West of the village of El-Ebek, [now called El-Tarif] the gorge or road terminates in an irregular area where the rock is perpendicular on all sides. In this basin, or dell, are excavated in a hard calcerous stone, which in some places has taken on a very fine polish, the tombs of the kings of Thebes: a situation exactly corresponding to that given them by Strabo, who places them behind the Memnonium. At the time that this geographer visited Egypt, it was commonly reported that there had been forty of these monuments, though the Theban priests give an account of forty-seven. Only eighteen, however, were then visible, the rest having been destroyed: at present there are not above ten which are accessible: but the site of several others is very easily determined: nor is there any reason to discredit the account which enumerates above forty of them. The space was amply sufficient; and it is plain that the entrances have been choked up by the loose stones that have fallen down in the course of time from the slopes of the mountain, and which have brought with them the chips and fragments of stones which had been thrown up at the time of the excavations. There is, however, one consolation arising from this circumstance; that if by the exertions of the curious and the liberal, they ever come to be explored anew, the sculptures and paintings in them must be untouched, and the tombs of sarcophagi themselves unhurt; for the greater part were certainly closed before the profane were allowed to enter and destroy.

Hamilton's trip to the Valley was necessarily brief, but the impression may be gained from his text that if he had possessed the time and provisions he would have dug in the Valley and searched for those tombs that he felt to be just under the stony surface. As it was, he contented himself with descriptions of some of the scenes in the open tombs, and commented upon Bruce's drawing of the harpist scene in the tomb of Ramesses III.

On visiting the sepulchre which contains the representation of The Harpers, first given in Bruce's Travels, and which is much the largest of all, we found that the character which his drawing has given of this subject very much flatters the original. There is indeed considerable expression and elegance in these figures, but by no means that pure Grecian taste which that indefatigable traveller has given them. The harps are of a very handsome form, and richly painted on the stucco, but the ornaments are exclusively in the Egyptian character. However unequal the originals are to Mr. Bruce's representation of them, he deserves at least the thanks of the lovers of antiquity for having first opened our eyes to the true merit of Egyptian artists, and for having ventured to oppose the notion so generally entertained, of their being incapable of executing, either with the chisel or the pencil, other than rude and shapeless figures.

Bruce's quick drawing was still exciting comment nearly forty years after his visit!

Following the departure of the French and British armies, Cairo was riven with riots and street fighting and Egypt was hardly a congenial place for the visitor. In the years after Hamilton's trip few visitors saw the Valley and none wrote accounts of their journey. One man, a John Gordon, cut his name in two royal tombs at the head of the Valley, but he wrote no account of his travels which, his graffito informs us, brought him to the spot in 1804.

One result of Napoleon's attack on the supply lines of the British Empire in the Far East was that British attention became focussed on the trade routes to India, particularly Egypt. The British initially attempted to restore Turkish rule in the land, vainly trying to return the country to earlier and quieter days. As a part of her widening strategy of empire, Britain's policy was to keep Egypt inside the weakening Ottoman Empire—the diplomat Hamilton's account of his travels, for instance, was entitled *Remarks on Several Parts of Turkey*—but once the vulnerability of the rich province had become apparent to the government of Britain, and its crucial position in world politics had made its full impression upon the statesmen of Westminster, Egypt would not be left unknown and unattended as it had been in the past.

As described by Sir Robert Wilson, the official historian of the British campaign of 1801, the land of Egypt was seen to be 'the natural emporium of the riches of three quarters of the world and, in her own soil could rival America'. The country, as the French had also realized during their brief stay, had enormous economic potential. Not only was it situated in a crucial position in world trading patterns, but the arable land was rich and fertile with a passive and excessively hard working workforce. It was a perfect target for the activities of the European entrepreneurs of the day. However, the paramount consideration was the buttressing of the Ottoman Empire, a Turkey of which Egypt was a central part. Declining to control the country directly, the British Army left Egypt shortly after the French, leaving a number of warring factions to their own devices.

When in 1807 a small force returned to attempt to reinstate the old and greatly admired Mameluke order to power it was surprised and brilliantly defeated by an Ottoman Turkish army led by an Albanian commander, Mohammed Ali. This victory was the climax of a ruthless struggle for power that Mohammed Ali had waged in Egypt since the British departure, and all his principal foes were now seen to have been defeated. British prisoners were executed by the hundreds, their heads jammed on to poles and placed in the streets of Cairo. It was hardly the time for tourism or scholarly contemplation of the monuments. In a few years the Albanian troops of Mohammed Ali had killed the last of the Mamelukes; the final massacres of these extraordinary slave princes of the Turkish Empire in 1811 being initiated by the famous slaughter in the Citadel of Cairo when five hundred of the principal members of the caste were trapped and killed upon their horses in a Delacroixesque welter of silk, steel, blood and horseflesh.

Nevertheless, so great was the West's fascination with all aspects of Egypt that it was not long before two English travellers were in the Valley, where they carved their names upon the much embellished tomb of Memnon, Ramesses VI. One of these men, Thomas Legh, returned to Egypt several times. He was typical of the Englishmen of his day who were visiting Egypt in larger and larger numbers.

Legh was a country squire from Cheshire, a Justice of the Peace and a Member of Parliament. He was a learned man; a Doctor of Law, Fellow of the Royal Society and a Fellow of the Society of Arts. His companion on his first voyage was Charles Smelt, a vicar, who on his return to England became a country rector in Nottinghamshire. Legh wrote a book of his first adventure: *Narrative of a Journey in Egypt and the Country beyond the Cataracts*, which was illustrated and included a map of his travels. It was published by John Murray, whose excellent presses seem to have virtually monopolized the writings of these early egyptologists. In his day Murray's travel books and the rest of his publishing ventures were a great success, prompting these immortal lines from an unsuccessful candidate for publication, Pierce Egan.

Thou, O Murray!
whose classic front defies
with terrific awe,
ill-starred, pale wan, and shabbily clad Genius
from thy splendid threshold.

Nevertheless, John Murray was good to his authors, and went to endless troubles and expended large sums of money on producing fine volumes and their accompanying folios of plates. Legh's book was moderately successful, went into a second edition within a year and was published in translation in Weimar. These literary squires were later caricatured by Thackeray in *Vanity Fair* in the person of Bedwin Sand who 'had published his quarto and passed some months under the tents of the desert'. Bedwin assumed oriental costumes on his travels, and Legh, too, may be seen in oriental dress in his portrait that hangs on the stairs of his house at Lyme Park. Legh and his fellow travellers often joined together into parties for their journeys and many books, both entertaining and frequently acute in their observations, were written about their adventures. But these travels were not to be undertaken lightly. Most of the participants were away from their homes for several years, many died of plagues and illnesses and were buried in odd Christian cemeteries throughout the Orient. Thomas Legh, however, survived his trips through the Middle East and was buried in his Cheshire parish.

After the killing of the Mamelukes, Mohammed Ali's hold upon the land of Egypt became absolute. The conditions in Cairo, through which every traveller had to pass, and those in the rest of the land, became as stable as could be expected. Nominally under the control of the Turkish Sultans, the wily Albanian turned Egypt back into a virtual private estate, as it had been in the period of the late Roman Empire. A cruelly efficient administration was set up and survived in gradually diluted form until the revolution of 1952. To aid the development of his stagnating country, Mohammed Ali sent agents throughout the Mediterranean searching for those who might serve the régime, and all manner of fortune hunters, soldiers, administrators and merchants came to Egypt to help this Pasha exploit his new won land. Until the British occupation of Egypt in 1882 Cairo, always the centre of modern Egypt, was a burgeoning booming community as dangerous as a renaissance city and holding more promise of illicit wealth and pleasures than ever the Italian city states had held out to a foreigner. Generally admiring the free-booting Mohammed Ali, the Europeans who gathered in his country seldom stopped to realize that the basic conception of his rule was of the land of Egypt as a large estate over which the owner held life and death control of the inhabitants. What was seen and recognized as exciting were the great developments of the age that were being introduced into the land: the birth of a fine cotton industry; the establishment of huge agricultural estates and the coming of railways. The latter arrived in the shape of two British locomotives imported to run between Alexandria and Cairo on rails designed by the son of George Stevenson. It was the first time that the impact of the industrial revolution that was taking place in Europe could be observed upon a non-western country. Mohammed Ali was seen as a modern despot attempting to race into modernity, and neither he nor his country was shackled by the restrictions that were being applied to the Europeans in their own countries.

As well as precipitating this drastic change of power, Napoleon's devastating plunge into the Egyptian scene had a further and somewhat happier effect upon the European consciousness. Not only was Egypt recognized as a potential source of great wealth, but now it could be seen as holding an ancient heritage of great splendour and especial significance for European culture. With the pragmatic attitudes typical of the 19th century, first-hand knowledge of the ancient cities and their treasures was becoming a necessary experience for scholars. It was now possible to verify and even correct the descriptions of the famous classical travellers. Later, Biblical authority would also be subjected to the processes of pragmatic scholarship, which added further impetus to the examination and recording of the remains of the Ancient Near East.

The 18th-century travellers in Egypt had announced the incredible wealth of monuments that still stood in the land and many of the major sites had been identified by them from classical descriptions. The work of the Napoleonic Commission verified and amplified these travellers' tales in great detail, and although the picture volumes of the *Description* did not begin to appear until 1809—and at its completion in 1825 the entire set cost 600 guineas, a price that it would not command again until the 1960s—the decorative styles and manners employed in the arts of ancient Egypt were becoming popular in European circles. Even before the Emperor had fled the land *le style égyptien* had taken France by storm and the writings and drawings of Baron Vivant Denon became a sensation upon their publication in 1802. Soon the rush to the monuments began and the great 19th-century passion to record and classify combined with the tremendous growth in the knowledge and science of egyptology, which culminated in the decipherment of hieroglyphics and the subsequent ordering of all Egyptian history, opened up the ancient Egyptian civilization. The first half of the 19th century was the heroic age of Egyptology, when a year more or less meant whole new worlds of knowledge and discovery for the scholars in Egypt and at their desks in Europe. Letters of dazzling erudition flew back and forth from Egypt to Europe among the charmed circles who were rediscovering the historical order of the ancient kingdoms and their rulers, their arts and the true ages of the massive ruined architecture. One of the prime targets in their researches would be the Valley of the Kings. But in the interlude between the visits to the Valley of Hamilton and Legh and the arrival in the 1820s of the scholars who could really read the texts on the great tomb walls, the Valley was host to its first archeologist, one of the most extraordinary men who ever dug in Egypt.

6

Giovanni Battista Belzoni

Among the wide variety of people whom the agents of Mohammed Ali encouraged to travel to Egypt to seek their fortune was an erstwhile hydraulics engineer from Padua, Giovanni Battista Belzoni. A dashing red-headed figure nearly six feet seven inches high, Belzoni was a well-known pantomime player and strongman in Regency London when he travelled south to entertain the Peninsular army of the Duke of Wellington. From the theatres of Lisbon and Toledo he eventually travelled to Malta, and it was there that he met the agents of the Egyptian Pasha, who persuaded him to travel on to Cairo. In the course of his adventures in Egypt Belzoni became the first man known to have excavated in the Valley of the Kings. His subsequent publicizing of his discoveries on his return to London led to the new science of egyptology being widely recognized as a subject of great drama and excitement.

In an extraordinary ten-day period in October 1817 Belzoni discovered and entered three magnificent painted tombs in the Valley, as well as numerous other rich burials. Thanks to his description of the work we are still able to share some of the revelations. This charming account of his work in Egypt was to be the mainspring of his later fame. It shows him to have been a simple man who, like many people with great physical strength, was gentle mannered, even meek. Yet, faced with the thrills of uncovering unknown monuments his enthusiasm and sheer physical energy exploded and sometimes became alarming for those who were around him. During one of his excavations at a temple site, he is reported to have jumped into the trench where the workmen were slowly clearing the sand and, in his impatience, scooped away fiercely with his bare hands for several hours until he had found the gateway for which he was looking.

His wife Sarah, though less flamboyant, was just as tough. With great courage and loyalty she stayed with Belzoni—or Mr B as she called him—throughout his Egyptian adventures. Her *Trifling Account* of her own travels in the Near East, tacked on to the end of Belzoni's own narrative, is an even more extraordinary tale than her husband's but she left the stories of the tombs in the Valley to him alone.

Belzoni loved his ancient Egyptians and the monuments that he uncovered. He greatly appreciated the grand size and scale of the ruins and with tremendous energy and skill he transported his casts of tomb walls, huge chunks of ancient Egypt, to England. Their exhibition, in an age when private galleries (the radio and television of their day) were displaying everything from the beautiful to the arcane and the gross, was a sensation. Part of Belzoni's success undoubtedly lay in the prevailing tenor of the public mood, which was in the process of turning to the manners of *le style égyptien* in many of its forms. Certainly he propelled Egypt and its monuments into popular consciousness with immense force and excitement. With his exhibition and his book, a childrens' version of which went in to nine separate editions and was being produced well into the reign of Queen Victoria, Belzoni made the mysteries of Pharoah a part of the popular culture of England, a fact for which British egyptologists should be most thankful. When, some thirty years after his death, the new Egyptian Galleries of the British Museum were opened, the popularity of the exhibition, especially the mummies, owed much to the scene setting of Belzoni's accounts of his gothick experiences in the mummy pits of Egypt, and the largest and most impressive sculptures shown were those that Belzoni and his workmen had taken from the temples of Thebes.

This new career was still unrealized when Belzoni arrived in Cairo in 1816 and tried to interest Mohammed Ali in a hydraulic lifting device he had invented. The Pasha was amused by the man but not by his waterwheel and so Belzoni was left without any visible prospects of employment. In search of work Belzoni went to the offices of the British Agency in Cairo and to the consul, Henry Salt. At that time several of the European consuls in Cairo, with the encouragement of Mohammed Ali, were engaged in digging at the ancient sites of Egypt. Very large numbers of antiquities were collected and usually offered to the European governments, or sold in a succession of huge auctions. The ancient Egyptian sites still held fine antiquities under a thin layer of sand or hidden among the stones of a fallen wall of a temple or tomb. In gathering these treasures pyramids were blasted open, tombs were pulled down and reliefs and paintings were cut from the ancient walls. The agents of the foreign consuls divided Thebes like the concessions of a gold rush. But the expenses of excavation and exportation were heavy and Consul Salt, who dearly wanted to join the scramble, could not afford to keep large gangs permanently at the sites, as did some of his counterparts. Before Belzoni's appearance at his office, the consul had, however, entered into partnership with John Lewis Burckhardt, the famous Arabist and pilgrim to Mecca, to bring the head and shoulders of a truly colossal statue from Thebes and ship it to England. This gigantic fragment which lay in the Memnonium had been presented to the Prince Regent by Mohammed Ali at Burckhardt's request during the course of a long interview, but no one had ever taken such a large piece from the temples before and the mechanics of the enterprise must have seemed almost insurmountable. So when Belzoni, both strongman and engineer, offered his services to the consul, Henry Salt knew just how to employ him. He gave Belzoni money for a trip to Thebes to collect the colossus and more funds to collect other antiquities that he might come across. Belzoni sailed to Thebes, found the colossus and moved it out of the Memnonium down to the river bank nearly two miles away. It was a tremendous feat of patience and strength that involved large numbers of workmen and took two weeks to accomplish. Next, Belzoni went to work in Bruce's Tomb in the Valley of the Kings.

This tomb of Ramesses III held the famous paintings of the harpists and the objects of courtly life so admired by the earlier travellers. It also contained the magnificent sarcophagus of the King cut from fine-grained pink granite and, doubtless, Salt had realized that such an impressive piece of antiquity from a celebrated tomb would fetch a good price in Europe, and he had just the man to do the job. To move the sarcophagus from the depths of the tomb, which at that time was the deepest known in the Valley and more than four hundred feet long, was

The box of the sarcophagus of Ramesses III, removed by Belzoni from that king's tomb

another challenge for Belzoni, but one that he rapidly accomplished. After bringing the huge box up to the surface of the Valley, he had a road cleared through the *Wadyein*, and the sarcophagus was dragged down it some four miles to the river. Later it was sent to Alexandria and sold by Salt to the King of France. It now stands in the Louvre, an elegant rectangular box, partly rounded into the cartouche shape that, in inscriptions, holds the name of the king. A fine high polish lightens its huge bulk and cut through the glassy finish, lightly engraved upon its sides, are extracts from the long religious texts that also decorate the walls of the royal tombs. The goddesses Isis and Nepthys sit at either end above a collar of beads, the hieroglyph for the word 'gold', their arms holding low-draped wings as if in mourning. They are fitting symbols for the careful wrapping of the pharaoh's body in such magnificence.

Isis and her sister Nepthys, whom Denon had seen carved over the doorways of the tombs, were the two principal mourners at the royal funeral, and may have been represented at the earthly ceremonies by members of the royal family. The goddesses were called the 'two kites' after the hawks that constantly circle in the sky of the Nile Valley, giving shrieks which sound like the cries of mourning uttered at the ancient funeral. Similar expressions of grief and mourning may still be seen at every village funeral in modern Thebes, and in the reliefs and paintings of the nobles' tomb chapels. The ancient gestures of mourning, as well as the cries called *zagreet*, were certainly seen and heard during the funerary ceremonies of the dead kings.

Long before Belzoni arrived to remove the sarco phagus from the depths of the dark tomb, water had entered it and deposited a layer of silt and stones over the floor of the burial chamber. He dug about in this debris and found, lying upside down where it had been thrown from the top of its box, the lid of the sarcophagus. Belzoni thought it to be a splendid piece of antiquity, considered it outside the brief that Salt had given him for the work, and claimed it as his own. Unfortunately, it shattered during its removal from the tomb but now, restored, it is on view in the Fitzwilliam Museum at Cambridge. Upon its upperside, running down the full length, is the figure of Ramesses III with Isis and Nepthys upon either side of him. The King is identified as the God of the dead, Osiris, the son of the sky and the earth. Close to him, in the darkness of his tomb, Ramesses III was surrounded with potent gods to help him in his journey to resurrection.

The lid of the sarcophagus of Ramesses III broken by Belzoni's workmen during its removal from the tomb

Perhaps it was this splendid discovery in the silt and stones of Bruce's tomb that led Belzoni to start to look for other buried tombs. William Hamilton had speculated upon the possibility of hidden tombs in the Valley fifteen years earlier and Thomas Legh, the Cheshire squire, had thought of the possibility too:

Most of the passages that have been opened penetrate far into the mountain, and generally contain a granite sarcophagus, but there are many which still remain untouched [Legh presumably meant part-filled] and as the specimens of papyri, that have hitherto been procured, come from this spot [?] it is not improbable that the discovery of many objects of considerable importance would be the result of further excavation.

Belzoni now came into his own. He examined the quality of the rock in the Valley and studied the patterns of the floods that would have covered the entrances of the tombs with debris. During the time when Belzoni worked in the Valley it rained more frequently than it does at present and he was certainly able to observe the actions of the flood waters. The road he had built to move the sarcophagus of Ramesses III, for example, was quickly swept away within a year of its construction by the floods that had followed a rainstorm. With a careful eye Belzoni realized that the huge basin above the southern end of the Valley was the catchment area for the slopes around the Valley's head and that here the water would build up into a big lake before flooding the Valley below. The ancient Egyptians had also realized the threat this posed to the monuments in the immediate vicinity and they had built a deflecting dam above the vulnerable tombs. None of the later workers in the Valley have seemed remotely aware of these facts. Indeed, one expedition actually demolished a section of this ancient dam exposing the tomb beneath it to the floods that will inevitably come again into the Valley. Belzoni also recorded, for the first time, that under the 'beautiful solid calcerous stone' of the Valley lay an unstable shale, a 'kind of black rotten slate which crumbled into dust only by touching' and doubtless with his sensitivity to mass and structure he realized the problems this would cause to the stability of those tombs flooded by water. Belzoni and many of his contemporaries were far more interested in these matters than the later archeologists who worked in the Valley. His eyes registered such phenomena as a matter of course; it was simply a part of the way of looking at and describing a landscape.

As many excavators would do after him, Belzoni walked the Valley searching for displacements and subsidences among the rocks that might betray a hole beneath them. He walked through the West Valley where less than twenty years earlier Jollois

The entrance to the tomb of King Ay

and de Villiers had found the open tomb of Amenhotep III. Further on into the grandeur of the lonely valley head Belzoni saw:

A heap of stones which appeared to be detached from the mass. The vacancies between these stones were filled up with sand and rubbish. I happened to have a stick with me and on thrusting it into the holes among the stones I found it to penetrate very deep. On removing a few stones we perceived that the sand ran inwards: and, in fact, we were so near the entrance into a tomb that in less than two hours all the stones were taken away and I caused some candles to be brought and I went in, followed by the arabs.

Belzoni had workmen with him and, as he must have had during his work in Bruce's tomb, supplied them with water and provisions. These simple logistics (still an essential ingredient of any archeological expedition) had defeated earlier visitors who, as we have seen, were left to speculate upon the possibilities of work they could never hope to perform. On the door of this tomb Belzoni proudly inscribed his name and the date of his discovery, as later excavators in the Valley would do but, to a man taken by the spectacular in Egyptian monuments, the tomb must have presented a sorry spectacle for it contained only heavily damaged wall paintings and a much broken and defaced sarcophagus. His 'Arabs' quickly dubbed the tomb the *turbet el garud* (the tomb of the monkeys) from one of the paintings on the wall of twelve apes in three rows; and since that time the Valley has been called locally *Wadi el Garud* (Valley of the Monkeys) which, as the address of our expedition house, has led to some amusement for us, the only inhabitants of this beautiful valley.

In fact Belzoni had discovered a unique royal tomb that had been decorated for King Ay, an elderly priest who took the throne upon the death of Tutankhamen. Ay had been a prominent courtier and state official during the reigns of several of the earlier Eighteenth Dynasty kings and a powerful figure at the court of King Akhenaten, whose reign had seen a most aggressive transformation of the orthodox state religion. The period is still one of the most controversial in Egyptian history; its beautiful arts and seemingly romantic court exciting a great deal of popular interest. The ambiguity of much of the surviving evidence from the period, which may almost be seen as a mirror image of orthodox ancient Egyptian culture, allows many differing interpretations of its 'real' history. The period has become a touchstone for the understanding of many of the different historical methods and viewpoints on the ancient culture. Akhenaten, a monotheist, has been claimed as a revolutionary, trans-sexual, philosopher, pacifist, poet, 'the first individual in history'. Indeed, it must seem that in such a highly stable ritualized society the impetus for such enormous changes in religion and art could only have been imposed by the highest power in the land. Many different elements were taken from the complex fabric of the ancient culture and, added to some truly radical innovations, were welded to form the new religious system and artistic style. In the course of the upheaval, which in a state controlled in large measure by religious offices, must have been felt throughout the kingdom, the economic and political framework of the land was swept away. In part the heresy seems to have been attempting a return to the ancient days of total royal supremacy, for the new religion stressed the dependence of the entire nation upon the personal communion between god and king, the sole conduit through which spiritual power could reach the earth. The centres of the old religion were attacked along with the priesthood which ran it. Akhenaten left Thebes and with a furious building programme, founded a new city away from the state temples that he had defaced and deprived of their huge revenues. His city, known by a corruption of its Arabic name as Amarna, was dedicated to his single god, the Aten—the sun's disc. When he died Akhenaten left the revolutionary state in great disorder and after three successive short reigns, which concluded with the brief term of Ay, the court officially returned to Thebes and the priests and their revenues were re-installed in the old state temples. The huge monuments of the new religion were attacked so systematically that they were eventually completely demolished. Akhenaten, the ever-ambiguous figure at the centre of the heretical faith, was struck off the official records and called simply 'the criminal'. However, the revolutionary art style that was created at his court had a profound influence upon succeeding generations. Today it is regarded as a most vital and intense period of ancient Egyptian culture.

King Ay had reigned only four years between 1339 and 1335 BC and his tomb was only half completed; its decorations hurriedly applied upon gritty and irregular plaster. The burial chamber of the tomb was in the position of the room normally called 'the chariot hall' in the plans of the finished tombs. Ay's tomb is quite regular in design until this point but the use of this room for the burial and the unusual position of the burial-chamber door shows signs of this quick adaptation for a hasty burial. Ay's burial chamber is much higher than the other 'chariot halls' because it has been adapted and enlarged to accommodate the big wooden shrines, which fitted one inside the other around the sarcophagus of Tutankhamen, and which were made during the reign of King Ay. It is eighteen inches higher than any of the other 'chariot halls' in the tombs of the period and, judging from the size of his sarcophagus, Ay's shrines would have been quite as big as Tutankhamen's. King Ay had ordered the burial of the last survivor of that long royal line, Tutankhamen, in a hastily adapted courtier's tomb in the Valley of the Kings, just a few years before he was laid in his own unfinished but nevertheless royal tomb. Whether or not Ay took over an unfinished tomb intended for an earlier king is presently impossible to say.

Ay's tomb gained greatly in interest after the discovery of Tutankhamen's tomb with which it can be usefully compared. Both share the same unusual style of decoration; the same distinctive drawing style and bright colour schemes that are not found in any other royal tombs. Many of the paintings' subjects are similar, although Ay's tomb has marsh hunting scenes upon the walls that are not found in other New Kingdom pharaohs' tombs although they are common in the private tombs. Ay had a fine private tomb made for him some twenty years earlier at the cemetery of Amarna, the city of the heresy. In that tomb, a masterpiece of Amarnan art, he appears with his wife worshipping the sun's disc. By the time that Ay was buried in a royal tomb he had seen three kings die along with the new religion of Amarna.

Ay's tomb has suffered that curious ancient vandalism in which the face and names of the dead person were chiselled from the tomb walls in an attempt to obliterate totally his name and person. It was the fate of kings who were believed by their successors to have been usurpers of the throne. Ay fell victim to the politico-religious disturbances which shook Egypt during the later years of his dynasty and which, it has been hypothesized, may also have accounted for the death of his predecessor. In Tutankhamen's tomb Ay was painted in the robes of a priest with royal titles, which showed him to be the new pharaoh helping Tutankhamen over his transition into the world of Osiris. This attempt at legitimization by ritual did not work for Ay and his tomb and sarcophagus were attacked early in the next dynasty on the orders of a later king, intent upon the suppression of his monuments.

It is likely that the desecrators of Ay's wall paintings also damaged the huge florid sarcophagus which Belzoni found lying damaged in the tomb. At the turn of the century, probably to satisfy the endless trade in souvenirs, local villagers further split the sarcophagus and some of the detailed fragments later found their way into European collections. Happily, many of these were returned to Egypt when the remains of the sarcophagus were shipped to Cairo for restoration and exhibition in the museum where it now stands. Other fragments have since come to light; one was found by our expedition during the work on the tomb of Ramesses XI, which is more than a mile away from Ay's tomb.

Belzoni left the tomb open and it became a regular historical puzzle for the early egyptologists who visited the monument soon after. At that time Ay was an obscure king and the unusual style of the tomb did not fit into place with the others. A relatively recent visit to the tomb was an impressive experience, even while waiting in the rough desolate gorge as the guards cleared away the rubble piled in front of the steel door, to protect it from illegal entry: today small fragments of decoration or a painted name of a king fetch absurd sums on the open art markets of Europe and the United States. To remove the debris from the iron grilles at the bottom of the entrance staircase took the guards about as long as it would have taken Belzoni's men to open the tomb nearly two hundred years ago. Then our party of egyptologists and friends could walk down the finely cut steps of the grand, carefully chiselled entrance and descend the long warm corridors, flashing our torches at the walls as we went, perhaps hoping to see an inscription or drawing overlooked by our predecessors. Loose stones rattled along the corridors under our feet. The strange gawky paintings, surprising in their awkwardness, had been most conscientiously defaced by the ancient vandals, and the white gouge marks they had left in the dusty plaster walls made it difficult to imagine the scenes as they once must have been. Fragments of the paintings were still lying on the floors of the decorated chambers until the tomb was cleaned in the 1960s. During this work several small fragments of the original burial equipment were found, making it virtually certain that the tomb had once contained the burial of Ay. He had at least been laid in his grave before the attack on his works was made. Since those days the entrance to Ay's tomb has been blocked by huge stones rolled down the entrance stairway and so the tomb lies quiet again in the dry air deep in the mountain.

Belzoni returned to Cairo in mid-December 1816. With him he took the colossus of the Memnonium which, after great difficulties in loading it at Thebes, was subsequently presented to the British Museum as 'the gift of Salt and Burckhardt'. As well as the colossus Belzoni had collected many other large statues by digging around in Thebes. He had also undertaken a trip to the temple of Abu Simbel in Nubia that Burckhardt had discovered some years earlier during a journey up the Nile. Salt must have been well pleased with his new agent and Belzoni was soon sent back to Thebes; this time in the company of Salt's secretary, Henry Beechey, who was to supervise both Belzoni and the other agents that Salt employed. After working in the temples the two men joined forces with a pair of British naval officers and together the small group sailed to Abu Simbel. This time Belzoni succeeded in opening the interior rooms and passages of the rock-cut temple that had been deeply buried in the sand. He was delighted and worked hard, carefully making measured drawings of the architecture and the sculpture that they had uncovered. Today Belzoni's drawings appear simple and unsophisticated but in their time they and the others that he made earned him a great reputation as a traveller and antiquarian. However, there was little in the temple for the consul's collection and the party soon returned to Thebes.

They arrived on Sunday 17 August 1817 and found themselves quickly caught up in the Byzantine world of dealers and diggers; of consuls' agents and local villagers, all intent on gathering up the lightly buried remains of the ancient empires and selling them abroad. Belzoni struck a bargain with his competitors whereby he agreed to leave the temples and tombs alone and work in the Valley of the Kings where he would not be disturbed. The French agents must have thought it was a good exchange, which left the giant Italian, who they had seen grow quickly from an innocent engineer into a skilled procurer of the very largest antiquities, with only the deserted tombs of the kings. Indeed, it was a temporary triumph; part of a scheme engineered to have the British consul's agents out of Thebes, but this, of course, was all part of the game. The following years saw Salt himself happily digging in several locations in Western Thebes, while his competitors were confined to the temples on the opposite bank of the river. Belzoni had his own ideas about the Valley of the Kings and quietly visited the site alone 'making observations, the results of which confirmed in me the opinion that there was a sufficient prospect to encourage me to commence my work.' Within a few days he was at work in the West Valley close to where he had discovered the tomb of King Ay in the previous year.

> *After a long survey of the West Valley, I could observe only one spot, that presented the appearance of a tomb. Accordingly I set the men to work near a hundred yards from the tomb which I discovered the year before; and when they had got a little below the surface, they came to some large stones which had evidently been put there by those who closed the tomb. Having removed these stones, I perceived the rock had been cut on both sides and found a passage leading downwards. I could proceed no farther that day as the men were much fatigued and we had more than four miles to return to Thebes. The next day we resumed our labour and in a few hours came to a well-built wall of stones of various sizes. The following day I caused a large pole to be brought and by means of another small piece of palm tree laid across the entrance, I made a machine not unlike a battering ram. The walls resisted the blows of the Arabs for some time, as they were not Romans, nor had the pole the ram's head of bronze at its end; but they contrived to make a breach at last and in the same way the opening was enlarged. We immediately entered and found ourselves on a staircase eight feet wide and ten feet high, at the bottom of which were four mummies, in their cases, lying flat on the ground with their heads toward the outside. Farther on were four more, lying in the same direction. The cases were all painted and one had a large covering thrown over it, exactly like the pall upon coffins of the present day.*

Belzoni's now infamous battering ram seems but a simple attempt to evoke the classical writers to bring images of immortality to his endeavours! In fact, the stone walls of these tombs, sealed with hard plaster, would have yielded easily to a steel chisel and would have certainly collapsed after a few blows with a palm log: indeed, the Arabs were not Romans, as Belzoni says, but he himself was listed as a 'citizen of Rome' on his travel papers! The tomb he had found was an extraordinary burial vault, far from the nobles' tombs in a lonely side valley of the royal cemetery. What was such a multitude of mummies doing in such an unlikely spot? Today the tomb is bare, the mummies dispersed, unknown. But by comparing several descriptions of the contents that are given by Belzoni at different points in his book, it appears that he uncovered a large cache of burials probably of

priests' mummies, from the period of the Twenty-first or Twenty-second Dynasty, when several other tombs in the Valley were also used for such intrusive burials. None of these other secondary burials, however, were as large or as perfect as this discovery of Belzoni's. The discretion with which these intrusive burials

The only tomb in which a large part of its original sealing is still preserved is this one, called West Valley A, *and situated close by the tomb of Amenhotep III. Such stone walls were usually coated with a hard impermeable white plaster, and the steps that lead down to them were filled with boulders and debris from the Valley floor. The location of the buried tombs were, therefore, easily missed, not least because the floodwaters which frequently passed through the Valley ran straight over the tops leaving the burials disguised but intact beneath them*

were placed among the royal tombs makes it probable that they were put there by people who knew of the sacred nature of the Valley, possibly the families of the priests who had taken such care of the royal dead at the end of the Twentieth Dynasty.

The tomb that Belzoni found, now number 25, was much older than the mummies it contained. Probably it is contemporary with the tomb of Amenhotep III close by, which had been found by Jollois and de Villiers. The measurements at the entrance door suggest that these two tombs are of the same group and the workmanship of the small precise diagonally-stroked chiselling upon their walls is certainly of that same period. The tomb of Amenhotep III had been initiated by his father when his son was still a prince, and it may well be that these two tombs were both originally intended for princes. One was finished and used for Amenhotep III's burial, but what of this mysterious tomb 25? Hardly half of the first corridor has been cut, but its workmanship is very fine. The steps and door jambs are a different design and show greater care and attention to detail than in the other tombs of the period. The tomb is perfectly preserved and the red ochre marks that the stonemasons have painted upon the walls to indicate their future lines of attack into the creamy limestone are a good example of work in progress. But we do not know why the work was stopped.

When the two naval officers who had accompanied Belzoni to Abu Simbel later visited his camp in the Valley they were shown this new tomb but they found it 'quite unworthy of notice'. The fascination of archeological remains, as opposed to the colossal or the picturesque was still, it would appear, not general! Even Belzoni, who showed a keen antiquarian interest in his work, also exhibited impatience to get his hands on some of the regal grave treasures that he hoped were buried nearby.

The result of my researches gave me all the satisfaction I could desire, of finding mummies in cases in their original position: but this was not the principal object I had in view: for, as I was near the place where the kings of Egypt were buried, I thought I might have a chance of discovering some of their relics.

And so Belzoni returned to the East Valley where he had worked before in Bruce's tomb. He carefully calculated the odds, as others had done before him, and as archeologists would, long, long after. From Strabo's account given him by the ancient priests, Belzoni knew that there were thought to be forty-seven kings buried in the Valley and realized that there should be other tombs beneath the loose rocks and silt as he had already discovered in the West Valley. Even counting the smallest pits and shafts that were open to view, the number of tombs he could identify still came to less than half the number of tombs that were claimed by the ancient Greeks. So he set to work and after three days, on 9 October 1817, he entered the tomb of Prince Ramesses Montu-hir-kopesh-ef. It is possible that Belzoni simply cleared away debris washed down from the slopes above it and that Richard Pococke had already drawn plans of the first parts of the tomb during his visits to the Valley some seventy years before. However, it was Belzoni who dug through all the dirt in the large corridors of the tomb until some seventy-five feet down the slope he suddenly came to a face of uncut stone—the end. The tomb had never been finished. Once again Belzoni was not to discover the 'relics' of the kings. However, the strong man had opened up a real treasure of Egyptian painting, and he had the taste to recognize it. 'The painted figures on the walls are so perfect, they are the best adapted of any I ever saw to give a correct and clear idea of the Egyptian taste'. The long wide corridor of the tomb is so well lit by the daylight that there is nothing to hamper a perfect view of some of the finest paintings ever made by the ancient Egyptians.

Prince Ramesses Montu-hir-kopesh-ef ('the arm of Montu is strong') was a commander in the Egyptian army and possibly the crown prince when he died. His tomb, of royal dimensions, may have been made originally for Ramesses VIII, for whom, at this time, there is no known tomb (but here we are left with the tantalizing possibility that this king is still lying in his tomb waiting to be found). The work in his tomb was brought to a halt while the workmen were still quarrying the blocks from the centre of the main corridor. The quarrying of the limestone, a method of laboriously taking block after block from an exposed face in a series of steps, each of which was more than two feet high, was stopped at a point just behind the second doorway of the tomb, at the beginning of 'the god's third passage' as it was anciently called (see Appendix, p. 279). There a trench was dug where, usually, a small step would have been cut at the back of the door jamb. Perhaps this trench—about four feet wide, nine and a half feet long and four feet deep—had held the coffins and the mummy of the warrior prince. Other accounts, almost contemporary with Belzoni's, describe two mummies lying in the tomb, and the archeologist Edward Ayrton, who later worked there, described the trench as being covered with flat limestone slabs set level with the floor. This arrangement hardly sounds like a prince's burial and judging from the brief descriptions these mummies were probably later intrusive burials, placed there after the end of the New Kingdom.

The finished corridors of the tomb were beautifully worked, the walls very carefully levelled and the finest white gypsum was plastered upon the limestone in a layer never thicker than one inch. This made a perfect canvas for the Ramesside draughtsmen who drew and painted seven scenes upon each of the two long walls—some of the finest drawing and painting ever made in Egypt. They are but the usual offering scenes so typical in ancient Egyptian monuments: the dead person adores the gods, pours libations to Osiris, offers a vase to Ptah, incense to Thoth, and worships many others. Here, though, the style of the prince's paintings are purely of their age, a period of refinement, elegance and a delight in the ephemera of leaves and plants, intricately pleated linen and elaborate fine-gold jewellery, inlaid with lapis lazuli and carnelian. The colours, too, enhance this depiction of a fresh, rich court of beautiful young men and elegant goddesses. At this time in the Twentieth Dynasty, the court was in the Nile Delta. There, the cities of the king, built of mud yet faced with glassy faiences and gold sheets, lay in the brilliant green farmlands with tall bright palms, luxurious perfumed vegetation and small, rapid flying, coloured birds. The paintings in the tomb seem to have taken on the quality of that landscape, adapting within the conventions of established style, the bright flashes of colour, the hard outlines and the sharpness of the light in the fields. It is these qualities that stand out in these paintings in the clean, light, tomb of the prince.

In his paintings the prince has a calm highbred face, elongated by the elegant traditions of a school of artists drawing with perfect, assured brush strokes. His eyes are lengthened beyond the size of earlier periods, the pupils are huge and less than half a circle, and he has the long, typically Ramesside profile that runs down into 'bee-stung' lips that are also found in the portraits of the kings of the period. The edge of a form was often used by the ancient artists to describe the texture within it. Here the prince's artists show us the woolliness of his natural-brown wigs, the fineness of his linen robes, held with small bows on to the slick gold necklaces. The transparency of the court robes is emphasized where it covers his flesh by a half-tone of brown skin, painted as it appears through the gauzy material. He is a child of his age, the period of the last Ramessides, and the names of two of his kings, Ramesses IX and X appear discreetly upon the jewellery worn by the painted figures on the tomb walls. Despite the formalities of the art the paintings in the corridor of this tomb are a curiously modern experience, the colours sing and there is an overall sense of order and organization not often found in Egyptian painting, which usually tends to sacrifice the total design to the details of its constituents. Here the master draughtsman has left us with his sense of order and his delight in colour, texture and crisply drawn shapes.

Behind the first door of the tomb, drawn upon the walls in thick black bands, there are two huge wooden doors. Their hinges, in the Egyptian manner, stick out top and bottom, and as if to guard these frail cedar doors from intruders, a row of spitting cobras is painted upon each jamb. It is, perhaps, the scene in the Valley which is closest to a curse upon intruders in the tombs. Even the simple black hieroglyphs above the cobras have the elegance of the wall scenes, their concise brushstrokes reminding one of the nonchalance of the Norwich glass painters or the quick drawings of Chinese potters. Poor Belzoni found a treasure trove but one he could not take from the tomb!

The tomb of Prince Ramesses Montu-hir-kopesh-ef lies in the easternmost section of the Valley, at an angle of the equilateral triangle that runs around the central hill. During Belzoni's time this area had large volumes of water occasionally passing over it and as there is not a large catchment area behind these tombs the rains must have been particularly fierce and powerful. It was in this area, covered in debris brought down by these storms that Belzoni concentrated his main efforts in the Valley.

As I had several parties of Fellah (farm worker) at work in different directions, I hoped to make farther discoveries; and indeed this first success gave me much encouragement as it assured me that I was correct in my idea of discovering the tombs. On the same day we perceived some marks of another tomb in an excavation that had been begun three days before, precisely in the same direction as the first tomb and not a hundred yards from it. In fact, I had the pleasure to see this second tomb on the same day, the 9th. This is more extensive but entirely new and without a single painting in it: it had been searched by the ancients, as we perceived at the end of the first passage a brick wall which stopped the entrance, and had been forced through. After passing

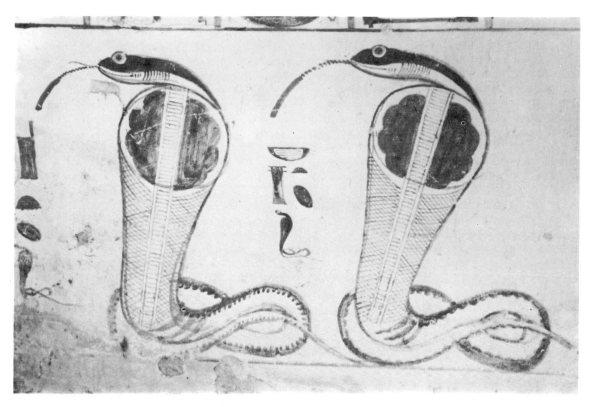

The spitting snakes painted on the left hand door jamb of Montu-hir-kopesh-ef's tomb

this brick wall you descend a staircase and proceed through another corridor at the end of which is the entrance to a pretty large chamber with a single pillar in the centre and not plastered in any part. At one corner of this chamber we found two mummies on the ground quite naked, without cloth or case. They were females, and their hair pretty long and well preserved, though it was easily separated from the head by pulling it a little. At one side of this room is a small door leading into a small chamber, in which we found the fragments of several earthen vessels and also pieces of alabaster, but so decayed that we could not join one to another. On the top of the staircase we found an earthen jar quite perfect, with a few hieroglyphics on it, and large enough to contain two buckets of water. This tomb is a hundred feet from the entrance to the end of the chamber, twenty feet deep and twenty-three feet wide. The smaller chamber is ten feet square: it faces the east by south and runs straight towards west by north.

As all of unknown ancient Egypt had lain before the gaze of Pococke while his boat drifted gently down the Nile, so now the Valley of the Kings lay before Belzoni. He worked very quickly, sometimes employing several gangs of labourers simultaneously and sometimes even leaving the Valley altogether during the course of the work. These practices, and Belzoni's own candid observations about his work, the 'weakness' of the mummies' hair and his description of using a battering ram to force his way into a tomb, have, however, given him a worse reputation than he deserves. It is true that he inadvertently destroyed much fragile important historical information, as did the other diggers of his day, but at least he did not mutilate the tombs as some of his more learned successors would do; and to complain of his lack of archeological method is to expect the stable door to be shut before the horse was even born: archeological procedures were simply not in existence at that time. In fact, work in the Valley has been poorly recorded by archeologists throughout its history and Belzoni's account is often nearly equal in value to some of the professional egyptologists who worked at the site some sixty years later. His contemporaries at Thebes left far scantier accounts of their activities despite the fact that they had dug these for more than thirty years.

What, then, had Belzoni's eyes lighted upon this time—the second tomb of that day in October 1817? The small tomb, numbered KV 21, is a courtier's tomb subsidiary to one of the two royal tombs of the Eighteenth Dynasty that are in the area but which were unrecognized or unknown by Belzoni. A few years after Belzoni, floodwater and debris once again blocked the entrance and by the late 1880s it was sealed and no one has entered it since. The two female mummies, probably people who had been close to the king, are still in the tomb in which they were placed some thirty-five centuries ago and the associated objects that Belzoni described may also still be there. These may contain the only clues to the identity of the mummies that we will ever possess.

The next day Consul Salt's secretary, William

Beechey, arrived at the camp in the Valley and Belzoni had to submit to the common fate of his profession; that of guiding parties of visitors around the monuments. For the first day the three Englishmen of Beechey's party were content to stay in the Valley and it was not until the following morning that they went out of the Valley to visit the temple ruins and the private tombs. He was with the group in the Temple of Hatshepsut at Deir el Bahari when:

About twelve o'clock word was brought me that a tomb discovered the day before was opened, so that we might enter it. On this we took the road over the rocks immediately [the magnificent cliff side path from Deir el Bahari to the Valley] and arrived in less than three quarters of an hour. I found the tomb just opened, and entered to see how far it was practicable to examine it. Having proceeded through a passage thirty-two feet long and eight feet wide, I descended a staircase of twenty-eight feet, and reached a tolerably large and well-painted room, I then made a signal from below to the travellers that they might descend, and they entered into the tomb, which is seventeen feet long and twenty-one wide. We found a sarcophagus of granite, with two mummies in it, and in a corner a statue standing erect, six feet six inches high, and beautifully cut out of sycamore wood: it is nearly perfect except the nose. We found also a number of little images of wood, well carved, representing symbolical figures. Some had a lion's head, others a fox's, others a monkey's. One had a land-tortoise instead of a head. We found a calf with the head of a hippopotamus. In the chamber on our right hand we found another statue like the first, but not perfect. No doubt they had been placed one on each side of the sarcophagus, holding a lamp or some offering in their hands, one hand being stretched out in the proper posture to hold something, and the other hanging down. The sarcophagus was covered with hieroglyphics merely painted, or outlined: it faces south-east by east.

This time Belzoni had found the tomb of the first King Ramesses, the old vizier who had followed the last rulers of the Eighteenth Dynasty to the throne and founded the second great family dynasty of the New Kingdom. Like Ay before him, the elderly king had ruled for only a few years before he died and time ran out for the workmen cutting his tomb. Once more the royal-tomb plan was hastily adapted to house the king. This time the burial chamber was made at the bottom of the second stair of the tomb, 'the god's fourth passage' and the two niches, 'in which the statues of the gods of the east and of the west repose' on the second stair were left half excavated. Only the improvised burial chamber was painted, and the huge granite sarcophagus that was placed in it was still unfinished, quickly painted with the two goddesses and the appropriate texts with a coarse yellow wash.

The burial chamber of the tomb of Ramesses I, photographed by Harry Burton about fifty years ago. This room is now filled with sturdy wooden beams that support a huge loose block of the ceiling

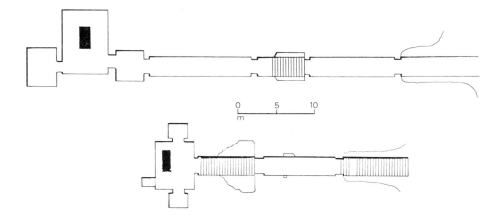

Plans of the tombs of Ay (above) and Ramesses I

Some of the measurements of the tomb's plan suggest that the old king had already seen his approaching end and was hastening the completion of his tomb—a race that he lost. The first corridor is the shortest of any royal tomb in the Valley, and the stairs that follow are steep and drop quickly. The burial chamber does not have the distinctive proportions of the other tombs in the Valley. Although the tomb of Ay was attenuated in its plan its corridors were still cut to their proper sizes, but he had reigned twice as long as Ramesses I, whose tomb is, like the paintings on the rough plastered walls, obviously a quick job. But the tomb has its own charm. The lightly painted burial chamber and its sarcophagus show the marks of the worker's hand, and it is a relief from the perfections of some of the other tombs in the Valley. It was one of the first tombs to be lit by electricity and it was popular with visitors, requiring little effort for the journey to the bright burial chamber with its cheerful walls and spacious proportions.

Ramesses I had ruled Egypt less than thirty years after Ay, and the intellectual and artistic turmoil of those earlier times was still being felt. Although the art of Amarna had changed the artists, stripping them of their simple vision of a single Egyptian style, it had opened new possibilities for them. They had seen a different manner of working but one that still lay inside the canons and traditional methods of Egypt. So for the first time there was a choice and the traditional ways were seen to be a part of that choice, not the totality. Certainly it was not one sanctioned in any way by the state, which had ruthlessly established the old order throughout the country, but nonetheless, there was a choice. It concerned, among other things, the way that shapes were drawn and

carved and the colours that were used, for these parts of the artistic language had been given new expression under the heresy. Prince Ramesses Montu-hir-kopesh-ef's tomb, painted some hundreds of years after that of Ramesses I shows these influences from Amarna happily assimilated into its style, and they become a part of typical Ramesside art. However, the tomb of King Ramesses I was decorated at a time much closer to the heresy, and the artists were deliberately attempting to exclude the ingrained manners of the new style, then some fifty years old, from their work. Strict orthodoxy was the rule and, thus, the paintings in the tomb are very sensitive in their attempts to exclude all traces of Amarna.

Nevertheless, the colour in the burial chamber is still hot, and the large-faced figures contain some of the nervous energy of the heretical style. However, it is very different from the tomb of Ay which is shot through with the mannerisms of Amarna: there the subject matter is confused, the religious content unresolved. By the reign of King Ramesses I no such bow towards the rival camps of tradition and heresy was necessary. The tomb returns to the old style, though the texts in the burial chamber are new and not those that were used by the kings before the period of the heresy. Ramesses I's tomb represents the beginning of a period in Theban art much beloved by earlier scholars. Like the arts of the Victorian age the ancient artists and craftsmen of this period were involved in the skilful re-creation of earlier styles, but they, too, were wiser and less innocent that those who had created the art they aspired to. Often these attempts at re-creation produced a scholarly, detailed and humourless art devoid of conviction and the breath of life.

The two plundered mummies that Belzoni found in the rough-hewn sarcophagus were put there after Ramesses I had been taken away for reburial with the other kings of the Valley. The red granite sarcophagus was still only partly shaped, awaiting its final cutting and polishing, unlike that of King Ay's which was finished. In its basic form the sarcophagus of Ramesses I, however, is different from Ay's, and returns to the shape employed in the Eighteenth Dynasty. This particular reprise was followed in the monuments of Ramesses I's successors; Belzoni had already taken a magnificent example of a sarcophagus of this type from the tomb of Ramesses III. But the sarcophagus of Ramesses I was unfinished with a poorly shaped and ill fitting lid which looked like a loaf of bread. Hardly a trophy for the museums of Europe.

The statues that were found by Belzoni in the burial chamber were gathered up by Salt and sold as part of a huge collection to the British Museum. Unfortunately no further records were kept of these discoveries, other than the account of the opening of the

Some of the statues collected by Belzoni from the burial chamber of Ramesses I's tomb drawn by Frederick Arundale and published in 1842

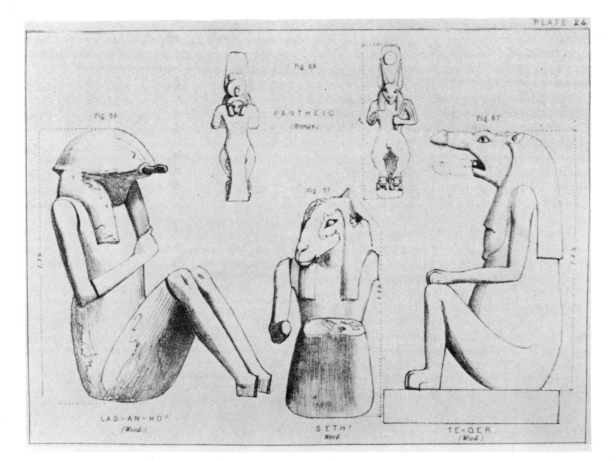

tomb by Belzoni, and by the time the collection was bought by the Museum in 1821 the exact provenance of most of the objects had been lost. It is difficult to identify positively pieces in the Museum today as being those which Belzoni mentions in his descriptions as being in the tomb of Ramesses I. A few sculptures may be identified, however: a strange tortoise-headed male god with its legs drawn up in a seated pose, and a god with flat pendulous breasts and the head of a hippopotamus, today languish in a small case in the British Museum with similar denizens of the other world having less specific origins. These are the statues of the gods that the king would meet in his journey towards rebirth. Thoueris, the strange half-hippopotamine goddess was the divine midwife. The wife of Horus' great enemy, his uncle Seth, this strange lady was also represented as a constellation in the night sky. The tortoise, too, was an animal associated with transformation and rebirth and may represent one of the forms through which the dead king passed in the process of his evolution from his beginning in the formless void to his entering the sky with the gods. Another seated figure with a strange full face, holding his beard as if it were the stick of a mask at a Venetian ball, is possibly the same deity that measures the hours of the night and the transit of the constellations in the huge astronomical charts in some of the other royal tombs.

All these statues had suffered greatly from the violence of ancient robbery in the tomb. Some of them had been covered with thin gold foil, as were the wooden statues in Tutankhamen's tomb. In Ramesses I's tomb they were thrown at the wall with such violence that this foil came off and stuck to the painted plaster, where it may still be seen; tiny fragments of gold glistening on the dented surface of the plaster walls. These figures of minor deities and demons are similar in function to the magnificent collection of statues found in the tomb of Tutankhamen. Since that time, however, theology had changed the destiny of the king to a grimmer future, more demons were stalking in the other world. They all had their special rooms and places in the royal tombs. By setting these gods around the dead king he was placed literally into the other world, surrounded by the cast of its characters.

Apart from these small statues there were two huge wooden figures of the King, at six feet six inches, almost as tall as Belzoni himself. These find ready companions in the two famous 'guardian statues' found later in the tomb of Tutankhamen and further examples have been found in other royal tombs.

Similar statues were buried with the dead at earlier periods of history, although there are no known examples from the contemporary private burials at Thebes. These statues in the royal tombs represent the continuance of the most ancient traditions of royal burial stretching back from the time of Ramesses I, for more than fifteen hundred years. Today, restored and chilly, the two sculptures guard a lift shaft by a stair in the British Museum. Damage and decay has turned them halfway back into the bulky cedar logs from which they were cut and they glisten with the strange shine of ancient desiccated wood. Like all the cedar used in ancient Egypt, these logs were cut from the forests of the Lebanon and brought across the eastern Mediterranean and up the Nile to Thebes.

Today the tomb of Ramesses I waits for the attention of restorers. It was closed some years ago when sections of the roof fell on the sarcophagus. Presently the burial chamber is filled with huge timbers that support further loosened blocks. The rockfalls were caused by movements along the joints in the limestone of the Valley cliffs. Our expedition made a special study of this problem that the tomb shares with several others. As the rock joints behind the plastered walls shift slightly, fragments of the painting that lie along the fault are easily loosened and detached. The plaster base of the paintings of Ramesses I is now very loose and it will require much conservation before the tomb can once again be opened to the public.

Opposite: royal vultures (above) on the ceiling of the tomb of Ramesses VI. The main corridors of the royal tombs of the Ramesside kings were called 'the corridor of the sun's path', and their ceilings are usually decorated with astronomical or aerial motifs. Below, a decorative border—called a heker frieze—in the tomb of Tuthmosis III. This unusual decorative device was also the hieroglyph which determined the ancient word for 'decoration'

Overleaf: Belzoni's coloured elevations of the tomb of Seti I and, on the right, Joseph Bonomi's elegant drawing of the bottom of the alabaster coffin of Seti I with the figure of the goddess Nut

Facing p. 67: Visitors to the 'tomb' of Seti I—the exhibition in the Egyptian Galleries, Piccadilly, 1821. Below, Bruce's harpists, accurately drawn by Wilkinson

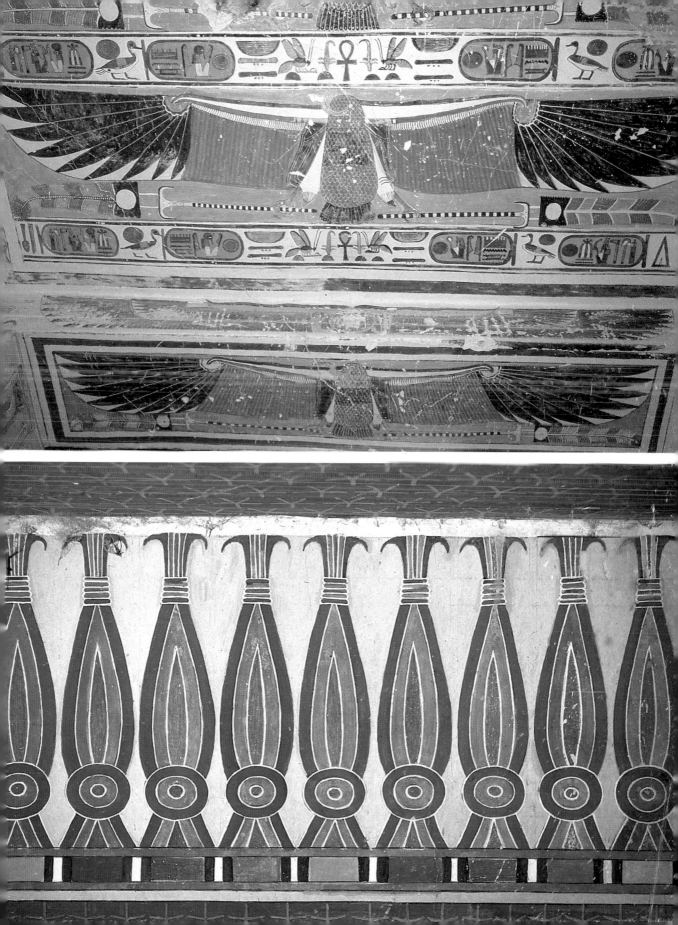

Plate 40.

Etched by A. Aglio, after a Drawing by G. Belzoni.

SECTION of the TOMB of SAMETHIS in the
Discovered and Opened by G. BELZONI, 1818.

London, Published 1820 by John Murray, Albemarle Street.

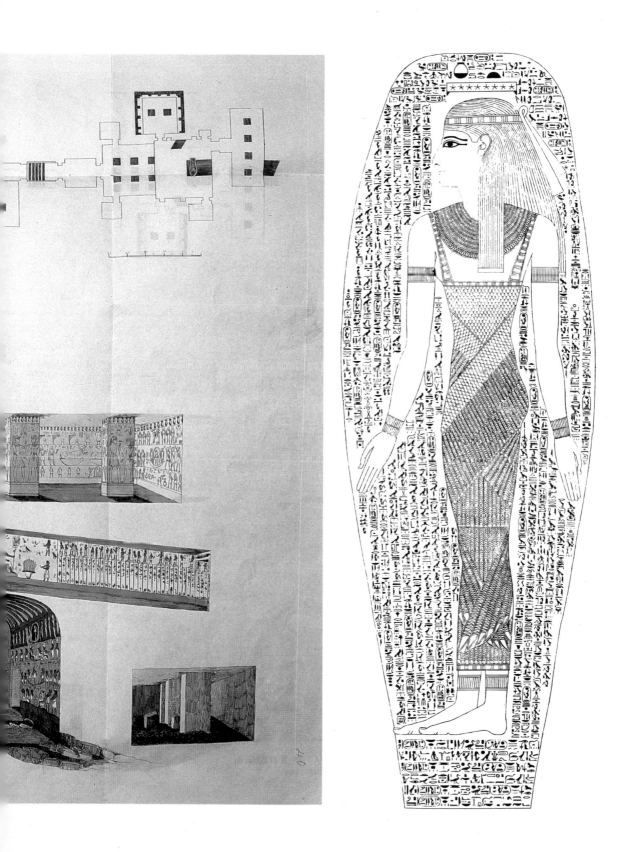

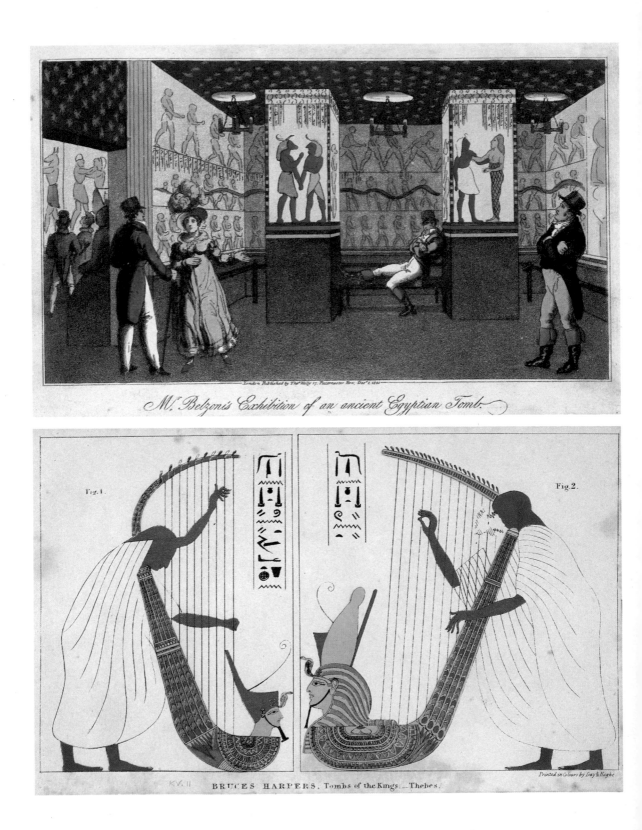

Mr Belzoni's Exhibition of an ancient Egyptian Tomb.

BRUCES HARPERS. Tombs of the Kings.—Thebes.

7

The Tomb of Seti I

Unfortunately the wind on the Nile died down on the day that Belzoni discovered the tomb of Ramesses I. Beechey's party was stuck at Thebes and Belzoni had to arrange further diversions for them. First he took them to see some of the painted chapels of the nobles' tombs and then on some ghoulish excursions through burial chambers and mummy pits. It was four days before he could return to his work in the Valley of the Kings.

So far in his excavations Belzoni had worked in a line down a small side valley that formed the southernmost side of a triangle of gullies that enclosed the centre of the main Valley. At the lower end of this gully lay Bruce's tomb from which Belzoni had taken the granite sarcophagus in the previous year. At the head of the gully some five hundred feet away lay the tomb of Prince Ramesses Montu-hir-kopesh-ef, at the bottom of the cliff which screens the Valley from the Nile. In the line between these two tombs Belzoni had found the small tomb with two female mummies in it and the tomb of Ramesses I. Also in this line of tombs were two more, those of Ramesses X and Amenmesse. Both were probably open when the tourists of the Classical period were in the Valley and both had long been flooded and filled with huge amounts of rocks and debris. They are still practically inaccessible beyond their first corridors. Belzoni continued his dig in the southern slope of this small valley hoping to find more tombs whose entrances had been covered by flood debris and blocked. Many later workers in the Valley would follow this example of digging through the hard flood debris and most would have good luck.

For his next dip into the hillside Belzoni started close by the entrance of the tomb of Ramesses I. By the side of this tomb's door was a low area of ground in the centre of which was a hole about five feet across and twelve feet deep. Flood water had drained into it and probably Belzoni saw evidence in the sand and debris in it that more water had swept down into this hole than ever could have been contained by such a small area. It was the vision of a hydrologist and Belzoni's early studies in the subject

(which had helped in a previous career when he had organized waterfall extravaganzas on the stage of Covent Garden and which had later led him to Cairo in an attempt to sell a water-lifting device to Mohammed Ali Pasha) now crowned his researches in the Valley of the Kings.

I caused the earth to be opened at the foot of a steep hill, and under a torrent which, when it rains in the desert, pours a great quantity of water over the very spot I have caused to be dug. No one could imagine that the ancient Egyptians would make the entrance into such immense and superb excavation just under a torrent of water; but I had strong reasons to suppose that there was a tomb in that place from indications I had observed in my pursuit. The Fellahs who were accustomed to dig were all of the opinion that there was nothing in that spot as the situation of this tomb differed from that of any other. I continued to work, however and the next day, the 17th in the evening we perceived the part of the rock that was cut and formed the entrance. On the 18th, early in the morning, the task was resumed and about noon the workmen reached the entrance which was eighteen feet below the surface of the ground. The appearance indicated that the tomb was of the first rule, but I did not expect to find such a one as it really proved to be. The Fellahs advanced till they saw that it was probably a large tomb, when they protested they could go no further, the tomb was so much choked up with large stones, which they could not get out of the passage. I descended, examined the place, pointed out to them where they might dig, and in an hour there was room enough for me to enter through a passage that the earth had left under the ceiling of the first corridor, which is thirty-six feet two inches long, and eight feet eight inches wide, and, when cleared of the ruins, eight feet nine inches high. I perceived immediately by the painting on the ceiling and by the hieroglyphs in basso relievo, which were to be seen where the earth did not reach, that this was the entrance into a large and magnificent tomb.

Belzoni stood in the first corridor of the new tomb. It was not as large as the other royal tombs that he knew. Its walls were covered in hieroglyphs cut so that they stood out from the surface of the wall in raised relief. This technique takes the light more easily than the heavy sharp-shadowed edges of the more usual sunken relief; it appears finer and small details show up easily. Where Belzoni now stood was lit from the daylight above and the effect of this very finely cut relief in such penetrating sunlight streaming down the dust-filled corridor must have impressed him as deeply as are visitors today. He had found a tomb like no others that were known in the Valley. Belzoni followed the corridor along and down a steep stair where the vertical columns of hieroglyphs on the walls changed first to rows of strange single figures then to the finely drawn half-carved representations of two goddesses and two jackels, in pairs either side of the doorway. The winged vultures, which had formed the ceiling decorations of the first corridor, here gave way to hieroglyphic texts. He passed down another steep corridor:

The more I saw, the more I was eager to see, such being the nature of man: but I was checked in my anxiety at this time, for at the end of this passage I reached a large pit, which intercepted my progress.

Belzoni had arrived at the brink of the well of the tomb, the first time that this feature of royal tomb architecture had been seen in modern times. The well was made like a small room about fourteen feet square with its ceiling at the same height as the one in the corridor which had brought him to its edge. The floor of the well, however, lay in pitch darkness more than thirty feet below his feet. By the light of a flame torch Belzoni could see a hole in the wall that faced him across the well; it was about two feet square and close to the ceiling. From it a rope hung straight down into the darkness. Laid at his feet, wedged behind the jambs of a doorway that stood before the well, was a large timber around which another rope was tied. This rope, too, dropped down into the well. To gain access to the hole on the other side of the well the Egyptians had climbed down this rope to the bottom of the shaft, then up another rope upon the other side. The ropes were ancient and brittle and had partly disintegrated where the flood waters that had

The gully in the Valley in which Belzoni concentrated his excavations. The tomb entrance in the immediate foreground is that of Ramesses III; the next two are, respectively, those of Amenmesse and Ramesses I

run down the tomb and into the well had lapped against them. Belzoni and Beechey, who had come over from Luxor to see what his master's headstrong prodigy was up to, had to leave the tomb, disappointed, to obtain planks and tackle to bridge the well. They could not have known what lay beyond that small black hole, but already the high quality of the wall reliefs in the upper corridors, their pure precise forms made even clearer by the absence of paint, must have greatly excited them.

The next day Belzoni and Beechey returned to the tomb equipped with beams and ropes obtained from a boat moored off Luxor. They pushed a plank across the well and into the small hole and persuaded a hapless workman to cross this precarious bridge and drop a new rope down from the hole in the wall into the well to hang alongside the ancient one. Then they climbed down another rope to the bottom of the well where they found nothing but some wood, anciently stacked against the side of the shaft to help the climber begin the long haul to the hole. The two men then pulled themselves up the shaft on their second new rope and scrambled through the small hole where the workman awaited them. There they found themselves in a low room with four square pillars, every surface of which was carefully engraved, finely smoothed and painted in bright strong colours which, and this is what really surprised them, were as fresh as the day they had been painted. The well and the sealing wall which cut off these lower sections of the tomb had been completely successful in preventing flood water passing beyond them and damaging the tomb.

Now, it was not uncommon to find new tombs in Egypt and many more will certainly be uncovered in the future, but few are undamaged and none, certainly, have ever compared in size and splendour with the monument that Belzoni and Beechey were now investigating. All around them in the pillared room were strange enigmatic pictures carved in relief. Each wall was divided into three horizontal registers, each one of which was partly filled with odd, unusually spaced figures, some of which were joined together by the coils of a gigantic snake. It was a section of 'The Book of Gates', a mystic story of the journeying of the bark bearing the dead king through the dark underworld to be reborn each morning with the sun. The bark, manned by personifications of different aspects of the body and soul of the dead king, held the fate of Egypt in it and its rhythms, the twelve 'chapters' of the book, were the night hours of the cosmic clock. The battles fought by the king in his bark and the daily revival of the king each morning were without ending, the eternal rhythm of the sun. For these two men from the 19th century who had intruded upon these scenes, they were but a further part of the mystery and magic of the discovery. Later Henry Salt described these walls in part of a long epic poem.

Genii with heads of birds, hawks, ibis, drakes,
Of lions, foxes, cats, fish, frogs and snakes,
Bull, rams, and monkeys, hippopotami
With knife in paw suspended from the sky;
Gods germinating men, and men turn'd gods,
Seated in honour, with gilt crooks and rods.

Those early commentators on the strange scenes could not read a word of the hieroglyphics and had only a vague understanding of the ancient religion gained from the classical writers, but they were still part of a society of peasants, courtiers and kings, one that was largely pre-industrial and based in craft and agriculture and so they were quick to comprehend a great deal of what they saw in the tomb scenes.

Belzoni and Beechey walked through this pillared hall and, passing down two steps they came to another room, which had two pillars in its centre. This larger room was covered with the finest drawings painted with a pure, black solid line upon flat white, plastered walls. There were life-sized figures and more strange symbols of the ancient religion all placed with great skill and extraordinary confidence upon the bright pure wall surface.

I gave it the name of the drawing room; for it is covered with figures, which, though only outlined, are so fine and perfect that one would think they had been drawn only the day before.

This room, the largest they had so far seen in the tomb, led nowhere. Belzoni had noticed, however, that the floor of the first pillared hall was disturbed along its left-hand side, the large blocks of stone that had been laid to make a level floor in that area were displaced, and in this rubble and rock there was a depression. Belzoni put his men to work and they soon uncovered another flight of steps leading down to a doorway, which, like the well wall above had been sealed and broken through. Beechey and Belzoni clambered through this breach and found themselves in yet more corridors and rooms covered with magnificent, perfectly preserved painted reliefs.

We perceived that the paintings became more perfect as we advanced further into the interior. They

retained their gloss, or a kind of a varnish over the colours, which has a beautiful effect. At the end of the corridor we descended ten steps into another. From this we entered a small chamber to which I gave the name of the Room of Beauties; for it is adorned with the most beautiful figures in basso relievo, like all the rest, and painted. When standing in the centre of this chamber, the traveller is surrounded by an assembly of Egyptian gods and goddesses.

And so they walked on, through a further pillared hall that joined the huge blue vaulted room which Belzoni christened the 'saloon' but which today is called the burial chamber.

This room is the architectural climax of the tomb. Its low, elegant barrel vault stands upon walls more than twenty feet high. You arrive in the room through a pillared hall and then down three steps. Surprised at the sudden extension of space—for the higher sections of the tomb are confining and slightly claustrophobic—your eyes run up the wall to the blue vault, the night sky. In this sky are painted the constellations of the stars laid out like a great zodiac with some signs that are still used by modern astronomers. The North Star is there, and the Big Dipper. Indeed, the whole night sky of Egypt is there, painted in broad, bold brush strokes in a gritty, yellow pigment, with the stars shown as large red dots. This change of scale, the relief from the confining smooth surface of the rest of the tomb is immense and it is some seconds before one notices the rest of the decorations—the fine hieroglyphs and reliefs of the walls, the two goddesses Isis and Nepthys, who spread out their protecting wings at either end of the great vault as they do on the great granite sarcophagus of Ramesses III that Belzoni took from his tomb nearby.

On their way to the burial chamber the two men had peered briefly into the two small side chambers that lay off the pillared hall; two more similar chambers lay off the burial chamber. One of these, on the left-hand side, was partly sealed, and later Belzoni had the plastered wall removed to expose yet another large room, again completely decorated with the fine fat relief, around the wall of which ran a deep shelf about three feet high projecting about three feet out from the walls behind it, to end in an elegant *cavetto* cornice. In his unaffected manner, Belzoni christened this the 'sideboard' room. By the entrances to the side

The burial chamber of the tomb of Seti I photographed by Harry Burton

chambers stood wooden statues, some with a deep hollow cut in their backs to hold rolls of papyrus, but these were empty even when Belzoni found them. The figures must have joined the collection of Consul Salt, but if they still exist their origins have now been lost and they are but blank wooden statues, perhaps lying anonymously in the reserve collections of a European museum. How much finer they would look back in the tomb for which they were made!

A blue-glazed ushabti of Seti I, now in the Salt Collection, British Museum

At the back of the vaulted burial chamber was another room, the largest in the tomb, nearly fifty feet long with four large pillars down its centre. This room was not decorated, though the perfectly smooth walls were covered with fine white plaster. On the floor lay the carcass of a bull, slaughtered to provide sustenance for the dead king. Scattered about in this huge white room were more than eight hundred small figures, each made in the shape of Osiris, that is, like a small mummy with legs together and hands folded across the chest.

The finest examples of these figures, which were all models of the king, were nearly a foot high and glazed with a glassy blue as bright as the Valley sky. On these figures, called *ushabtis*, were drawn the outlines of the king's features in a fine purple blue line, and hieroglyphic texts, which swathed the lower half of the figures, like the bandaging of a mummy. Although there were many variants of the central theme, a typical text upon one of these figures might read:

> *Osiris who illuminates the King, the Lord of the Two Lands, this Men-Maat-re [Seti's first name] the justified [title given to the dead] says, 'Oh you ushabti, if the Osiris, the son of Re [the sun god] Seti, the justified is counted or called to do work or drafted to fulfil any tasks in the underworld; to till the fields, to irrigate the banks, or to transport sand from east to west; since hardships come in the course of such duties, if at any time I am called, say "Behold I am present."'*

In other words: Seti I commands the ushabti to take his place in the other world when work is required by the spirits who inhabit it. The next world was made, as all must be, in the image of society upon earth, and in Egypt from ancient times until almost the end of the last century, the population was required to work, when agricultural activity was mimimal, upon public works projects. These little stand-in figures for the king do not hold the sceptres of kingship across their chests but two hoes, the perennial tools of the Egyptian labourer. On their backs are the palm-leaf baskets in which the dirt scraped into them with the hoes, would be moved to whatever location the lords of the underworld should require. Once the ancient Egyptians accepted such notions as this into their burial rituals the concept was carried through to a logical conclusion. The fully elaborated form of this custom includes small shrine-shaped 'houses' for the ushabti figures, which were divided into gangs to serve under special foremen figures. Sometimes figures were made for each day of the year, three hundred and sixty-five of them, which could be accompanied by replacement model tools that, occasionally, were beautifully fashioned from the most precious metals. When one is confronted with the odd fragments of such elaborate rituals—a single model tool or part of a miniature shrine-house—it is sometimes necessary to stand back from these details and attempt to find the basic conception that encouraged the manufacture of such extraordinary paraphernalia. Such care and attention to detail is but one aspect of the thoughtfulness and affection that the Egyptians showed towards their dead and is typical of the religion of the New Kingdom, which is filled with such highly elaborated and complex provisions which, by their very multiplications, seek to encompass the mystery of the underlying ineffable truths in which they believed.

When Belzoni first walked wonderingly through Seti I's tomb he was probably its first visitor in nearly three thousand years and followed directly in the footsteps of the ancient priests who had removed Seti's mummy and most of what remained of his burial equipment. After the funeral the tomb had been carefully filled with the same types of objects that were found in the tiny tomb of Tutankhamen, which have delighted the world ever since their discovery in the Valley in 1922. These objects were either directly connected with the burial rites, food, statues and other ritual pieces connected with the king's death and journey to the next world, or were domestic objects, the property of the living king, left in the tomb with their owner. Normally all these things were placed in different rooms, each according to custom and each category with its special place.

Seti I reigned much longer than the young Tutankhamen and would have had far more objects for his burial. Certainly there would have been more personal belongings, chariots, clothes and all the accoutrements of ancient kings. The special religious objects made to go with the king into his tomb were similar to those in Tutankhamen's tomb although the images were probably more diverse and complex reflecting the increasingly complicated destinies of this later period. Most of these courtly objects had long since been smashed or taken from the tomb and Belzoni found the empty halls and corridors littered with statues and fragments of broken burial equipment.

He turned his attention away from the long white room with its slaughtered bull and went back to the vaulted burial chamber:

> But the description of what we found in the centre of the saloon, and which I have reserved till this place, merits the most particular attention, not having its equal in the world, and being such as we had no idea could exist. It is a sarcophagus of the finest oriental alabaster nine feet five inches long, and three feet seven inches wide. Its thickness is only two inches; and it is transparent, when a light is placed in the inside of it. It is minutely sculptured within and without with seven hundred figures, which do not exceed two inches in height and represent, as I suppose, the whole of the funeral procession and ceremonies relating to the deceased, united with several emblems, etc.

A drawing by Joseph Bonomi of the alabaster coffin of Seti I. The lid is a reconstruction based on the surviving fragments

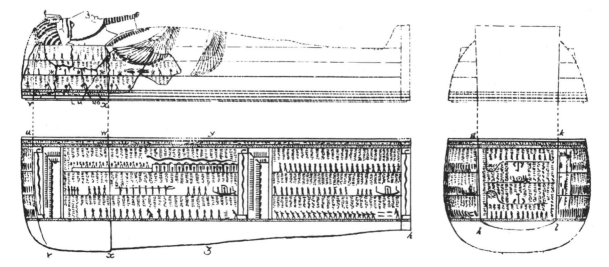

Here he had found a beautiful and rare example of Egyptian art, made to hold the body of a king. Belzoni's term 'sarcophagus' came from the classical writers, who used it in its literal sense of 'flesh-eater', after a type of sarcophagus reputedly used in Asia Minor that was supposed to consume the body it held in forty days. Presumably such sarcophagi, if they existed, contained a corrosive chemical in their stone. It is truly the reverse of any intentions the Egyptians had for their burial arrangements and, indeed, what Belzoni called a sarcophagus, egyptologists today would call a coffin; a sarcophagus being a larger container into which the coffins were placed. Egyptian coffins were generally made in sets like Russian dolls, fitting closely one inside the other and shaped in the form of the mummy that they were designed to hold. Belzoni, then, had found a mummiform coffin, unusual but not unique, in that it was made of stone.

The distinction between coffin and sarcophagus is an important one. For if Belzoni had found only an internal coffin of the king, where was the real royal sarcophagus? These sarcophagi were as carefully designed as the architecture of tombs themselves, each one being developed from the design of its predecessor. The coffin that Belzoni found is not part of this tradition. It lay across the entrance to another stairway that he had encountered in the upper sections of the tomb, and in common with the others, was filled with debris and had been covered with slabs of stone to make a flat floor in the great vaulted room. Again Belzoni cleared the debris from the mouth of this buried doorway but this time he and Beechey did not find further decorated rooms beneath. The limestone stratum in which the tomb was cut finished about three feet above the floor of the vaulted chamber. Beneath the limestone was a stratum of unstable soft brown shale that was almost spongy in its horizontal bedding and as unsuitable for excavation as would be a mountain of newspapers. Even before he could examine this section of the tomb Belzoni had to clear away the heaps of shale that had fallen from the walls and ceilings of the dark tunnel. The ancient masons who had cut this tunnel had quarried in shale before and well understood the problems involved in such work. It was better, for example, to cut corridors with a steep angle of descent as the horizontal strata easily collapsed from flat ceilings with very little warning. Perhaps the masons were intending to cut straight through this 180-foot shale band into the soft white chalk which, from experience of the landscape of Thebes, they knew lay beneath it.

Whether or not the ancient workmen succeeded in this we do not know, for Belzoni was forced to stop his progress down the dangerous irregular tunnel after three hundred feet. The rock was extremely loose and the air was very bad; he was, after all, more than 650 feet from the entrance of the tomb in the Valley above. Conditions in the tunnel have remained sufficiently unpleasant and dangerous to discourage further excavations, although one attempt made in 1960 did extend Belzoni's original clearance by about one hundred feet. This tunnel has remained one of the great mysteries of the Valley. Local tradition, going back at least two centuries, asserts that it leads through the mountains of the Valley and comes out of the rock by the temple of Hatshepsut which stands upon the exposed shale at the foot of the cliffs that look across the Valley of the Nile. But this is a folk story and has little to do with either the needs of the ancient religion or the designs of the royal tombs or temples. In every known royal tomb there is only one entrance, and after the royal burial was made it was quite unnecessary to obtain regular access to it again. Similarly there is no known function that such a second entrance to the tomb could have served.

Ali Abd er Rassul, the local sheik who dug in

A plan of the tomb of Seti I showing, in dotted line, the beginning of the mysterious tunnel that runs down from the burial chamber

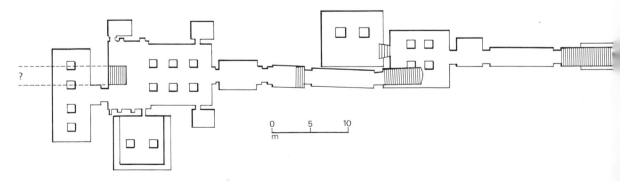

the tunnel in 1960 did so in the belief that he would find gold and other treasures there. Several fragmentary antiquities were found but they may well have been washed down into the tunnel during a flood that occurred in the tomb shortly after Belzoni had opened it. The sheik's interest in archeology was probably spurred by boyhood memories of conversations between the elders of his family who had discovered a cache of royal mummies in their younger days, and like many *Gurnawis* he must have made endless speculations on the possibilities of finding more treasures. However, the air pump purchased to improve conditions, while the workers cut away at the dusty face of the rock-hard flood debris at the bottom of the tunnel, did little to speed the work, and then the money ran out. So the tunnel still holds its secret and we are left to speculate upon its possibilities from our knowledge of the other monuments of the Valley and elsewhere.

Such speculations are the stuff of egyptology; old and new evidence is reviewed and from it fresh possibilities are constructed. Precedent and tradition were very strong forces in ancient Egyptian culture but it is as well to remember that the monuments were designed by responsive, living people and so there is always a chance of a difference, a variation, in the pattern. Indeed, a basic test of a forgery of an ancient work of art is that a genuine original always contains the spark of something new in it; a variation on the theme, a small surprise. On the other hand, a forgery, unless made by a real master, is essentially imitative, merely an assemblage of copied parts. An understanding of the ancient elements of design and their possible permutations is one of the great attractions of egyptology. With every correct solution of puzzles such as the long corridor in the tomb of Seti I—and the correct solution can, in this case, be verified by excavation—the archeologist shows real insight into the world of the ancient architects and priests, comprehends their motives and problems and the alter-

native solutions open to them. This understanding of a part of the ancient experience is surely worth all the treasure of Pharaoh.

An enquiry into the possible purposes of the tunnel in Seti's tomb would, therefore, deal with all the evidence, old and new, and weigh this against our knowledge of ancient precedents and traditions. Let us begin with some fresh evidence that may have a bearing upon this mysterious tunnel.

During the geological survey conducted by our expedition in the Valley in 1978–9 we found evidence that another tunnel, previously unknown, lay off the burial chamber of the tomb of Seti's son Ramesses II. This tunnel, the entrance to which is hidden under piles of flood debris, was detected by a study of the broken limestone rock from above the shale. Ramesses II's tomb, like Seti's, has its lower sections resting on the upper surface of the shale, and our geologists were puzzled by the collapse, in the burial chamber, of part of one limestone wall that had fallen onto the shale floor. For it to have dropped down, there simply had to be a void under the limestone and, indeed, it was this void which, when the limestone was under stress following the flooding of the burial chamber, had been the cause of instability in the rock above it. Almost certainly this void is the entrance of another tunnel similar to the long-known puzzle in the tomb of Seti I. Unfortunately, Ramesses II's tomb is ruined, dangerous and full of flood debris. Its clearance would require a major excavation with little hope of discovering anything that would justify such an undertaking. Apart from occasionally being host to a torch-bearing egyptologist trying to check a hieroglyphic text, the tomb remains shut and empty.

It is probable, therefore, that there are at least two of these tunnels in the Valley tombs, and perhaps others because there are several other tombs that have not been sufficiently cleared to determine whether or not they share this mysterious feature. Most of the royal tombs, however, never had their burial chambers completed in ancient times, let alone the additional work of further tunnels beyond the vaulted rooms, which now hold the royal sarcophagi. Of the few that were completed, Bruce's tomb, that of Ramesses III, for example, was like Seti I and Ramesses II, completely finished; it has a succession of long narrow chambers running back from the vaulted burial hall. Another tomb, that of Queen Tausert also has these rear chambers, but here they form the first corridors of another complete tomb, cut for King Setnakht who was eventually buried there. So it would seem that the ancient architects and the priests sometimes continued the design of the royal tombs behind and beyond the vaulted burial chambers and that, at least in one example, these chambers led to another burial place. The obvious differences between the steep tunnel in the tomb of Seti I and the narrow rooms that lie beyond the burial chamber of other royal tombs could be partly due to the nature of the rock in which they were excavated, the shale requiring angles of descent different from those in the solid limestone—as we have already seen. Indeed, it may have been these enormous problems that this unstable shale posed to the ancient workmen that led them to abandon the whole idea of long deep tunnels in the later tombs. When, later in the Valley's history, they excavated a deep shaft in another tomb, that of Ramesses XI, the quarrymen stopped their work exactly where the limestone rested on the soft underlying shale.

But what purposes would these long tunnels have served? The plan of Seti I's tomb, the tunnel apart, is quite in keeping with the traditional scheme of design for the series of royal tombs that preceded it. There are, however, certain innovations which show that a programme of religious and ritual exploration was being adopted in the tomb. In the tomb of Ramesses I, Seti I's predecessor, the text traditionally painted upon the walls of the burial chamber, the *Amduat*, which is also known as 'The Book of What is in the Otherworld' was not used; another text, 'The Book of Gates', was painted there in its place. In Seti I's tomb the discarded texts reappeared, carved upon the uppermost corridors of the tomb—these were the fine columns of hieroglyphs that Belzoni had seen when he had first entered the tomb. Down in the burial chamber in Seti's tomb 'The Book of Gates' was used again and a magnificent innovation, the astronomical ceiling, appears in the Valley for the first time. The 'Sideboard' room, designed to hold specific ritual objects upon its shelves, also shows the continuing process of the development of ritual and religion through changes in the tomb's traditional decorations and architecture. The long tunnel beneath the tomb is also a part of this same process.

Other monuments of the reign of Seti I also contain architectural/religious innovations. Some of his buildings attempt to express the oldest rituals and beliefs of the state religion through the architecture of the day; a reassertion of some of the most traditional elements of the faith after the heresies of the Amarnan period. At Abydos, a religious centre close to Thebes, which had been the burial place of kings in ages even before the rise of the Old Kingdom, Seti in common with other kings, had a cenotaph built deep in the ground behind a magnificent temple that he also had erected at the site. These cenotaphs were alternative 'tombs' for the dead kings, a kind of *doppelgräber*. Some of the earlier royal cenotaphs excavated at Abydos had been tunnelled down deep into the rock in a manner similar to the last mysterious corridor of Seti's tomb in the Valley of the Kings.

Seti I's cenotaph at Abydos, however, employed water as an element in its design: water which seeped through the soft rock beneath the temple to form a great pool around the symbolic sarcophagus of the king, the primaeval lake from which all matter had been born with the royal sarcophagus as the central element in the drama of creation. But this was hardly the intention of the architects of the tunnel in Seti's tomb which was hundreds of feet above the water table of the Nile and many miles away from it. Nevertheless, the cenotaph at Abydos may still provide an important clue in the mystery, for it demonstrates, as do some of the other tombs in the Valley, that the ancient architects were quite prepared to continue the architecture behind and beyond what would normally be considered as the prime focus of the temples or tombs—the shrines in Seti's temple at Abydos or the vaulted burial chamber in his tomb in the Valley of the Kings. Seti, as we have seen, had two tombs made for himself, in common with many of the earlier kings of Egypt, and it is quite possible, therefore, that the great tunnel at the back of his tomb in the Valley leads to yet another burial chamber. But which room in the tomb, the vaulted burial chamber or the hypothetical room at the end of the long tunnel, actually held the dead body of the king?

The traditional answer must be: the vaulted chamber above the tunnel—for every precedent of tomb architecture supports this opinion, and most of the huge sarcophagi of the kings could never have fitted into the small tunnels that may have been planned to run down from the vaulted burial chambers. However, none of these tunnels have yet been excavated and there are many indications, as we have seen, that the concept of such tunnels and their place within Seti's monuments fit well into the somewhat innovatory architecture of the period. It is as well, then, to examine all these possibilities to determine the actual location of the royal burial, for egyptology is filled with surprises and significantly, in this case, the obvious traditional answer to the question of Seti I's burial leaves many important issues unresolved.

Seti I's underground cenotaph at Abydos, called the Osireon

Neither the sarcophagus of Seti I nor that of Ramesses II, nor of his successor Merneptah, have ever been found although in the tomb of the latter there were once at least three huge granite lids. It is possible, of course, that the granite boxes of the sarcophagi, each weighing many tons, were all taken out of their burial chambers in antiquity but it would have been incredibly difficult to raise these sarcophagi from the depths of their tombs. Another alternative that should be considered is that these kings never possessed normal sarcophagi, consisting of a box and lid, but that large lids were placed over small crypts cut in the rock of the tomb that held the coffins and mummy of the king. This system was used for the burials of some of the later kings in the Valley.

Some years ago I found a dozen blocks of sandstone in Seti I's tomb which, judging from their measurements that showed great similarity to other examples, may originally have formed the base upon which the king's sarcophagus rested. Many such blocks were removed from the tunnel during restoration work in the tomb at the turn of the century and several are now stacked in a side chamber in the tomb; accurately and finely-made sandstone slabs that had been brought to the tomb from quarries some sixty miles south of Thebes.

There are two other small, perhaps significant clues which may point to the possibility of a second

77

burial chamber in Seti I's tomb. First, when Belzoni discovered the alabaster coffin it was lying across the end of the mouth of the tunnel, a position that suggests it may have been dragged up from the constricting lower section of the tomb to a place where it could be conveniently handled on a flat surface and in a large space. Possibly this event occurred when Seti I's mummy was removed from the tomb to be reburied with the other kings in one of the two royal caches made at the end of the New Kingdom. If Seti I's mummy had already been plundered it is probable that its removal would have been a delicate task that required space in which to manœuvre. In earlier royal tombs, coffins and sarcophagi have sometimes been discovered at the top of the final descent into the burial chambers. In some of the smaller pyramids of the Middle Kingdom, for example, the burial chambers were often so small that it was impossible to raise the lids of the sarcophagi or the interior coffins once they had been installed in their final positions. Thus, the sarcophagi and the coffins were left outside the burial chambers to receive their occupants. In order to remove these mummies from their burial chambers once they had been put into place, it would have been necessary to take the complete burial out of the chamber or to smash the stone and wooden lids where they lay. The lid of Seti's alabaster coffin was smashed into small pieces, which may suggest that whoever robbed the burial was working in a small enclosed space. The thin and brittle piece of alabaster would not have been difficult to lift from the coffin had there been sufficient room.

The second clue is the most unusual and compre-hensive decoration of the coffin itself. The loose shale of the tunnel and the chamber that, perhaps, lies buried at the end of it, could hardly have provided a suitable surface upon which to paint or sculpt the texts that would have been placed in the royal burial chamber and in these circumstances the Egyptians usually painted some of the intricate burial chamber texts on the coffins. Seti I's alabaster coffin was carved in fine detail and extraordinary care with the entire 'Book of Gates'—the text that had replaced the *Amduat* as the standard text for the royal burial chamber. Was the surface of the coffin a substitute for the normal place of the texts, the walls of the burial chamber?

Many questions remain to be answered before it is possible to state definitely that Seti I and his two successors were buried in their great vaulted burial chambers and not in another room cut into the brown shale some hundreds of feet below. All we can do now is to survey the evidence, some of it quite contradictory, and weigh the possibilities. Further excavation in the tomb of Seti I would, of course, supply the answer to the riddle, but it would be an expensive operation and the tomb, yet again, would be placed at great risk from such activities. It has already suffered more damage from the casual attentions of millions of visitors than any other in Egypt and with so many tombs in distress in the Valley there are much more urgent tasks for archeologists. The mystery in the tomb of Seti I should, therefore, be allowed to lie; as far as we know, one of the last mysteries that the Valley holds—perhaps, indeed, its ultimate hidden ritual.

8

Seti in London

Belzoni considered that the tomb of Seti I was the finest ever discovered in Egypt. Most people of the time agreed with him, and it soon took pride of place over Bruce's tomb as the most admired and visited monument in the Valley. In their accounts of the tomb some of these early visitors wrote lengthy descriptions of the dazzlingly fresh wall scenes, texts that are part explanatory, part anthropological, occasionally mystic, sometimes moralistic, mostly dull and as so often happens with descriptions of ancient monuments telling us more about the authors than they do about the tomb.

The first visitor who wrote of what he had seen in Belzoni's tomb was a member of the party of Lord and Lady Belmore who were engaged on a very grand tour of the Middle East with their doctor, priest and family servants, all packed into a huge yacht that Lord Belmore's brother, Captain Amar Lowry-Corry had sailed into the Mediterranean. Salt made good friends with Belmore while he was in Egypt and several crates of Salt's antiquities, including some from Belzoni's excavations in the Valley, were stowed aboard the earl's yacht and shipped to England.

Lord Belmore's party arrived in the Valley just a few weeks after Belzoni's great discovery and were accompanied by Beechey who, forewarned of their approach, had gone to Luxor from the camp in the Valley to guide the party around the monuments. Lord Belmore was keen to collect some antiquities of his own and he employed one of Salt's agents, who now had many groups of Arabs digging in different areas of Thebes on his behalf. Belzoni, too, helped the English lord to find some souvenirs.

I pointed out two likely spots of ground in the valley of Beban el Malook [Valley of the Kings] but they turned out to be two small mummy pits. This proves that small tombs were permitted to be dug out in that valley where, it was supposed, that none but the tombs of the kings of Egypt were to be found.

Belzoni's observation is still pertinent today, for many people believe that the Valley holds only the tombs of the kings. Certainly, some of the more than fifty private tombs known to be in the Valley were open in Belzoni's day, but they were so unimposing that they were never placed in the early maps of the Valley or counted by the travellers. Similarly, the positions of Belmore's two small tombs were not recorded, but presumably they are among the open private tombs that dot parts of the Valley floor.

It was during one of these sallies into the Valley landscape that Lord Belmore and his brother wrote their names on the door jambs of a small ruined tomb, but it was not these little amusements that provided the most memorable experiences of their visit. The discovery of the huge tomb had been local knowledge within a few days of its opening. Already Belzoni had received a flying visit from the Turkish Governor of Kena who had ridden directly from his house in the capital of the province some fifty miles away and, with a troop of his cavalry, thoroughly searched every room and corridor of the tomb. His hard two-day ride had been unfruitful and the reports that Belzoni had found a golden cockerel filled with diamonds and pearls proved false. With his usual good humour Belzoni convinced the Governor that the rumour was but a countryman's dream, and when the disappointed Mohammed Aga left the tomb at the end of his quick inspection he expressed his opinion that at least the tomb might make a good harem because 'the women would have something to look at'. Lord Belmore's party arrived hard on the heels of the Turk but they were filled with far loftier sentiments as his doctor, Robert Richardson, makes abundantly clear with every page of his Grundyish account. Richardson's two volumes describing the sightseeing of this eccentric excursion are not the work of a great diarist, but one cannot but enjoy his account of the visit to Seti I's tomb by Bernadino Drovetti, the first of the foreign consuls in Egypt to excavate and collect antiquities and Salt's principal rival in Luxor. Lord Belmore was very pleased to show this Frenchman their consul's impressive discovery.

On the 20th we revisited the newly discovered tomb, in company with the ci-devant French Consul, whom

*we found an agreeable and intelligent man, and one
of the most zealous and successful collectors of
antiquities in Egypt. He is the only Frenchman that
I ever saw in all my life completely run out of the
small change of compliment and admiration. He was
so lavish of his civilities on entering the tomb and
everything was so superb, magnifique, superlative
and astounding, that when he came to something
which really called for epithets of applause and
admiration, his magazine of stuff was expended and
he stood in speechless astonishment, to the great
entertainment of the beholders.*

Drovetti was not alone in his astonishment, for the
tomb of Seti I greatly impressed most of its visitors. It
was fresh, pristine and filled with extraordinary
highly finished visions, and as well made as the finest
European craftsmanship. It underlined the enigma
posed by the situation of these royal tombs, all filled
with intimations of an ancient courtly life of great
luxury and grandeur yet hidden away in a rough
desert valley at the end of a winding, waterless track.
These contrasts intrigued and puzzled many visitors.
Richardson, in common with many of his day, would
not believe that such an enormous amount of skill
and effort had been destined only to be sealed up
and left after the funeral rites. Why had an obviously
cultured and refined people made such immense
complicated tombs for their kings? Was there, in
these ancient places, a significance that had previously
gone unnoticed? The problem of the 'true purpose'
of the royal tombs occupied many authors after their
visits to the Valley. Even Browne, that very level-
headed traveller, imagined that the royal tombs contained reference to 'mysteries' but by this he had
simply proposed that a centre of ritual initiation had
existed in the Valley, such as had been common
throughout the classical world. However, in 1830
James St John, who had walked through most of
Egypt in his day and knew many of the leading
scholars of the time, put the case for the 'true purpose'
clearly:

*With what object were these gay and costly palaces
constructed? For the reception of a corpse; to be
closed like other receptacles of the dead, until
doomsday. This seems wholly improbable. In my
opinion they were made for the use of the living,
not for the dead.*

The classical writers had, in fact, already given a
clear and correct answer to these questions. The great
monuments in the Valley of the Kings were tombs of
the kings of Egypt and, thanks to these classical
writers, when the very first European travellers
entered the Valley they knew exactly what they were
seeing. The local Arabic name for the Valley, *Biban el
Moluk* (Gates of the Kings) had also transmitted the
germ of this knowledge directly from the ancient
past. During this century thousands of texts written
by the community of workmen who built the tombs
and mummies of kings and found sealed in the tombs
where they had been buried in ancient times, have
been translated. However, in the period before the
1850s there was insufficient evidence for people who
were loath to take the often prosaically expressed
opinions of scholars as the final word on such exciting
and romantic monuments. Unwilling to view the
royal tombs with the detachment that scholarship
can provide, they trusted entirely to the vision of their
own times, and found many different purposes for the
tombs. It is an early example of the failure of scholars
to communicate more than the barest of their
findings to the general public and one which still
leads to the advancement of strange misinformed
theories concerning ancient monuments. A part of
Richardson's account of his first visit to the tomb of
Seti I shows how such confusions can be born.

*It is impossible adequately to describe the sensations
of delight and astonishment that by turns took
possession of the mind as we moved along the
corridor and examined the different groups and
hieroglyphics that occur successively in every
chamber of this most perfect of all ancient relics.
During the whole of our visit, the eye was constantly
at variance with the ear. We had been told that
what we saw was a tomb, but it required a constant
effort of the mind to convince us that it was such.
Only one sarcophagus in one chamber, and twelve
chambers, exclusive of the long corridor, all highly
ornamented for nothing! It may have been a
subterraneous temple, exhibiting the religious creed
of the worshippers, or the rites of initiation. It may
have been a subterraneous palace, like those for the
king of Troglodyta; but never was such a monstrous
supposition, or such a superfluous waste, as to fancy
that all this was done for the reception of this one
sarcophagus.*

The standards by which Richardson judged the
plausibility of the explanation that the royal tombs
of the Valley were only tombs had been brought
with him from his native Scotland, where the proper
way to accommodate a burial was in a church crypt,

with, perhaps, a neo-classical urn and plaque in the nave of the church above to mark the place of interment. More than this was 'lavish', less was 'poor' or 'modest'. Seti I's burial arrangements obviously failed to meet Richardson's commonsense values. He was unable to conceive that the ancient Egyptians, in common with many other races of the world, placed different values on death and hence, that their royal tombs had a different purpose and function. The royal tombs of ancient Egypt were not megalomaniacal funerary vaults but the underworld itself magically made by paintings and the rites of priests. The dead king was not a mere corpse waiting through the ages for the Last Trump, but a body which, once certain ritual requirements were met, underwent constant revivication and thus manifested a deep power that ran through Egypt.

The arguments of these early travellers and several of the contemporary popular writers upon antiquity are identical. First, the reader is flattered by an appeal to his 'commonsense', then he is told quickly that the usual explanations of the purposes and technology of the tombs are wanting in this powerful quality and therefore, are unbelievable. Thus the flood doors are opened for any explanation that

'commonsense' might provide: all opinions carry the same weight since scholarship has been shown to be a fool. But this 'commonsense' has never been common to all mankind and those who use it to explain the past can only make a modern world in an antique costume. Similar confusions exist about the ancient technologies. Some writers, unable to concede that the ancient people possessed sufficient intelligence and ability to make their own monuments, suggest that they were aided by intelligences from other nations, or even from other planets. A bunch of shoddy mysteries which may rob us of the true sense of wonder and admiration for the civilization of our own remote ancestors is a very poor swap for knowledge hard won by centuries of study. It is little more than a sad appeal to extra-terrestrials to enable people to comprehend their own past.

In the last century, however, man was still firmly on the ground and God alone inhabited the realms

A plate depicting the Valley of the Kings from a popular history book published about 1830. Though primitively drawn, the sketch shows the main features of the Valley: the path over the mountains, the peak of the Gurn, and the cliffs encircling the Valley's centre

Cantù. St. Univ.   Tav. 14.

D. Bonetti inc.

Tombe di Bibau el-moluk

of the extra-terrestrial. So, in the Reverend William Jowett's *Christian Researches*, written in 1822, it is God himself who is called upon to give an explanation for the royal tombs, which Jowett had first visited in the same year as Richardson. Dr Jowett, a well-known and conscientious protestant missionary who worked in Egypt for many years, believed that the tombs were the 'scene of idolatrous rites performed in the dark'. He quoted the authority of the Old Testament to support his views but one might fairly observe, however, that he does take the words of the Prophet somewhat out of context:

> *Then said He unto me, Son of Man, dig now into the wall; and when I had digged into the wall, behold a door.*
> *And He said unto me, Go in, and behold the wicked abominations that they do here.*
> *So I went in and saw; and behold every form of creeping things, and abominable beasts, and all the idols of the house of Israel, portrayed upon the walls about—*EZEKIEL 8, 8–10

Dr Jowett made the Bible sound like a celestial excavation report and, at the same time, delivered the single most severe opinion upon the tombs that has ever been written!

Happily, it is unlikely that such complications ever entered the practical mind of Giovanni Belzoni who, after some time away from the Valley, in Cairo, had been having a quite different set of thoughts about the tomb. Belzoni's earlier career in show business had endowed him with some understanding of the popular imagination and he now realized he had the means of exploiting a vein of public curiosity to the full. Enlisting the aid of a fellow Italian traveller, a Siennese doctor and artist named Alessandro Ricci, he returned to the Valley and stayed there for nearly a year, living in the tomb of Seti I with a small group of people that included Sarah, Ricci and a group of their personal servants, one of whom, an Irish boy, silently shared nearly all of Belzoni's Egyptian adventures. Using a mixture of beeswax, resin and dust, which Belzoni had concocted to stand the desert heat and the effects of travel, they made casts of the wall reliefs in the tomb, unfortunately stripping some scenes of much of their colour; an indignity which, in the end, turned out to be the very least they would have to suffer. The moulds, made with this special mixture, were to enable Belzoni to recast the walls of the tomb in England, for he intended to exhibit the tomb of Seti I to the public for whom he had once acted. It was a completely novel idea and one which

modern museum curators are beginning to take up again in the interest of conserving the real monuments.

Although Belzoni eventually removed the alabaster coffin and most of the other antiquities from the tomb, it is greatly to his credit that he did not cut away any of the wall decorations or carry off the loose fragments that later fell from the walls and ceilings. The four hundred drawings and casts that were made from the decorations still remain a valuable archeological record because some of the scenes and texts that he recorded have since been damaged or have disappeared. During this work it occurred to Belzoni that the tomb, its door now completely cleared of stone chippings and rubble, was vulnerable to flooding by the waters that regularly poured off the high desert and down through the Valley, so he set his men to work building a series of dykes around the tomb entrance to deflect the torrents.

As they worked in the Valley the little group was

Belzoni's own map of the Valley, showing the general positions of the tombs as they lie under the ground. His discoveries are shown in solid black and the previously opened tombs are in hatched lines

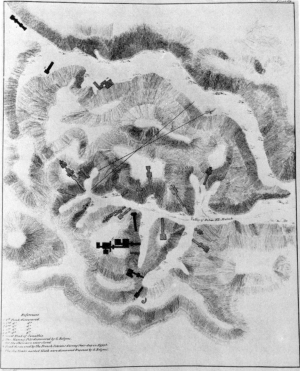

visited by an Arab miner who had come from a remote ancient emerald mine that had recently been rediscovered close-by the ruins of a Roman town by the Red Sea. The first reports of the site gave the impression of a major archeological discovery with hints of great natural wealth and ancient treasures, 'a new Pompeia' thought Belzoni and, encouraged by the information gained from their visitor, he set off in September 1818 with Ricci and Beechey on a long hard camel ride through the Eastern Desert. Sarah also left the Valley at this time and made a remarkable journey of her own to Syria and Palestine, where she visited many of the biblical sites. The men found the mines and the city, a ruin on a wild and beautiful seashore, but there was no treasure and, disappointed, they returned empty-handed to Thebes.

While he had been away Belzoni found that Salt himself had been digging about at Thebes. The Consul-General had brought a group of friends from Cairo, one of whom, William Bankes, was visiting Upper Egypt for a second time. Bankes, heir to large estates in Dorset, had studied at Cambridge and, after serving as aide-de-camp to Wellington in Spain had been travelling throughout the Middle East for some years. He had been buying antiquities on a large scale and now he was returning to Philae to remove a huge obelisk that he had discovered there three years earlier. Belzoni was swiftly hired to put the obelisk on board a barge for Alexandria and Salt's large party left Thebes for Philae in three boats. Belzoni soon accomplished this task and returned to the Valley where he found that Sarah had set up house in the tomb of Seti I, having herself returned from Palestine just a week before. He recounts that 'It was then Christmas and we passed the solemnity of that blessed day in the solitude of those recesses, undisturbed by the folly of mankind'.

Since they were last together in the Valley there had been many changes. When Sarah had returned to the tomb she found, to her great dismay, that it had been flooded, for the dykes that Belzoni had begun to build around its door had never been finished. Sarah had experienced the same heavy rains that had caused this flood as she sailed upstream to Thebes in a small boat hired in Cairo. During one night a violent electrical storm soaked all her belongings and, although the rain stopped within a few hours, she had seen water pouring off the deserts for several days afterwards. The tomb of Seti I had suffered especially badly in these flash floods because Belzoni had filled up the protecting well—the water trap— with the debris he had taken out of the lower sections

of the tomb. The water had even penetrated the tunnel that ran down from the vaulted chamber. The shale that underlies the limestone of the tomb, as it does the whole Valley, expands and exerts great pressure when wet. Recent investigations by our expedition in the Valley shows that the limestone, to a lesser extent, is also subject to expansion, its creamy colour betraying the presence of a small percentage of the expansive mud in the body of the stone. Apart from damage to the lower sections of the tomb walls, where the incoming flood water and debris had abraided the delicate paint and relief, the expansion that occurred during the hours that followed the soaking of the tomb had forced up the limestone walls that stood upon the shale floor of the lower rooms into the ceilings with tremendous pressure. Pieces of the tomb began to fall; small fragments at the junctions of columns and ceilings, door jambs, pieces of the vault in the last decorated chamber, even sections of the walls themselves. Like a flower the tomb had lost the first bloom of its uncovering and had slowly started to die.

Mrs Belzoni found that 'the only thing I could do was to order a number of boys to take the damp earth away, for while any damp remained the walls would still go on cracking.' Unknowingly she was on the horns of a dilemma, for by removing the damp earth she caused the wet walls that were buried in silt and rubble to dry out quickly, causing the mud in the limestone to shrink rapidly; this sudden relaxing of pressure at the top of the shattered walls and columns brought further rock falls. The instability of the walls of the lower sections of the tomb was further increased by the partial disintegration of the shale at their base, causing some of the walls to overhang the layer of disintegrated shale beneath by more than a foot.

A few years later another archeologist, James Burton, finished the work of dyke-building begun by Belzoni outside the tomb. Inside the tomb the well was cleared of its filling and the lower parts of the tomb have not been floooded since; the continuing destruction since that time has been mostly caused by the hand of man. But the century-slow action of desiccation in the lower sections of the tomb, which was accelerated by the clearance of the tunnel beneath the vaulted room in the 1950s, still causes great concern for the stability of the tomb. The cracks in the walls plugged at the turn of the century, have opened once again and the decay slowly continues.

Belzoni was 'not a little vexed to see such a thing happen' and he gathered up some of the fallen fragments to protect them from further damage. It was the first of a series of calamities suffered by Belzoni and Sarah. Soon after Christmas the harassment to which he had been continually subjected by the other excavators at Thebes reached a climax. While the barge with the obelisk from Philae was still lying at anchor at Thebes, he was attacked by a gang of workmen led by two of Drovetti's agents who had always considered that Bankes' obelisk had belonged to them. The agents were becoming concerned at the continuing success of this comparative newcomer to Egypt; even Salt felt that the giant was taking too much for himself. Then Sarah fell ill with jaundice. Medicine was sent for from a doctor living a hundred miles or more up river, but the messenger returned 'after five days with about half an ounce of cream of tartar, and two teaspoonfuls of rhubarb. Fortunately [says Sarah] two English gentlemen happened to arrive and gave me some calomel, which was of great service to me, and which I remember with much gratitude.' The hardy couple, away from their own countries and the mental ease of living in their own society for more than seven years, began to look longingly towards Europe. Belzoni, too, was dispirited by the endless rivalries and quarrelling that had accompanied his work and taking advantage of the barge that held Bankes' obelisk, they quickly decided to embark and drift down to the port of Alexandria.

> Having put all things in readiness, and all the models of the tomb being embarked, I took out the celebrated sarcophagus [coffin] which gave me something to do (in consequence of it being so very slender and thin), lest it might break at the smallest touch of anything: however, it was safely got out of the tomb and put in a strong case. The valley it had to pass is rather uneven for more than two miles, and one mile of good soft sand and small pebbles. I had it conveyed on rollers all the way, and safely put on board . . . I had the pleasure to walk over the remains of old Thebes and I must confess that I felt no small degree of sorrow to quit a place which was become familiar to me, and where, in no other part of the world, I could find so many objects of inquiry so congenial to my inclination. I must say that I felt more in leaving Thebes than any other place in my life. It was on the 27th of January, 1819, when we left these truly magnificent ruins, and we arrived in Cairo on the 18th of February.

When they finally arrived at Alexandria Belzoni and Sarah found a letter from Salt and Bankes awaiting them. The attack on Belzoni at Thebes, a violent public dispute between the agents of the two most powerful Consul-Generals in Egypt, had provoked a minor political scandal and Salt asked the Belzonis not to leave Egypt until the matter had been settled. Salt also wanted to divide the huge collection of antiquities that Belzoni had brought with him to Alexandria. Belzoni, on his part, was waiting for Bankes to pay him for moving the obelisk. With time on his hands he went on another desert journey in search of an oasis of classical fame—Siwa, the city in search of which an entire Persian army had been engulfed and had perished in a great sandstorm and where, it was said, Alexander the Great lay buried. However, this second trip, during which Belzoni visited two of the western oases, did not make his fortune for him either. Reluctantly he returned to Alexandria for a final, miserable meeting with the disputing consuls and to collect his payment from William Bankes.

> At last, having put an end to all my affairs in Egypt, in the middle of September 1819 we embarked, thank God! for Europe: not that I disliked the country that I was in, for on the contrary, I have reason to be grateful: nor do I complain of the Turks or Arabs in general, but of some Europeans who are in that country, whose conduct and mode of thinking are a disgrace to human nature.

However, despite all these problems. Belzoni had accomplished great things while in Egypt. During his brief stay of four years he had found and opened more important monuments than all his contemporaries put together, and the account of his work which he later wrote is by far the best of its time. In the Valley of the Kings alone he rediscovered three royal tombs and at least three others, the first to be opened since ancient times and his work at other sites was equally productive.

In Europe Belzoni was already a celebrity, news of his exploits in Egypt having preceded him. He returned to Europe through Venice, where he was introduced to Lord Byron, and then he travelled on to his home town of Padua where he was publicly greeted at the town gates by the civic dignitaries. A relief portrait of him was sculpted and placed in the Palazzo Pubblico. In return for these honours he presented the town with two life-sized black granite statues from Thebes, a mere fraction of his extensive baggage which, at the time, must have weighed several tons. He reached London later in the same year and there he mounted an exhibition of his treasures in the Egyptian Galleries in Piccadilly, which was a sort of stucco égyptien extravaganza some fifteen years old, mounted over the façade of a Regency town house, and was one of the most popular exhibition halls in London. Belzoni devoted great time and trouble to this show which was principally composed of the huge collection of plaster casts that he had made in the tomb of Seti I, as well as a model of the tomb itself and some assorted mummies and other antiquities. He remodelled the galleries in the Egyptian style and in them he constructed from his casts a facsimile of the main room of the tomb, which was over two hundred feet long and more than eight feet high. Part of the show was lit by gaslight, still very much a showman's novelty in those days.

At the grand opening Belzoni unwrapped a mummy before a distinguished audience. Later he presented a folio of his drawings to one of the sons of the old King George III and finally, to crown his success, John Murray published a magnificent quarto volume, accompanied by a fine folio of engravings and maps: *Narrative of the operations and recent discoveries within the Pyramids, Temples, Tombs and excavations in Egypt and Nubia*. Within a year French and German translations were published in Paris and Jena. Like his exhibition, the book was a great success and went into several editions. Its lively style and candid observations still have their sparkle today, although in comparing it with some of Belzoni's personal correspondence, it is obvious that the Paduan who never mastered his adopted tongue, had some assistance, perhaps from Sarah, in its preparation. Be that as it may, Belzoni worked hard for his success, applying himself with the same furious energy with which he had conducted his work in Egypt.

Despite this popular success, Belzoni considered himself to have been badly treated both by Consul Salt and by the Trustees of the British Museum who now held the alabaster coffin from the tomb of Seti I. Belzoni, who had claimed a share in the coffin, dearly wanted it for his Piccadilly show, but little notice was taken of his requests. When Belzoni had first found the tomb of Seti I the Consul had published an article about the discovery in a popular London magazine; Salt considered both the discovery and the antiquities to be his, Belzoni being merely an employee. Belzoni, however, had simply shrugged these awkward facts aside when he returned to London where he was seen as a great traveller and discoverer on his own account, which he undoubtedly was. To his credit, Salt was never vindictive towards his head-strong employee, though he did call him the 'Prince of ungrateful adventurers', which must have seemed all

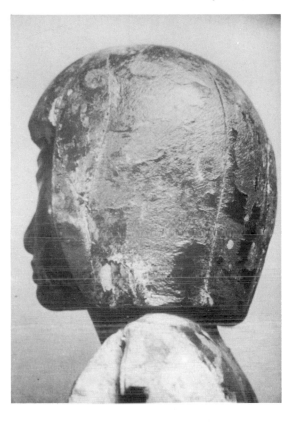

Salt sold many of the antiquities that Belzoni found in the royal tombs to the British Museum. This fine head from a broken statue of a young god or king was carved in cedar wood and coated with black resins. Unlike the similar figures found in Tutankhamen's tomb these statues were not, apparently, covered in gold leaf

too true. At his post in Egypt Salt must have looked anxiously towards London where his previous employee was sensationalizing a pursuit of gentlemen in a Piccadilly gallery. Belzoni, on the other hand, felt thwarted in his claims, both by Salt's London agent and the all-powerful Trustees of the British Museum who had taken the sarcophagus for exhibition along with the colossal head and the rest of Salt's collection.

Bitterly he turned his back on Egypt and its antiquities and planned another journey to a fabulous ancient city of treasure. Set on reaching the city of Timbuktu, the market town of salt and gold on the edge of the south Sahara, Belzoni and Sarah managed to join a caravan crossing the Sahara that was bound for that fabled place. At Fez, failing to gain the friendship of the wild Tuareg who terrorized the Sahara and at this time controlled Timbuktu, the caravan

The explorer Belzoni—a portrait published as a frontispiece to a catalogue of his Piccadilly exhibition

was forced to halt. Belzoni sent Sarah back to England and embarked on a British brig bound for West Africa, planning to reach his El Dorado by ascending the Niger river, a trip of over a thousand miles.

It was a wild plan. Only a few years earlier the experienced West African explorer Mungo Park had died wretchedly with his entire thirty-man expedition travelling the rivers of the same region. Disease and hostile villagers had accounted for hundreds of Europeans, but the naive and gentle Belzoni persevered and with his usual energy and ability to make friends he reached the savage city of Great Benin where, dressed in his Egyptian robes, he was honoured by the chiefs and provided with an escort for his journey. His drawings of the extraordinary shrines of that city show that his eye was still possessed of the charm that haunted his Egyptian plates, but already he was ill and within a day's journey of Great Benin he was brought down by dysentery. In a short while the giant died and was buried in a grave at the trading station of Gwato by the Benin River. He was forty-five years old.

After Belzoni had left Egypt, Salt returned to the Valley and for several months he excavated and drew. There, he was visited by the Comte August de Forbin, the Director-General of the Museums of France who was travelling in Egypt to acquire antiquities for the French collections. He described the Consul-General with his 'numerous suite, having taken up residence under tents . . . superintending researches relative to the chief and most valuable remains of Thebes': Yet despite this encouraging rhetoric, Salt found nothing. On a column in the tomb of Ramesses VI, where so many of the ancient visitors had also left their names, Salt pencilled his own, the only memorial of either the Consul-General or his mercurial agent that still remains in the Valley. A few years later, other workers in the Valley believed that it had been Salt's expedition that had dug down deep into the tomb of the son of Seti I, Ramesses II, which was half filled with the debris of successive ancient floods. If this is true, it is possible that Salt had recognized among the columns of hieroglyphs carved upon the wall of this ruined tomb the same group of signs that were also to be seen in the famous Temple of Memnon below the Valley in the plain of the Nile. If Salt had noticed this similarity of signs he may well have been digging in this tomb for the sarcophagus of this celebrated king which he would have expected to find lying under the deep layers of flood debris. Certainly he would not be the last person to search for this trophy. Such observations about the hieroglyphs upon the monument held great interest for the scholars and the travellers of the day despite the fact that still, some eighteen years after the discovery of the trilingual stone at Rosetta, no one could yet read the ancient signs. The investigation of the ancient writing by European scholars was, however, well under way. Salt himself took a keen interest in the progress of the decipherment and wrote a pamphlet on the subject.

While the Consul-General researched into the monuments of Egypt his London agent was negotiating with the Trustees of the British Museum over the purchase of his huge collection of antiquities. The Trustees had just been heavily criticized in the Houses of Parliament for the large sum they had paid Lord Elgin for the Athenian marbles, which William Hamilton had shipped to London some years earlier. They declined to buy the alabaster coffin of Seti I and gave Salt such a low price for his collection that he complained that the sum did not cover his expenses. Later he sold his other collections, with the aid of the Comte de Forbin, to the French museums and at public auction at Sotheby's.

When the alabaster coffin had first arrived in London on board a Turkish frigate, it had been immediately displayed to the public at the British Museum where it had been much admired, but following the Trustees' refusal it became difficult for Salt's agent to sell the large and awkwardly fragile *momento mori* for a suitable sum. Eventually it was sold for £2,000 to Sir John Soane, the eccentric architect who had designed the corinthian façade around the Bank of England and the strange architecture of the Art Gallery at Dulwich. Soane delightedly took the coffin to his London house where, after demolishing a section of the wall to obtain its entry, it was installed at the bottom of the main rectangular stairwell. It is still there today, probably the finest piece of Egyptian art in England; it is encased in an extraordinary glass box that vies uncomfortably with the jumble of innumerable fragments of classical and mediaeval mouldings and architectural details, all mixed up with other bric-à-brac and curios, and close by, a roomful of Hogarth's finest paintings.

Sir John Soane's purchase of the alabaster coffin had been more than the passing whim of a magpie collector. Many architects of that time were returning to the fundamental principles of architecture in an attempt to simplify the elaborate classicism of the time. Soane was particularly interested in stripping away all the decorative clutter from architecture and returning to pure 'primitive' style. The alabaster coffin with its elegant streamlined shapes without one cornice or moulding must have represented ancient Egypt to him as the age of pure form; he placed his coffin in the lowest part of his house, literally at the root of his collection.

Some fragments of the smashed lid of the coffin, found by Belzoni outside the tomb, were kept with the coffin, and they too may still be seen at Soane's house at 13 Lincolns Inn Fields, which, following his bequest to the nation, is now an extraordinary museum. Since Belzoni's day fresh fragments of the lid have occasionally been found, but these have since been scattered through the European collections and no attempt has ever been made to join them back together again.

Soane gave a three-day viewing party upon receiving the coffin, which was by far his greatest prize. The guest of honour on these occasions was the widowed Sarah Belzoni. Later she tried to re-exhibit Belzoni's Tomb of Seti I in another gallery, but without his energy and whimsical flair the venture failed and poor Sarah had to sell the huge collection of casts and drawings. However, she still enjoyed some powerful friends and received a regular income from the continued success of Belzoni's book. She eventually outlived all her contemporary egyptologists and died in 1870 aged eighty-seven. Poor Henry Salt had died in Egypt, in a small village close to Alexandria, just four years after Belzoni.

In nineteenth-century Egypt the Consul-Generals held wide powers that stemmed from the so-called Treaties of Capitulation with the Sublime Port of Istanbul. Under the terms of the Capitulation foreigners in Ottoman territory were not subject to the national laws, but were accountable solely to the Consul of their own countries. It is an example of the extent to which the Ottoman Sultans were prepared to concede their sovereignty in order to restrict the contact of their citizens with the Christians of the West. The Consul-Generals in Egypt were usually directly responsible for negotiations with Mohammed Ali's administration which in practice was performed in audience with the Pasha himself. Salt maintained British commercial interests in Egypt as well as giving endless help and hospitality to travellers and scholars. Along with Belzoni, Henry Salt became something of a butt for later egyptologists. He had shown, however, a quite genuine enthusiasm for this budding science, an enthusiasm that was unique among the cupidic contemporary excavators. He was on friendly terms with many of the scholars of the day and corresponded with several of them. While in Egypt Salt had inherited a fortune, which had allowed him to take a part in the traffic of antiquities as well as pursue his scholarly interests. However, the early egyptologists never really admitted this trader into their small circle and he cuts a comic figure in many of their memoirs. The Comte de Forbin, who greatly profited from Salt's connections and collections in Egypt described him as 'an enlightened character in matters of general observation, but not equally successful in the finer shades and more precise determinations of profound research'. More recent researchers in the Valley have been unable to see the wood for the trees: Salt, it seems, had the reverse problem.

It must be said that the Consul-General was never a scholar, despite his pretensions and his enthusiasms. One of Drovetti's friends, the employer of the man whose tales had led Belzoni on his fruitless three-month search in the Eastern Desert, played a scholar's trick on Salt when he sold him a tobacco pipe engraved with hieroglyphs. Belzoni had to suffer many embarrassing interviews with Turkish officials about the hieroglyphic pipe that had made his employer a laughing stock in Egypt. Perhaps even now the unfortunate object is stored with the contents of the royal tombs and the rest of Salt's first collection in the British Museum.

In September 1827, a month before he died, Salt offered some rooms in his house to Sir Moses and Lady Judith Montefiore who were travelling to Palestine for the first time. Lady Judith's journal gives a small glimpse into the home and habits of Henry Salt who, when he had been first appointed Consul-General of Egypt in 1816, had considered that 'to stagnate thus at a distance from all science, literature, arts, knowledge, delicacy and taste is a punishment almost to drive one mad'. Yet in a few years he had made his home in Egypt, cultivated an interest in its ancient civilization and financed the excavation of one of its finest monuments.

> We were shown into a large room: its furniture bespoke it Turkish; divans were placed all around, with a small rich carpet in the centre; little other furniture was observable, except books and maps, the numerous and choice assortment of which testified both the country and character of its owner, who soon made his appearance, and welcomed us most hospitably. As Mr. Salt was conducting us to the apartment we were to take possession of, we passed the dining room, which at one end had a handsome marble fountain: the water could be let in at pleasure: and it was in play, diffusing an agreeable freshness around, well adapted to the clime . . .
>
> The dinner hour in Cairo is at one, after which Mr. Salt took his siesta, with his legs folded under him, à la Turc. In the evening he amused us by explaining some of the hieroglyphics: and in pointing out the great progress that had been made by Dr. Young, M. Champallon [sic], and himself in elucidating and deciphering their signification. He then showed us some of his drawings, which displayed infinite talent.

Salt's misfortune was that he was but an ordinary man in a circle of brilliant scholars all caught up in the heat of the decipherment of the hieroglyphs that was then under way. Salt's simple enthusiasm for the new-born science and Belzoni's innocence of spirit are both affecting in their ways, and it is sad that for the most part such lively characters disappear as these personal enthusiasms are transformed into a scholarly discipline and egyptology becomes a career. Already during Salt's lifetime one may detect in the letters of some of the scholars the beginning of a new kind of dispute. Disputes not in the manner of the consular agents, about the ownership of antiquities, but about the ownership of intellectual discoveries. The results of research would become the commerce of scholarly careers and hence more valuable than the ancient stones themselves.

Salt published very little; indeed, a two-volume biography of him contains far more words than he ever committed to paper, but in an Alexandrian publication of 1824 he commemorated Egypt and her monuments in a long lumbering poem that perhaps sums up the admiration that these early excavators felt for the monuments. *Egypt, a descriptive Poem, with notes* is the only poem which, at least in part, celebrates the Valley of the Kings in verse, and its air of awkward innocence and old fashioned fustiness is a suitable epitaph for one of the most extraordinary periods of the history of the Valley which came to its end with the beginning of the decipherment of hieroglyphics and Belzoni's colossal show in the Egyptian Galleries in Piccadilly.

> Hail to thee, lonely valley of the dead!
> Compass'd with rugged mountains, where the tread
> Of man is rarely heard, save his who roams
> From foreign lands to visit thy lone tombs —
> Tombs of long perish'd kings, who thus remote
> Their sepulchres have set in barren spot,
> Where not a blade of verdure ever grew:
> To me thou hast a charm for aye that's ever new
> For I have cast, for days, weeks, months, my lot
> Among thy rocks secluded — oft at night
> Hath the still valley met my awe struck sight,
> Lighted by silver moon that seemed to cast
> A lingering look upon the 'antres vast',
> While many a blast blew, not unmixed with dread
> That bore, methought, a chiding from the dead.

Part III

SCHOLARS AND HIDDEN TREASURES

9

Champollion and Hieroglyphs

Just ten years after Belzoni's camel ride from Thebes to the shores of the Red Sea in search of the Emerald Mountains, an East Indiaman out of Bombay, the brig *Thetis*, put in at a small sea port on that same coastline and discharged her dirty cargo of Welsh steam coal on the beach. The coal was to fuel the steamers that would ply between Port Suez and India, one half of the express journey from England to the East. Forty years later the great canal was cut through the isthmus of Suez and the big ships would steam directly from Britain to the Eastern Empire. Egypt was Europe's highway to India and the Far East.

On his arrival in Egypt, Salt had found just a handful of British merchants, some left behind, with their French competitors from the days when they had served as victuallers to their countries' soldiers in Egypt. However, with the transformation of the Egyptian economy by Mohammed Ali, European businessmen began to frequent Cairo and Alexandria in ever increasing numbers. During Salt's consulship the first bales of raw Egyptian cotton were shipped from Alexandria to Europe and, aided by the continually rising prices of the world market, it quickly became Egypt's principal cash crop and a staple of its developing economy. After Salt's death the post of Consul-General in Egypt became a tough career-diplomat's appointment, deeply involved in international finance and the politics of the Ottoman Empire of which Egypt was still a part. With this rapid expansion of foreign trade and the great influx of foreign managers, mercenaries and businessmen, Egypt quickly changed. Egyptology, too, was undergoing a revolution.

Belzoni had never known the name of the king whose huge tomb and alabaster coffin he had discovered and for several years after its opening it was simply called 'Belzoni's tomb'. When he had first arrived in London from Egypt, his collection of drawings of the tomb and its inscriptions were shown to Thomas Young, a renowned physicist and doctor on the staff of St George's Hospital, London, who in correspondence with several other European scholars, had been studying the hieroglyphs since the turn of the century. Since that time these decipherers had made considerable progress and had particularly concentrated their attentions on the texts engraved upon the trilingual stone from Rosetta, which the British Expeditionary Force had taken from Napoleon's army. The elongated rings that enclosed whole groups of hieroglyphs were of especial interest to these scholars, for it had long been assumed, and quite correctly, that these contained the names of the ancient kings. The Napoleonic scholars called these rings *cartouches*, because they were similar in shape to the charges of the same name with which their artillerymen loaded their cannons, and this is the name that they have borne ever since.

From his study of the inscriptions upon the Rosetta stone, Young was able to identify tentatively the hieroglyphs of the name of just one king, Ptolemy, for only one royal name, enclosed in a cartouche, had survived in both the Greek and Egyptian versions of the damaged texts. This enabled Young to compare the Greek name with the hieroglyphic version and to suggest phonetic values for those hieroglyphs. Only one of these signs that Young had tentatively translated on the Rosetta Stone appeared in the copies of the cartouches that Belzoni had brought from the great tomb in the Valley of the Kings; and this, a simple rectangle, was the sign of the letter 'p'. With this single exception all the other signs inside the cartouches from the tomb were completely indecipherable and Young vainly toyed with the many Greek names of the ancient kings listed by the classical writers, hoping to find some small connection.

Eventually, in agreement with Belzoni's own views upon the subject, Young decided that a part of the tomb's decorations depicted a group of four 'Ethiopian captives' and he knew that in Herodotus' description of Egypt there was a reference to a king who had captured that nation and whose name, Psammis, started with the letter 'p', the hieroglyphic rectangle. Thus the tomb in the Valley was proclaimed as 'The Tomb of Psammis', Young confirming this opinion in a special appendix that he wrote

Plate 8.

FROM THE TOMBS OF THE KINGS AT THEBES, DISCOVERED BY G. BELZONI

*One of Belzoni's drawings of the 'foreigners' from the
walls of the tomb of Seti I*

*Account of taking the obelisk from the Island of
Philae to Alexandria. Arrive at Thebes—set off for
the first cataract—Arrive at Aswan—Proceedings of
the agents of Mr. Drovetti at Philae [Belzoni's
competitors]—Commencement of operations for
removing the obelisk—difficulties encountered—It
falls into the Nile—Preparations for taking it out—
descriptions of the operation—Again Embarked—
Preparation for launching it down the cataract—
observations on the various colours of the cut
granite—Launch the obelisk—arrive at Aswan and
voyage to Thebes.*

for the second edition of Belzoni's *Narrative* published
by Murray in 1821. In fact, the tomb was very much
older than Young thought—his guess was some eight
hundred years, or seven dynasties, in error. However,
such procedures, connecting a king named by the
classical authors with the small clue of the single
hieroglyph with a known phonetic value, was one
of the very few rational methods of procedure available to the early decipherers.

Probably the first people since ancient times to read
hieroglyphs on the standing monuments of Egypt
were Henry Salt and his friend William Bankes—
several years before the full decipherment. While
Bankes was at Philae with Belzoni in 1817, collecting
the obelisk for his Dorsetshire house, he was able to
identify the cartouche of a King Ptolemy using a
paper written by Young some three years earlier
which he had carried with him to Egypt. To move
this six ton, twenty-six-foot granite obelisk from the
temple where Bankes had found it had taken all
Belzoni's skill. The extraordinary undertaking,
accomplished with manpower, ropes and palm logs,
is most graphically described by the chapter headings
in Belzoni's *Narrative*:

From Alexandria where the Nile barge had taken
it, Bankes had the huge obelisk shipped to England,
where it was dragged from Southampton on a special
wagon pulled by large teams of dray horses down
the narrow Dorset lanes to his country house at
Wimborne Minster and there, in the presence of the
Iron Duke himself, it was re-erected.

The subsequent publication by Bankes of the hieroglyphic texts upon his obelisk and the Greek text cut
upon its stone base considerably enlarged the meagre
list of identified hieroglyphs. A Queen Cleopatra was
named in the Greek text and it was correctly assumed
that the long cartouche upon the shaft of the obelisk
contained the numerous hieroglyphs which, phone-
tically, spelt her name. Several of these hieroglyphs

91

FRANÇOIS CHAMPOLLION.

Champollion

phered the hieroglyphs, after years of devoted work. And it is altogether appropriate that the achievement was his, for he had dedicated himself completely to the study of ancient Egypt and later he held the first university chair in the subject that he himself had created. Jean François Champollion was the founder of the science of Egyptian linguistics and the first professional egyptologist, a man for whom the subject was a life's work and not a gentlemanly diversion.

In 1822 Champollion was sent a copy of the inscriptions upon Bankes' obelisk and its base and pencilled in the margin of the hieroglyphic text next to the long and, as yet, unidentified cartouche was the word 'Cleopatra?', another of Young's suggestions which this time proved to be correct. Possibly such nudges to his mind helped Champollion to extract the essential sense of the hieroglyphs from the rag-bag of alchemical lore, small and often damaged texts, and the poorly drawn copies of inscriptions which, in common with the rest of the small group of scholars, he was using to work towards a proper understanding of the ancient language. But it was Champollion alone who understood the nature of the task of decipherment sufficiently to start a proper study of the ancient Egyptian literature, and it was a study in which he left his contemporaries far behind.

The first decipherment was, however, inevitably a quick affair, a flash of realization quickly verified. Champollion had been applying the theoretical values of some of the hieroglyphs which he had tentatively translated on the Rosetta Stone and Bankes' obelisk in an attempt to translate the names of kings in other unknown cartouches and to establish the correctness of these trial interpretations he was comparing the results with the names of kings given in the works of the classical writers. The connections between the kings' names in the Greek texts and the vocalization of the hieroglyphs that he eventually established were far from obvious and may well have escaped the notice of other scholars engaged in the work, but Champollion had a wide experience of many ancient languages and was used to such processes. When he was sixteen he had delivered a paper before the Academy of Grenoble upon the similarities shared by the written Christian Coptic language of Egypt and the ancient language written in the hieroglyphs and this knowledge of Coptic also stood him in good stead at twice that age when, in September 1822, he received a copy of some texts that had been recently discovered in Egypt.

Champollion had long believed, without real proof,

were identical to those in the name Ptolemy, which appeared on the obelisk as well as on the Rosetta Stone. By a process of comparison, the phonetic values of the twelve enclosed hieroglyphs could be tentatively identified. Further comparison of other cartouches and the names given by the classical writers allowed more hieroglyphs to be identified. Thus Bankes' obelisk played a major role in the decipherment, but one often unacknowledged by early accounts of this work—perhaps because some years later he had to flee England following a scandal from which even the influence of his friend the Duke of Wellington could not extricate him. Bankes was discovered, just a stone's throw from the Houses of Parliament, where he had been a senior member for some twenty-five years, publicly engaged in an illegal sexual act with a soldier from a nearby barracks. Exiled from his large collection of antiquities and works of art that he had assembled with such enthusiasm during his earlier travels, Bankes lived for the rest of his life in Venice, where he died in 1855. Eventually it was a young Frenchman who deci-

that the hieroglyph for the words 'give birth' or 'to bear' was rendered by the untranslated sign, 𝔥, which represented three foxes' skins tied together. This sign was also present in several cartouches in the copies of the new-found texts that he had just received. In one cartouche the circular sun sign, ○, in Coptic, *Ra*, was followed by this sign for 'to bear', in Coptic, *Mise*. He put the two words together—*Ra Mise*—and made the name of the King called Ramesses by the Greek writers. Another cartouche in these new copies showed a hieroglyphic ibis, long known as the bird of the god Thoth, and before the same sign this conjunction gave him *Thoth Mise*: the Tuthmosis of the Greek writers. Champollion was reading the ancient language for the first time in nearly two thousand years, and not by guessing from the signs of a bilingual text but with knowledge applied to the hieroglyphs gained from other sources! And his translations were corroborated by the Greek writers. The copies of the texts that he had used for this experiment came, incidentally, from the Great Temple at Abu Simbel which Belzoni had opened just four years earlier.

This small but momentous event led Champollion quickly on to the decipherment of the entire hieroglyphic alphabet. He recognized that the ancient language was written with a mixture of phonetic signs and others, called determinatives, which identified with a hieroglyphic picture the word spelt out by the alphabetic signs. It would be another sixty years before advances in the study of the ancient grammar enabled scholars to understand something of the nature and significances of the long religious texts in the royal tombs but Champollion had provided the first link in this chain of understanding and, after a silence of fifteen hundred years, had rendered the ancient language accessible.

It would now be possible to place the ancient monuments in their correct order, and to establish their relative histories. In the year that followed his decipherment of the alphabet, Champollion published a short pamphlet in which he outlined his discovery and the further progress that he had made, and subsequently his interpretation of the hieroglyphs became the centre of a number of ferocious debates. At first the interpretation met with great opposition, not least from many of the members of the Napoleonic Commission who were still in the process of publishing the last volumes of the *Description*, and from such prominent men as the Comte de Forbin, then Director General of the Museums of France. After this row had died down, another concerning the relative achievements of Young, Champollion and the other scholars who had participated in the decipherment, came to the fore, and this largely Franco-British rivalry was still alive at the turn of the century. One by one, almost every member of the group of decipherers was pushed forward as the true decipherer of hieroglyphics: he who had first understood the phonetic nature of the signs; he who had first recognized the cartouche as containing the royal name; he who had first used Coptic equivalents when working upon the hieroglyphs; and so on. But it was Champollion who had taken these disparate discoveries from a whole jumble of hypotheses and organized them into the correct cohesive order. Where others had been making stabs in the darkness, Champollion was confident enough of his system to state with full force the truth of his decipherment. He had taken segments from the studies of other linguists and bound them together with his own knowledge to create the new subject of egyptology. The written history and literature of ancient Egypt was to occupy the rest of his brief life; he deciphered the hieroglyphs at the age of thirty-two; ten years later he was dead.

One of the more immediate results of Champollion's discovery was to open up the written records of more than two thousand years of Egyptian history. Periods that had previously been considered as barbarous and remote could now become the subjects of historical research. Obviously the establishment of the royal chronologies was a top priority. Young's guessing games with the cartouches of Belzoni's tomb had involved the names of Egyptian kings, Psammis, Ramesses, Sesostris and the like, which had survived in Greek literature. But the histories of these kings were not known at all and neither was it known whether they had been earthly rulers or kings in a mythical land of gods and giants. Certainly nothing was known about their dates in history and their relationship to each other was still obscure.

Of especial interest to the early egyptologists, therefore, were the surviving ancient chronologies: row on row of cartouches, which some of the early travellers had occasionally found cut into the walls of the temples. William Bankes had copied the first of these king lists to be discovered in a temple of Ramesses II at Abydos and shortly after two more were found, one more at Abydos and another in the Great Temple of Amun at Thebes. By far the most important, and also the most tantalizing, of these lists was found in a box in a museum in Turin; a heap of papyrus fragments, the broken remnants of a roll that had been found at Thebes by Drovetti and damaged by the carelessness of his agents. Champollion had discovered these precious flakes of papyrus while studying the collections and quickly recognized their significance. The list was far more comprehensive than any of the others in existence and had contained nearly one hundred royal names, all in order. On the fragments that could still be read and rejoined the decipherers found a general agreement between the papyrus and the stone lists cut into the temple walls. But all these lists were official compilations from the ancient state archives and would not include the names of monarchs who were officially obliterated from the records for politico-religious reasons. However, many of the cartouches of these officially expunged rulers were still to be found upon the standing monuments of Egypt.

In the Valley of the Kings alone there were more than twenty different cartouches to be seen in the tombs, some of which had been half obliterated and overcut by their successors or otherwise disfigured. For students of Egyptian history during the 1820s, the ancient monuments were a huge puzzle of building blocks and inscribed walls which, with hard work and long study, could all be fitted into the correct sequence. Not only the political history of the rulers of ancient Egypt waited to be rediscovered, but the history of the monuments themselves. Such an understanding of the dates of the monuments would provide a real key for the appreciation of the antiquities of Egypt which, scholars and travellers, in ever increasing numbers, were braving the dangers of a difficult journey to experience at first hand.

At this time the usual route taken by the English travellers journeying to Egypt was through Italy, embarking at either Venice or Naples for the voyage to Alexandria from where a Nile boat could be hired to sail upstream to Cairo, Thebes and Nubia. While at Naples, visiting perhaps Roman Pompeii or the great collections of antiquities that were in the area, any serious scholar of antiquity would wish to meet Sir William Gell, a retired English diplomat and celebrated classicist who, during the course of his missions in the eastern Mediterranean, had travelled widely and written copiously upon the antiquities of Greece and Turkey. Gell had been a friend of Dr Young since before the turn of the century when they had lived near one another in London. Champollion, too, became a good friend of the amateur antiquarian, when he was visiting Italy in 1824 to study the Egyptian collections. Gell's house at Naples and his hospitality to travelling scholars were famous; he was awarded the title of 'resident plenipotentiary' in Italy of the famous Society of Dilettanti. During the 1820s Sir William was particularly interested in the process of decipherment of hieroglyphs and its application to the monuments of Egypt and several scholars actively concerned with this work were in correspondence with him. Naples was a port between East and West and Gell had his foot in both camps. Henry Salt wrote from Egypt of his work, as did many of the European scholars, some of whom were *Champollionistes*; others were suspicious and antagonistic to the Frenchman's achievements. Gell passed information and opinion from one correspondent to another, copying hieroglyphic texts from one letter to the next, redirecting enquiries among his correspondents, and all with such diplomacy and tact that the group which he had formed around him remained his friends, even though individually they were often bitter critics of each other's work.

In 1820 Gell encouraged a twenty-three-year-old would-be army officer, John Gardiner Wilkinson, to travel to Egypt from Naples to further an interest in hieroglyphics that the young man had maintained since his schooldays. For his first visit to Egypt the young man stayed for twelve years, and he subsequently returned to the country for three further long trips: Gell had certainly pushed Wilkinson to follow his own inclinations. During his first visit, Wilkinson wrote and had published several books on hieroglyphics and ancient history while he was still working in the field. On his return to England he completed his magnificent work *The Manners and Customs of the Ancient Egyptians*: a five-volume masterpiece of cultural and historical anthropology that has never really been surpassed. He became the first egyptologist to be knighted, shortly after this work was published in 1837.

For the most part Wilkinson worked alone. He was a clergyman's son, educated at Harrow and Oxford with a private income from his mother's family that allowed him to live well while he was in Egypt, but only to excavate there on a small scale. This may account, to some extent, for his great interest in the tombs of Thebes, for even in the 1820s a large number of the small private chapels were either generally accessible or half buried in rubble and stone chippings, and in the Valley of the Kings many fine monuments were wide open. Wilkinson was the first scholar to study these tombs in any detail and describe his work in publications. He learnt his egyptology, studied the hieroglyphs and the subjects of the ancient paintings and sculptures, at the walls of the monuments themselves, and fre-

Wilkinson as a young man, 'à la turc'

quently, by intimate first hand knowledge, he was able to correct the errors of scholars working in Europe. He was a happy, patient man who worked hard at his personal enthusiasms. In middle age, when he was back in England, he gained a reputation for his fine clothes and kid gloves. After years of living rough in the desert or in the tombs themselves, it is easy to see why such delights of his own culture would appeal to him. Joseph Bonomi, an old friend of Wilkinson's from his Egyptian days described the now famous scholar at a visit to a country house in England: 'We have got Wilkinson down here with an immense variety of waistcoats, some of them very distinguished ones too'. When in London, Wilkinson frequently visited the house of Samuel Rogers, one of the centres of London literary society; several of the later scholars and travellers in the Valley of the Kings started their journeys in conversation with him in this London drawing room. When he died he left a splendid collection of small antiquities to his old school, for the encouragement of the study of

ancient Egypt; a study that, as a boy, he had enjoyed with his headmaster who was a friend of Dr Young.

In a letter from Henry Salt to Sir William Gell, written from Alexandria in 1822, the twenty-five-year-old Wilkinson, using Young's early publications as his guide, is described by the Consul-General as 'working like a horse . . . I have not indeed seen any person here who has entered with so much spirit into the study of hieroglyphicks' and the interest he takes in 'our Egyptian antiquities far exceeds that of ordinary travellers'. How right Salt turned out to be. In the first few years of his stay Wilkinson went on a survey of all Egypt: the Nile Valley, the Delta, the deserts and the oases. Even with the meagre information that he could glean from Young's pamphlet, Wilkinson must have realized exactly what the decipherment would mean for the study of the ancient monuments and the civilization that made them.

Wilkinson had begun his researches in Egypt at the same time as the decipherment was rapidly advancing in Europe and the new direction and impetus that he would provide for the study of the standing monuments in Egypt was an exact parallel to the studies of Champollion in Europe. He was a practical man, as his deep interest and understanding of the material culture of ancient everyday life shows, and he could readily see that, armed with the names of the kings, the order of and histories of the monuments that bore their cartouches could be established. When, in a series of papers, the full decipherment of the hieroglyphic alphabet was published by Champollion it must have represented a revelation to the young Englishman as they arrived at his camps in Egypt. By 1824 Wilkinson was living at Thebes, daily copying the inscriptions and drawing the scenes upon the walls of the ancient tombs and temples. He concentrated much of his attention on the royal cartouches, examining their relative order on the monuments by studying the successive building periods or reconstructing damaged or defaced texts, and was constructing king lists of his own from evidence completely independent of the sources used by Champollion.

In a dazzling series of letters to Gell, written between 1826 and 1828, Wilkinson placed the kings of the New Kingdom dynasties at Thebes in their correct order for the first time. In an impatient and businesslike hand he rapidly wrote an exciting text illustrated with firm clear hieroglyphics, making the whole thing as vivid as scholarship can ever be. Frequently his first-hand experience of the monuments caused him to disagree with the published chronologies of Champollion, which were also appearing at this time, but he always acknowledged the extent of his debt to the studies of Champollion. However, it was Wilkinson who took the Frenchman's key and turned it cleanly in the Egyptian lock.

While Wilkinson worked at Thebes, Champollion continued his studies in France and Italy among the huge collections purchased from the consuls and the antiquities agents. He quickly made progress in the decipherment of entire texts and in this respect his intuition and scholarship placed him far above any of his contemporaries. But, inevitably, he was hampered in his appreciation of ancient Egypt and especially in his historic studies by the limited range of monuments that were available to him in Europe and the, usually, inaccurate copies of texts that were still in tombs and temples he had never seen. To Champollion it was obvious that after his years of study in Europe he had to travel to Egypt and see the objects of his life's work at first hand. There, this great scholar and linguist would meet the pragmatic Englishman whose extraordinary energies and abilities were transforming the study of ancient Egypt and its archeology. As was to be expected they did not make good friends or working companions. The Frenchman had fought hard for his system of decipherment in France and had spent years studying in the museums and libraries of Europe. He expressed his views with oratical force and some impatience; also he had access to areas of special knowledge from literary sources such as papyri that were quite new to Wilkinson. On his part the Englishman, although deeply impressed by Champollion's scholarship, was

disturbed by the insistence of his views and by his numerous errors of simple fact, which Wilkinson knew from his own experience to be wrong. In a long letter to Gell, Wilkinson, the old Egypt hand, describes Champollion wildly theorizing, in literary fashion about some rough drawings commonly found upon the monuments that, although they were well known and understood by the early field workers, were quite new to the French scholar.

In wry celebration of Champollion's erudition some small verses were written in Egypt, probably by Wilkinson, and sent to Gell in Naples. They expressed the temperamental differences between the two men, the writer and the one described. Champollion, absorbed in study, passionate, talking absent-mindedly almost in a series of footnotes; Wilkinson, while no less hardworking, affecting an ease of scholarship, not as work but as an enjoyment for himself and others. Gell would often travel from Naples to visit a friend in Rome who was also at that time an enthusiastic observer of egyptology, the German Consul, Josias Bunsen. There, we may imagine, in the course of a warm summer evening, Gell played the small organ in Bunsen's music room while his friends gathered around him to sing these verses, which he had wittily set to music. This verse is spoken by Champollion, the speech marks indicating a phrase of which he was particularly fond:

The pyramids 'without a doubt'
Whatever effort they cost
Are seven thousand years of age, or something more
The proof is in a papyrus.

A painting from the tomb of Montu-hir-kopesh-ef: the prince offering to the gods

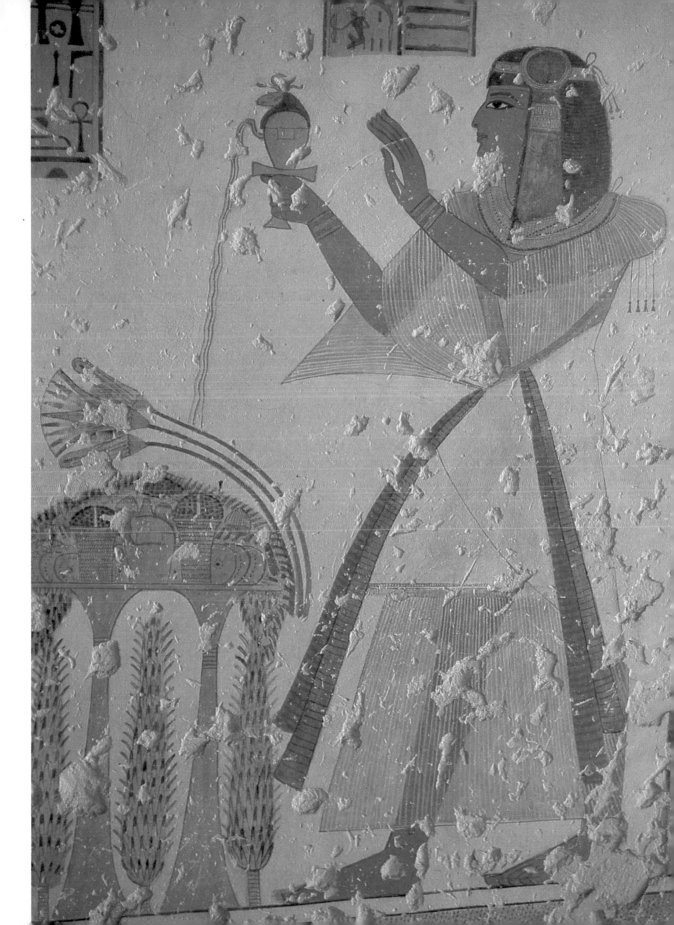

72

BELZONI'S.

10

John Gardner Wilkinson

Wilkinson visited the Valley of the Kings many times during his first years in Egypt and in 1826 he settled at Thebes for some considerable time and began a detailed study of the royal tombs. On the hill of Gurna, among the private tombs, he built a large walled house made of the local mud brick, with two turreted towers that overlooked the Nile and its green valley. From here he could walk to the Valley of the Kings in half an hour along the steep white path that follows the diagonal rock fault that runs up the cliffs at Deir el Bahari and over the ridge that separates the royal Valley from the Nile. It is still a walk that is one of the most vivid experiences of ancient Egypt.

Undoubtedly Wilkinson's greatest contribution to the Valley was his numbering of the tombs and the ordering of the kings that had been buried in them. For the first time he also established correct modern dates for the royal tombs. In his description of Belzoni's tomb, one of the oldest then known in the Valley, he estimated that it had been built from about 1385 BC; a modern dating for the beginning of work upon the tomb would be *circa* 1315 BC. After this information he adds that the tomb 'was excavated for the father of Remeses [Ramesses] II', whom he called King Osirei which, if it does not correspond to the modern Seti was at least gleaned from a phonetic reading of the hieroglyphs in the king's cartouche. Many of the royal names have been changed since Wilkinson's day by more than a century and a half of research and in some cases the numbers assigned to some of them have also been altered as the order in the line of kings has shifted. The modern divisions of the dynasties also varies slightly from that used by Wilkinson, but none the less it is clear that essentially he had ordered and established the entire sequence of the open royal tombs; a remarkable achievement considering that Champollion's publication of the decipherment was less than ten years old.

For the chronology to be established, the first essential was for a catalogue of all the large open tombs in the Valley. This Wilkinson accomplished in the most simple and direct manner. In 1827 he walked around the Valley carrying a brush and a pot of brown oil paint with which he wrote, upon the entrances of the tombs or on a nearby rock, in large clear letters and numerals, the number that he had assigned to each tomb. He started his numbering at the lowest tomb in the Valley and as he walked further up the central path he crossed right and left to draw his numbers by the open tombs, until he reached the highest point in the Valley at which there were known to be tombs. At this point in his system the numbering had reached fifteen. Then he returned to the central area of the Valley and proceeded down the gully where, a few years before, Belzoni had uncovered the tomb of Seti I. Passing by this door to which he gave the number 17, Wilkinson continued up the slope of the side of the Valley to the tomb of Prince Ramesses Montu-hir-kopesh-ef, numbering it 19, then back again down to the lower slopes of the Valley, marking further tombs on the way.

Wilkinson numbered the four tombs of the West Valley uncovered by Belzoni in a separate system, because he thought there would be later additions to the list. He also numbered many of the prominent

Wilkinson's number painted on the door jamb of the tomb of Ramesses VII surrounded by other graffiti

A water colour drawing by a member of Robert Hay's expedition of the burial chamber of the tomb of Seti I

nobles' tombs and both this system and the one in the Valley of the Kings have survived to this day. The number of tombs in the Valley has now reached sixty-two. The list of numbered private tombs has been enlarged by an even greater amount: today there are more than four hundred, and many more await inclusion.

WILKINSON'S TOMB LIST IN THE
VALLEY OF THE KINGS

Number	King	Dynasty
I	Ramesses VII	20
2	Ramesses IV	20
3	a prince of Ramesses III	20
4	Ramesses XI	20
5	time of Ramesses II (this tomb has been lost since the beginning of this century)	19
6	Ramesses IX	20
7	Ramesses II	19
8	Merneptah	19
9	Ramesses VI (anciently called the tomb of Memnon)	20
10	Amenmesse	19
11	Ramesses III (Bruce's tomb)	20
12	anonymous	19
13	Chancellor Bay (unidentified by Wilkinson the name was later read in faint hieroglyphics on the tomb door)	19
14	Tausert & Setnakht	19
15	Seti II	19
16	Ramesses I	19
17	Seti I (Belzoni's tomb)	19
18	Ramesses X	20
19	Prince of Ramesses Montu-hir-kopesh-ef	20
20	Hatshepsut (unidentified by Wilkinson)	18
21	anonymous (contained two female mummies, found by Belzoni)	18

In his house on Gurna, Wilkinson must have written out a list of tombs similar to the one above and compared its columns with his chronology of kings to find out what had been caught by his system:

The tombs of the Kings of Thebes are principally of Pharaohs of the 18th and 19th Dynasties; [now 19th and 20th] the oldest in the eastern valley, where they are nearly all situated, being that of Remeses I, [Ramesses] the grandfather of the conqueror of the same name. That of the third Amunoph [Amenhotep] is in the western valley, with two others of an old and uncertain era.

Like all the historians of his day, Wilkinson found the Amarnan period with its complicated erasure of texts and changed inscriptions on the monuments somewhat puzzling, and King Ay, 'of an old and uncertain era' was eventually one of the last to be fitted into the historical sequence of New Kingdom Kings. The tomb of Amenhotep III 'of the vocal statue' stood out for Wilkinson as being the oldest royal tomb known. He thought that it was 'certainly singular that none have yet been met with of the first kings of the eighteenth dynasty' and suggested that 'it is perhaps in this [the West] Valley that others of the oldest royal catacombs may someday be discovered'. In the next few years several archeologists would test this theory for themselves.

There seemed little point in digging further in the East Valley, for none of the Eighteenth Dynasty kings were known to have tombs there and the list of the later kings was almost complete. Belzoni himself had said:

It is my firm opinion, that in the Valley of the Kings, there are no more [tombs] than are now known, in consequence of my late discoveries; for previously to my quitting that place, I exerted all my humble abilities in endeavouring to find another tomb, but could not succeed; and what is still greater proof, independent of my own researches, after I quitted the place, Mr. Salt, the British Consul, resided there four months and laboured in like manner to find another.

The siting of the tombs that Belzoni had known in the Valley fitted neatly into two groups which divided conveniently upon the turn of the Nineteenth and Twentieth Dynasties. The Nineteenth Dynasty group were situated in the lower parts of the Valley floor and, in consequence, were extremely susceptible to flooding. Wilkinson himself had seen water pouring into the tomb of Merneptah from a small fissure in the cliff face directly above the door. Indeed, this was a common enough occurrence, for many of the royal tombs had been cut into cracks in the limestone rock that served as convenient quarrying points. But in times of flood many of these same cracks acted as drains and consequently became enlarged into small ravines by the abrasive action of rock and other debris as it was swept down into the lower sections of the Valley. Thus many of these tombs were situated under waterfalls and several of the Nineteenth Dynasty were flooded and choked with hard-packed debris.

The ancient Egyptians had understood the problem

of these flash floods in the Valley and had made allowances for them, sometimes building dams above vulnerable tombs to deflect the water away from its natural drainage path. In addition the tomb doors were blocked with dry stone walls and sealed with a hard grey plaster that was quite impervious and very strong. The flood waters passed easily over the sealed entrances, depositing debris that soon obscured them and blended with the natural desert landscape. Only a few of the priests and necropolis officials knew where some of these hidden tombs were located, and they could only be inspected for security purposes with considerable difficulty. During the Nineteenth Dynasty, however, the tombs' entrances began to be designed as imposing architectural features in their own right. From the steep steps that lead into the small corridors of the tomb of Seti I, the design was transformed into a broad shallowly sloped entrance that gave access to the now enlarged interior corridors. The entrances themselves, which in Seti's tomb had been left undecorated, were embellished with the elegant reliefs that Denon had so vividly described in his account of his trip to the Valley: two goddesses and the king worshipping a central sun disc were placed over the splendid doorways, the 'corridors of the sun's path'. At this time the secure but rather unprepossessing plaster sealings were abandoned in favour of two tall thin cedar doors which were sealed across their bolts with rope and clay seals that bore the impressions of the necropolis authority. The effect upon the tombs was disastrous, for though it was now possible to openly inspect the doorways of the tombs and thus ensure that they had not been illegally entered, they were easily flooded and tomb after tomb was wrecked by water and debris. It is even possible that one tomb, that of Ramesses II, which had been partially excavated by Salt, had been flooded even before the royal burial had taken place. The ancient answer to this new problem was to change the locations of the tomb mouths, which is what the architects did. Moving out from the central part of the Valley, which in any case was becoming somewhat filled with tombs, they situated the huge tombs of the Twentieth Dynasty at the end of the rock spurs left between the gullies down which the water passed. None of these huge open tombs was seriously flooded, and the problem was solved, but towards the end of the dynasty the quarrymen ran out of suitable spurs in which to excavate the tombs, and once again flood-prone locations were chosen.

The question of 'filling up' the Valley with tombs is rather more real than a map of the site would indicate. The ancient Egyptians had no surveying equipment and therefore had no accurate way of telling whether or not their excavations would hit previously dug tombs whose entrances had been lost under the loose debris. In fact this happened on at least three occasions, and on one of these, work on a partly decorated tomb was abandoned. Usually, the direction in which the tomb was quarried fanned out away from its neighbour, but with unlocated tombs lying in many places under the ground in the Valley, there was always an element of hit-or-miss.

Belzoni's opinion that the Valley held no more tombs was, provided we bear in mind where he considered the royal tombs to be located in the Valley landscape, correct. Virtually no more would be discovered in the type of location where Belzoni had dug and if the ancient Egyptians had shared his views, the story of the excavation of the Valley would finish here. But happily they did not, and when a discovery in another part of Thebes pointed to the likelihood of more royal tombs lying buried in the Valley the royal necropolis was re-excavated bringing fresh surprises, and treasures that had never before been imagined were taken from newly discovered tombs.

These as yet undiscovered tombs were still lying secure in the ground under Wilkinson's feet as he worked in the Valley during the 1820s and '30s. He spent much of his time copying inscriptions and wall scenes that interested him and these records, along with material collected by him from the rest of Egypt, are preserved in fifty-six large volumes. These careful copies are all too frequently the only surviving record of ancient documents long since damaged or destroyed.

When he was not studying or drawing in the tombs, Wilkinson wrote a series of books and articles while still in the field, scratching away with a blunt quill upon the rough, locally made paper, seated cross-legged on the ground, like Salt, à la turc. Recurring bouts of opthalmia, a very common problem in Egypt, occasionally forced him away from the Nile Valley to the higher sterile environment of the desert. In 1828 he wrote a letter to Gell from a lonely desert valley and in it he bemoans the fact that his friend and one-time mentor has not come to see him, as he was expecting him to. In a few pages he ranges from gossip, 'Champollion has arrived', to some remarks about the goddesses of local towns and temples, the identification of some Ptolomaic cartouches, an error of Champollion's, a daydream about the beautiful goddess Isis falling in love with the ugly Bes, further ruminations about Champollion and Salt, now dead, the ancient Egyptian calendar and methods of designating hours of the night, the fact that he had found a brick arch far older than the classical examples and, 'what will the dons say?' As an example of the difficulties of working in remote Upper Egypt at that time he complains to Gell that Young had not returned some of his papers to him, and that if he does not do so he will have to return to Nubia to make fresh copies—and this a dangerous river journey of over five hundred miles!

By 1830 Wilkinson had completed his brilliant *Topography of Thebes and General View of Egypt*, which included his classification and numbering of the Valley's tombs. The book was the first account of the Egyptian monuments with their histories accounted for, a guidebook to the remains of ancient Egypt. He planned to publish it in Egypt, but his Alexandrian printer contracted cholera and died and Wilkinson finally sent the manuscript to John Murray in London, who published it in 1835, after Wilkinson had returned from Egypt. In 1837 his other major work, *Manners and Customs of the Ancient Egyptians*, completed his overall plan; the *Topography* described the land and its monuments, and *Manners and Customs* the ancient society and its technologies. He also wrote on the geology and geography of Egypt and, in his early days in Egypt, contributed to the succession of slim volumes of hieroglyphic texts copied from the monuments in Egypt, which were the lifeblood of the European scholars of the day who were engaged in the study of the ancient Egyptian language and history.

Manners and Customs was probably Wilkinson's most influential work; re-edited, revised and translated into several European languages, it introduced entire generations of egyptologists to their subject over a period of more than fifty years. The work treated nearly all aspects of the ancient culture employing mainly the surviving evidence from New Kingdom times. Some of the small volumes contained a history and description of the ancient religion, others detailed the daily life of the people who had made the great monuments that were so magnificently described in the *Description*. From the information contained in the ancient paintings and sculptures and the abundance of ancient objects, still to be found in Egypt at the time, Wilkinson virtually reconstructed the material culture of the New Kingdom, supplementing his studies of this ancient material with commonsense and a wide knowledge of the contemporary peasant life in Egypt.

The Valley of the Kings provided Wilkinson with much diverse material for this great work. He was not greatly interested in the somewhat esoteric texts on the walls of the royal tombs, of which he could probably make little sense, but what he did describe was the ancient artists' techniques and the subject matter of those paintings that would provide evidence of the everyday life of the court and its officers. More than any other single thing in the Valley, he was fascinated by the six small side chambers in Bruce's tomb, the tomb of Ramesses III (number 11), one of which had on its walls the celebrated scenes of the harpers playing before the gods.

In this cluster of tiny rooms Wilkinson found endless subjects for his studies. They are, he said, 'unquestionably the most interesting parts of the tomb' and 'throw considerable light on the manners and customs of the Egyptians'. Here, as bright as new, were pictures of some of the smaller domestic treasures, long since destroyed, of a strong empire with a rich court. Some of the chambers were filled with paintings of objects from the royal household, the kitchens, the armouries, and the paraphernalia of the royal audience chamber. Pictures to which Wilkinson, in common with the earlier travellers, could directly respond. For although they were glimpses of an ancient eastern court, they were but different versions of objects that were still in use in many of the great houses of Europe. Slaughtering scenes, cooking, bread making—all were known not only from the daily scenes of Egyptian village life but also from personal experience in his home. Wilkinson, for example, was impressed with the size of the cabins shown in paintings of the ancient boats; they were, in fact, probably larger than those of the Nile boats in which he had travelled and complained of the consequent discomforts. Keenly, he noticed that the drawings of spear heads were painted blue; probably steel, he remarked, which is certainly likely, for the importation of iron into Egypt from kingdoms to the north was well under way during this reign. He also observed that some of the tables in the paintings used during the preparation of food were suspended from the ceiling by ropes 'to guard against the intrusion of rats and other destructive predators'—not, perhaps, an observation that many archeologists could make from their own experience today. Next Wilkinson described some of the extraordinary household goods of those times:

The next chamber has [paintings of] chairs of the

most elegant form, covered with a rich drapery, highly ornamented, and evincing admirable taste: nor can anyone, on contemplating the beauty of Egyptian furniture, refuse for one moment his assent to the fact that this people must have been greatly advanced in the arts of civilisation and the comforts of domestic life. Sofas, couches, vases of porcelain and pottery, copper utensils, cauldrons, rare woods, printed stuffs, leopard skins, baskets of a very neat and graceful shape, and basins and ewers, whose designs vie with the production of the ancient cabinet maker, complete the interesting series of these frescoes.

Then the description passes to the next chambers, until he comes to the chamber of Bruce's harpers.

The principal figures in the last [chamber] are two harpers playing upon instruments of a not inelegant form. From these the tomb received its name. One has eleven, the other apparently fourteen strings, and one (if not both) of the minstrels is blind.

For the first time the harpers were observed by the eye of a true copyist. Wilkinson counted the harp strings and looked carefully at the eyes of the musicians to detect that, in common with many other representations of harpists, the minstrels were shown as blind. Wilkinson published copies of these scenes in fine colour illustrations that may be enjoyed today, not only as pictures of delightful ancient art that is no longer in such good condition, but also as exceptionally good examples of the book plates of their day. The heraldic images of the groups of objects, the bizarre oriental costumes and exotic nationalities of the people depicted, the sheer splendour of the accumulation of the arms and furnishings of royalty, all greatly contributed to the creation of a powerful image of the ancient court that quickly took an important place in the historical imagination of Europe.

The travellers and scholars delighted in the airy elegance of the royal tombs which, to them, seemed far more impressive than the private tomb chapels that were often cramped and not infrequently inhabited by the villagers of Gurna and their animals. Admiration for the royal tombs grew and grew. Typical of this enthusiasm is the eloquent description of the Valley and its tombs by Dean Stanley, who first visited Thebes in 1853:

Nothing that has ever been said about them [the royal tombs] had prepared me for their extraordinary grandeur. You enter a sculpted portal in the face of these wild cliffs, and find yourself in a long and lofty gallery, opening or narrowing as the case may be, into successive halls and chambers, all of which are covered with white stucco, and this white stucco brilliant with colours, fresh as they were thousands of years ago, but on a scale, and with a splendour, that I can only compare to the frescoes of the Vatican Library.

In all, *Manners and Customs* contained more than six hundred plates and many of these were lithographed in bright colours, the accuracy of which was controlled by cakes of ancient pigment that had been brought from Egypt by Wilkinson. He had made these colour samples by scraping paint from the 'fallen stones' in the tomb of Seti I where he says, 'sufficient numbers still remain to enable any future traveller to make a similar experiment'; this observation being made in a special footnote 'least the reader should suppose I had defaced any of the figures in the ruins.' Wilkinson showed a care for the monuments not shared by many of his contemporaries.

It was typical of Wilkinson that he sent these ancient pigments for scientific analysis, as well as using them to aid the printer. Wilkinson's friend 'Dr. Ure' made a series of simple analyses of the cakes of paint that agree in every respect with the modern analysis of other ancient pigments. Dr Ure's tests preceded the later analysis by more than fifty years, and they are still the only ones performed on pigments used in the Valley of the Kings. He discovered that the ancient paints were basically composed of two types of pigment: naturally occurring minerals and chemical compounds. These two stable types retain their colour much better than some complex modern paints—as the brightness of the colours in the tombs clearly shows. However, they have a severely limited colour range, which the Egyptians exploited for its maximum effect.

The binders that held the pigments to the tomb walls have not been accurately identified, and there were certainly several alternatives. The ancient craftsmen doubtless thought of such substances in terms of the world they knew rather than in the abstractions of modern chemistry. All the naturally occurring binders that were available—gum acacia, egg white, beeswax, and animal glues may well have been used by the ancient painters. These organic substances have changed in a millennia-slow chemical reaction with the atmosphere and are no longer identifiable in the paints that remain upon the tomb walls. Nevertheless, they still perform their task well.

The pigments too were mostly obtained from everyday sources. For example, the black used in Seti I's tomb for the beautiful free line drawings as well as a colour in the scenes of carved relief was a carbon made of burnt bone, one of the many forms of black still used by artists today, and completely permanent. The red pigment also used for the drawings in the tomb as well as a flesh colour in the finished scenes was, Dr Ure found, a naturally occurring red pigment composed of oxides of iron, sometimes called haematite and ochre by artists, and still in wide use. The white pigment used for preparing the walls, as well as a colour in its own right, was merely a very pure chalk; the yellow, like the red, a naturally occurring pigment, another ochre or oxides of iron. The blue was rather more complex in its constituents. It was described by Dr Ure as a 'pulverant glass, made by vitrifying the oxides of copper and iron with sand and soda', which is a basic description of the beautiful blue glaze commonly used by the Egyptians and called 'Egyptian faience' or, rather more prosaically, blue frit. Had Dr Ure continued his tests he would have discovered that the iron oxides, if present in more than a trace, would have turned the glaze green. In fact, the composition of this long celebrated production of ancient Egypt had already been investigated by no less a person than Sir Humphrey Davy, and doubtless Dr Ure had access to this great chemist's paper on the subject, which had been published some twenty years before. After being pulverized, Dr Ure discovered, the powdered glaze was mixed with some white chalk to lighten its dark hue: simply mixing the same powder with the yellow pigment had given the ancient artists a fine green.

The pigments made paints of varying consistencies which would have to have been applied in different ways. The colours without blue frit in them were finely ground into a paste so soft that its grains could not be felt when the pigment was rubbed between two finger nails, a sure way of testing the fineness of any paint. After mixing the pigment with water and whatever medium was chosen, it was left for several days to mature and saturate properly so that when the artist came to use it the colour flowed smoothly, as fine as satin, from his stiff reed brushes. The grains were so light and small that the hairs of the brush did not filter them out of the medium as would be the case with less thoroughly ground paints. Thus the brush marks normally retained their intensity of colour right through the long elegant strokes of the master draughtsmen, until the brush became quite dry and required recharging. The paints with frit in them, however, required quite different handling. They had a much coarser consistency and were applied to the walls and ceilings in a thick layer that could hardly have been used for drawings. These coarser colours have changed with age, and the brilliant blues have darkened or, sometimes, turned green. Unusually, some of the figures in the tomb of Seti I were coated with beeswax used as a kind of a glaze, which has darkened and, unfortunately, collected a great deal of dust upon its surface that now obscures the colour beneath. But, thanks to the simplicity of the ancient techniques and the thoroughness of the craftsmen, the paints have survived the battering of one hundred and fifty years of tourism with remarkable resilience.

In his study of ancient painters, Wilkinson not only includes Ure's revolutionary chemical analysis, adding that the ancient paints were 'certainly bound with gum', but also such information as the types of ancient brushes, paint boxes, the laying out of wall decorations, even the information that 'as in the modern studio or the counting house of a European town, we find it was not unusual for an ancient artist, or scribe, to put his reed pencil behind his ear'.

In the indexes of a standard modern work on the materials and industries of ancient Egypt, Wilkinson's name occurs in connection with an extraordinarily wide range of activities: from brewing palm wine to the wide occurrence of ancient sawdust in linen bags; from the aquamarine mines of the Red Sea hills to 'mummies of the lower orders'. It is an inadvertent commentary upon a truly remarkable career of great breadth but one curiously neglected by many writers upon egyptology. In his lifetime Wilkinson received many scholastic honours for his work, but it is probably as the author of a fat little brown-covered guide book that he is best remembered. 'Murray's Handbook for Travellers in Egypt, being a new Edition, Corrected and condensed of Modern Egypt and Thebes, by Sir Gardner Wilkinson, F.R.S., M.R.S.L., F.R.G.S. etc.' was one of a series produced by John Murray, whose father had published both Belzoni and Wilkinson, designed for the ever growing tourist trade that was rapidly taking Egypt into its orbit. The book first appeared in 1847 and thousands upon thousands of travellers and scholars who visited the Valley carried a copy. During the remainder of the century 'as Wilkinson says' was one of the most popular refrains in the literature of Egyptian travel, and it is most appropriate that these travellers were guided through the tombs by the man who, perhaps more than any other, made ancient Egypt live again.

11

Burton and Hay

Another scholar who worked in the Valley of the Kings, sometimes alongside Wilkinson, was James Burton. Their work complemented each other's, for while they shared a common interest in history and hieroglyphics, Wilkinson was principally interested in scenes of daily life and Burton, at least in the Valley, was more interested in the architecture and archeology of the tombs. Burton was in a good position to appreciate the ancient techniques of building and quarrying for he had been born into a family of builders and architects. His father, also called James Burton, had developed large areas of Regency London and in association with John Nash had laid out many of the squares and terraces of Bloomsbury, one of whose streets still bears the family name. Although the elder Burton had designed several buildings in this development, he was not an outstanding architect, but another of his many sons, Decimus, became well known and was responsible for the pretty neo-classic gateway to Hyde Park which now stands by Apsley House at the end of Piccadilly. In designing the details of this screen Decimus had received his inspiration from the Greek temples, and the reliefs on the gate emulated the marbles that Elgin had recently shipped from Athens. Scholarship was very much part of the architecture of the time and brother James, growing up in this same climate of practical scholarship after a long career at Cambridge, opted for the study of Egypt and its monuments.

Burton's father had made a fortune and had considerable influence. Following a hugely successful London development he had moved his family first to Tunbridge Wells, where more building schemes were developed, and finally to St Leonards, which he transformed from a village to a seaside town and where he was appointed High Sheriff of Kent. When his son James discovered the third tri-lingual inscription to be found in Egypt, embedded in a mosque in Cairo, the elder Burton was to enlist the aid of the British Consul-General in Cairo to secure its release by writing to the Secretary of State in London. At Thebes young Burton excavated far more than

Wilkinson. At Karnak he exposed whole walls of the great Temple of Amun, including the huge battle reliefs of Seti I, and he found a long list of kings in the same temple. He also made excavations in the Valley. Outside the tomb of Seti I, he uncovered a large amount of broken pottery, lying in a heap of shale which, Burton surmised, Belzoni had removed from the tunnel at the bottom of the tomb. Inside the tomb he cleared the well of the debris with which Belzoni had filled it, and to protect the monument from flooding, completed a series of dykes, started by Belzoni, around the entrance of the tomb. Another small tomb attracted his attention, this time situated in the cliff above Prince Ramesses Montu-hir-kopesh-ef. Wilkinson had numbered this tomb KV 20 and, in their day, the French expedition had recorded its entrance on their map. However, it was filled with flood debris. Burton tried to clear it out to test the local belief that the passage was supposed to connect with the temples on the other side of the ridge. But he had to stop the work after cutting his way through some 75 feet of flood debris 'owing to the danger of mephitic air which extinguished the lights'. He was far short of the end of the tomb which lay deep in the rock some 300 feet beneath him along a corridor more than 500 feet long. The mephistophelean climate of the tomb is still present for it is inhabited by swarms of bats whose guano fills the air with the sharp smell of ammonia, and is an extra hazard to climbing in the steep corridors.

Despite these surroundings Burton's enthusiasm for the tomb stemmed from the fact that he had understood that the two niches cut into the walls of the upper corridor were designed to hold a beam used as an aid in the lowering of the sarcophagus into the tomb. These beam slots, as they are called, are found in most of the royal tombs and, in their simplest form, consist of a rectangular hole in one side of the corridor and a slot on the other side into which the two ends of a beam were inserted. The beams of Lebanese cedar wood were necessarily huge baulks of timber designed to take the large palm-fibre ropes that were wrapped around the sarcophagi as they were slowly rolled down into the tombs on logs of palm wood. The Egyptian workmen who moved large boulders and heavy rocks for our expedition in the Valley of the Kings displayed the same skill in manoeuvering large heavy objects in confined spaces as had their ancient counterparts. The knowledge of how to move heavy weights accurately and with the simplest of equipment is an instinctive art that westerners have largely lost. It takes patience and intelligence and, these days, is accompanied by much singing of songs and invoking of the local holy sheiks.

Burton, the first person to recognize the significance of the beam slots, left the intractable tomb still blocked up and it was some eighty years later that Howard Carter managed to cut through the hard flood debris in the winding corridor and reach the burial chamber below. Yet his careful observations in the tomb was typical of Burton's work and most of the tombs that were open in the Valley received similar attentions as he went around them, clearing dirt and making notes of what he found. In the tomb of Ramesses I, uncovered by Belzoni just a few years before, Burton found that the two mummies still lay in the granite sarcophagus, and the remains of the plaster-sealed dry stone wall at the entrance to the tomb was still in position. Nearby, in the tomb of Ramesses VI, he found many pieces of the original burial equipment, mixed with the piles of loose chippings that still lay in the corridors. The piles of chippings and natural debris in these open tombs held much of real interest and value. Burton records that in the great tomb were 'small figures similar to those in Belzoni's tomb'; there were vases, much pottery, many small alabaster ushabtis painted with coloured waxes and a miniature coffin, also for ushabtis, painted with the same materials—a common technique of the period. After another sixty years of visitors digging about, all the debris was eventually cleared out, but if modern archeological methods had been practised in Burton's day we should now possess a remarkable record of the contents of these huge Rameside tombs. Unfortunately, our knowledge of most of these tombs has suffered from lack of records. Even the smallest fragment of an object, once recognized by comparing it with others of the type (and the tomb of Tutankhamen has supplied us with an excellent check list of objects that were buried in the Valley) can tell us what was originally laid in these Rameside tombs.

Burton was not the first to realize that the ceiling of a part of the tomb of Ramesses VI was hollow, and that by means of a small rough hole high in the wall

of the corridor it was possible to crawl through into another tomb that crossed over Ramesses VI's, high above in the rock. To avoid this hidden tomb, which they had run into during their quarrying, the masons working in the tomb of Ramesses VI were forced to increase greatly the angle of descent of · the main corridor so that the tomb above them was not further exposed to view. This smaller, older tomb was neither carved nor painted, but it was so extraordinary in both its size and design that Wilkinson, not usually impressed by blank monuments, had included it in his numbered list as tomb 12; other earlier travellers had also included it upon their maps.

The proper entrance to this strange tomb lies up the slope of the gully to the south of the tomb of Ramesses VI, and it was from there that Burton commenced his plan of the tomb, still the only one in existence. At a date later than the original work of excavation, a chamber was cut into the upper section of the first corridor of the tomb, a huge column was left in its centre, and three rough side chambers were cut into its walls. These alterations were very roughly made, cut out with the same careless workmanship with which the first corridor was enlarged and the doorway cut back, as if to admit something large into the tomb. It is a bewildering beginning to a strange tomb that is a long (some one hundred and seventy feet) and low monument, quite unlike any other in the Valley. The entrance is steep and roughly stepped, the light barely penetrates beyond the first rough room, and the rest of the tomb, partly blackened by smoke, is in pitch darkness. The plan is eccentric and unique and visitors are disoriented; there is no centre to the tomb, one room leads to another and many smaller side chambers lie off them. It is a blank, dateless, empty tomb all beautifully cut with great precision but the intended recipients of this care and attention have left no record of themselves—not a mark. The walls are a tangible enigma which, while they speak of the skill and effort of their manufacture, stand perfect, blank, as if waiting.

Since Burton's day the tomb has been completely swept out; doubtless by archeologists searching for the smallest of tell-tale joints in the floors or walls that might cover the entrance to hidden chambers but, in their search for treasure they have left us no records of their activity. Previously the tomb had been lightly flooded and its end rooms covered with fine sand washed in. Some of this deposit was streaked down the walls of the tomb of Ramesses VI which passes almost at right angles underneath it. When Burton was in the tomb in the 1820s it was still partly

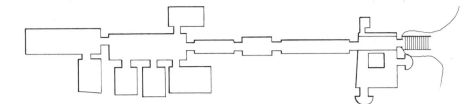

The plans of the two tombs that interested James Burton:
number 12 (above) and 5 (below)

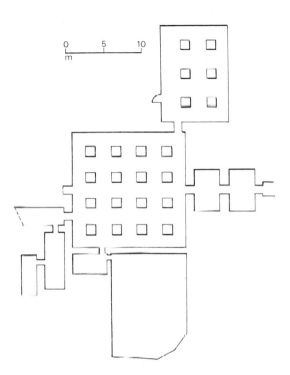

filled with the chippings left behind by the ancient quarrymen; and the workmen's laying-out lines may still be seen in the tomb—outlines of doorways that were never cut out were painted on the walls. Exactly down the middle of the ceiling of the entire tomb is the centre line, the main reference point for working measurements during its excavation. The line was carefully positioned, marked by plucking a string soaked in red ochre paint against the white lime-stone rock. In common with most of the large monuments in the Valley, the tomb is very precisely cut and the final careful finishing work, done with copper chisels rather than the flints and granite pounders used in the coarser work of roughing the tombs' shape out of the rock, proceeds neatly and deliberately from the ceiling and down the fine flat walls. The area where modern surveyors would habitually measure for their plans—at the bottom of the wall—is frequently the least accurate part of a royal tomb, whereas the most accurate points, with tolerances well within those of modern architecture, are in the angle between the ceiling and the top of the walls. The system of measuring the tomb from the top down, though not always adhered to, followed naturally from the usual quarrying techniques of the ancient Egyptians in the Valley, which was to cut the face of the rock in a series of steps the approximate height of the corridor and to proceed into the rock face by removing blocks of stone from the top down; the finishing process simply continued this same order. Burton understood this method so the plans he drew are, therefore, accurate and informative.

In his note upon the tomb he reports that he found 'writings' on one of the walls, and one might expect a list of workmen, perhaps even a date of a king drawn in the abbreviated cursive version of hiero-glyphic used by the scribes in the Valley. I once spent several days searching the tomb walls by torchlight to find these texts but saw nothing but the masons' marks and their usual signs for north and south, written in the traditional hieroglyphs. Perhaps

Burton's 'writings' have been covered over by the soot from the fire that burnt deep in the corridors of the tomb and whose oily smoke blackened the outer rooms and the ceilings of the upper part of the tomb. With no texts to provide a clue, the identity of the tomb's intended occupant remains unknown. Prob-ably its numerous side chambers were each intended to hold separate burials of members of the royal family or the court. One of the rooms, the last in the long straggling tomb, was anciently sealed with mud plaster, and we may suppose that this chamber, at least, once held a burial. However, it is all a mystery and to visit this strange place, pitch black and com-pletely empty in the warm rock, is an eerie experience as the noise of voices filters wordlessly through the small hole in the floor that runs down into the great tomb of Ramesses VI beneath.

Burton's greatest service to his successors working

in the Valley is the record he made of another strange tomb that has since been completely lost. Just visible at the turn of the century, the tomb is now probably buried somewhere under the car park. Burton's plan showed it to be a quite extraordinary monument, with a very grand entrance corridor that led to a square room with no less than sixteen pillars in it and from which further chambers ran off. There is certainly nothing like it to be seen in the Valley today, nor indeed in the rest of Egypt. The tomb's position, low in the Valley and close to the narrowest part of the central area through which all the flood waters drained, made its flooding and destruction inevitable. Burton's plan of the tomb has unfortunately lost its scale and there are no measurements drawn upon it, but it is possible to estimate its approximate size. The columns of the other tombs in the Valley range from between two and a half feet to, exceptionally, six feet wide. In this tomb they are the same width as the doorway in the great hall, so three and a half feet would be a good approximate figure, giving us the dimensions of the hall as being more than forty feet in both its measurements (the two sides being 12×13 column widths). It has, therefore, the same proportions and size as the burial chambers of the Nineteenth Dynasty kings. Burton gives a graphic description of the tomb's interior:

The tomb is all in a state of ruin. On the ceiling alone which has in general fallen in vast masses are to be seen small remains here and there of colouring. The substance of the rock between the small chambers and the large ones above cannot be more than eighteen inches. Being full of mud and earth the descent from the pillared room to those underneath is not perceptible. The Catacomb must have been excavated very low in the Valley or the Valley very much raised by the accumulation of earth and rubbish brought down by the rains.

Happily Burton persevered in these difficult and probably dangerous conditions and 'found part of the name on a stone in the inside and the other part on the doorway'. It was the cartouche of Ramesses II, son of Seti I, whose tomb close by had been flooded. Salt had cleared a path into that king's tomb, but no one bothered to dig this ruin out and it has slowly been lost to small slides of rocks and pebbles, floods and, lately, tarmacadam.

Other accounts of the tomb before it was finally choked up, describe a goddess by the left of the entrance door sculpted in relief, a goddess whose identifying insignia is a feather in her headband:

Ma-at. She is found in most royal tombs in the Valley, one of the group of deities who welcomes the king to his tomb with promises of endless life, power and magic gifts. Here she is gracing a tomb situated low in the centre of the Valley, of grand and unique design, bearing the names of Ramesses II—a ruined, unexplored monument that does not fit the normal royal tomb plan. There are some similarities in these two tombs of which Burton drew plans; both lack a focus—an architectural climax—the point at which the sarcophagus stood, and both have numerous side chambers which suggests that they were intended for more than one burial. In some ways, the second tomb, numbered 5 by Wilkinson, is similar to the tomb of Ramesses II. The huge square pillared hall is reminiscent of the great vaulted chamber in that king's tomb, but in this tomb there are two extra rows of columns running through its centre.

When Seti I invested his young son Ramesses II as co-regent, in 1302 BC, he gave his son a harem 'like the beautiful ones of the palace'. Ramesses was proud of his numerous children and by the end of his long reign the walls of some of his temples boasted of more than one hundred princes. His lengthy reign of nearly seventy years would ensure that many of his offspring would have died before him and perhaps the king had provided this tomb, number 5, as a joint monument for some of them in the Valley close by his own. There is, of course, another more extraordinary explanation for this second tomb of Ramesses II in the Valley: it could be another tomb that he had made for himself, for it has the royal name on it and the goddess in relief by the entrance is only seen in that exact position in other royal tombs. Also, there is the question of the form of the royal name. In the tomb of Ramesses II in which Salt dug, the name of the king in the upper sections is written in a way different from that in the lower sections and shows, unlike the other tomb in the Valley that bears his name, that this one was started very early in his long reign. This would correspond well with the fact that the tomb is one of the few in the Valley that was completely finished—after all, the workmen had nearly seventy years in which to complete their task! Obviously they and their children would have finished long before the reign had ended, and they might well have then been put to work upon the second tomb with its strange pillared hall. Perhaps the tomb was meant for some of the princes; perhaps, even, the earlier tomb was already destroyed by floods, for, after all, the sarcophagus of Ramesses II has never been found . . .

In common with some of the tombs which he studied so carefully, Burton is something of an unknown quantity. His papers—nearly seventy volumes of notes, plans and drawings—were presented to the British Museum after his death, by his brother Decimus. A large collection of antiquities, which he gathered together while he was in Egypt, and some of which were drawn by Wilkinson and depicted in *Manners and Customs*, were sold in the year following his return to Britain in some four hundred and twenty lots at Sotheby's. Like Wilkinson, his good friend, he published a volume of hieroglyphic texts at the time of the decipherment but, unlike his friend, Burton never wrote again and, in fact, even the *Excerpta Hieroglyphica* contained only hieroglyphs and no words of English. He gave some of his drawings and plans to friends while he was still in Egypt and worked, it seems, solely for personal pleasure. During the course of two long trips Burton spent seven years in Egypt, some of the time alone, travelling in the desert. When he returned to Europe he lived in Edinburgh from where, one hundred years before, his grandfather had left to found the family fortune. There he adopted the old family name of Haliburton that had been discarded by his father and, although he still kept himself informed of egyptological matters, he spent much of his time researching the genealogy of his family. He died, unmarried, in Edinburgh in 1862 and was buried with the epitaph: 'A zealous investigator of Egypt and of its language and antiquities'.

In 1824, two years after Burton had arrived in Egypt, a distant relative, Robert Hay, also came to the Valley to study the great tombs. Hay, the fourth son of a Scottish land-owning family, had gone to sea but had forsaken this career when he unexpectedly inherited the estate of Linplum in West Lothian from an elder brother. Many members of the family had served in the eastern Empire, in India and Ceylon, and an uncle had been killed during the landing of the British Expeditionary Force in Egypt that expelled the French. Hay first became interested in visiting Egypt and its monuments after meeting two young architects and seeing their drawings of a trip up the Nile, from which they had just returned. He was different from Burton—gregarious and vocally enthusiastic about many aspects of Egypt and over a period of fourteen years he made several journeys in Egypt and spent much time drawing in the tombs in the Valley of the Kings, where he set up house.

Great numbers of young architects and artists visited Egypt during the 1820s and '30s. People were very interested in the ancient civilization and its style was very much admired but except for the plates in the huge volumes of the *Description*, it was virtually unrecorded and, therefore, had to be seen at first hand. One of the first English architects in Egypt had been Sir Charles Barry who, as a young man, had taken the opportunity of a trip up the Nile offered to him while he had been drawing in Greece. Later, when Barry was successfully ensconced in his London practice, where he later designed the Houses of Parliament, he, in common with other architects, encouraged the young professionals in their offices to see the ancient monuments for themselves. Eclecticism was the order of the day and the young architects travelled far and wide, later celebrating their experiences in a multitude of decorative styles, that eventually embellished many of the buildings of the Industrial Revolution.

Like Robert Hay, many of these men, aged twenty-four or twenty-five, were extremely skilled draughtsmen. Some carried the *camera lucida*, a drawing aid invented just a few years earlier by Dr William Hyde Wollaston, the eminent physicist and chemist of the Royal Institution. Its four-sided prism enabled the draughtsmen to view the object of their work as an image superimposed on the paper on which they drew. In practice it was a simple device—the prism, mounted on a holder above the corner of the drawing board, was positioned under one eye of the draughtsman who, with the other eye shut, could view both the image of the object being drawn and his pencil and paper simultaneously. As one enthusiast of such optically aided drawing methods proclaimed: 'By means of this instrument, a person of moderate skill in drawing, but habituated to the effect of it, can do more work, and in better taste, whilst executing views of ruined architecture, in one hour, than the readiest draughtsman, unassisted, could do in seven'. The *camera lucida* was widely used in Egypt some thirty years before the photographic camera and even after that time it had many advantages over its mechanical rival. The *camera lucida* relied on the hand and brain of man to construct a meaningful drawing, whereas the photographic camera simply records light falling upon a sensitized paper. Thus, when drawing ancient objects that are damaged or stained with dirt, a concentrated inspection and drawing of the original can render visible scenes and hieroglyphs that photographs may never record. In the words of Sir Mortimer Wheeler: 'The basic trouble is, of course, that the camera is an awful liar'; in other words the camera's optical distortions and the

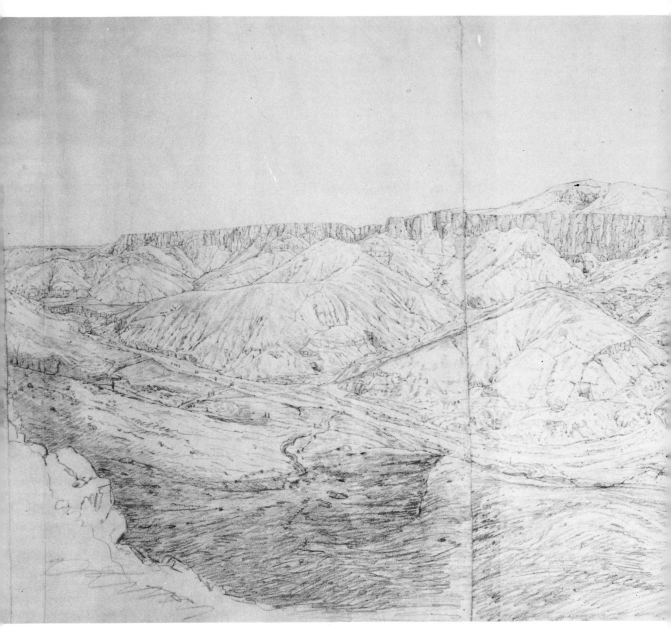

A panoramic view of the Valley, drawn by a member of Hay's expedition. The artist was seated on its western side; the entrance to the Valley is at the left and its southern head on the right. Such old records are extremely valuable in showing the Valley as it was before the extensive excavations and alterations of the past hundred years. To protect the tombs from future flooding it will be necessary to change the present shape of the Valley floor and remodel it so that it will drain as efficiently as it did during the last century

effects of different illuminations must be interpreted with great care.

At different times Robert Hay hired many of these journeying architects and artists to help him in his work, and when his group stayed in the Valley they were often joined by Burton and Wilkinson. Several of these young men, initially very willing to stay and draw in the country that they had travelled to see, were enthusiastic enough about their work to con-

tinue in the profession for the rest of their lives. For egyptologists and travellers coming to Egypt there was always a pool of skilled adventurous draughtsmen available who were pleased to extend their travels by working in the monuments. One such traveller, and one of Hay's earliest draughtsmen, who later wrote *The Manners and Customs of the Modern Egyptians* as a modern companion-study to Wilkinson's work, was Edward Lane. He had worked as an engraver before travelling to Egypt and later he became the greatest Arabist of his century—the learned translator of *A Thousand and One Nights* and compiler of a magnificent Arabic dictionary. As a young man he was greatly fascinated by the tombs in the Valley, and for a time had been a companion of Burton's. Owen Jones, who was to produce the influential pattern book, *The Grammar of Ornament*, was a supervisor of the Great Exhibition of 1851

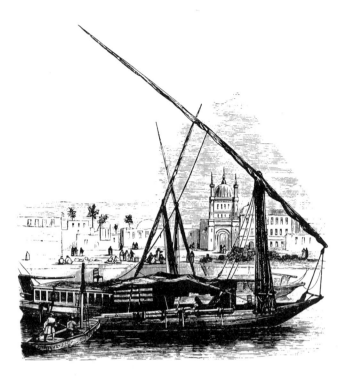

*An example of the type of Nile boat used by travellers in the
19th century*

and designed and supervised the exhibition in the
Crystal Palace when it was later moved to Sydenham.
Frederick Catherwood, who was one of the architects
who first encouraged Hay to visit Egypt, later worked
with him at the Valley before leaving the Mediterranean and taking his epigraphic skills with the
camera lucida to South America and the Mayan
monuments. They were a vigorous and talented
group of men and for ten years, after 1825, they
haunted the ancient monuments of the Nile, copying,
translating, measuring and, always, drawing.

For the trip to Upper Egypt and the Valley a boat
was hired in Cairo. Because many of the boats were
filled with vermin and insects of all kinds, Wilkinson
recommended having the hired boat washed clean
and painted—he suggested using red ochre bound
with egg, which the ancient artists had sometimes
used—and all the cracks and crevices filled with putty.
He also suggested that the traveller should bring an
iron rat trap from Europe for use on the boats; one
traveller found that vermin had killed a dozen
chickens that had been put in the hold. Though they
travelled through one of the most beautiful landscapes
in the world, it must have been something of a relief

to disembark at Thebes. Here there was a choice of
staying either in the temples, 'At Karnak the traveller
may take up his abode in the north-west tower of the
great temple' or in the tombs where 'he may take a
bed, or mat or carpet, with a small stock of provisions:
if he makes any stay there he may procure bread . . .
A lantern, a small broom (in order to have one of the
grottoes swept, which makes a tolerable abode) and
above all, a mosquito net and umbrella are requisite'.

At Gurna, on the west bank of the Nile, the 'troglo-
dytes' were no longer as 'tumultuous', as an earlier
visitor had complained, and the villagers provided a
useful source of labour to the expeditions. Living was
easy; both servants and food were very cheap.
When he was not living in the Valley, Hay took over
the house built by Salt some years before at the foot
of the hill of Gurna, a few hundred yards away from
Wilkinson's mud castle. Here the artists could unpack
their possessions which, Wilkinson suggested, should
include the following:

*A camp bedstead, bedding, and mosquito curtain, a
camp stool and drawing table; umbrella, double or
lined; drawing paper, pencils, and Indian-rubber;
and if he intends to follow European customs a
plentiful supply of tea, wine, cognac, aromatic and
distilled vinegar and as many luxuries as he may
think proper.*

The full list also included chronometers, measuring
tapes, sextants, 'and in their cases, nails answer
better than glue.' The medicine chest included remedies for diarrhoea, constipation, sunburn, blistering
and ophthalmia as well as remedies for cuts and
wounds.

*The choice of his library will depend, of course, on
his occupations or taste; I shall only, therefore,
recommend Larcher's Herodotus, M. Champollion's
Phonetic System of Hieroglyphs, Pococke, Denon,
Hamilton's Aegyptiaca . . . to which may be added
Browne, Belzoni, Burckhardt, Ptolemy, Strabo and
Pliny; but of course these last three, as well as of
Diodorus, extracts will suffice, if he considers them
too voluminous.*

Hay's party often stayed in the tomb of Ramesses
IV which, more than a thousand years earlier, had
been the centre of the small Christian community in
the Valley. They set up sun screens in the open
entrance of the tomb and their camp beds in the
shaded corridors inside. Dogs, doubtless brought up
to the Valley by their servants, sat and played by the
door of the tomb and by their barking told of a stran-

ger's approach. Chickens and ducks ran around the open tomb entrances. Inside, pegs were banged into the cracks in the walls from which their rifles and pistols were hung. Carpets, bought in Cairo, were spread upon the clean swept floor, a Turkish mirror and thermometer were hung on the wall. Bookshelves held the volumes of the earlier travellers. Long straw-filled pillows and divans were placed Turkish style against the walls, and meals, cooked in a nearby tomb by one of the servants of the expedition, were shared by the group in the shade of the corridors.

Behind them, in the dark burial chamber stood a colossal sarcophagus, the largest in the Valley. Robert Hay was intrigued by these huge granite boxes and had one of his draughtsmen, Catherwood, measure and draw all that were visible. The sarcophagus of Ramesses IV was eleven and a half feet long, about nine feet high, and box and lid weighed many tons. The ancient thieves had broken into it by lighting a fire to one side and then shattering the hot granite with cold water. The remains of seven sarcophagi, mostly broken and stained like Ramesses IV's, were visible to Hay in the Valley. Since his day two more of this type have been dug from flooded tombs. The earliest sarcophagus that he could see in the Valley was that of Ramesses I, in which Belzoni had found the two intruded mummies; it was unfinished and somewhat amorphous in shape. Nevertheless, the bulky cartouche-form of the box and lid set the basic style for the succession of sarcophagi that followed and its material, rose granite, was also employed by successive kings. All the royal sarcophagi that were made after Ramesses I's had sculptures of the king upon them, which stood up from the slightly convex form of the lid, like the effigies of the knights and kings in European churches. But the Egyptian figures were not twisted in attitudes of muscular tension like the European effigies. They lie in the static mummiform pose of Osiris, the ruler of the Underworld with whom the identity of the dead king was fused. Many of these figures are finely sculpted portraits and are the best examples known to us of the monarchs they portray.

On the underside of the arch of the lid was a figure of the goddess Nut, the goddess whose body was the sky. Her sensuous smooth form ran down the full length of these lids in a pose: arms above her head and legs closed together in a straight line that stretched directly over the coffins of the kings lying beneath. Her dress was sometimes covered in the stars of the night; she is, indeed, the night sky through

which the king will journey. In many of the larger royal tombs she is also painted on the ceilings, stretched between sunset and sunrise, the bark with the king and the sun is shown entering her mouth upon the western horizon and, passing through her body, is reborn upon the eastern horizon.

In one ancient text, Re, the sun god, begets himself, 'Joining his seed with his body to create his egg within his secret self'. This is, perhaps, a difficult image for us to comprehend—the creator creating himself. In another form Nut, the mother of Osiris, 'spread herself over [the king] in the form of a heavenly mystery': the goddess of the sky closes over the king in his coffins so that he may be born again.

The whole earth lies beneath thee.
Thou hast taken possession of it.
Thou enclosest the earth and all things in thy arms
Mayest thou put this king into thyself as an
    impenetrable star.

Sometimes this mother goddess appears as the sky in the form of a cow, Hathor, and the boat sails through this heavenly cow to be reborn each day. Then the dead king is 'the bull of his mother', the king Horus, son of Hathor, whose name literally means the 'House of Horus'.

Reign by reign the size of the sarcophagi increased, if somewhat erratically, and eventually they became, by their sheer tonnage, an effective part of the security arrangements of the tombs, whose entrances now closed only by light cedar doors were guarded by the watchmen in the Valley. As the physical size of the sarcophagi was increased, the two goddesses, Isis and Nepthys, took up their places upon the gigantic lids, gently holding and protecting the figure of the king on either side. Between their figures and that of the king were carved the snakes and demons that he put to flight in his nightly combat in the Underworld.

The last sarcophagus that we know to have been installed in a royal tomb is that of Ramesses VII. Subsequently the kings were buried in small crypts cut into the burial chamber floor and closed over with huge granite lids, all of which have been shattered during the opening of their burials. The sarcophagi of Merneptah were apparently precursors of this system. His burial arrangements consisted of three granite lids, the largest over twelve feet long, which were probably intended to fit over each other and over a crypt with stepped sides to hold the enlarging lid sizes. Small fragments of alabaster bearing 'The Book of Gates' and Meneptah's name have survived and suggest that an alabaster coffin similar to that

A Hay expedition drawing of flood-borne rubble and debris covering the floor of the tomb of Ramesses III. One of the expedition's architects has dug through the debris at the door sill to obtain a proper measurement for his plan. The columns with cows' heads that flank the entrance door have almost disappeared today. They probably represented a part of the ancient symbolism that identified the cow, goddess Hathor, with the Western Mountain, a mother goddess who received the dead king back into the womb-like Western Mountain for his daily rebirth on the horizon

of Seti I's may have been placed inside the crypt, under the three granite lids. The quality of the workmanship of these three lids is magnificent. The largest, outer, rectangular lid is covered with small hieroglyphic texts, finely polished and beautifully engraved. The second cover bears a fine effigy of the king and symbols of his travels through the Underworld and, like the outer cover, is still in the tomb. The third, innermost, lid was taken to Tanis, a town in the Delta, some two hundred and fifty years after Merneptah's burial and reused in a later royal tomb. This is certainly the finest lid of its dynasty and gives a hint of what the missing examples from the tombs of Seti I and Ramesses II may have looked like.

The design of the sarcophagi of the last kings of the New Kingdom, is still unknown. In the ultimate royal tomb of the Valley, that of Ramesses XI, our expedition found that the huge shaft in the burial chamber simply stopped, unfinished, at a depth of forty feet, leading nowhere. It is possible that the shaft itself was considered to be the burial crypt for the coffins of the king, a theory borne out by the presence at the corners of the pit of small deposits of ritual objects that had been made to accompany the burial of the king. Unfortunately, as we discovered, the burial of the king had never been placed in the tomb.

Catherwood measured and drew most of the sarcophagi for Hay but it is unlikely that they could either read the religious texts on them or that they had any deep interest in doing so. Indeed, it is only in the last twenty years that many of these texts have been translated in a manner that makes them intelligible. As for the sarcophagi themselves, they still lie much as Hay saw them, mostly fragmented, filthy and displaced, almost unrecorded by photographs and very little known in any of their details even among specialists.

For scholars unable to visit the tombs, then, the drawings of Hay's artists and architects still retain great practical value and all forty-nine volumes of them are deposited with Burton's in the British Museum. During Hay's later trips to Egypt, he was accompanied by his wife, Kalitzia, the daughter of a Cretan nobleman. One imagines that she did much to add to the exotic quality of Hay's encampment in the Valley. One visitor who later visited the Oasis with Hay and Catherwood, namely George Hoskins, carefully described the life of these early egyptologists in the Valley, a life that was fast disappearing as the professional egyptologist working at a speed born of competition and ambition, brought a different tenor of life to the tombs.

When engaged among the tombs of the kings, I resided in the sepulchre of Ramesses V [VI] which is very comfortable. . . I will briefly mention the manner of living there. Generally before sunrise my Arab boy used to come into my bedroom. 'e'Shams, Effende; e'Shams, Effende'—The sun, sir, the sun; . . . Others soon followed with a cup of hot strong

Frederick Arundale's plan of the Valley and its tombs—a detail of a large map that he drew for Robert Hay. Arundale was an architect, a pupil of Pugin's, who spent more than fifteen years travelling and drawing in Europe and the Near East

coffee and a pipe. To use the expression in the East, 'having drunk' both, and also taken a more substantial English breakfast, I mounted my ass and rode to a tomb . . . an hour after sunrise I was able to commence my labours, sometimes standing over the camera lucida table, otherwise squatted on a carpet, and finishing the outlines made with the instrument . . . the pencil in my hand was no obstacle to having between my lips the amber mouthpiece of the shibouk; and really a pipe of high-flavoured mild Gible tobacco (disgusting as the habit of smoking may be in Europe) is in these regions an inexpressible comfort, as the Arabs say, it reconciles you to fate, soothes down the asperities of life, and endows you with powers to build more castles and light airy structures, than even all the talent of our British architects.

At twelve I dined . . . I found it advisable to live almost entirely on fowls; and except a glass of light French wine, I drank no other beverage than water . . . Rice and Italian maccaroni are well adapted to the climate; and if a traveller is fortunate in his choice of cook, he will not say, that an Arab pillof is a bad dish. The water of the Nile agrees with every person; and however hot the day may be, it is better to drink it cold and pure than to mix it with brandy. When cooled in the porous goolahs, no draught can be more wholesome or delicious . . . It is imprudent to make any excursion, or even take a short walk, without being accompanied by a boy carrying two goolahs of water, one for his master and one for himself.

It is the custom of the East to sleep for at least half an hour after dinner. After this repose on the luxurious divan . . . I clapped my hands and at the well-known call my servant again brought me a cup of coffee and a pipe. Thus refreshed, I resumed my labours with the pencil.

After drawing almost from sunrise to sunset, I spent the evenings in reading and writing. Sometimes Mr Hay smoked his pipe with me; and on Sunday, which we invariably made a day of rest, I dined with him. On Thursday evenings also the artists and travellers at Thebes used to assemble in his house, or rather tomb I should call it; but never was the habitation of death witness to gayer scenes. Though we wore the costume, we did not always preserve the gravity of Turks; and the saloon, though formerly a sepulchre, threw no gloom over our mirth. The still remaining beautiful fragments of the painted room were illuminated by the blaze of wax lights; and the odour of the mummies had long been dispelled by the more congenial perfume of savoury viands.

Notwithstanding the great civilisation of the ancient Egyptians, I question whether their divans were more comfortable, or their fare more relished, than that of my friend Mr Hay. We were all fond of the arts, and had proved our devotion to antiquarian pursuits by sacrificing for a time Europe and its enjoyments, to prosecute our researches in this distant land. Our conversation therefore never flagged; and assuredly I reckon, not among the least happy hours of my life, the evenings I spent in the tomb at Thebes.

12

Books of the Tombs

The studies of the British scholars in Egypt such as Wilkinson and Hay were not supported by the British Government—neither the expeditions nor the subsequent expenses of publication. Curiously, throughout the long years that Britain held the lion's share of foreign trade with Egypt and wielded such great power in her councils and ministries, she invested not one penny in the study of the culture or ancient civilizations of the land. However, several other European countries held very different attitudes and while Britain manifested its national pride in vast home-based exhibitions which included gigantic replicas of ancient architecture and works of art, the governments of France, Tuscany and Prussia subsidized the production of a series of magnificent folio volumes, each masterworks of scholarship and crafts-manship that reflected many facets of national pride and skill. These volumes of superb drawings remain, to this day, the very bedrock of egyptological studies around the world. Bedrock, because the volumes contain fine copies of a large number of the essential historical documents of ancient Egypt recorded in the condition in which they were preserved over one hundred years ago. Since those days many of the scenes and vital historical texts have greatly deterior-

The left side of the scene on the main lintel of the tomb of Ramesses X. The ruin of this fine scene, shown complete on p. 40, underlines the value of such accurate drawings; frequently they are the sole surviving record of ruined monuments. The black shape at the left upper corner of the photograph is a part of a buttress that supports the entrance of the tomb

ated—some have been taken out of Egypt and others damaged or destroyed. A great part of the elegance and splendour of the ancient court was portrayed in these books and to publish copies of such splendid texts and pictures, records of state, home and military expeditions, was to participate in some small measure in the glories that they described. The ancient notion of 'living for ever' once again proved true, and several European states successfully hitched their wagons to the ancient star. The national publications of France, Tuscany and Prussia, in part complementing both the *Description* and each other, brought, for the first time, the basic materials required for the study of ancient Egypt into the libraries and universities of Europe.

Although Champollion's expedition to Egypt during the late 1820s had not been state subsidized, the Grand Duke of Tuscany had financed the party of Italians that joined Champollion's group under the direction of Niccolo Rosellini, a great friend of Champollion's and Professor of Oriental Languages at the University of Pisa. The Grand Duke subsequently financed the publication of drawings made by the combined Franco-Tuscan expedition but in his folios no proper acknowledgment was given to Champollion, who had been the real instigator and mover of the work. Subsequently, the French Government voted a large sum of money to reproduce the records of the French contingent under the guidance of Champollion's elder brother. Nearly twenty years later King Wilhelm IV sent an official Prussian expedition into the field in Egypt. This was greatly aided by direct diplomatic representation, a part of a wider *entente*, between the two nations, and the Prussian archeologists were allowed to remove many thousands of antiquities, many of which had been uncovered in hasty excavations at the ancient sites. Not only were vast collections added to the public museums in Berlin, but also the expedition documented and published many of the large monuments of Egypt for the first time.

Champollion arrived in the Valley in 1829 accompanied by a group of young artists from Paris, students of Baron Gros whose huge paintings had glorified the Napoleonic campaigns in Egypt and Europe. Augmented by the Tuscan party, the expedition doubled its size and the two groups collaborated happily and the amalgamation was a complete success. Champollion went to Egypt principally to copy major wall scenes and important texts that he planned to publish on his return to Europe. He envisaged that his expedition should document both the political history and culture of the ancient civilization, each in several separate volumes. Because, it is said, the pious French King did not want to disturb the 'biblical chronology' which placed the birth of Adam in the era of the pyramids, Champollion's group concentrated their efforts on the New Kingdom period, and especially Thebes. Virtually nothing had been published of the scenes in the royal tombs, apart from the drawings in the volumes of the *Description*, and the expedition, settling down in the tomb of Ramesses VI at the centre of the Valley, spent much of its time drawing in the royal tombs.

Under the guidance of Champollion the artists drew selected details from the tombs. The long religious texts held little interest for him and they concentrated on the larger scenes of the kings meeting the gods and others, such as those in the small side chambers in the tomb of Ramesses III which, at that time, were still not published. Champollion was particularly interested in the portraits of the ancient kings, which were still to be seen painted in bright colours on the walls of their tombs. His artists made elegant copies of the heads of the pharaohs and each one of these was published with their cartouches above their heads—a portrait gallery of the ancient kings. In the tomb of Amenhotep III in the West Valley the black line-drawings of the young royal head were faithfully copied and in the Valley itself the reliefs in most of the tombs were drawn and, if necessary, the drawings of the king's features were slightly restored to make them perfect. Champollion was probably the first

Amenhotep III— a drawing in his tomb copied by Nestor l'Hôte of Champollion's expedition

The goddess Nut from the burial chambers of the tomb of Ramesses VI (above) and Ramesses IX (below). Though bound by strict canons and conventions, Egyptian artists still made widely differing interpretations of the same subjects—in this case, the head and shoulders of the great goddess whose bodies span the vaults of the later royal burial chambers

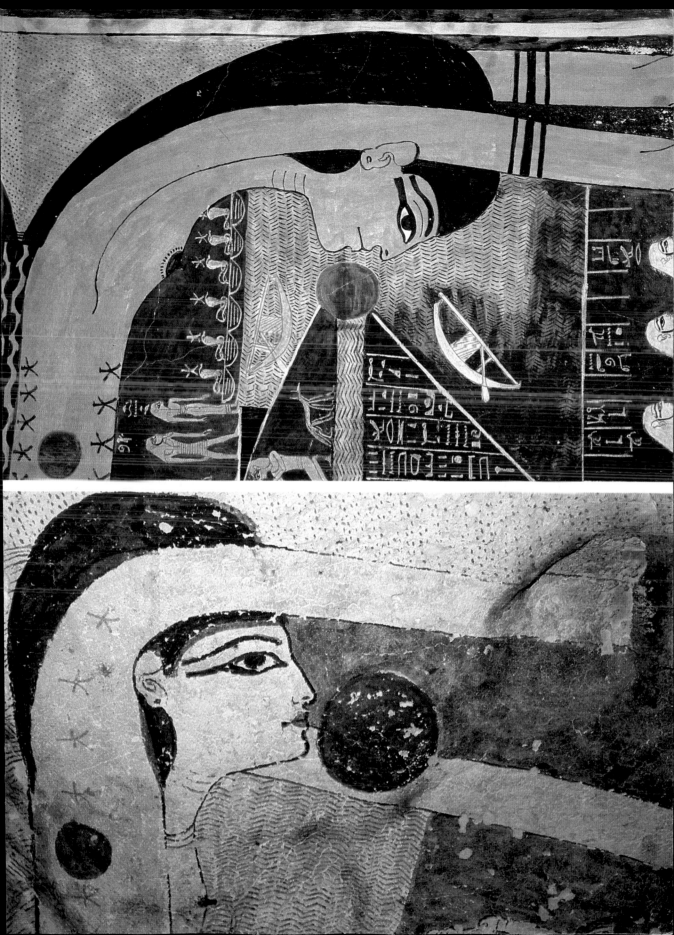

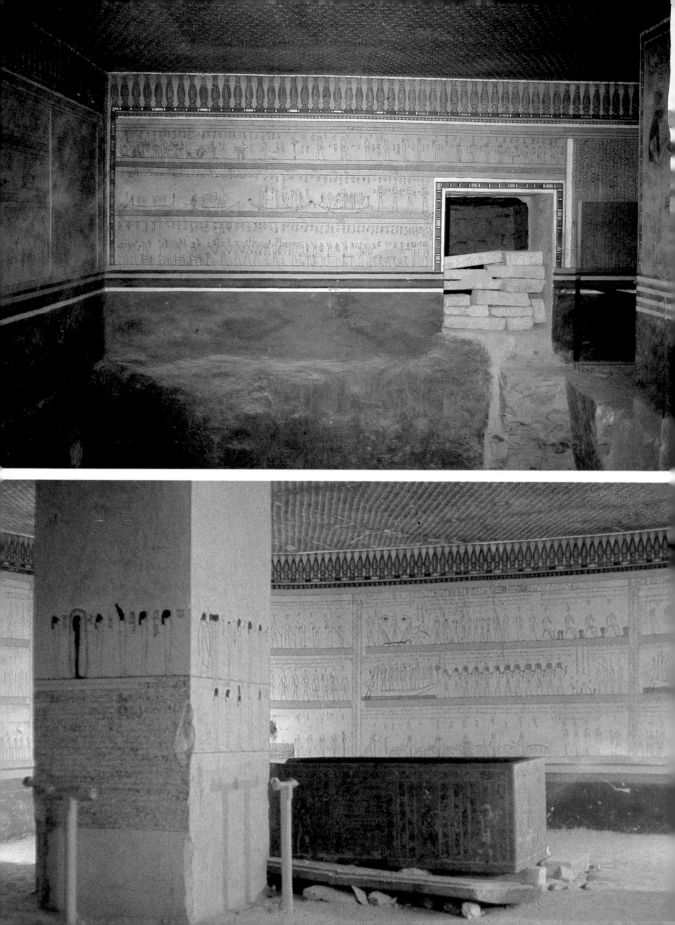

person to recognize that these Egyptian relief figures were sometimes portraits and indeed, to eyes more accustomed to European portraiture with its often precise realism and careful control of light, it is easy to see why this had been previously overlooked.

The Egyptians made their portraits by drawing the distinctive features of an individual on to an idealized figure. Across the millennia the 'idea' for the basic figure sometimes changed, the frame was drawn to appear younger or heavier, and often the facial features of individuals were partially modelled on the king, but always there is the usual Egyptian self-restraint; the reticence that is a hallmark of their art; the desire to create images without tension and with carefully controlled simplicity. King Siptah, as we know from his mummy, had a club foot and buck teeth but such deformities would never appear in pictures or sculptures of him.

To our eyes the method produces an 'idealization' of the individual which must, inevitably, flatter the sitter. But after a short acquaintance with the portraits of the kings of the New Kingdom it is still usually possible to recognize the features of a particular king or, at least, of a number of kings from a particular period of history. It is also true that the Egyptian sculptors would frequently re-use royal sculptures, altering only the cartouches in the inscriptions and leaving the features of the kings as they had been made originally. The sculptor enjoyed a special place in Egyptian society and was called 'he who keeps alive' (by the making of images). A person represented and named on his sculpture would survive for ever, as the ancient kings had done. The phrase is one close to the deepest wish of children as portrayed upon funerary monuments 'to make their father's name live for ever'.

The special rituals that were intended to vivify reliefs and statues were carved upon the walls of several of the tombs in the Valley. In the tomb of Seti I, a series of scenes like a strip cartoon caught Champollion's eye; these showed many of the stages of the ritual of 'the Opening of the Mouth', a rite that was also performed upon the mummies of the dead kings. Many of the objects used during this complex ritual were placed in the royal tombs and were probably the ones that had been used at the funeral. These rituals were an ancient conglomeration of rites

The burial chambers of Amenhotep II (above) and his father Tuthmosis III (below). The room in the burial chamber of the tomb of Amenhotep II, still partly sealed, held the cache of kings discovered by Loret

and spells in use since pre-historic times. In Champollion's drawings of this ritual from the tomb of Seti I, a statue of the king is lustrated with water, purified with balls of natron—a substance used in embalming to dissolve body fats—and presented with various ritual objects, including a flint adze and the front leg of a calf freshly cut from a living beast, while the performers, accompanied by spells and incantations, change costumes. At one point in the ceremony a priest entered into a trance-like state in an attempt to find the spirit of the person who was being called to inhabit the representation that was undergoing 'the Opening of the Mouth'.

A strange accretion of spells and mumbo-jumbo perhaps, but so old and retained from such a distant age, that in the minds of the participants and the believers such rituals represented a part of the wisdom of mankind, a part that was not necessarily understood by man: hence a mystery. There are many such rites and rituals in any civilization, though usually less involved and codified than those of the practical and highly organized Egyptians. The rituals were central to the faith; indeed, the organized religion of ancient Egypt might properly be viewed as a series of ceremonies rather than as statements, dogmas or abstract beliefs. Ritual was a central feature of Egyptian religion and Champollion perhaps recognized the importance of this series of scenes in Seti's tomb as representing one of the fundamental activities of this ancient society. In some ways Champollion's volumes are like a deluxe newspaper of ancient Egypt—a mixture of history, names, portraits, representations of ancient life and precious objects. The role of the Valley in this work was to supply the models for the portraits, and pictures of some aspects of the religion, for there was no history in the royal tombs.

It was Alessandro Ricci, the same man who had helped Belzoni make casts and drawings of the Opening of the Mouth ritual in the tomb of Seti I, who drew them again for Champollion. It must have been Ricci who guided the Franco-Tuscan expedition through Egypt, for most of the members had never visited the country before. He is one of the few adults recorded to have died of a scorpion bite at Thebes, for although the Egyptian scorpions are large and somewhat alarming, the effects of their poison usually die down after twenty-four excruciating hours.

Champollion died two years after his return to France, leaving the work of publication uncompleted. One of his artists, Nestor L'Hôte, later returned to Thebes on two separate occasions to complete the

117

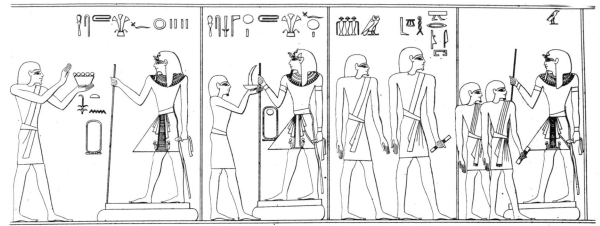

Lith de Kaeppelin et Cie

Ricci's drawing, published by Champollion, of a part of the 'Opening of the Mouth' ceremony from the walls of the tomb of Seti I. This drawing employs the convention of two line thicknesses—so-called 'sun' and 'shadow' lines—with a theoretical light source at the top left. This technique enables a copyist drawing relief sculpture to describe a line as standing out from the background or being sunk into it: this drawing shows that the reliefs are raised

drawings for his own projected egyptological folios, but he too died before his work was made into printing plates and these priceless manuscripts, like the drawings of the British scholars, remain unpublished. L'Hote was highly strung and had found expedition life difficult, nearly leaving the team while they were still in the field. However, Egypt had captivated him and when he returned he went again to the tomb of Ramesses VI, where a few years before he had lived with Champollion, and mourned his dead friend and colleague. Champollion's death from a stroke at the age of forty-two was a grievous blow to the new science. He had been recognized as the pre-eminent authority on the ancient language and his great talents as a field worker, posthumously witnessed by the publications of his expedition, were equally extraordinary. Following the publications of the Franco-Tuscan expedition and the near contemporary volumes of Wilkinson, there was to be no more study or documentation made in the Valley and its tombs for more than twenty years.

However, the academic establishment that Champollion had engendered did not stand still. The collections that had been purchased from the consuls and the merchants many years before were now further studied and a new generation of scholars came upon

the scene. Few of them, however, studied the monuments in Egypt and a wealth of texts and art remained largely undocumented and unrecorded. In the Valley only the works of Wilkinson and Champollion showed pictures of the tombs. The *Description*, though it contained excellent plans of the tombs (wanting in accuracy rather more than their elegant drawing might suggest), had few plates of the wall scenes and even these were badly copied. Apart from this the huge tombs were undocumented and, thus, inaccessible to scholars and workers outside Egypt.

One of the most distinguished scholars at this time and, it is said, 'with the exception of Napoleon, the most famous man in Europe', was the Prussian nobleman, Alexander von Humboldt. Early in his career Humboldt had intended to travel to Egypt with Napoleon's scholars and he had greatly admired the volumes of the *Description*. Thus, when Bunsen, the Prussian diplomat and scholar, had proposed that a protégé of his, Richard Lepsius, should undertake a national expedition to Egypt to collect and document the antiquities, Humboldt willingly joined with him to press the king, with whom he had great influence, to sanction the plan. Wilhelm IV was a romantic, an essentially old-fashioned monarch who did not believe in the political reforms that were being demanded throughout Europe at that time. The image of ancient Egypt, as it was revealed in contemporary scholarship greatly appealed to him. As Crown Prince, he had purchased a huge collection of Egyptian antiquities from Giuseppe Passalacqua who had gathered them principally at Thebes, where he had also pencilled his name in a fine copperplate hand in a tomb in the Valley. In 1843 Wilhelm sanctioned the project and Lepsius was appointed organizer and director.

It was a happy choice. Lepsius was a brilliant linguist and, like Champollion before him, had spent years in the European collections studying the available Egyptian material. He had the reputation of being the best egyptologist alive and a sound administrator. The grant awarded to him for the project must surely have surpassed his expectations. In the end, the expedition was a resounding success and immortalized the name of the King of Prussia on the elephantine volumes that stand as a true monument to Prussian scholarship and artistry. The expedition lasted for three years and travelled throughout Egypt, Nubia and Sinai. It visited Thebes from October 1844 until February 1845 and during that time drew and excavated in the Valley of the Kings.

Lavish as the expedition was, Lepsius sensibly chose not to duplicate the work of his predecessors but to enlarge and expand the corpus of published material. Thus, his excellent architect and surveyor, Erbkam, who was responsible for some of the finest plans ever to have been drawn in Egypt, did not map the Valley; this work having already been accomplished by the Napoleonic scholars. Neither were the tombs that the French had drawn resurveyed, but some of the monuments that had been ignored, being choked with dirt and chippings, were cleared and measured for the first time. Salt had never known the name of the king whose tomb in the Valley he had dug but Lepsius certainly understood that the tomb, which he also excavated, was that of the celebrated king, Ramesses II—'the Great' as he was then called. Like Salt before him, Lepsius would certainly have carried off the sarcophagus of the king had he found it, but like his predecessor, he did not. Erbkam made a plan of this large tomb and also mapped tomb 20, which Burton had partly cleared some twenty years before. Seti I's tomb was also surveyed for the first time and the beautiful plan in the publication belies the innaccuracies that, given the pressure of work upon Erbkam, were inevitable. An artist brought especially to Egypt by Lepsius to draw views of the ancient sites prepared a nondescript view of the Valley with dark, heavy shadows cast across the landscape in the manner of the day. The greatest contribution of the Prussian expedition to the documentation of the Valley was, however, the drawings of some of the wall and ceiling scenes which, although the accuracy of the smallest details may sometimes be wanting, have never been bettered for their mode of presentation and the sheer excellence of the published plates. In its clarity and skill the *Denkmäler aus*

Aegypten und Aethiopien has set the standard by which all such works have since been judged. Naturally, it was just a little larger than both the *Description* or the Franco-Tuscan volumes, a situation that later prompted the French scholar Mariette to remark that when he consulted the *Denkmäler* he needed the help of a corporal and four men.

The plates of the *Denkmäler* basically complement Champollion's work with more portraits and more copies of the finer offering scenes—with the focus always upon the kings themselves rather than the religious texts. Lepsius did, however, have two of the fine astronomical ceilings in the tombs drawn. Previously, Champollion had copied the inscriptions of another example, but Lepsius' artists drew the complicated patterns of grids and stars with sufficient accuracy to enable astronomers in Europe to calculate the dates that the star charts had been drawn from the pages of the published volumes.

The elaborate texts and diagrams on the star ceilings in the Valley of the Kings fall into two types: the drawings of the major constellations and the drawings of the star clocks by which the twelve hours of the night, the 'chapters' of the book of the journey of the Kings through the Underworld, were counted. As these stars moved round the heavens so the ancient calendar moved around the year. They might also have provided the ancient Egyptians with an accurate clock but the charts were not properly maintained and thus some of the star patterns painted in the royal tombs were hundreds of years out of date,

Although Lepsius' expedition made no new detailed survey, Erbkam included this small plan of the Valley as a part of his magnificent map of Thebes. It is a fine example of the excellence and accuracy both of the expedition fieldworkers and of the Prussian engravers and publishers

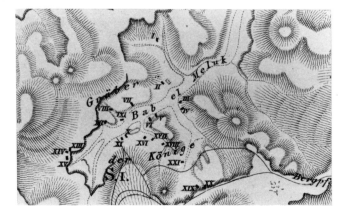

The centre of the astronomical ceiling (above) in the burial chamber of the tomb of Seti I. Some of the images drawn around the constellations of the ancient Egyptians have survived to this day as astrological signs

The decan figure of the 16th week of the month of Thoth. A detail from the astronomical ceiling in the tomb of Ramesses VI. The decan constellation is laid out in the grid to the right of the figure

having been observed at the beginning of the Eighteenth Dynasty.

In the tomb of Seti I the vaulted ceiling had large and splendidly drawn pictures of the constellations in the Egyptian sky, some of which are different from the ones recognized today. But some, the Great Bear, Cygnus, the Pleiades, and Scorpio among them, are recognizable but represented by different images: the Great Bear by an Ox (called the Ox's Leg), Cygnus by a man with arms outstretched, and so on. Planets were also recognized, called the 'stars that never rest' and some were identified with different aspects of the god Horus; the names given to the circumpolar stars also emphazises their connection with the royal destiny: 'the imperishable stars' are identified in religious texts as a part of the cosmos to which the dead king would join. The Dog Star, Sirius, is especially beloved by egyptological historians because it was the rising of this star that the ancient observers used to fix their New Year's Day. Happily, the small cumulative error of a quarter of a day per year that subsequently resulted from this arrangement sent the ancient civil year right around the seasons in a 1,460 year cycle, known as the Sothic Cycle. Thus, the ancient records that show the first day of the ancient civil year coinciding with the great rising of Sirius have given us the only absolute fixed dates in ancient Egyptian history.

The length of time that Sirius was invisible in the Egyptian sky—seventy days—was also roughly the period of time selected for the invisibility of the constellations of the Egyptian star calendar system. This was composed of thirty-six separate star groups known by scholars as the *decans*, which were selected so that they appeared in successive ten-day cycles. In this way the Egyptian civil year was measured out by the appearance of the *decans*: 36×10 days plus five additional days to give a 365-day year. The *decans* also marked the twelve hours of the night by their rising. Lepsius also recorded another simpler star-clock system in the later royal tombs derived from the *decans* that consisted of a star chart, represented in the form of a seated, full-faced giant figure, which recorded the positions of certain stars in their transits through the hours of the night. Above the drawing of this figure, a grid of lines held symbols that showed the positions of the stars which, with reference to the giant below, could then be described as being in the co-ordinates of 'opposite the heart', 'upon his left eye', 'the neck' or other locations. The centre line of the giant represented the meridian of the grid with the observer facing south.

Serious discrepancies between the civil year length and the difficulties of accurate sighting meant that the system could not function with the degree of accuracy necessary for modern requirements and in common with ancient Egyptian mathematics, it is full of errors. In the royal tombs the star charts, hundreds of years out of date, were painted for reasons of ritual rather than for practical time telling. As one observer has commented: 'It is appropriate to the Egyptian genius that the elegant pictorial element survived whilst the crude astronomical one vanished'. In due course the methods and calculations of Egyptian astronomy gave way to the more accurate Greek ones but its images formed a part of the astrological hieroglyphs of the Middle Ages and still survive in the Zodiac.

For his journey to Egypt, Lepsius had chosen to embark at Southampton, where, as Wilkinson remarked, 'the traveller will find greater comforts and less civility on board an English line than a foreign vessel'. Lepsius had collected two members of his expedition in England. One was a young architect, James Wild; the other, Joseph Bonomi, was an old Egypt hand who had worked with Hay in the Valley some eighteen years earlier. Bonomi had a wide and varied career in Egypt and his experience must have greatly aided Lepsius. A native of Rome, Bonomi was apprenticed in Piccadilly, London to Joseph Nollekins, the sculptor, and had made several celebrated memorials for a number of Indian Army officers which were erected in Calcutta Cathedral. After Nollekin's death in 1823 Bonomi returned to Rome, and then travelled to Egypt where he lived for many years drawing and exploring with the traveller-scholars. In the 1850s he was responsible for the erection of the huge plaster statuary in the Egyptian court at the Crystal Palace, a task he performed in company with Owen Jones, another of Hay's one-time draughtsmen and James Wild, then appointed as architect for the exhibition. Also at that time, Bonomi drew many of the pieces from Salt's collections for the publications of the British Museum, and the plates for Wilkinson's works and many others. A genial and popular man who could recall seeing in his youth Belzoni's exhibition of Seti I's tomb in Piccadilly, Bonomi was eventually appointed curator of the museum in Soane's house where he drew and lithographed the plates for the publication of the great alabaster coffin of Seti I, the centrepiece of the collection. After Bonomi died his post at the Soane Museum was filled by Wild who, until his death in 1892, was the last surviving member of the great Prussian expedition, some forty years before.

13

Scholars and Vandals

After the frantic efforts of the consular agents during the first quarter of the 19th century, excavation on a large scale in Thebes died down. Occasionally travellers still dug here and there and the villagers of Gurna plumbed the tombs in the hope of finding objects to sell, but the fascination with the study of the ancient language had greatly outstripped the work of excavation. Even after the visits and publications of the French and Prussian expeditions, Belzoni's *Narrative* remained a main source of archeological information on the royal tombs. Slowly, however, people became aware that carefully made and recorded excavations could greatly complement the records of the ancient culture that were revealed in the texts and could also provide information of a different sort. But the study of both the language and the archeology developed very slowly; it was not until the late 1850s that the Vicomte de Rougé formulated working methods that could be applied to ancient texts so that a standardized continuous translation might be obtained in modern languages; and it was exactly at this time that the beginnings of the practical science of excavation in Egypt could be detected in the work of Alexander Rhind, a young Edinburgh lawyer who had gone south for the benefit of his health and had become interested in Thebes and its archeology.

Rhind lived on Gurna, in Salt's old house, and made several excavations in that area as well as in the Valley of the Kings. He had studied the work of earlier excavators and recognized the need for careful recording of the processes of discovery. Probably for the first time in egyptology, Rhind had understood that an object that had been recorded in the position in which it was first found was of infinitely more value to science than the same object, anonymous, in a showcase of a European museum. Thus, while working on the hill of Gurna, Rhind made some remarkable discoveries which, for their day, are exceptionally well described. He recorded such accurate observations of some of his excavations that it is possible to identify what he had discovered although, at that time, Rhind himself was unable to furnish a proper explanation.

'From all times the Tombs of the Kings have been the central point of interest in the Theban Necropolis', remarked Rhind, and it is not, therefore, unexpected to find him digging in the Valley during the winter of 1855. Like others before him, he had speculated upon the probability of the existence of buried royal tombs and he re-read the classical texts that gave descriptions of the royal necropolis. Although he thought the Valley had been thoroughly searched he started work in some small areas that were still undisturbed with two gangs of twenty men each. The results were disappointing and he described his daily trip of inspection as 'a round of laborious duty unrelieved by interest'. Then one day, as he watched another of his excavations close to his house, a messenger ran down the path from Deir el Bahari to bring word that his workmen had found an entrance to a tomb.

Rhind immediately went to the excavation and found, to his delight, that the men had uncovered an area and chiselled rock face similar to that which stood above the tomb of Seti I close by. A palm frond, thrust into the sand at the edge of the face disappeared tantalizingly into the sand, 'Expectation was great, and the *fellahin* needed no stimulus beyond their own excitement to work with vigour'; watched by Rhind, they cleared away the loose sand from the chiselled rock face for two days. Then, to their great disappointment they discovered that the deceptive rock formation was, after all, a natural one and that the frond had simply probed a small fissure in the rock that ran deep into the ground. Rhind was dismayed, but his appetite for royal tombs had been whetted and he planned to set to work in the West Valley where, Wilkinson had speculated, there must surely be more tombs. Unfortunately at this point Rhind's health, never robust, broke down completely and he was forced to abandon work in such a remote location.

Rhind's instinctive sympathy for the antiquities in their ancient situations, his realization of the importance of the context of the monuments and their contents also led him to ponder the effects of the antiquity collectors upon the monuments. Some five years before Rhind arrived in Egypt, the American Consul in Cairo, George Gliddon, had published a pamphlet: *An Appeal to the Antiquaries of Europe on the Destruction of the Monuments of Egypt*, in which he had brought the problem to the attention of many people for the first time. Unfortunately Gliddon was already known in Cairo for his outspokenness on a wide range of subjects and no one had taken much notice of his arguments. Indeed, since the earlier days of the consular rivalry at the ancient sites the whole issue seemed to have died down and the vast collections of statuary and ancient objects were no longer being assembled. But a new problem had arisen with the decipherment of hieroglyphs. Now the hitherto meaningless inscriptions upon the ancient walls were suddenly transformed into valuable historical documents and scholars were keen to remove examples of the finest quality to the European collections. While they were in Egypt both Champollion and Rosellini had gathered many antiquities of this type and the collections of the Grand Duke of Tuscany at Florence and the museums of France were greatly enriched.

The Valley of the Kings suffered particularly from a type of looting that it had not undergone in the past. Perhaps it was because Champollion and Rosellini were fresh in Egypt and regarded the monuments of the Valley as being in such a remote location that they felt at liberty to so deface the tombs. At the foot of the stair that ran down from the first pillared hall in the tomb of Seti I, they had the two door jambs of the corridor sawn from the walls. It was the beginning of a spiteful tradition of despoiling the antiquities which, though illegal, has continued to this day. The soft limestone of the Valley is an easy material to cut with a steel saw and the work would not have taken them long. Today, the left-hand door jamb is in Florence, the right one in the Louvre. The fragments from the tomb that had fallen from the walls when it had flooded and which Belzoni had

A drawing, by one of Hay's draughtsmen of the stairway from the lower sections of the tomb of Seti I to the 'Hall of Beauties'. Here, the two door jambs at the bottom of the steps still have the beautiful reliefs that were later cut from the walls by the Champollion and Rosellini expedition

A recent photograph of a wall in the tomb of Amenhotep III showing the defaced paintings, scarred by collectors, bats, flooding, and the torches and fires of visitors

gathered together and left in the tomb, were also examined; Rosselini took one for his Duke. In the West Valley it is, unfortunately, highly likely that some of the heads of the King which Champollion had so admired and which were beautifully copied by his friend Nestor L'Hôte and published in the *Monuments*, were also cut from the wall at this time. Robbed of their royal heads the paintings, each with white rectangles where the portraits were removed, make an unhappy sight and there is little incentive now to restore the tomb and clean the blackened

paintings when a major element of the decoration has been removed. Shortly after Champollion's death some of these portraits were presented to the National Collections of France, by his friend Letronne. The monuments were suffering because they had been deciphered; the knowledge, for example, that the owner of the decrepit tomb in the West Valley was none other than Amenophis 'the Magnificent' and the great interest in portraiture, had prompted the desecration and in Egypt at that time there were few controls and no concern about such matters.

Appeals had been made to Mohammed Ali Pasha to control such depredations but he was puzzled: 'How can I do so, and why should you ask me, since Europeans themselves are their chief enemies?' Now this was, to some extent, true but at the same time the rapid erection of factories to process sugar cane in Upper Egypt had caused the destruction of many ancient monuments that were used for foundations and rendered into quicklime. European collectors could counter criticism by maintaining that they were actually protecting the ancient heritage from further destruction by transferring it to the safety of their museum! It is an argument still offered by some people today, and in the 1840s it may have made some sense.

There was also a growing problem arising from the increasing number of visitors. In 1845, while on a tour of the Valley, Isabella Romer found that the entrance to the tomb of Ramesses VI was of such a gradual and easy slope 'that I was able to ride my donkey through its long and spacious galleries to the first chamber', where presumably she dismounted and left the animal to stand stabled in the chariot hall while she explored lower in the tomb. In order to supply a better light in the large vaulted burial chamber of Seti I's tomb, the guide obligingly 'set fire to a pile of dried brushwood of which he keeps a provision there for that purpose, and the merry blaze it threw around lighted up every corner of the chamber'. The bright clean walls were sooted with the dirt from the flames of the tourists' fires and torches, some of the visitors even recording their names with the smoke from their lights on the low ceilings of the tomb's side chambers, where they can still be seen. Wealthier tourists brought strips of magnesium to the tomb which burnt briefly, but with a sharp white light and intense smoke. During the visits of the Prince and Princess of Wales in the 1860s hundreds of them were burnt in the tomb of Seti I alone. One member of the Duke's first party commented:

*Ours is probably
the last generation which
will be permitted to see the glory of
Egyptian sculpture, as they were first
revealed to the explorers at the beginning
of the century . . . the smoke of the
travellers' torches and the disfigurement by
travellers' names, and the injury by travellers'
spoliations, have rendered the 'fine gold dim' in
many of the paintings and inscriptions.*

It was, indeed, a melancholy fate that the royal
tombs were now having to suffer. Scores of books
such as Isabella Romer's were encouraging more and
more tourists to visit Thebes and the Valley, a development that eventually led to the establishment of
Luxor as a major tourist resort. Although it was not
until the 1880s that Thomas Cook's company
started to invest heavily in the hospitals and the
hotels of the town, the travel bureau had been
operating 'Cook's tours' down the Nile on steam boats
since 1840.

The final realization of the need of legislation to
protect the antiquities came some years after Lepsius'
expedition had left Egypt. So splendid had his expedition been and, as a major Prussian diplomatic mission,
so courteously received in Cairo, that Mohammed Ali
had given him the pick of Egyptian antiquities, with
government labour and barges to transport his collections back to Germany. Fifteen thousand antiquities
were taken to Berlin, officially presented by Mohammed Ali to the King of Prussia. It was a major part of
the work of the expedition and one that Lepsius
vigorously defended on the grounds that others were
doing the same thing clandestinely and that his was a
scientific collection made by scientists for a major public museum. The openness of Lepsius' activities and the
unfavourable publicity that they provoked attracted
attention to the whole problem of the traffic in
antiquities. In 1857 Auguste Mariette, a curator at
the Louvre who himself had been sent to Egypt to
collect, appealed to the Khedive Said to establish an
organization to tend the standing monuments of
Egypt and to found a museum to hold those antiquities that were in need of greater protection. Strongly
backed by his Consul-General and prominent French
businessmen in Egypt, Mariette was given a grant

for the work and a house at Bulak, a small port on
the outskirts of Cairo, for his museum. It would be
the first national museum in the Middle East.

For Westerners of the day Cairo was a real novelty;
within a three-day journey by steam boat from
Europe all the splendours and mysteries of a great
Islamic city could be enjoyed from the comfortable
terraces of modern hotels and fine villas. The tourist
trade was large and increasing yearly. Originally
drawing upon the resources established to cater for
the overland route to India, by the 1870s it was

turning into a grand industry in its own right. Innumerable guide and travel books were popularizing the delights of the country, and the land was considered to be one of the healthiest places in the world. The journey up the Nile, which thirty years earlier had taken several months, could now be made in a few weeks or less with the introduction of river steamers and a railway system. In the 1840s all travellers had eaten around the same table in Mr Shepheard's Hotel, but by the late 1870s European society with all its fads and manners had arrived and, well away from the feudal country system of peasantry and Turkish overlords, this new transient society ran an efficient and enterprising system, like smart new paint on an old house. However, this measure of modernity had been bought at an appalling price. Many of the schemes were financed by British and French interests who extracted the maximum rewards from a country that lacked many of the fiscal controls of European law. By the 1870s the country was near to bankruptcy and its lifeblood, the agricultural resources, were badly run down. An indigenous nationalist movement was taking shape.

Mariette's career in Egypt spanned this second phase of national development. He moved with his family to Cairo in 1856 and lived there until his death some twenty-five years later. During his extraordinary career he supervised excavations at thirty-five major sites and, with the aid of a group of loyal assistants, such as Bonnefoy at Thebes, he stopped the wholesale depredation of the monuments and created the foundations of the *Service des Antiquités* which, transformed and greatly enlarged, is still in existence today. Never again would national treasures be taken in such copious quantities to other countries and all the excavations undertaken in Egypt were agreed between Mariette and the excavator. In the field Mariette's methods were crude, very much of their day and possibly inferior to those being employed by excavators elsewhere at that time, but he did stop large-scale looting for ever.

At Thebes he excavated the treasures of some of the Seventeenth Dynasty Kings, rescuing some of the jewellery from the harem of the Governor of the Province at the town of Kena, for a place in his museum. He had whole temples cleared of choking rubbish and dirt and began the long job of putting the ruins of ancient Egypt back together again. It is not generally realized by the visitor how much of the ancient architecture is restored, or how much monuments such as the royal tombs owe their present existence to Mariette and the *Service des Antiquités*.

He was 'rather a stern and terrifying figure with his great height, his red tarboosh [fez], his stern face, his staccato talk and his tinted spectacles, but when he was in the mood he sparked with wit and gaiety'. As well as his herculean labours with the antiquities Mariette was the joint author of the libretto for Verdi's opera *Aida*, commissioned by the Khedive Said for the great festival that accompanied the opening of the Suez Canal in 1869. After his death his body was placed in a great Egyptianesque sarcophagus brought, curiously enough, from France, and he lies today in the grounds of the great Cairo Museum (hereinafter called the Museum) that is the successor to the one which he founded and which he filled with so many of its most famous works of art.

Mariette did not excavate in the Valley, but he certainly saved it from further depredations. Virtually nothing has been removed from the walls of the royal tombs since Mariette's time, and the attentions of the guardians of the *Service* has helped to save them from the casual damage of visitors. In a small guide to Upper Egypt, which Mariette wrote to complement Wilkinson's *Topography*, he devoted pages to such subjects as 'respect for the monuments' and 'the vandalism of tourists', recording for their lasting shame some eminent people who had written their names in large letters, sometimes with tar and brush, across the front of temples and tombs. He noted that some of the tombs had suffered more during the 1860s than in all the millennia of their previous existence. Seti I's tomb, he observed, is 'almost entirely disfigured'. Yet today what would one give to see the tomb even in the condition that Mariette described one hundred years ago! Mariette too, believed that the West Valley held the tombs of the Eighteenth Dynasty Kings 'and is alone worth exploring, pick axe in hand' but he added that 'all excavations are interdicted in Egypt and no permissive firman [Ottoman permit] has even been given'.

Mariette continued: 'one might imagine that opportunities of purchasing papyri can never present themselves. Such, however is not the case'. He was disturbed about illicit excavations that were being conducted by villagers which resulted in a continuous traffic in small, sometimes valuable antiquities such as papyri, a business in which some of his friends and employees were themselves deeply involved. Mariette was hard on this trade, confiscating all antiquities offered for sale that were known to have been recently discovered, but once they had been bought by Europeans he was virtually powerless, and with the failing finances of the Khedival Government the resources of his *Service* could not maintain the increased surveillance that became necessary with the steady increase in tourist traffic.

During the 1870s many unusual objects began to appear on the international market, antiquities that had obviously come from a royal tomb. Mariette himself had negotiated with a dealer from Suez the purchase of two papyri for his museum, papyri that came from this tomb. He felt that papyri were especially precious antiquities:

> *We have no advice to give to those travellers who wish to buy antiquities and take them home as souvenirs of their visit to Egypt. They will find more than one excellent factory at Luxor. But to travellers who really wish to turn their journey to some account, we would recommend the search after papyri.*

Many of these ancient written scrolls had been dug from city ruins by villagers taking the rich earth of the ancient decayed mud bricks to fertilize their fields. As a possible source of historical information such documents held enormous potential.

The papyri that Mariette had bought at Suez were different; these were two large rolls that had accompanied the mummy of a Theban queen, Henutowy, to her grave. They contained ritual information essential to the dead if they were to succeed in the ancient afterlife. Such papyri were usually about a foot wide and sometimes over one hundred feet long. They were filled with texts—columns of hieroglyphs interspersed with carefully drawn scenes of a ritual and funereal nature. 'Gods and demons of the next world, a farrago of wild mythology and amulitic defence' as one bemused scholar later commented, but they held the very keys to the Egyptian afterlife. Such papyri, especially those with fine pictures painted on them, like the two that Mariette had bought at Suez, were greatly sought after by museums and collectors because they were often magnificent examples of the most ancient books and the illustrations, both in their quality and their subject matter,

A scene from another papyrus from the plundered burial of Queen Maatkare. This shows her funeral procession in the lower register, and above, she is receiving offerings

were similar to the scenes in some of the famous tombs. In Mariette's day, as more and more marvellous examples of these funerary papyri appeared upon the market, they commanded prices of up to £400 per roll.

In 1876, Gaston Maspero, a professor at the College de France, received from a friend some photographs of a papyrus that had been offered for sale by an antiquities dealer in Beirut. It was another of the same type that Mariette had bought at Suez, this one made for another queen, Nojmet, the grandmother of Henutowy and the sister and wife of Herihor, a member of the priestly family that had succeeded the Ramesside kings at Thebes. The dealer, Antoun Wardi, eventually divided it into three pieces to sell separately and these pieces are now in the Louvre, the British Museum and the Munich Egyptological Museum. That same year Maspero was shown another complete papyrus by General Archibald Campbell, an Englishman who had bought it during a trip to Egypt undertaken to observe the transit of Venus. It had also been bought from Wardi and it had been made to accompany the mummy of King Pinejem II, another member of the same royal family, and probably a grandson of Queen Henutowy. Many ushabtis of this same king were also appearing on the European antiquities market. Now, Wardi had lived for a time on Gurna and since the kings and queens of the papyri were Theban, it was obvious that either a family vault had been uncovered or that a whole series of tombs had been found and Wardi was selling off their contents.

Two years later Maspero published in a scientific journal an interesting hieroglyphic text that guaranteed another member of the same royal family all the privileges normally reserved for those who had been judged 'good' in the afterlife. The inscription was written upon a small wooden plaque, probably originally part of a coffin, and it was one of three that were eventually sold to European collections. In his article Maspero stated openly that the panel had come from the tomb 'close to the as yet unlocated tombs of the Herihor family'. However, at this time Mariette, an old and ill man, was not interested in returning to work again at Thebes and was attempting to open the smaller Old Kingdom Pyramids built above Memphis which had been closed since ancient times. Perhaps he hoped to crown his long career with a final magnificent discovery, for he had begun his excavations in Egypt in the same area by uncovering the extraordinary subterranean labyrinth cemetery of the Apis bulls, which had caused a sensation some twenty years before.

In France there was concern that on Mariette's death the directorship of the *Service* that he had created, should remain in French hands, thus continuing the brilliant tradition initiated by Champollion. Acting on advice from their diplomatic officials in Cairo, the French Government voted a sum of money for the creation of a French School of Archeology in Cairo and Professor Maspero was appointed its first director. He left Paris for Cairo in 1881 with two of his young ex-students of egyptology and two arabists. When Maspero arrived in Cairo, Mariette was mortally ill. The old man was still very concerned about his excavations, however, and shortly before he died his friend Heinrich Brugsch, the great German egyptologist, told him that two of the pyramids that the *Service* had succeeded in penetrating contained unexpected treasure; the interior walls were covered with inscriptions, the first ever found inside the pyramids. Later, Maspero had three more of these inscribed pyramids opened which contained more texts and slowly, over a twelve-year period, he collected and translated all the examples that were known. The 'Pyramid Texts' as they are now called, are the most ancient religious literature of Egypt. They provided a much needed key for the study of later religious texts that were, in part, derived from them.

Very early in his work on the pyramid texts Maspero realized the great importance of the texts that covered the walls of the royal tombs in the Valley of the Kings. During the 1880s these were still lying unexamined and the observation of Dean Stanley in 1856 was still completely true: 'Only a very small proportion of the mythical pictures of the tombs of the kings has ever been represented in engravings. The mythology of Egypt, even now, strange to say, can be studied only in the caverns of the Valley of the Kings.'

However, such scholarly concerns as these were overshadowed by the uncovering at Thebes of probably the most extraordinary archeological find of that, if not any, century and once again the Valley of the Kings was looked upon by archeologists as a site with potential where fresh discoveries might be made and new tombs found.

14

The Royal Cache

Maspero had already decided to search for the plundered royal tomb before he had arrived in Egypt. The task would not entail excavation for no one except the robbers knew where to start such work, but a careful, persistent, enquiry conducted among the modern inhabitants of Thebes, from where all this valuable material was coming. Egypt was very new to Maspero who had not yet visited Thebes and obviously he had to rely largely upon the help and advice of old-established Egypt hands. These were principally the Marquis de Rochemonteix, a French diplomat who had worked closely with Mariette since 1875, and Heinrich Brugsch's younger brother Émile, Mariette's assistant who knew the antiquities trade well. De Rochemonteix, an ex-student of Maspero's had lived in Upper Egypt for some years and as a member of that small enclosed society must have had a good idea exactly who was peddling the royal antiquities. Maspero also enlisted the help of another newcomer to Egypt, Charles E. Wilbour, an American who, after a chequered career in New York politics, had abandoned the USA for egyptology and became a student of Maspero's in Paris. As a wealthy tourist showing an interest in the antiquities market, Wilbour, who greatly enjoyed dabbling in the trade with all its dramas and gossip, might well be shown antiquities from the unknown tomb and he would try to locate the source of the precious objects.

Other pieces from the unknown royal tomb were constantly being sold. When Maspero first arrived in Egypt a funerary papyrus of a princess had just been bought by an English building contractor working on Alexandria Harbour. This magnificent specimen, subsequently presented to the British Museum and called the Greenfield Papyrus, is the longest example known to have survived from ancient times, being over 123 feet long when completely unrolled. It contains more ritual texts than any other single papyrus and its pretty vignettes are wonderful examples of the free and intimate drawings of the ancient artists.

At Luxor, too, tourists had been buying objects and papyri from the unknown tombs for some time.

A papyrus roll from the plundered burial. This magnificent text—written in a cursive form of hieroglyphic called hieratic by scholars—did not command as much money as illustrated papyri and so the tomb robbers found it more difficult to sell. It was made for Queen Eskhons

In 1874 Amelia Edwards, a well-known writer of the day who later devoted years of her life to raising funds for excavations, had bargained with a 'grave arab' for yet another papyrus, this one accompanied by a mummy! But the grave Arab was playing Miss Edwards' party off against another group of visitors who were also sailing up the Nile. The outcome of these protracted and thrillingly illegal negotiations was, as Miss Edwards announced, that the Misses Brocklehurst 'bought both mummy and papyrus at an enormous price; and then unable to endure the perfume of the ancient Egyptian they drowned the dear departed at the end of the week'. One wonders if it was the mummy of a king that was sacrificed to the ladies' sensibilities.

Amelia Edwards' party had to console themselves with a hoard of fine blue royal ushabtis, a wooden figure with a small papyrus roll in a panel in its back and a score of tall vases all inscribed for the same family of kings and queens. It was, of course, well known that it was illegal to buy antiquities; a fact that must have added zest to the whole proceedings of inspecting and bargaining for such regal relics.

Before their game was up, the local Theban dealers had sold hundreds of the precious antiquities from these royal tombs to more than thirty private collectors. And these objects really were precious, for nothing like them had been seen before. Further, the excellent condition of the numerous papyri gave a strong indication that the tomb or tombs, were very well preserved, at least until the recent rediscovery. Now the burials were being stripped of their small valuable antiquities year by year and it was imperative to discover them as soon as possible before they were completely emptied or destroyed by the villagers to hide the last evidences of their plundering.

Wilbour, who had left Cairo as Mariette lay dying in his house by the Museum, arrived at Thebes by steamboat on 21 January 1881 and put up at the Luxor Hotel. Between gazing at distant views of the landscape and the magnificent temples 'looking wonderfully like their photographs' he attended a *fantasia*—an Arab party of dancing girls, coffee and sweet cakes—given by the Vice-Consular Agent at Luxor for Britain, Belgium and Russia. Mustafa Aga Ayat, the ubiquitous Vice-Consul lived in a house which, according to William Russell, the reporter from *The Times* who had been entertained there as a member of a party of the Prince of Wales, was 'planted like a swallows nest against the eaves of the Luxor Temple'. When Wilbour attended the *fantasia*, probably at the prompting of De Rochemonteix, Mustafa had been a Vice-Consul for more than forty years. In that time he had befriended the much-celebrated Lady Duff Gordon during her last lingering illness and had been friend and host to a great number of other travellers and scholars. Mustafa was, 'next to the ruins, the best known object in Luxor', according to Russell, and he dispensed his hospitality, always in the Arab manner, with a charm and good humour that is typical of so many of his race. As British Vice-Consul in the largest tourist resort in Egypt after Cairo, he had a difficult and sensitive job that he performed with great tact and discretion, soothing arguments and helping bewildered tourists. He was also, Wilbour

soon discovered, with his son, at the centre of the trade in antiquities, an occupation that he shared with some of his Vice-Consular colleagues who stocked antiquities 'for the convenience of travellers'. However, local gossip told that Mustafa had gone much further. With a family who lived on the hill of Gurna, he was slowly selling the treasures from the unknown royal tomb. Mustafa was, however, protected from the law of Egypt and the processes of interrogation by his consular status and so it was necessary to discover the next link in the chain; the source of Mustafa's antiquities.

Six days after the Vice-Consul's *fantasia*, while Wilbour was sightseeing in the Temple of Karnak, a dragoman, or local guide, told him that a certain Ahmed Abd er Rassul had a papyrus and 'lots of good things to sell', so the next day he went to a house on the hill of Gurna to see what was for sale. 'After much preparation of coffee, etc. in the little white house behind the Ramesseum [the temple of Ramesses II, the Memnonium], we were ushered into a gate closed tomb and seated whilst a funerary papyrus in an admirable state of preservation was unfolded inch by inch to me.' Abd er Rassul asked £350, slightly less than the others, but then this one had no pictures drawn upon it. Wilbour thought that the papyrus had already been cut into several pieces and this portion was a long religious text which did not interest him. He wrote to a friend in Cairo describing the roll and received a reply that it was 'not worth forty pounds'; a comment which comforted Wilbour in his own judgement. In the same post he also received a modest letter from Maspero telling him that following Mariette's death, he had been appointed his successor. The French and British Consuls had, on this occasion, jointly pressed the Khedive to make the appointment and now Maspero would quickly establish himself in the post by investigating the looting of these royal tombs and, he hoped, start his new career with a major archeological coup.

A week later, while he was visiting some of the private tombs of Gurna, Wilbour was shown two leather straps, mummy wrappings which had decorated the folds of the outer shrouds. Embossed into their fine red leather were the cartouches of Pinejem I 'so fresh that they must have been opened lately and I am going to try to find the tomb, now unknown except to the *fellahs* [villagers] who found it'. At first Wilbour had thought it was the cartouche of another king but Maspero, to whom he had sent a copy of the inscription, had read the names correctly. Wilbour then telegraphed Maspero in Cairo for permission to dig for the tomb but in reply Maspero said that he would shortly be arriving in Luxor himself.

While Wilbour waited for Maspero he asked the villagers who had shown him the leather straps to take him to the tomb and show him the mummy from which they had been taken. The *fellahs*, realizing that they had made a mistake in showing the straps to the inquisitive scholar in the first place, obligingly produced a mummy in a small tomb which, they said, was the one. Wilbour was not impressed with their mummy, but was further bemused by Mustafa who, in a burst of confidence, told him of a fabulous tomb that he had discovered out in the desert. Everyone in Luxor knew by this time that Mariette had died and that his successor Maspero had left Cairo by boat and was coming to Upper Egypt. By this time Wilbour was on such good terms with Mustafa that the Vice-Consul was taking some of his freshly acquired antiquities to him for translations and comments! Nervously, Mustafa put it to Wilbour that he should ask his friend Maspero to grant them both an official permit to dig in Upper Egypt and then they could split the proceeds of the work with the Museum!

Maspero arrived in Luxor on 3 April. He had come with a large party which included Émile Brugsch, now his assistant at the Museum, de Rochemonteix, and the two egyptologists who had come with him from France—Loret and Bouriant. It had been a leisurely cruise, the first of many excursions that the officers of the department would undertake in the steam boat of the *Service*, *Nimro Hadacher*, Number Eleven as she was known along the river bank, a fine old boat that in the 1840s had been one of the first steamers on the Nile. On these trips the *Service* archeologists and scholars would take their wives, relatives and friends, journalists and occasionally Wilbour, who wrote with great affection of their good company, the fine library on board and the delights of the cruise.

Egyptologists in the Temple of Luxor, close to Maspero's boat mooring. Left to right: de Rochemonteix, Gayet (a student of Maspero's and a member of the French archeological mission), Insinger (a friend of Maspero's and a resident of Luxor), Wilbour, and Maspero

On Maspero's first night in Luxor Wilbour joined the party on board where he was warmly welcomed by his old professor. It was an unusual combination: Maspero—a brilliant, hard working ambitious professor just embarked on a new career fraught with diplomatic and scholarly rivalries and Wilbour—with his long white beard looking older than his forty-eight years, a kindly, if somewhat cynical figure, in happy retirement from a business career in New York. They ate their supper together sitting on deck looking across the Nile to the great golden line of cliffs that framed the cultivation and behind which the Valley of the Kings, and probably their unknown royal tomb, lay. Maspero invited his American friend to join them on their trip which was to continue to Aswan and then return to Cairo. Wilbour was to occupy a small cabin on the boat, which Madame Maspero had completely renovated for the trip. She was, Wilbour notices, tired; unused to Egypt and its climate and looking forward to returning to Paris in a month or so.

Wilbour was pleased to see his friends, but some of the other inhabitants of Thebes were very apprehensive about the arrival of the new *Mudir*, the new Director of the *Service*. For ten years the Abd er Rassuls had held the secret of their tomb but as their profits had mounted from the treasures and the papyri were displayed in the finest museums of Europe, their chances of remaining anonymous were greatly diminished. One Gurna dealer told Wilbour that 'Mohammed Abd er Rassul, whose house is next to his, found some years ago a tomb in which there were £40,000 worth of antiquities'; he himself 'saw with these eyes' thirty-six papyri from it. They could all feel the tension mounting in the air and they wanted to disassociate themselves from the whole business. The villagers, on the other hand, could feel the long exploited wealth of the tomb slipping away from them. It was as if they knew that Maspero had come to take their treasure away, as indeed he had.

For the villagers of Upper Egypt, life had been very hard for many years. The Khedive Ismail, by his indebtedness to his creditors, had lost the control of the government and Egypt was virtually in the hands of a group of European banks. In 1879 one of these bankers decided that Ismail should go, and subsequently he was deposed by order of the Sultan in Istanbul; his son Tewfik assumed the office with greatly reduced authority and the vast Khedival estates were placed in the hands of receivers. The ever mounting debts incurred by the Khedive had been paid by constantly increasing the taxation in his country. The main burden had fallen upon the peasants and in one of the most fertile places in the world, the people whose labours had supported his whole lavish system of government, were now reduced to near starvation, unable to afford to buy the wheat from their own fields. There was, in Upper Egypt, a famine of money.

For the villagers of Thebes, the tomb represented an extraordinary source of wealth during this terrible period, for in the strong extended family units in Egyptian village life the money from the sale of the illicit antiquities ensured that the entire family, about a fifth of the village, would never, like so many of their contemporaries, suffer or starve for lack of money. The family had already built a new house, close by Wilkinson's old house on the hill of Gurna, with an arched courtyard where the men could sit and talk on long wooden benches and the family ceremonies of circumcisions, funeral wakes and religious festivals were held. It was the house that Wilbour had visited to view the papyrus the family had offered to sell to him, and there, during a later visit he had written out a sign for them: 'The New White House, Abd er Rassul, Proprietor'. In the pages of Wilbour's diary one can sense the mounting apprehension with which the members of the family had greeted the arrival of the new *Mudir*, and in befriending Wilbour they obviously hoped to win over a friend to their cause. But Wilbour, fresh in Egypt, did not understand their anxieties.

On the day after Maspero arrived he visited Wilbour at the Luxor Hotel. As the friends drank lemonade under the arches of the verandah and Madame Maspero picked roses from the flamboyant tropical gardens, Maspero sent an order for the arrest of Ahmed Abd er Rassul to the Chief of Police in Luxor, and a telegram to the Governor of Kena and the Ministry of Works requesting permission to open an enquiry against Ahmed and his family.

Ahmed was brought to Maspero's steamer and interrogated by Brugsch and De Rochemonteix, but to no avail. Ahmed was told that he had been named by many tourists as the person who had been selling papyri and ushabtis from a grand tomb, but he denied all knowledge of such a place. Guided by his two tough colleagues, Maspero held up the threat of interrogation with the accompanying prospect of torture and imprisonment at Kena to frighten Ahmed into revealing the location of the tomb, but the brave Abd er Rassul denied any knowledge of the matter and left the boat that evening for 'The New White House' on Gurna.

The gardens in front of the Luxor Hotel, from a contemporary postcard

Oblivious of all this, Wilbour decided the next day to make a little excavation of his own and have a private tomb chapel dug out from the debris which buried it. He crossed the river and visited Ahmed who, ever anxious to help, showed him where the tomb lay and gathered together some men for the work. Wilbour left them to dig away while he walked to the foot of the path that led over the cliffs to the Valley of the Kings. There he met Maspero with his party who had been visiting the Valley for the first time. Together they walked back to the tomb which they found the workmen had cleared and settled down to copy the inscriptions. Ahmed appeared with 'coffee and a cloud of Arabs' and later they left for Luxor after a pleasant day.

Some of Maspero's party now believed that 'The New White House' on Gurna was built over the tomb itself; the family tomb, they suspected, of Pinejem I, and Maspero had accepted Ahmed's offer, made during the interrogation to search it but they found nothing but a small hole in the floor with a few worthless antiquities in it. In the evening Wilbour went off to Mustafa's for a feast of lamb, turkey and apple pie and there he was told by his host that Ahmed had finally been arrested.

Next day Maspero received the full warrant to open the official enquiry against the Abd er Rassul family and again Ahmed and a brother, Hussein, stood before the Frenchman. Yet they would not talk, and after a few more days were sent in chains to Kena, the provincial capital, to be further questioned by the Governor. He, a successor of Mohammed Aga, who had visited Belzoni in the tomb of Seti I, was Daud Pasha, a man feared throughout the province over which he had absolute control. Daud had taxed the province, already the poorest in the land, so heavily that in the late 1870s many villagers had starved. Tourists, who had found the price of food so low, were surprised to find people dying of hunger in the streets of Kena itself. Daud Pasha's reputation for the pursuit of justice was widely feared and, in the case of Ahmed and Hussein, their trials were, as Maspero reported, 'soundly pursued'; one of the brothers subsequently limped for the rest of his life as a result, it was said, of having the skin torn in strips from the soles of his feet. Many of the notables of Gurna and Luxor went to Kena to testify on the brothers' behalf. They were, they said, honourable men from a fine old family. For their

133

part, Ahmed and his brother claimed that they were in the employ of Mustafa Aga and vainly tried to invoke the same diplomatic immunity that the Vice-Consul enjoyed, but to little effect and they were thrown into prison and left to meditate upon their fate.

Maspero, returning to Paris in early June as he had planned, had left a country in a state of near revolt. The general condition of Egypt and the lack of pay and prospects in the army had led to the rise of a new armed nationalist movement that the Khedive Tewfik was quite unable to control. Anxiously, the great powers looked on as the government, which was so indebted to them, collapsed in a welter of outrage and anger. In their 'White House' the Abd er Rassul family had other problems. After two months of imprisonment, Daud Pasha had provisionally released the two brothers into the custody of two Gurna elders and they returned to their village having told nothing of the tomb. However, Maspero, Brugsch and de Rochemonteix had left the Abd er Rassuls in no doubt that if they did not surrender their treasure, they would have to face another enquiry the following year, possibly of an even more vigorous nature. The family argued and quarrelled about the situation for it was obvious that the Vice-Consul could not protect them from the Governor, as they had hoped. Then, the eldest of the brothers and the head of the family, Mohammed, went by himself to Kena and told Daud Pasha that he knew the whereabouts of the site, which had eluded the authorities for so long. He said it was a single tomb that contained not one or two mummies but about forty, and many of the coffins had golden serpents upon their heads, the sign of kingship. Daud Pasha immediately informed the Minister of the Interior who, in his own turn, told the Khedive Tewfik. Though Maspero had left for France, his assistant Brugsch had been invested with the necessary powers of action and left for Luxor with two other assistants.

First they visited Daud Pasha at Kena and much to their surprise were presented with three huge funerary papyri, all inscribed for members of the same royal family as the earlier examples that had been sold on the antiquities market. Daud had taken

The small valley just south of Deir el Bahari, where the royal cache was hidden. The great shaft that leads to the tomb is hidden in the chimney in the cliffs at the end of the bay, to the right of the centreline of the picture.

them from the Abd er Rassul house during a search. Doubtless the brothers had rifled the tomb for the last time before informing the authorities and Daud, outwitting them, had searched the house immediately after Mohammed's confession. In the company of some of Daud Pasha's soldiers the three arrived at Luxor on 4 June where, in the heat of summer, the temperature must have been well above $100°F$ both day and night.

Two days later the three men were taken by Mohammed and a group of workmen to a remote and arid bay which lay behind the hill of Gurna. In a yellow desert landscape of patinated limestone, chalk and sand, two long ridges of rock stuck out from the high cliffs like the two arms of a great sphinx. The northern arm, about five hundred feet long, is, on its outer side, a part of the great circle of cliffs that contain the temples of Deir el Bahari. Up the centre of the southern arm runs a precipitous path that is a short cut over the high cliffs to the Valley of the Kings behind. It is a dangerous climb, but one still made daily by the guardians of the royal tombs as they go to and fro from their work. Unbeknown to them, it has been christened 'Agatha Christie's Path' as it figured in one of her stories of criminal detection set around the tombs of ancient Egypt. During the Middle Kingdom, hundreds of years before the Valley of the Kings was used for royal burials, the rocks high up on this path were inscribed by priests as they stood waiting for a first sighting of the golden temple barges that were carrying the Gods of the eastern bank on trips to their counterparts across the river. But the slender sun-baked valley that these ancient priests overlooked was completely remote from any of the works of man. Its steep shadowed sides and long blank terraces led nowhere but to the bottom of the face of the great cliffs. The bay is a sun trap, seldom cold; the rocks are warm to the touch, the sand hot and springy underfoot. The steep sides cut off all sound from the nearby temples and villages; the noises of the living. It is a lonely but strangely hospitable place, quiet, uncommunicative, undisclosed.

For a short while the party of men walked along this valley's floor, then, guided by Mohammed, they took a path that ran along the inside of its northern arm. This they followed until they were almost at the foot of the great cliffs at the head of the bay. Then, suddenly, the path turned sharply right between two large rocks and they arrived in a small nook hidden in the apparently sheer rock face. Above them a natural chimney rose 150 feet to the top of the ridge. To their right was the top of a rough rectangular

0   10   20
m

A plan of the huge tomb; originally excavated to hold the burial of an Eighteenth Dynasty queen, the tomb was enlarged to take the royal mummies

shaft, about ten feet across and eight feet wide. This dropped nearly forty feet and its smooth sides were laced with cracks and small fissures on which large jagged fragments of loose rock were perched. The ancient masons who had cut this shaft had utilized a natural rock fault that ancient floods had eroded to form the great chimney which rose above them. The edges of the shaft were dangerously sloped and slippery, covered in loose stones and small rocks and the narrow chimney limited the space around its edge.

Carefully, Mohammed bridged the top of the shaft with a palm log that his men had carried with them; then they tied a rope around it and descended to inspect the sand and debris that covered the floor. Soon his men had cleared this away and the tomb was surrendered to Brugsch and his two assistants. Led by Mohammed they were lowered into the shaft. At the bottom was a tiny doorway which gave access to a low corridor that ran northwards through the rock. Dropping to their knees the party of men led by Brugsch scrambled through the opening, which was less than three feet high. Just inside and half filling the corridor lay a huge whitewashed coffin decorated in yellow paint and inscribed for a priest, Nibsony. Behind this mummiform box, with the carved head of the ancient priest appearing rather bashfully over his crossed arms on the cover, lay three more coffins of a finer quality. Brugsch inched carefully past these bulky objects and, lighting a candle, turned right into a second corridor and away from the light in the shaft. This long corridor, though as narrow as the first, was much higher but although they could stand they still had to bend over to walk down the irregular passage that was strewn with numberless antiquities among which the fine blue glazes of the ancient faiences and glass glittered in the light of their candles. After some seventy feet they went down a short flight of steps that led into a taller corridor, in one of whose walls a chamber had been cut. This room, more than seventeen feet square, was piled high with more coffins, some of them of quite colossal proportions that must have fitted through the tiny doorway of the tomb like corks in a bottle. Brugsch raised his candle over the coffins and

read some of the cursive inked inscriptions that ran over the centre of the lids.

It was like a roll-call of New Kingdom history. On the different coffin lids he read, one by one, the royal names: Amosis, founder of the New Kingdom; the first three Tuthmosis'; Ahmose Nefertari who, with Amenhotep I, whose mummy was also in the room, was the revered patron of the ancient necropolis workers; and other later kings, the first two Ramesses' and several more. Brugsch, stunned, had already read the cartouche of Seti I, Belzoni's king, on a large white coffin by the doorway.

The head from a beautifully made cedar wood royal coffin of the late Eighteenth Dynasty, perhaps originally intended for Horemheb, which held the mummy of Ramesses II. It was photographed by Brugsch, the discoverer of the cache. Many of the coffins in the royal cache held mummies other than their intended occupants

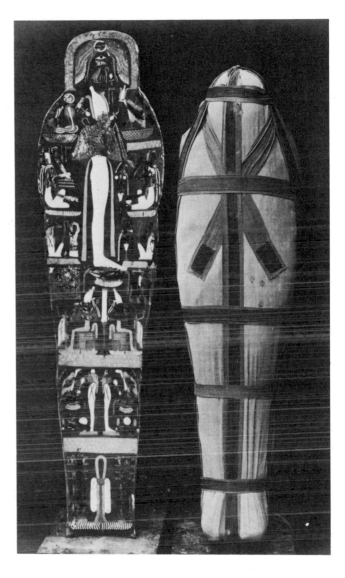

The tomb which held the royal cache was used by Pinejem's family as their burial vault. The coffin and mummy of Queen Esiemkhebi, daughter of Pinejem I, is a fine example of the workmanship of the period

Standing against the wall or lying on the floor, I found an even greater number of Mummy cases . . . Their gold covering and their polished surfaces reflected my own excited visage that it seemed as though I was looking into the faces of my own ancestors. The gilt face on the coffin of the amiable Queen Nefertari seemed to smile upon me like an old acquaintance. I took in the situation quickly, with a gasp, and hurried to the open air lest I should be overcome and the glorious prize still unrevealed, be lost to science.

So Brugsch's recollections of those extraordinary minutes were retold in Edward Wilson's account, written for a popular magazine of the day. Its value, perhaps lies in the fact that we rely on some things of Brugsch's description sticking in the mind of the journalist, for his story was far richer than any imaginings.

Brugsch's sudden retreat from this chamber full of mummies was due, he explained, to the fact that the party were all holding candles and in the tinder-dry environment deep in the tomb there was a real danger of sudden fire if one of the party should stumble or faint. This impulse to leave the tomb is one that Brugsch shared with many archeologists who have been suddenly confronted with such ancient treasures. Carnarvon, and Carter too, recorded the same emotion in Tutankhamen's tomb when they first entered it and almost every excavator has at some time felt the embarrassment of uncovering a secret thing to be an act of intrusion as the past stared them straight in the face.

Brugsch returned to the inside of the tomb and continued past the stacks of kings and walked further along the corridor, which was now higher and of more generous proportions. This was also littered with more objects, as the first section of the corridors had been. Carefully and slowly, they penetrated nearly a hundred feet further into the rock until they eventually entered a very large room, some sixteen feet high and more than twenty feet long. Here, at last, they found the coffins of the royal family of Pinejem whose burials had supplied the antiquities market with such

riches. Rifled but not broken the kings and queens still lay in their brightly decorated coffins, some of which had been badly disfigured by the Abd er Rassuls. All around them were thousands of small objects: ushabtis, garlands of flowers, bronze vases, cups, glass jars—a truly incredible welter of antiquities. These were the remaining burial goods in the chamber, the rest had been loosely strewn through the corridors of the tomb by the Abd er Rassuls.

Later, at the museum, some of the boxes and rush baskets which had lain in the chamber were opened and were found to contain voluminous brown wigs of carefully curled human hair, meats and other foods, and one held the pet gazelle of a young queen. Brugsch and his two companions looked around the room then walked back through the tomb. By the coffin of Seti I, where the corridor turned into the light, lay, 'all twisted together like a useless piece of lumber which had been thrown carelessly aside by a priest who was in a hurry to get out', a large tent made of gazelle hide decorated in patterns of red, blue and green. It was the very tent used at the funeral of one of the princesses. For Brugsch the frail leather object was the one piece in the tomb that really impressed him. The gap in time between the last burial of these mummies and his visit to the tomb contracted to the same shared moment.

They had been in the tomb for nearly two hours when Brugsch realized the true urgency of their situation. The disturbed conditions in the country and the fact that the villagers of Gurna now knew that a great treasure was being taken away from their community by foreign beys and pashas made him understandably nervous. In some ways it was a microcosm of the Egyptian situation at that time and in the end, sadly, archeology suffered and a part of ancient history was lost to us all. Brugsch decided to move the entire contents of the tomb to the surface, from where it could all be taken to the Nile and loaded on a boat for Cairo and the safety of the Museum. Thus 'three hundred Arabs were quickly assembled by Daud Pasha's men and put to work'. The liveried soldiers from Kena must have whipped most of the male population of Gurna up to the small lonely valley to carry away the kings. The secret of the Abd er Rassuls was out and every man must have been looking to see if he could not take a small piece of the treasure for himself.

The Museum steamboat, summoned earlier from Cairo, had not yet arrived, but one of the pilots, Reis Mohammed, a Nubian who had worked with Mariette for many years, was in Luxor ahead of the steamer. He was sent down the shaft and into the tomb to pack up the coffins and the antiquities and put them upon the hoist to be hauled to the surface At the top Brugsch and his assistants supervized the wrapping of the coffins in matting and had them sewed into white sailcloth. Then they were carried to the bottom of the small valley and laid out in the sun in a long row. It took two days of hard work, some of the coffins were so heavy that twelve men were needed to lift them, but slowly in little processions that looked much like the ancient funerals that they were now dismantling, the coffins were all taken out into the heat of the little rock bay and down through the fields to the river bank. From there they were taken to the East Bank to await the arrival of the Museum steamer at the Luxor quay. On 15 June the steamer docked and it was quickly loaded up with the mummies and set off again bound for the museum at Cairo.

> When we made our departure from Luxor, our late helpers squatted in groups upon the Theban side [west bank] and silently watched us. The news had been sent down the Nile in advance of us. So, when we passed the towns, the people gathered at the quays and made most frantic demonstrations . . . the women were screaming and tearing their hair. . . .

The three men were witnessing a common enough scene: the wailing and gesturing that accompanies the funeral processions of Upper Egypt—rites that have not changed since New Kingdom times, when the artists drew in the tomb chapels figures in the same mournful poses, and the scribes of the texts described the same shrill kite-like cries. It was strange, but the times were fraught and there, in front of the villagers passed both a treasure and the bodies of the very kings who had built the tombs and temples around which they lived and about whom they had woven a tradition of folk stories. There is also a less romantic possibility. In a letter to *The Times* describing conditions in the same area just a few years before, W. J. Loftie wrote:

> When children are reduced to skin and bone, the famine indeed must be sore in the land. At every village the cry of the mourners was heard as we passed.

Faces of Pharaoh

The true story of the discovery of the hidden tomb by the Abd er Rassuls was never told though several writers of the day made up their own imagined versions of the drama, short romances filled with 'wily' Arabs and the like. In his later years Ahmed, who became locally celebrated as a great tomb robber, would often yarn to groups of tourists about the discovery. Many of the stories can be discounted, but there are certain common factors in some of the recorded accounts that may be pieced together to form a likely tale of the event.

It seems that the tomb had been discovered in 1871, ten years before Brugsch had entered it. At that time some of the Rassul brothers worked as local guides and it is likely that one of them had first noticed the chimney above the tomb while climbing up the 'Agatha Christie' path, a well known short cut to the Valley of the Kings. Several other tombs had been found in similar chimneys in the cliffs and it would have been easy for the brothers to organize a party of men and discreetly clear the sand out of the bottom of the chimney, where they would have discovered the top edge of the shaft without much difficulty. The problem of persuading their accomplices in this excavation that there was nothing in the shaft was, according to Ahmed, accomplished by a number of rural ruses; either he told them that he had seen a malevolent spirit, an *afreet*, in the corridor and convinced them of the truth of this story by subsequently placing a stinking dead animal in the tomb; or that one of the brothers had noticed the entrance to the corridor in the shaft when the other excavators had not, and thus they became disheartened at their lack of success and stopped the work. It is more probable, however, that the workmen at the tomb were all gathered from their own family and that the knowledge of it was shared by a large group of people. The brothers claimed that they only entered the tomb on four occasions and, although it was well plundered, no papyri, for example, were found by Brugsch; the objects and the mummies that they had left behind were not smashed in the normal manner of tomb robbers.

Ahmed Kamal, one of the Government Inspectors, who accompanied Brugsch on his first trip to the cache, poses elegantly with the coffin of the great Queen Ahmose Nefertari. These colossal outer coffins held small ones within them which, in turn, held the royal mummies. They are of a type commonly used for the queens of the early Eighteenth Dynasty

Some of the objects they took were damaged by their great haste; apparently the funerary shroud of Tuthmosis III was ripped quickly off the mummy, portions of it being left behind in the coffin. But apart from this, the brothers handled their discovery in a calm, collected way. And as Mohammed eventually revealed, he had kept other secrets, some almost as extraordinary as this cache of kings.

Mohammed Abd er Rassul received £500 for revealing the tomb and doubtless this had been negotiated at some point in an earlier meeting. He was also given the post of foreman of the Museum's excavations at Thebes, and, Maspero observed 'if he serves the Museum with the same skill that he had used for so many years against it, we may hope for some magnificent discoveries'. Ahmed, the tormented brother who had successfully shielded the head of the family from the authorities right through the enquiries, would probably not have objected to such a settlement for it was Mohammed's duty as the eldest to ultimately decide matters for them all. The reward money would be available to all the family if it were needed and, in fact, much of it was given away in small sums to friends and relatives.

When the Museum steamer arrived in Cairo, the government customs officer, whose job it was to tax the comings and goings of everything that passed through the city, saw the royal coffins and was placed in a quandary. They were unclassified in his lists of excise duties. Eventually he decided to tax the mummies as dried fish, *farseekh*, a Cairene delicacy. And so it was that the ancient kings came, at last, to Cairo. After an inspection of the coffins and their contents, the coffins of the principal kings were arranged side by side in cases in a small room in the Museum, the others were placed into store. Maspero returned to Cairo some weeks later and after a brief inspection of the incredible hoard of kings, set off again for Thebes.

During his second trip to Thebes, Maspero— accompanied by Brugsch—was taken to the tomb by Mohammed and it was probably during this visit that he was told the details of the tomb's discovery and clearance; information that was never, for the most part, recorded. Maspero, a stocky, muscular figure

Maspero sitting by the edge of the shaft, accompanied by the Abd er Rassul brothers and Émile Brugsch. The engraver of this plate, made from a photograph since lost, has substituted a loose slide of rock for the sheer walls of stone which rise up from the chimney that holds the shaft

was lowered into the shaft to walk through the strange, ever-enlarging tomb, shaped like a telescope. After some two hundred feet he arrived at the great burial vault of the priest kings. There were still many fragments of mummy cloth and coffins lying in the corridors, as well as many of the garlands of leaves and flowers that had formed a part of the ancient burials. Maspero had most of this cleared out and, since that time, the tomb has only been entered once. Twenty-five years after Maspero's visit the tomb was examined by an expedition from the Metropolitan Museum of New York. They found it in a dangerous condition with the roof partially collapsed, due probably to the desiccation of the rock in the tomb following its opening and clearance. In the sand at the bottom of the shaft the expedition found fragments of an early Eighteenth Dynasty coffin 'evidently from the original occupation of the tomb'. The study of the inscriptions written on the other coffins from the tomb had already showed that it had originally been the tomb of Inhapy, a little-known queen, and the characteristic chisel marks of the masons who worked on this smaller and neater excavation may still be seen on a part of the shaft, a remaining portion of the little tomb that was later so grossly enlarged to hold the royal mummies.

Early on in his studies upon the tomb and its contents Maspero distinguished between two separate groups of mummies: first, a group of kings and courtiers who had originally been buried in their own tombs in the Valley of the Kings; second, a large number of the members of the family of priests, all descended from Herihor, who had reigned at Thebes under the authority of the Delta kings after the end of the Twentieth Dynasty. Only this second group, who were buried in sets of distinctive, highly decorated coffins that fitted tightly one inside the other, had their complete burials about them and had occupied the ultimate chamber of the tomb. It is possible that the other kings had originally all been stacked in the other room of the tomb, and that it had been the Abd er Rassuls who had scattered them through the corridors, dragging them towards the light that filtered down from the shaft and through the little door.

During his visit to the tomb Maspero made a copy of the groups of hieroglyphic script, known as hieratic, around the tiny door at the bottom of the shaft. They were of a type with which Maspero would become very familiar during the next four years as he studied the dozens of small texts written upon the coffins and the wrappings from the tomb.

The graffito at the bottom of the shaft. From a photograph, taken by the American journalist Edward Wilson, who visited the tomb with Maspero

Year 10, fourth month of the winter season, day 20, day of the burial of the Osiris, the High Priest of Amun-Re, King of the Gods, the great chief of the army, the leader, Pinejem, by the divine father of Amun, the scribe of the army, the chief inspector, Nespekeshuty; the prophet of Amun . . . enamun, the divine father of Amun, Wennefer; by the king's scribe in the place of truth, Bekenmut; the chief workman, Pediamun; the chief workman Amenmose; the divine father of Amun, the chief of secrets, Pediamun, the son of Enkefenkhons.

The inscription recorded the burial of Pinejem II in the tomb by a group of necropolis officials and priests. The descriptive 'Osiris' referred to Pinejem, now identified with the god of the Underworld and was a pious euphemism for 'deceased'. Pinejem was a 'High Priest of Amun Re [the] King of the Gods', which was an administrative as well as a priestly function. The officials named by the scribe in the inscription were listed in their approximate order of seniority: Nespekeshuty was a major state official, who came from a long-established noble family. He it was who bore the ultimate responsibility for the burial. The other men listed also came from long-established families of priests and necropolis workers. The two chief workmen were the principal foremen of the workers on the royal tombs, and they also held considerable authority in the village where the community of royal tomb-makers lived. This appointment of two chief workmen reflected the organization of the work in the royal tombs, where there was 'a gang of the right' wall and 'a gang of the left' wall. At the time of this inscription the life of that some 500-year-old community was nearing its end, for no more grand tombs were being excavated and decorated in the Valley of the Kings. The 'King's

scribe in the place of Truth' Bekenmut was an official of the same community of workers. He it was who kept records of the work, rations and other activities of the workmen. There were normally at least four scribes attached to the tomb gangs, two to each gang. Bekenmut is the last known official to hold this office, again the final link in a chain that stretched back to the beginning of the New Kingdom. The last official named in the inscription was a senior member of the priestly caste of the Great Temple of Amun Re on the East Bank. Presumably he officiated at the rites of the burial, hence his title 'chief of secrets'. This party of notables, accompanied by a number of necropolis workmen and religious officials buried Pinejem on a day in October, about 987 BC. After more years passed similarly composed burial parties returned to the lonely tomb with further royal burials to add to the huge cache. The mummies of the priestly family who then ruled Thebes lay in great honour, surrounded by their royal ancestors.

Maspero discovered an entire history written on the mummies that had been taken from their tombs in the Valley of the Kings. In the series of written notes and dockets scribbled in hieratic upon the remaining possessions of the mummies, there was an elaborate record of restorations and re-wrappings and of the shifting of the kings from one tomb to another. Several of the kings had been taken to the tomb of Seti I, and had been restored, presumably after plundering by thieves, when they were in that tomb. Many of the mummies were moved on different days and over a great length of time, perhaps as much as seventy years. The earliest texts recorded restorations of the royal mummies; then under Pinejem II they were gathered up and taken, one by one, to the tomb of his wife, Neskhons, who had been buried in the enlarged tomb of Queen Inhapy, who had lived some five hundred years before. The last mummies to be added to the tomb were those of the great kings Seti I and Ramesses II, and Pinejem II must have been so sure of the security of the huge tomb with its tiny

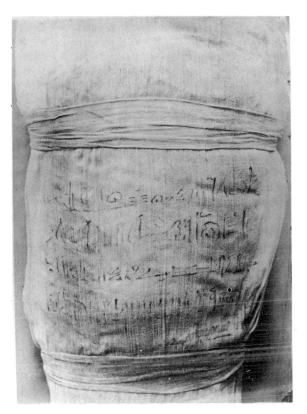

*A typical hieratic inscription from the royal cache.
This example was written on the wrapping of the mummy
of Ramesses II*

door that, when he died, his mummy, too, was added to the august assembly. After Pinejem II's burial party, the next visitors were the Abd er Rassuls, nearly 3,000 years later.

These ancient dealings with the dead had been conducted by Theban civilian authorities and priests for, although the government of that time was far away in the Delta, the religious supremacy of Thebes does seem to have been recognized. The records of the peregrinations of the mummy kings are, however, dated with reference to the reigns of the Delta kings who are sometimes described as having ordered the whole activity. At one point in their travels the royal mummies were taken to the huge fortified mortuary temple of Medinet Habu, which at that time was the home of the community of royal tomb workers and the centre for the administration of the west bank at Thebes. Perhaps it was there in the precincts of the temple, that the mummies were carefully restored and re-wrapped for many objects from the royal

tombs have been found in that locality. This whole procedure of restoring the damaged burials of the ancient kings was an act of great piety and many of the new shrouds that were placed on the kings had been woven and decorated by the daughters of the principal officials of Thebes.

Long before they were left in the hidden tomb, the royal mummies had been almost completely denuded of their rich burial jewellery, some of the patterns of which could still be seen indented on their limbs and bodies. Despite the obvious evidence of brutal handling visible on some of the mummies, which suggests a thorough pillage of the burial, the care with which others of the royal dead had been relieved of their jewels strongly suggests that it was the commissions of refurbishing and reburial that had been the ultimate and possibly even the major spoilers of the mummies. Certainly the final hacking away of nearly all the gold foil from the exteriors of the coffins was the work of the reburial parties, for the names and titles of the kings were occasionally carefully left while the rich gold patterns were hacked away, showing a care not to be expected of normal tomb robbers. The Abd er Rassuls found practically nothing in the coffins or among the shrouds and bandages of the mummies from the Valley of the Kings. Their prime antiquities had all been taken from the second group of priest-kings and queens who lay in the large room at the end of the tomb, and which was very badly damaged.

During our expedition's clearance of the tomb of Ramesses XI in the Valley, we found strong evidence that some of this work of stripping-off the gold foil from the coffins and other pieces of funerary equipment had been performed in that tomb. In the huge shaft at the end of the tomb we found fragments of statues, coffins and boxes from several royal burials, some of the very finest workmanship, and all chopped into pieces that resembled kindling. At the top of the shaft, all around the vaulted burial chamber, we found scores of small pieces of gold foil that had slipped down between the chippings that had covered the floor and had never been retrieved. This foil, incidently, is far thicker than modern gold leaf and would have been well worth the work of scraping it from the coffins. That this workshop in the tomb of Ramesses XI was not simply a thieves' hideaway, for which it would have been a very poor choice, seems to be proven by the articles belonging to workmen of the royal tombs that were mixed in with the broken objects. Further, there is in the first corridor a text naming Pinejem I, the last hieroglyphic inscription in the Valley of the Kings, and one that is

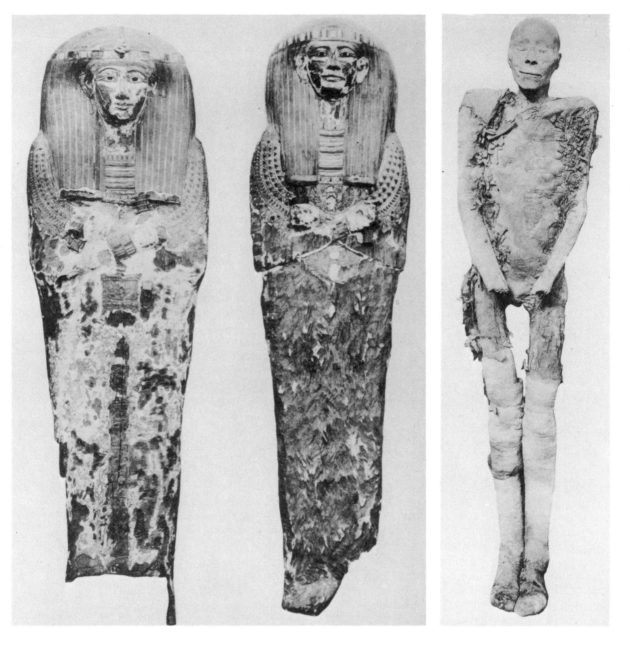

The coffins and supposed mummy of Tuthmosis I. The rewrapping at the end of the New Kingdom had hidden its real condition. The original wrappings had been torn away along with the king's hands and his burial jewellery. But Tuthmosis' coffins had been re-used some five hundred years after their manufacture by Pinejem I—an antiquarian gesture that demonstrates the interest shown in the earlier royal mummies during the Late New Kingdom. The hacking away of the thick gold foil with which Pinejem's workmen had embellished the old coffins was, perhaps, done by the Abd er Rassul brothers

also unique in that it is the only occurrence of a restored inscription in any of the royal tombs. Perhaps Pinejem I was planning to take over the great empty tomb for himself, a notion that he later abandoned since his mummy was found with other members of his family in the Abd er Rassul tomb.

There was an especially strong interest in the royal burials of the Valley of the Kings during the reign of Pinejem I. Not only was much of the restoration and rewrapping of the royal mummies accomplished during this time, but the king himself was buried in an antique coffin which was, even at that time, nearly five hundred years old and had belonged to Tuthmosis I of the Eighteenth Dynasty. The greater part of the plundering in the Valley of the Kings seems to have taken place during the reigns of the later Ramesside kings for papyri records of tomb inspections tell that many of the royal burials were still intact at quite late dates in the New Kingdom. The amounts of gold and other precious substances removed from the royal burials by the reburial commissions remain unknown. That they were happy to re-use some of the finer pieces is evident from Pinejem I's own coffin and it is probable that a lot of this recycled wealth went north to the Delta to embellish the palaces and burials of the kings of the new dynasties.

The precise ordering of these reburial commissions, the tours of inspection and removal of the mummies remains a terribly confused business. Never simple in their movements in the first instance, the ancient records of the activities of the commissions were badly documented during the last century and some of the most important texts are lost or damaged. Indeed, it was only in 1939 that a proper copy of the inscription concerning the burial of Pinejem II was finally obtained from the wall of the shaft of the cache tomb. The rapid clearance of the royal cache by Brugsch and Reis Mohammed was a true archeological disaster. It is ironic that although Brugsch was a skilled photographer not one photograph of the interior of the tomb as it lay before the little group of men was ever made. So much more would have been known about these dead kings and their complicated destinies, if only they had been carefully examined where they lay, or even, if a simple plan or list had been made of the order of the coffins as they were discovered in the tomb. As it is, there is not even a proper architectural plan of the tomb itself, and certainly no record of what it once contained. Scholars have been left to puzzle over poor photographs of half rubbed inscriptions written upon the whitewash abraded by the passage of the mummies first into the tomb then, later, on their journey to Cairo. The standard of the reports upon the hidden tomb and its contents is so poor that we are left wondering whether there were facts concerning the cache and its robbery that Maspero and the authorities felt that they had to conceal. There may have been Europeans directly involved in its exploitation; people of nationalities who, at that time, were not accountable to Egyptian law and who Maspero certainly could not have named. Mustafa Aga, in his position of British Vice-Consul in Luxor may well have given a stolen papyrus as a present to a member of one of the parties of the Prince of Wales, when they visited Luxor. Certainly Ahmed always claimed a long-standing friendship with the Prince himself, dating back to an earlier career as the Prince's donkey boy, many years before! Whatever the truth, it is very curious that none of the people who first entered the tomb left even a personal memoir of their experiences for, despite the ravages of the Abd er Rassul family, the tomb was still one of the most extraordinary archeological finds in history.

The wrapped mummy of Tuthmosis III showing the hole torn in the bandages by the Abd er Rassul brothers as they searched for the king's heart scarab

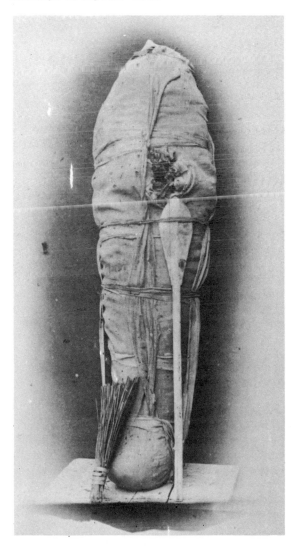

In the Museum at Cairo Maspero pondered over the cache that Brugsch had secured. Apart from his study of the texts, which even today remains an indispensable source of information on the royal mummies, and the hidden tomb, he organized several unwrapping events as Belzoni had done in Piccadilly some sixty years before. The first king to be revealed to modern gaze was Tuthmosis III, the great warrior whose reputation for valour and bravery has survived through his inscriptions to this day. The Abd er Rassuls had attacked this mummy in the tomb, cutting through the outer wrappings at the left side of the chest in a knowledgeable search for the large scarab that was normally placed near the heart. It is very unlikely that they found one and certainly, if they did, it has never surfaced in a museum. However, the fine shroud inscribed with the name of the king suffered badly and its torn pieces are now in several different museums. The wrappings that the Abd er Rassuls had cut had been hastily folded and carelessly wrapped around the mummy by the ancient priests. Stuffed into the outer wrappings was a small hand broom and two oars which, originally, had been put into the king's tomb to guide the royal bark through the hours of the night. They now served to stiffen the smashed mummy.

The unwrapping was a haphazard and unskilful affair. After cutting through the bandages of the rewrapping, they exposed the body of the king and found his legs broken off at the pelvic joints and the head snapped from the neck. The king's hands, slightly raised and folded across his chest, had hidden a few strings of carnelian and gold beads which had thus escaped all of the robbers. But all in all it was a depressing sight and it so disheartened Maspero that he did not unwrap another king for several years, fearing that underneath their bandages all the royal mummies would prove to be similarly smashed. The bandaging, which they had cut from the mummy and which Maspero described as being as fine as the best cambric, lay all around the king like the results of a gruesome explosion; this was the linen that had been placed upon the mummy by the commission of priests. The original wrappings, such as remained, were saturated with resins and oils and lay quite dried adhering to the skin of the king. The king's coffin which had held the re-wrapped mummy was probably the original one used at his burial in 1450 BC. It was made of thin planks of cedar wood

The pathetic mummy of Tuthmosis III after being unwrapped by Maspero and his colleagues in the Museum

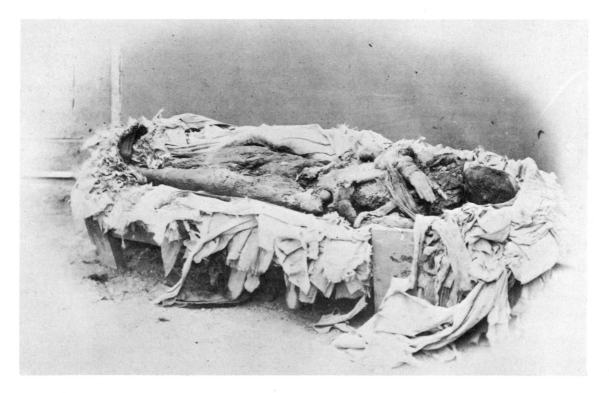

that had been beautifully made by the ancient carpenters. It had suffered the fate common to many royal coffins—its entire surface had been hacked away with a small sharp adze, and all the original gold covering was gone. In the tomb of Ramesses XI our expedition found several fragments of the burial equipment of Tuthmosis III and it must be likely that this miserable work was performed in the darkness of that tomb.

The next occasion on which Maspero organized the unwrapping of some mummies was in June 1886. Assisted by Brugsch, the Museum conservator, Alessandro Barsanti, unwrapped several of the most famous kings. The researches of the first day were held in the presence of the Khedive Tewfik and many other illustrious personages. It was the sort of gathering about antiquity that greatly appealed to Maspero, an occasion to match the ancient grandeur of the long-dead participants—later such gatherings would be repeated in the Valley of the Kings. The first mummy to be unwrapped was that of Ramesses II. Maspero showed the Khedive the inscription on the coffin, which dated from the reign of Pinejem I and which named the king. This inscription was one of three. One told of a restoration of the royal mummy during the reign of Pinejem's grandfather Herihor, another told of the removal of the mummy to the tomb of Seti I and the last of the removal of the mummy from that tomb to the tomb where Amenhotep, the patron of the necropolis, lay. The coffin itself, though of very beautiful work, had not originally been made for Ramesses II, for it has the features and style of the last kings of the previous dynasty of Tutankhamun, Ay and Horemheb. 'To ascertain whether the mummy really was that of Ramesses II, Maspero detached a part of the wrappings which seemed to be loosely fastened and found, on the breast of the original shroud, a hieratic inscription written in ink which put the matter beyond any possible doubt'. The explorers did not stop here. They rolled off bandage after bandage, sheet after sheet, including one which had a fine line-drawing upon it of the goddess Nut, such as was carved into the coffin lids. Under this the bandages became spotted with the resins that had been used at the embalming. Then, under these stained wrappings, the king was exposed. The unwrapping of Ramesses II had taken them less than one quarter of an hour. Ramesses' extraordinary head, thus revealed, regarded them across the centuries; and Maspero regarded Ramesses:

The chest is broad; the shoulders square; the arms are crossed upon the breast; the hands are small and dyed with henna; the feet are long, slender somewhat flat soled and dyed, like the hands with henna . . . The head is long, and small in proportion to the body. The top of the skull is quite bare. On the temples there are a few sparse hairs, but at the poll the hair is quite thick, forming smooth, straight locks about five centimetres in length. White at the time of death, they have been dyed a light yellow by the spices used in the embalm-ment. The forehead is low and narrow; the brow ridge prominent; the eyebrows are thick and white, the eyes are small and close together; the nose is long, thin, hooked like the noses of the Bourbons, and slightly crushed at the tip by the pressure of the bandages; the temples are sunken; the cheek bones very prominent; the ears round, standing far out from the head, and pierced like those of a woman for the wearing of earrings; the jawbone is massive and strong; the chin very prominent, the mouth small but thick lipped, and full of some kind of black paste. This paste being partly cut away with the scissors, disclosed some much worn and brittle teeth, which, moreover, are white and well preserved. The moustache and beard are thin. They seem to have been kept shaven during life, but were probably allowed to grow during the king's last illness; or they may have grown after death. The hairs are white, like those of the head and eyebrows, but are harsh and bristly, and from two to three millimetres in length. The skin is of earthy brown, splotched with black. Finally, it may be said the face of the mummy gives a fair idea of the face of the living king.

They proceeded to another, anonymous, mummy that had been smelling rather badly in the storerooms and Maspero decided to open up its bandages. Although there had been some confusion about the ordering of the mummies, some of the inscriptions upon the coffins differing from those upon the shrouds, it was later agreed that the mummy that lay before them was that of Ahmose Nefertari, the queen who with her son Amenhotep I had been the deified patron of the ancient necropolis workers. The mummy was quickly unwrapped 'but the body was no sooner exposed to the outer air than it fell literally into a state of putrefaction, dissolving into black matter which gave out an unsupportable smell. It was, however, ascertained to be the corpse of a woman of mature age and middle height, belonging to the white races of mankind'. The atmosphere of Cairo, more humid than the oven-dry valley where the mummies had

The head of Ramesses II

lain for three thousand years was having an effect upon the royal dead. The mummy was subsequently buried for a few months under the storehouse of the Museum. After this time it 'was found to have lost these disagreeable symptoms' and it rejoined the others in the collections.

Excitement now ran through the group of scholars. By a process of elimination they had decided that another mummy found with Nefertari in the same colossal sarchophagus, which was over ten feet high, must be that of Ramesses III.

Ramesses III was thus placed erect and photographed in his bandages. Short as was the delay, it seemed too long for the impatient spectators. The strange revelation [of the identity of the mummy] had astonished and excited them to the uttermost. All had left their places and gathered around the operators. Three thicknesses of bandages were rapidly unwound, then came a casing of sewn canvas covered with a thin coat of cement. This casing being cut with the scissors, more layers of linen appeared. The mummy seemed to diminish and reveal its forms

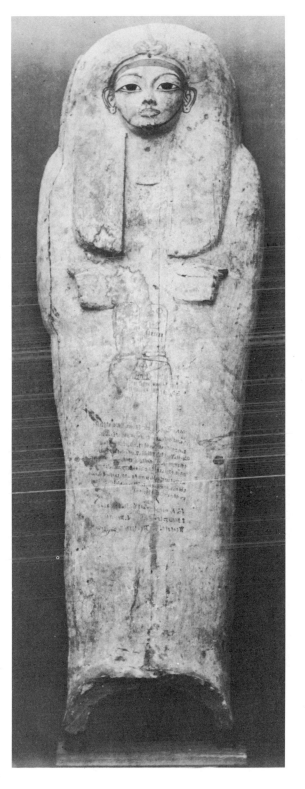

The coffin of Seti I

under our fingers. Some of the wrappings were inscribed with legends and groups in black ink, notably the God Amun enthroned, with a line of hieroglyphs below, stating that this bandage was made and offered by a devotee of the period, or perhaps, by a princess of the blood royal:— 'The Lady Songstress of Amen Ra, King of the Gods, Fa'atenmut, daughter of the First Prophet of Amen . . .' Two pectoral ornaments were laid in the folds of the wrappers, one of gilt wood, bearing the usual group of Isis and Nepthys adoring the sun; the other in pure gold, inscribed with the name of Ramesses III. One last wrapper of stiffened canvas, one last winding sheet of red linen, and then a great disappointment, keenly felt by the operators; the face of the king was coated with a compact mass of bitumen, which completely hid the features. At 20 minutes past 11 His Highness the Khedive left the hall of mummies.

In the afternoon Maspero examined the bandages they had cut from the mummies earlier and found more inscriptions upon them. Then, 'The tarry substance upon the face of the mummy being carefully attacked with the scissors was detached little by little, and the features became visible.' The unwrapping of other mummies followed this grand beginning. One king was found to have been killed by a succession of dreadful wounds to the head, and it was a suitable death for a monarch known to have lived during a period of war and civil disturbance. Amenhotep I, still lying garlanded with flowers in his restored coffin, was left wrapped. Among the garlands, with their blue flowers still arrested in bloom, was an ancient wasp that had been attracted to their scent and had been trapped in the royal coffin when the lid was fixed.

The extraordinary coffin of Seti I has achieved, by the strange process of robbery and restoration, a beauty of its own. An original part of the king's burial equipment, it had been scraped of its gold. The restorers finding the face irretrievably scarred, re-modelled it, cutting down its size and leaving the huge elegant inlaid eyes of blue glass and white limestone, with black obsidian pupils, strangely large, floating in the bland whitewashed countenance. The hasty but highly competent drawing of the details of the ears and the chin line fixed the great eyes in the small, newly-modelled face; the two cartouches drawn at this same time upon the middle of the coffin

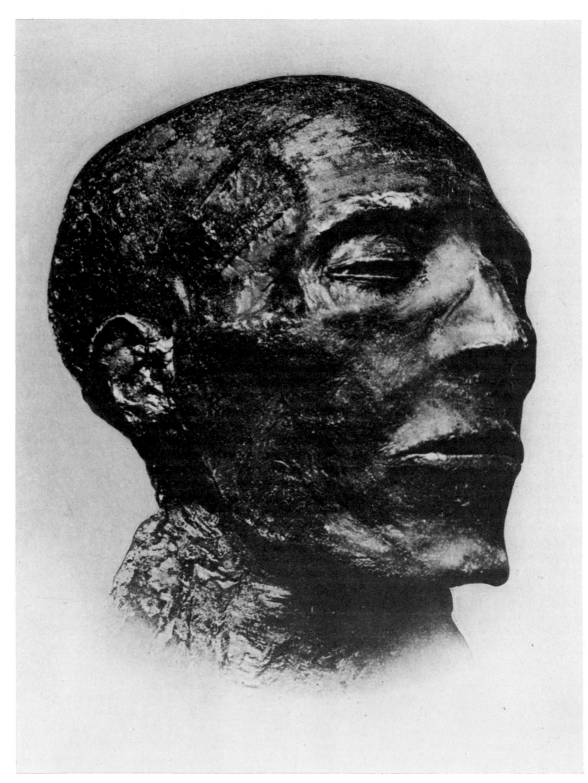

tell, as do the long hieratic inscriptions below them, of the pious work of the reburial commissions. The remarkable mummy of Seti I amazed the investigators by its beauty. It still remains the most fortunately preserved and the finest faced of all the ancient kings to have survived:

It was a masterpiece of the art of the embalmer, and the expression of the face was that of one who had only a few hours previously breathed his last. Death had slightly drawn the nostrils and contracted the lips, the pressure of the bandages had flattened the nose a little, and the skin was darkened by the pitch; but a calm and gentle smile still played over the mouth, and the half opened eyelids allowed a glimpse to be seen from under their lashes of an apparently moist and glistening line, the reflection from the white porcelain eyes let in to the orbit at the time of burial.

The descriptions of the ancient kings given by Maspero and his contemporaries are often marvels of the historical writing of the period. How sure these people were of their subjects of study and the soundness of their own judgements! It is sad that scholarship has had to retreat from such noble sentiments; today we do not even feel sure of the identification of the kings they unwrapped, let alone of our understanding of the politics and ethics of those ancient times. Ramesses II, probably the most famous of all the kings of Egypt before Tutankhamen was discovered, particularly caught the attention of the day. One writer using Maspero's description of the king, ruminated:

The mask of the mummy gives a fair idea of the living king; the somewhat unintelligent expression, slightly brutish perhaps, but haughty and firm of purpose, displays itself with an air of royal majesty beneath the sombre materials used by the embalmer.
The hero of the battle of Kadesh [Ramesses II] must in his prime have been a man of large and powerful frame. Even after the coalescence of the vertebrae and the shrinkage produced by mummification, his mummy still measures over 5 feet 8 inches; so that we may picture him as a formidable figure over 6 feet in height, perhaps nearly 7 feet with the high war helmet of the Pharaohs crowning his head, as he charged with arrow drawn to the head, in his rattling war chariot upon the Hittite ranks. His conduct at Kadesh suggests a good

The head of Seti I

trooper, but a dull general, and his mummy does nothing to cause a revision of the judgement.

This account of Ramesses at war, written at the time of the last cavalry charges of the British army in the Sudan, and drawn from the reliefs of Ramesses II in his chariot charging at his enemy, clearly had more immediacy for the people of those years than they have for us today. With such assurance they read character in the face of a mummy and reviewed Ramesses' conduct from the ancient accounts as if it were a school report, for these people, too, were the masters of an empire, like Ramesses before them.

It is only during the last ten years that the royal mummies have been subjected to modern scientific investigation, at a time when so much of the peripheral evidence that once surrounded them has disappeared. Unfortunately, it seems that some of the kings were muddled in their coffins and are thus wrongly labelled. However, with biologists able to analyse and compare hair and blood samples from the mummies and with a careful analysis of such inter-relationships as may emerge from detailed bone measurements, it may yet be possible to reconstruct the royal bloodlines and retrieve the biological order of the mummies of the same families. Most of the mummies from the hidden tomb were unwrapped within fifteen years of their arrival in Cairo. Eventually they were all properly photographed and studied by an anatomist, the eminent Victorian anthropologist, Sir Grafton Elliot Smith. He published the results of his enquiries as a part of the Museum Catalogue.

It may well have been a symbolic gesture that Ramesses II made when, as he was being unwrapped yet again by one of Elliot Smith's assistants, the long compressed fibres in the royal arm retracted suddenly causing the scientists to start away from him. Certainly, if he could speak, the ancient king would command a return to the quiet Theban Hills. Shortly after his unwrapping the king was found to contain lice, and he was bathed in mercury as a cure. Lately, in the course of an investigation to determine whether the king was fit to be flown to France to appear in an exhibition of the arts of his reign, the royal mummy was found to be infested with all manner of insects and he was taken to Paris for restoration rather than exhibition. He is now back in Cairo, cured, but doubtless just a little lighter as the delicate fibres of hair and skin are slowly frayed and flaked.

The presence of the royal mummies on exhibition in the museum at Cairo has, however, turned that building into something other than simply a showcase of art and artefacts. Perhaps because it has become the repository of so much of ancient Egypt that is fragile, transitory yet preserved, the building, shrine-like, seems almost imbued with the spirit of the ancient past.

In the end it may be this quality of wonder that the royal mummies have provoked ever since their rediscovery that is more important for us than the establishment of the exact movements of the ancient committee or the unedifying information that such-and-such a king had pimples or fallen arches. Shortly after the royal cache arrived in Cairo, the newly appointed director of the French Institute of Archeology, Eugène Lefébure, composed a short, evocative piece of prose upon the discovery which, perhaps, brings us closer to those earlier days of greater certainties and greater wonders:

There was nothing as pretty as this covering, made of a slightly yellowed linen cloth (of a shade known today as the colour of cream) under a coquettish arrangement of crossed-over rose-coloured filets. The effect reminded one, so to speak, of those boxes of bonbons knotted with ribbons which are given out after a christening, or better, Arab brides who are still led through the Cairo streets to their grooms, entirely veiled and masked.

Nearly all the mummies that were so decked, were covered with dry garlands and withered lotuses which had lasted intact through the thousands of years, and there was no better way to understand the suspension of time and the halting of decay than to see these immortal flowers on the eternalised bodies. It was really the image of an endless sleep. A mummy, that of Amenophis I, whose yellow mask with enamelled eyes moulded his adolescent face, seemed, weary of his sleep to be awaking with a smile, in his bed of flowers.

This graceful tableau sums up the basic impression of the work at Deir el Bahari. Apart from some precious historical documents of the Twenty-first Dynasty and some prayers on linen that were chanced to be found with the Eighteenth Dynasty mummies, there is perhaps no material to sustain long research, nor will there be great conclusions. The interest in the discovery lies elsewhere. It is in the piece of theatre, the dramatic and sudden bringing to light of the assembly of kings which brings close to us that which we had thought so remote. It is the Egyptian vision of death that we see in this poetic entourage. Framed again for our eyes are the most fleeting relics of life, from the fly swash of Tuthmosis found in his coffin, to the smile of Amenhotep.

Part IV

ARCHEOLOGISTS

16

Littérateurs

(1883–98)

Although Maspero did not visit the Valley of the Kings for more than two years after his brief trips during the Abd er Rassuls' interrogations he made plans for the documentation of the royal tombs and the copying of their texts to complement his own researches upon the Pyramid Texts. This work was to be undertaken by the French Archeological Institute, which Maspero had left to become the director of the *Service*. His successor was a *Lyonnais*, Eugène Lefébure, at forty-three some eight years older than Maspero. Lefébure, previously a civil servant, had been a professional egyptologist for only one year before his arrival in Egypt. He was also a poet and a close friend of Stéphane Mallarmé, and shared that poet's fascination with language and the hidden structures of written communication. With the support of Maspero he obtained a grant from the French Government for the documentation and the publication of the royal tombs and their long religious texts.

Work started at the end of January 1883 with the recording of the hieroglyphic inscriptions in the form of a modern hieroglyphic handwriting known as

Lefébure's published record of the lintel over the entrance to the tomb of Ramesses X. The poor technique and lack of interest shown in any of the qualities of the relief, save that of its text and iconography, indicate the way in which the monuments were, increasingly, being drawn at this time. For the Champollion expedition's drawing of the same subject see p. 40

'hand copy' to distinguish it from the more laborious process of precisely drawing the ancient texts exactly as they were made by the ancient artists. Two of the archeologists of the Institute, Loret and Bouriant, and an artist, Bourgoin, were to help Lefébure. Their aim was to copy two tombs completely—those of Seti I and Ramesses IV—and the rest were to be examined for variations and additions to the texts already copied. Lefébure's methods were extremely quick and often careless but he worked hard and with great dedication. At the beginning of his work he set up house, as many had done before him, in the tomb of Ramesses IV but it proved to be very cold during the winter nights, when temperatures in the Valley can drop to freezing point, and he soon abandoned the pharaohs for the White House of the Abd er Rassuls. Lefébure's hectic pace quickly discouraged his assistants, who retreated to the hotels in Luxor, and soon he was left to work largely by himself. He seems to have been an obsessive figure and although Maspero thought him ineffective he was utterly dedicated to the work in the Valley. He had left his wife with their newborn baby in Cairo and never once crossed the river to Luxor where his assistants spent so much of their time. Within two months he had copied every line of every wall in the tomb of Seti I and the greater part of the texts in the other tomb and during the rest of the year he completed his survey of the entire Valley. Every tomb was inspected and its contents listed and copied. As well as his work upon the texts, Lefébure

also noted the physical conditions of the tombs and made rough plans where there had been previously none available. Wilkinson's tomb list had stopped at KV 21, Lepsius had added the two royal tombs in the West Valley as 22 and 23, and Lefébure added two more West Valley tombs to the list, 24 and 25, one of which Belzoni had opened. Wilbour, who was back in Thebes at this time, visited the West Valley with Bouriant who was working erratically for Lefébure and they crawled into the open pits and small tombs, examined the tomb of Ay, where they copied all the texts that Lepsius had not bothered with, then visited the tomb of Amenhotep III and copied the remains of the texts that had survived the floods and the attentions of collectors. Later, for his publication of the royal tombs, Lefébure enlisted the help of two of the leading authorities upon Egyptian religion, Édouard Naville and Ernesto Schiaparelli. His complete survey was published during the next four years. It was an extraordinary feat, quickly done but one that Lefébure was not destined to repeat at other ancient sites for he was replaced at the Institute by another scholar, Grébaut, in the following year.

In 1886, two days after the last of his great mummy unwrapping ceremonies at the Museum, Maspero resigned. It had been a difficult five years. From an auspicious beginning with the revelation of the royal cache, egyptological studies had been inevitably overshadowed by the political events that had shaken Egypt. In 1882 the British Navy bombarded Alexandria and subsequently an expeditionary force had beaten the Egyptian Army and taken Cairo. Tewfik was still nominal ruler of the country, but a British administration controlled the government. At Thebes, Maspero had been faced with Mustafa Aga, just one year after his exposure as a grand despoiler and trafficker in antiquities, directing excavations in the temples of Deir el Bahari for Lord Dufferin, the British Ambassador to the Ottoman Empire, who had been sent to report on the conditions and possibilities that now faced occupied Egypt. A British civil administration was quickly established, staffed in part by civil servants brought from India. The British Agent and Consul-General who now effectively governed the province of Egypt was determined that the country should pay the huge debts of the deposed Khedive and set about creating an administration that would produce the cash. Government expenditure was greatly reduced and in the later years of his directorship Maspero was annually awarded for excavation £500—the same sum he had given to the Rassuls for revealing the location of the royal cache in 1881.

After Maspero left for Paris the Directorship of the *Service* passed to Grébaut, another of his students and still very much under his influence. The work of recording the inscriptions in the Valley of the Kings was continued by two younger scholars of the Institut who were charged with the copying of all the thousands of graffiti in the tombs. Jules Baillet studied the Greek and Latin texts and he later produced a brilliant study of them, and Georges Bénédite, copied the graffiti written in the demotic script but unfortunately never wrote upon the results of his work, which is a pity as the history of the later Pharaonic Period in the Valley is very little known.

As well as these studies, Grébaut sent the Deputy Director of the Museum, Georges Daressy, to Thebes to clear out the tombs of Ramesses VI and IX. These two tombs were among the most visited monuments in the Valley but their entrances were choked with chippings and rubbish, which also lay in lesser amounts in the interiors. The clearance would not only allow tourists to enter with greater ease, but also permit a great deal more light to enter the tombs. Sixty years earlier James Burton had found some of the original burial equipment lying in the tomb of Ramesses VI and it is not surprising that Daressy found the remains of more when the tomb was completely cleaned out. Until this time all the ancient objects in the tomb lay on the floor mixed with the limestone chippings that were constantly being trodden down by visitors. It was surprising, nevertheless, what still remained in the tombs, even after some three thousand years of neglect.

Deep in the chippings of the tomb of Ramesses VI Daressy's men found an ancient fire-making device, a block of wood with holes drilled in it into which a stick was pressed and revolved to produce embers by the friction. There were also some ancient brushes still packed in their box; they were made of reed whose fibres had been separated by the careful chewing of their stems. This method provides a brush whose tip is much harder than a modern sable or hogshair brush and when used it produces a firm equal line, something like that of a felt pen. Among the other remains of workmen's equipment was a large collection of funerary furniture, smashed vases, and statues and the cabins from model boats. Ramesses VI had taken over this tomb from his predecessor Ramesses V, and it is interesting to note that Daressy also found a piece of a box with the earlier king's name written upon it, which may suggest that at one time there was a joint burial in the tomb, for it would seem unlikely that Ramesses VI would take over his predecessor's funerary goods without even bothering to change the name. The finest pieces were some ushabtis of Ramesses VI, both in wood and alabaster, similar to those that Burton had already found. Nearly forty of these are now known, spread through the collections of several museums, which show that the original burials of these Ramesside kings must have been large and lavish for such a large number to have survived.

Daressy also found a similar heap of fragments in the tomb of Ramesses IX, and there, surprisingly, his team also discovered two huge runners from a wooden sledge—part of the funeral procession that had brought the king, encased in his coffins, to his tomb for burial. Undoubtedly Daressy's greatest find was nearly three hundred limestone flakes called *ostraca*, the detritus of the quarrying of the tombs by the stonemasons, which bore sketches made by the artists who had worked in the tombs, and the jottings of the scribes of the tombs, lists of equipment, provisions, workmen and the like. The range of subjects in these sketches is quite remarkable. They do not often relate directly to sections of the decoration on the tomb walls, but include small religious scenes, like little votive pictures showing the artists' or scribes' offering to the gods, and many small and wonderfully sure sketches of the king, hieroglyphs or ritual furniture from the temples and the great tombs. The most extraordinary and delightful of these images are those that show small simple subjects which the artists themselves chose: lighthearted and skilfully drawn pictures of animals, or sometimes caricatures of religious ritual and battle scenes, with animals playing the parts of the king and other delightfully absurd rural imaginings. These more personal and informal *ostraca* complement a similar series excavated from the village of the tomb workers. They cover all aspects of the life of this extraordinary community. On these stone flakes we see the people of the village, one man, even, with his hand stuck deep in a pot; the workmen, the dancing girls, women suckling their babies, lovers in sinuous complicated embraces, a great section of ancient life caught by the quick eye and sure hand of the master artists who worked in the royal tombs. The permanence of their stony sketches has ensured their survival in great quantities and now there are thousands of such *ostraca* spread throughout the museums of the world. Every excavator in the Valley found further examples as the ground was cleared in the search for more tombs.

It was Mohammed Abd er Rassul who provided Grébaut's directorship with its most extraordinary discovery. In January 1891 he pointed out to Grebaut a depression in the sand that lay between the huge courtyard of the two temples at Deir el Bahari, and before the Director left Thebes he asked Daressy to clear it out. Another cache, one far larger than that of the kings was uncovered and, as in that earlier tomb, the Abd er Rassuls had long pilfered the coffins before they gave their secret away. However, the sheer quantity of this second cache, known as the *Bab el Gasus* (the Door of the Priests), must have daunted the tomb robbers for the *Service* eventually removed nearly two hundred statuettes and large numbers of papyri and stelae from the tomb. The encoffined inhabitants were the priests of the great temples of Thebes who had lived at the end of the New Kingdom. Numbering nearly one hundred and sixty, more than a hundred had been buried in double coffins, all beautifully made and finely decorated with small exquisite paintings similar to those upon the funerary papyri. It represented an impossible haul for the Museum and large numbers of the mummies and their coffins were presented to other museums around the world. Many of these ancient priests had been members of the same families that had organized the burial of the royal mummies and this tomb, tunnelled deeply into the rock under the temples was a part of the same concept. The care and richness of the burials emphasized the power of the priesthood at this period of Egyptian history; if the first Abd er Rassul cache of kings was a Theban Westminster Abbey, this second was its St Paul's Cathedral.

Mohammed Abd er Rassul's second revelation did him no good, however, for in a few years the *Service* rid themselves of a *Reis* that they could not trust. Grébaut, too, resigned from the Directorship after a few years; he had no experience as an archeologist and his unpopular decisions concerning the excavation permits, that as a department of the Ministry of Public Works the *Service* issued, caused many complaints to his minister. For the first time the directorship was given to an archeologist, Jacques de Morgan and in a series of excavations that he and the British archeologist, Flinders Petrie conducted, some of the earliest royal tombs of Ancient Egypt, those of the First and Second Dynasties and periods even older, were excavated but all at sites far from the Valley of the Kings. The honeymoon with archeological method, however, was brief. De Morgan returned to Persia where he had started his career and in 1898 the post of Director devolved upon Victor Loret, another of Maspero's pupils.

Loret had arrived in Egypt with Maspero in 1881

and in the eight years that he spent in Egypt he had acquired a great deal of knowledge and experience. He had worked briefly with Lefébure on his survey and later he had recorded many of the private tomb chapels at Thebes. He had also observed the communities of villagers at Thebes very closely and had studied different aspects of their lives. Loret had also seen fragments of the royal ushabtis of Amenhotep II of the Eighteenth Dynasty appearing upon the antiquities markets for several years. Many other fragments of that Dynasty's royal burial equipment, including the better part of a bed decorated in part with gold and silver foil had been taken from Thebes, sealed with the protection of consular seals, from under the gaze of Grébaut himself. These pieces, several of which were known to have been found in the Valley of the Kings, posed a question; obviously they had been taken from the burials of the Eighteenth Dynasty kings, many of whom had been found with the later kings in the Royal Cache, but where were their tombs? Once again the Abd er Rassuls may have known at least a part of the answer for at this time Mohammed was claiming to visitors to Luxor that he knew the existence of an unknown tomb of a king—and this in the Valley of the Kings itself!

Loret, too, knew the Valley well and may long have suspected the existence of more buried tombs which, as Director of the *Service* he could now excavate. It is not known whether or not he dug in the West Valley testing the theories of Wilkinson and Mariette but if he did he was unlucky and it was in the main Valley that all his discoveries were made. Loret adopted the system of excavation where soundings, or *sondages*, were taken in the debris of the Valley by digging circular pits about a metre across through the debris down to the bedrock. It was certainly quicker than clearing out complete gullies in the Valley, which were partly filled with ancient quarry chippings and flood debris, but far less effective than the system of trenching that was later employed. Of course, none of these method were ever more than techniques for removing the archeological strata to discover whether or not it covered a tomb. Real archeological excavation, recording these strata and all the finds as they were discovered during the course of excavation has never been performed in the landscape of the Valley of the Kings. It is a sad loss for the history of the Valley, and an unnecessary one because there were excellent archeologists working at that time who could have performed such work efficiently.

In early February 1898, as previous excavators had done before him, Loret accompanied by the local Inspector Hosni, walked the ground of the Valley looking for indications of buried tombs and, from the positions that he chose for his first *sondages*, Loret certainly had prior knowledge of the general areas where tombs might be located. He took Hosni to the southernmost end of the Valley, far from the known tombs, and on to the top of the terrace of cliffs that ringed the central area. The main drainage area of the entire hillside above the Valley started high on the slopes behind them. The rainwaters ran into a huge natural bowl above the Valley, and then to the Valley floor through an eroded rock crevice, gouged and worn by the tremendous force of the floods.

The path that led to the tomb of Tuthmosis III. The loose scree that ran down from the cleft that holds the tomb was laid with a stone block staircase to enable visitors to climb to the mouth of the tomb. The scree was deposited by ancient floods, the largest of which occurred during the Nineteenth Dynasty, and the Eighteenth Dynasty tombs that had been cut in the floor of the wadi beneath were buried under several metres of rock and debris. These thick deposits were cleared away during Howard Carter's excavations. This photograph, by Harry Burton, was taken during the first decade of this century

Loret gave orders to sound the upper half of this narrow crevice, perhaps in the knowledge that the area around the top of this natural drain had been carefully dammed and anciently filled with chippings, possibly to shield an unknown tomb that lay below. Loret decided to begin the lines of the *sondages* at the top of the crevice and continue them down the gully that lay in the floor of the Valley below. At that time there were no known tombs in this section of the Valley and when studying the maps of the Valley, Loret had noticed a second large blank area around the mysterious tomb 12 that James Burton had measured and mapped some fifty years before. Walking along the path around the top of the cliffs that ring the Valley, Loret may well have noticed another water deflection arrangement above this second blank area, a kind of small cutting with a little dam built above. Later he dug under these cliffs.

Leaving Hosni in charge of the digging Loret then left Thebes by the Museum boat for the annual inspection of the antiquities of Egypt. Four days later on 12 February 1898, when Loret was at Aswan, he received a cable from Hosni announcing the discovery of a tomb. Loret directed the Inspector to cover the doorway and await his arrival. He returned to Thebes on 20 February after a voyage up the Nile to the first cataract. The next day he went to the Valley to see the site of the tomb and Hosni showed him a covered depression in the cleft high above the Valley in the very centre of the crevice down which the water drained. It took the workmen several hours to reach the entrance to the tomb again then suddenly a small black hole appeared under the flat carved lintel of the entrance way. From this hole came an intense heat and a strange odour, which they later discovered was of the cedar wood and other materials of the ancient tomb furnishings, still smelling of their life some three thousand years before. Slowly the workmen enlarged the hole until Loret and Hosni could scramble through into the darkness below.

Climbing over the spill of dirt that had fallen from the opening the two men found themselves in a steep slippery corridor that dropped down out of sight. They scrambled and slithered down the half-filled but well-made corridor, cautiously climbing over the heaps of debris and rock that had entered through the doorway above. After some forty feet they slid down a steeper slope which, they later found, covered a flight of steps. This led them into another corridor and, as in the tomb of Seti I, spilled them on to the edge of a deep well. The well was carefully plastered but decorated only with an ornamental frieze and a pattern of stars on its ceiling. Loret had a ladder put down into the pit, then crossed the floor and climbed up the other side and through a rough doorway into a pillared hall. In their haste to enter the tomb, the workmen had tied a supporting rope around an ancient beam that stuck out from the wall but it held Loret long enough for him to climb out of the well into this next section of the tomb.

Like Belzoni before him, Loret now found himself in a hall supported at its centre by two large pillars. The room was covered in debris, the ancient tomb furnishings, ritual equipment and the masons' limestone chippings all mixed together. In the centre of the room stood a large wooden statue still standing on its base. The walls were painted, but in a style different from the other tombs then known in the Valley. The pictures, drawn upon the shiny smooth plastered walls, were all divided into grids, each separate compartment of which held the figure of a god and above them were drawings of rows of pots containing burning incense. The drawings were elegant, spare; the limbs of the figures represented only by single lines—'stick figures' but of such elegance as had never before been seen. The room is a most curious shape, none of its walls being the same length, and Loret took some time to appreciate what he had come to. Then he saw a great black rectangle gaping in the floor along the left side of the room and he realized that the tomb continued beneath the room in which he stood. Again he slid over debris spilled on a broken and roughly covered flight of steps and this time he was ejected into the final room of the tomb, a huge cartouche-shaped chamber painted in warm browns and pinks, some thirty-seven feet long and twenty-five feet wide. Loret, the first person to walk in such a strange shaped room since ancient times, was amazed. He described it as being like a 'monstrous papyrus' and the stick figures upon its walls also helped to create that strong impression. All around him, in the texts on the walls and the two massive square columns in the centre of the room, was the cartouche of the king, Tuthmosis III. All over the floor the pathetic remnants of the original burial were thrown and smashed. They had been broken against the walls with such force that its plaster was dented. Even the lintels that had been set into the plaster over the doors of the four chambers that ran off this main room, had been wrenched from the walls. The ugly gaps from where they had been extracted were outlined in the flickering light of their torches. Walking slowly through the chamber Loret finally saw the sarcophagus behind

The burial chamber of the tomb of Tuthmosis III

the second pillar. It was made of stone and very shiny. Excitedly, he first thought it was made from a block of carnelian, but later, after taking a small broken fragment with him to the surface and washing it, he found that its colouring turned the water red. The sarcophagus, fine-grained yellow quartzite precisely cut in a marvel of fine workmanship, had been stained with ochre, perhaps to imitate the pink softer granite of Aswan.

Loret then went into the four side chambers that were still filled with broken statues and funerary goods. In the first room on the right were nine broken statues and the remains of a large ape. In the room next to it was a great quantity of pottery jars, originally filled with food and provisions, and in the centre

of the floor lay a slaughtered bull. The two rooms on the other side of the burial chamber had been anciently swept quite clean, and in the one close to the sarcophagus Loret found two coffins which, until they were unwrapped later at the Museum, he imagined to be from the family of the king. They were, in fact, two mummies of a later period, placed into the cleaned-up side chamber of the old royal tomb in a secondary burial.

In the dust on the floor of the tomb Loret traced out a grid and in the next three weeks cleared out all of the objects. The positions of the objects were recorded upon gridded charts. The list of the discoveries includes statues of the kings and gods covered with black resin; vases of glass and alabaster ceramic jars for food storage; sticks and staves both for practical and ritual purposes; sandals; many plants; some fragmentary jewellery; boxes of beef, veal and birds; the baboon; at least twenty-one model boats (and some of these, judging from their fragments, were more than six feet long); natron, which was used for drawing fats from the body during embalming and during parts of the 'Opening of the Mouth' ritual. The tomb had been very heavily robbed and this list represented but a fraction of its original contents. No records were kept of smaller fragments that might have told us of the other goods, such as chariot harness and body armour, which one would have expected to find in the tomb. Neither, strangely, were any ushabtis found nor have any been seen of this king. Cleared of its ancient objects in three days, the tomb was completely swept of its dirt and chippings in another eight.

While Loret was still occupied with the tomb of Tuthmosis III, he gave orders for *sondages* to be made in the second blank area in the Valley that he had noticed earlier. The hill above the old bare tomb 12 was peppered with *sondages* but with no success, then the gangs of workmen tested the foot of the cliffs that ran straight up from the Valley floor to the terrace

The mummy of the prince that had been flung onto one of the royal funerary boats of Amenhotep II

above. By early March Loret was sure that he had found another tomb. Slowly his workmen uncovered an area against the foot of the cliff where a large pile of loose boulders had been piled up. The white, un-patinated colour of these limestone rocks clearly showed them to have been cut and broken by the hand of man. As they dug lower, taking away the stones from the cliff face, they found that the rock had been carefully chiselled and smoothed and by the evening of 8 March they had exposed an entire cut surface of rock, the top of a tomb's doorway.

The next day they exposed more of the entrance. So far only small pieces of faience had been found that bore a royal cartouche but these were so broken that the fragmentary signs could have belonged to any one of three kings. Then the workmen found an ushabti in the dirt bearing the name of Amenhotep II, the son of Tuthmosis III whose tomb they had found just a month before. Obviously with broken grave goods scattered all around its door they could not expect to find the tomb intact and Loret was also aware that objects from this king's tomb had already appeared upon the antiquities market in Egypt and Europe. But the workmen persevered and they were nonetheless excited for all that. By the evening, at seven o'clock, they at last managed to clear

enough of the doorway to allow entry to the first corridor of the tomb. Loret and the foreman entered the warm dark hole and again they slithered down steep corridors, over rubble and broken antiquities to the edge of a well. Then Loret decided to continue the work into the night.

They crossed the well with a ladder and once more found themselves in another room with two square pillars at its centre. All around were more smashed items of funerary equipment, a wooden head, a serpent, lotus flowers carved from cedar wood and many pieces of large wooden boats.

I went forward [between the two columns] with my candle and, horrible sight, a body lay there upon the boat, all black and hideous its grimacing face turning towards me and looking at me, its long brown hair in sparse bunches around its head. I did not dream for an instant that this was just an unwrapped mummy. The legs and arms seemed to be bound. A hole exposed the sternum, there was an opening in the skull. Was this a victim of a human sacrifice? Was this a thief murdered by his accomplices in a bloody division of the loot, or perhaps he was killed by soldiers or police interrupting the pillaging of the tomb?

It had been a long day, and Loret's imagination was running at full pelt in the flickering candlelight. In fact, the body was a mummy, perhaps that of Prince Webensennu who, in his lifetime had over-seen the royal chariot horses and had been buried in the royal tomb. The mummy had been robbed while the resins and oils that were poured into it were still fresh and, on being thrown across the room, it had adhered to the top of one of the king's funerary boats. For the next ten years or so the mummy on the boat was a prime sight for visitors to the Valley.

Loret continued down the staircase that ran from the left-hand side of the room; they passed through two more chambers, then:

At the bottom the door opened into blackness. We advanced, the light grew greater, and with stupefaction we saw an immense hall entirely decorated, held up by two rows of three pillars on which were painted life-sized groups of a king in the presence of a god. It was really him, Amenhotep II, there were his cartouches. There was no more doubt. It was the son of Tuthmosis III. It was the beginning of the strange chronological series that marked my work that winter.

Everywhere in the large hall lay a thick layer of broken objects, funerary statues in wood and ala-baster, pottery, glass, ancient garlands and plants, splintered wood. Beyond the two last pillars, steps led down into a crypt and there, surrounded by further heaps of broken objects lay the sarcophagus similar to that of Tuthmosis III but larger and more sparsely decorated.

The sarcophagus was open, but was it empty? I did not dare to hope for the contrary, because royal mummies had never been found in the necropolis of the Valley, all of them having been moved in antiquity to a safe place. I reached the sarcophagus with difficulty being careful not to break anything underfoot. I could partially read the cartouches of Amenhotep II. I leant over the edge, bringing the light a little nearer. Victory! A dark coffin lay in the bottom, having at its head a bunch of flowers and at its feet a wreath of leaves . . .

Loret retreated from the royal presence and in-spected the side chambers where, once again, he found the basic divisions of their contents that he had seen in the tomb of Tuthmosis III; one chamber for food and meat, among which was identified the earliest known olive branches in Egypt; another for ritual objects, faience and statues of the king and great black leopards.

We passed to the rooms on the right. In the first one we entered an unusually strange sight met our eyes: three bodies lay side by side at the back in the left corner, their feet pointing towards the door. The right half of the room was filled with little coffins with mummiform covers and funerary statues of bitumined [resin painted] wood. These statues were contained in the coffins, that the thieves had opened and rejected after having searched in vain for treasures.

We approached the cadavers. The first seemed to be that of a woman. A thick veil covered her forehead and left eye. Her broken arm had been replaced at her side, her nails in the air. Ragged and torn cloth hardly covered her body. Abundant black curled hair spread over the limestone floor on each side of her head. The face was admirably conserved and had a noble and majestic gravity.

The second mummy, in the middle was that of a child of about fifteen years. It was naked with the hands joined on the abdomen. First of all the head appeared totally bald, but on closer examination one saw that the head had been shaved except in an area on the right temple from which grew a magnificent

161

tress of black hair. This was the coiffure of the royal princes [called the Horus lock]. I thought immediately of the royal prince Webensennu, this so far unknown son of Amenophis II, whose funerary statue I had noticed in the great hall, and whose canopic fragments I was to find later. The face of the young prince was laughing and mischievous, it did not at all evoke the idea of death.

Lastly the corpse nearest the wall seemed to be that of a man. His head was shaved but a wig lay on the ground not far from him. The face of this person displayed something horrible and something droll at the same time. The mouth was running obliquely from one side nearly to the middle of the cheek, bit a pad of linen whose two ends hung from a corner of the lips. The half closed eyes had a

strange expression, he could have died choking on a gag but he looked like a young playful cat with a piece of cloth. Death which had respected the severe beauty of the woman and the impish grace of the boy had turned in derision and amused itself with the countenance of the man.

A remarkable fact was that the three corpses, like the one on the boat, had their skulls pierced with a large hole and the breast of each one was opened.

The three mummies that Loret found in one of the side chambers of the tomb of Amenhotep II. Loret had them drawn as they were found lying in the tomb but this photograph, with the mummies set on one of Loret's packing cases and lit by candles, has not been published before. It was recently discovered in a pile of old photographs in a shop in Luxor

This extraordinary old lady, majestic and although severely damaged, inadvertently given great presence by the processes of age and embalming, has recently been proved to be the mummy of Queen Tiy, the powerful and beloved wife of Amenhotep III, mother of the heretic king Akhenaten. Tests made upon hair samples of the mummy proved it to be from the same head as a small lock of hair of the queen carefully preserved inside a set of four miniature coffins that were placed in the tomb of Tutankhamen.

One of the four side chambers remained unexamined, that to the right of the sarcophagus which had been anciently sealed with limestone blocks. Loret hauled himself up to the opening at the top of this wall and looked into the darkness.

> *The room was rather large, three metres by four, the taper hardly illuminated it. I distinguished nevertheless nine coffins laid on the ground, six at the back, occupying all the space, three in the front, leaving to the right a small free space. There was only room in the length of the room for two coffins, in the width for six so that the mummies touched at their head, shoulders and feet. Five coffins had lids, the other four were without. It was not for the moment possible to think of entering the room and looking at the coffins at closer quarters. I said to myself that they were probably members of the royal family analogous to the two princesses found in the tomb of Tuthmosis III . . .*

Realizing that he could not attempt to move these mummies before the rest of the tomb was cleared, Loret returned to his other work and was occupied in the tomb of Tuthmosis III, which was still being emptied of its objects and its debris. When he eventually returned to the tomb of Amenhotep II he again divided the rooms into a series of grids and cleared the objects, labelling the maps and marking the position of the objects as he went. More than 2,000 pieces were recovered from the tomb, some smashed and broken into many fragments that were scattered throughout the tomb while others were represented by only the smallest remnants. Finally, when everything had been packed, taken out of the tomb and put aboard the Museum boat, he gave his attention to the mummies in the two side chambers.

First, Loret supervized the lifting and boxing of the three mummies that had lain in the open side chamber. These 'as rigid as wood' were lifted into boxes lined with cotton wool and taken out of the tomb to the boat. Then Loret turned towards the king in the sarcophagus.

> *The flowers which garlanded the coffin had already been removed with a process shown to me by Dr Schweinfurth; they were put in damp silk paper and then into cardboard boxes of the right size. In my examination of the coffin I had noticed that the part covering the feet was pierced by a large hole. I slid my hand into the hole and to my great chagrin I found that it was empty. The mummy, had it been taken? Was it one of the four that I had just packed up? I lifted the lid . . . the mummy was there— smaller than the coffin, it did not reach down to the foot—intact, carrying around the neck a garland of leaves and flowers, on the breast a little bouquet of mimosa which hid the prenomen of Amenhotep II written on the sheet, the name which I later read.*

There only remained the walled chamber.

> *I had been in there alone some days after the discovery, through the narrow aperture. On the other side of the wall I found myself in a very narrow space, and several objects which were hidden from view from outside the wall became apparent . . .*
>
> *The coffins and the mummies were a uniform grey colour. I leant over the nearest coffin and blew on it to read the name. The grey tint was a layer of dust which flew away and let me read the name and prenomen of Ramesses IV. Was I in the hiding place of royal coffins? I blew away the dust of the second coffin, a cartouche showed itself, illegible for an instant, painted in a matt black on a shiny black ground. I went over to the other coffins, everywhere there were cartouches! Here the name of Siptah, there the names of Seti II, further, a long inscription bearing the complete titles of Tuthmosis IV. We had fallen on a royal cache, similar to that of Deir el Bahari. Several people could not be contained in the little room at one time. It was impossible then to lift the covers and examine the mummies nearer to. I contented myself with taking the measurements of the coffins and I gave the order to the Luxor carpenter for nine new cases . . .*

Loret had a part of the wall taken down and the mummies were carried one by one into the burial chamber where the lids of the coffins were lifted.

> *Each shroud was photographed, each mummy measured, described, examined in all its details. Some inscriptions were found on the bindings. I copied them patiently, mechanically, without giving myself time to study them in depth. It was thus that I discovered on the mummy shut in the coffin of Seti II, a long legend saying that in the year XII, fourth*

*month of the winter, day six, the first priest of
Amun Re, Pai-Noudjem [Pinejem I] wrapped the king
Amenhotep III . . .*

Loret had found another smaller cache of kings,
the Cachette as it came to be called, where the reburial commissions had placed eight kings and an
anonymous woman. They were the missing links in
the chronological line of royal mummies which, in
conjunction with the kings found in the Abd er Rassul
tomb, virtually completed the list of New Kingdom
kings, from the early Eighteenth Dynasty to the late
Ramessides. Inscriptions on the mummies stated that
they had been placed in the tomb under the same
circumstances and at the same time as those found
in the great cache of Deir el Bahari.

After three weeks of clearing and packing, the
boxes of mummies and antiquities were transported
some four miles down the dusty track to the river for
loading into the Museum boat. Loret had come to
the end of his first season's work in the Valley.

*Everything was well carried out, foreseen, organised.
It only remained to leave. We nailed up the last
planks on the last cases hastily, because the Nile
was sinking and we were pressed for time—when I
received from the Minister of Public Works the order
to replace the mummies in their ancient place and
to seal the tomb . . .*

Loret's *Service* came under the control of the
Ministry of Public Works and Sir William Garstin, an
expert in irrigation. Garstin's order was a reaction to
political statements concerning the royal dead and
their antiquities: foreigners, it was said, were robbing
Egypt's royal tombs and the popular general sentiment was that the burial of a dead king should be
left to lie where it had been placed with all the majesty
of his empire some three and a half thousand years
earlier.

Loret, though no doubt angered at this last-
minute order from Cairo, returned the mummies to
their tomb and resealed the monument. He would not
be the last archeologist to encounter political troubles
in the apparently innocent work of excavation in the
Royal Valley. But the Valley had fascinated him and
the following year he was back again digging for
more royal tombs. Meanwhile he left the *Service*'s
architect, Émile Baraize to draw a new map of the
Valley and plot every known tomb upon it.

Loret's discovery threw open the door to speculation
about the existence of the unknown royal tombs.

Virtually all the mummies of kings of the Eighteenth
Dynasty had now been found and it was clear that
there must also be some of their tombs still lying
undiscovered and that the two splendid tombs uncovered by Loret promised further marvels. The
discovery of the tomb of Tuthmosis III high in a cleft
above the valley floor had also opened a new possibility for the location of other tombs. This tomb was
the last of a line of earlier royal tombs and at the
same time the first of the great decorated tombs of
the Valley: last in a series of tombs that were all
hidden away in rock clefts and whose architecture
consisted of a rough progression of corridors snaking
deep into the rock; first, in that in the architecture of
the tomb was the first example of the almost complete
set of architectural elements that is common in the
designs of all the later royal tombs in the Valley.

The tomb of Tuthmosis III is a series of carefully
made inter-related rooms spaced apart in the rough
corridors and stairways that run down to the burial
chamber. The approach to the tomb is through a
narrow, hidden cleft in the cliffs, the entrance suddenly burrowing down into the rock as the fissure
turns sharply left. The entrance stair is steep and
irregular, the first passageway of the tomb, though
well made, runs steeply down and is small, hot and
dark. The first decoration of the tomb seen by a visitor
is a frieze, painted on the first fine plastered wall of
the tomb, that runs around the top of the walls of the
well. This consists of a large row of beautifully painted
heker hieroglyphs, which in themselves signify the
word 'decoration', painted above the forty-foot pit.
At the end of the corridor at the top of the well one
is faced with these huge decorations at the top of
these high walls, sheer and inaccessible. This alarming
scale is deliberately reversed in the small irregular
room beyond, called the antechamber, which is supported by two strong square pillars and decorated
with a carefully detailed catalogue of ancient gods.
The decorative *heker* frieze in this room is exactly one
third as high as its counterpart in the well, and the
grid system that holds the neat little pictures of the
gods consists of rectangles just a few inches high.
The room's scale is neat and jewel-like. Its rough
finished floor and the odd angles of its walls are a
result of the necessity to finish the work upon the
room quickly—the room was never completely
quarried from the rock and the walls were smoothed
down and plastered flat at irregular angles to each
other. In the area around the doorway to the well the
borders of the panels that hold the catalogue of gods
were never finished. The two columns, which were

marked out to receive drawings of the king being welcomed into the Underworld by the gods, were never painted. But the columns are cut so precisely that, with tapes and rulers it is impossible to detect any error in them. The fine precision of the stone work and plastering, and the sure warm colours of the decoration all mixed in with the rough and haphazard workmanship of the corridors and stairwells, are the essence of the tomb's great beauty and the burial chamber that lies below the small painted ante-chamber is one of the supreme examples of ancient Egyptian architecture that has survived.

After the dramatic contrasts of the previous rooms and corridors the burial chamber seems very still and weightless, floating deep in the cliffs. The great cartouche-shaped wall swings around the two columns, its rhythms carefully controlled by the vertical dividing lines of the wall texts which are separated in a manner that is in harmonious relationship to the architecture of the room. These vertical divisions of the wall scenes were precisely drawn at the principal points of the geometric scheme that underlies the architecture of the burial chamber and this is the key to the aesthetic attraction of the tombs. It owes its outstanding qualities neither to garish decorations nor to mere bombastic size, but to perfect proportions and fine craftsmanship. Its essential modesty of size and materials form the greater part of its beauty. It is a simple, spare product, excellently made.

The wall texts of the burial chambers are painted in a manner reserved principally for royal tombs of the earlier Eighteenth Dynasty and some of the funeral papyri of that period. The taut spare style has nothing of the light colourful qualities that were being explored in the paintings of private tomb chapels of the same period. They are skilfully drawn in black lines as sure and as workmanlike as the pencil marks of a carpenter. This style was a true innovation though, on a much smaller scale, a somewhat similar type of burial chamber decoration had been used in some nobles' tombs some three hundred years before. Two of the succeeding royal tombs also have the same text, drawn in the same spare manner, upon the walls of their burial chambers but these later tombs used a background plaster of a greeny-grey colour which was enlivened in the details, somewhat vulgarly, with the use of bright white paint. In the tomb of Tuthmosis III, however, a warm yellow plaster was used for the walls, which were smoothed down carefully in the manner of a fine papyrus. The effect is roseate, warm and generous.

Drawn upon one of the columns of the burial chamber is a small scene that shows Tuthmosis III with some of his queens and, by its side, a strangely touching little picture of the king being suckled by his mother Isis; she is in the form of a tree and her breast hangs from a branch. This brief scene of the king and four of his queens is the nearest that any in the Valley tombs come to recording biographic details; the inscriptions indicate whether the queens were alive or dead. At the end of the New Kingdom, the tomb was visited by a scribe, Amenhotep, probably as a member of the reburial commission that had come to take the royal mummy. On the wall of the burial chamber he scratched his name and re-marked appreciatively 'A thousand times beautiful is this painting below!' Amenhotep is probably the first recorded art critic of history.

The two texts that the scribes drew in the tomb were 'The Book of What is in the Otherworld', usually called by its ancient name, the *Amduat*, and whose twelve sections were drawn on the burial chamber walls, and the Litany of Re, a far shorter text that was drawn upon the two pillars of the burial chamber. The gods in the upper chamber are the cast of hundreds that appear in these two texts of the burial chamber. This great assembly of gods was culled from

Some of the mysterious drawings that illuminate the Litany of Re, a strange text that describes the various phases that the king passes through between death and resurrection, a metamorphosis described in a succession of frequently baffling images

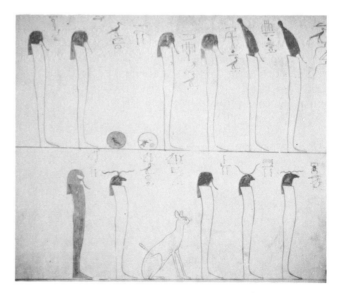

early less organized religious writings and belief to form the casts of the great theological compositions of the New Kingdom. The *Amduat* was the first of these compositions and it survives in its first complete version in the tomb of Tuthmosis III. The drawing of this verion is certainly the finest of the existing copies.

The twelve chapters, or 'hours' of the *Amduat* that correspond to the hours of the night, are separated from each other in the tomb by vertical divisions between the columns of texts. Each hour is also horizontally divided into three registers and it is the central register that usually contains the king in his bark as he sails through the Otherworld to the morning horizon. The book begins:

The writings of the hidden chamber, the places where the souls, the gods and the spirits stand. What they do. The beginning of the Horn of the West, the gate of the Western Horizon. This is the knowledge of the power of those in the Netherworld. This is the knowledge of what they do: the knowledge of their sacred rituals to Re; knowledge of the mysterious powers: knowledge of what is in the hours as well as of their gods, knowledge of what he says to them; knowledge of the Gates and the way on which god passes; knowledge of the powerful ones and the annihilated . . .

Powerful information! The complete scenario of the Otherworld; all the knowledge that the king would need to overcome his fate and achieve immortality. The 'hidden chamber' where such mysteries were revealed—the royal burial chamber—was the scene of this great cosmic drama and in the wall texts it is laid out in great detail for the dead king.

At the beginning of the book, in the first hour, the Sun God just descended from the western horizon, orders his physical body, the dead king, to open the doors of the Underworld for him. He enters and 'the darkness is lit' and 'the netherworld breathes', for here is its salvation come again. From this point on the borders of the book are represented as sand, the sand of the horizons under which this drama takes place. Already in this first hour the long recital of the god's names begins. Knowing the gods, however mysterious they may be, is so important that often mysterious poetic epithets, mere hints of a half-perceived presence of the myriad unknown gods, are written down—even those that have no name at all.

The beautiful west
The one who swallows without rest
The chief of those in the Netherworld

She who swallows the dead
She who gives birth to herself
She who frightens the souls
The Orders of Osiris
The Crook of Osiris

Some of these minor figures may sometimes be explained by reference to other much older texts. They are all present in the *Amduat* because their very mystery was felt to hold a religious validity.

Already in the Second Hour the narrative states that the king will emerge victorious from the Eastern Mountain at the end of the night. For the Egyptians were never so foolish as to imagine that the outcome of this adventure was in doubt; that the sun might not rise; that the cosmos would grind to a halt in a world without belief in these dramas, without the performance of constant rituals in the temples and the activities of everyday life. But the Egyptians knew that in such circumstances their world would lose its validity, its carefully measured order. If all the rituals of the tomb and the temples, and the identification with the elemental processes of the world were stopped, mankind would float in formless terror.

Slowly, throughout each of the hours of the *Amduat*, the Sun on his journey revives the gods in the Otherworld and restores such vital aspects of the dead king as his mind and his will. The sun glows and warms the spirits of the Otherworld, just as it will cause the crops to grow in the fields. In the Fourth Hour further deeper doors of the Otherworld are opened and the king slides downwards into the sombre sandy regions where the larva of the scarab beetle, Sokaris, awaits. Here the royal bark sails in darkness. 'The flames coming out of the mouths of the barge guide him towards the mysterious ways. He does not see their forms. He calls to them and it is his words they hear'. In this blackness the mysterious processes of the royal rebirth are beginning and in the fifth hour is the climax: Sokaris is reborn from the larva:

The image is like this, in utter darkness. The egg [larva] which belongs to this God [Sokaris] is lighted up by the eyes in the head of the Great God, his flesh shines, his legs are inside in coils. Noise is heard inside the egg after the Great God has passed by it, like the sound of roaring in the sky during a storm.

Finally the king emerges in the form of the creator god upon the back of the Eastern and the Western Mountains, and so powerful is this rebirth that the

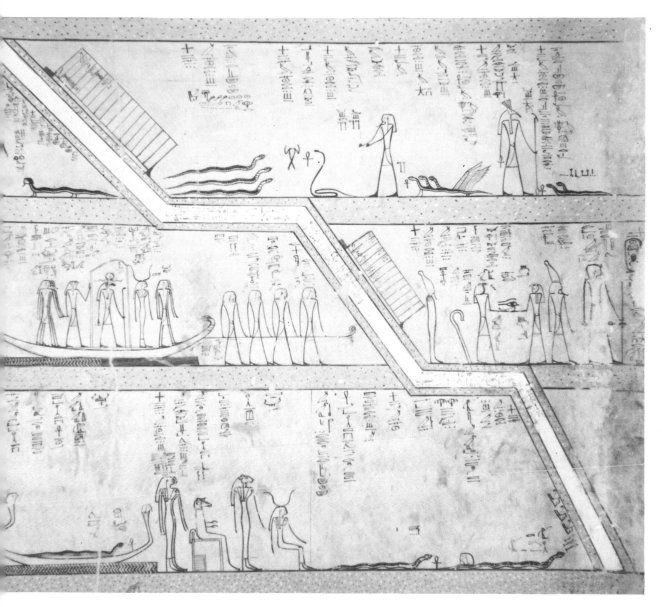

The Fourth Hour of the Amduat *in the tomb of Tuthmosis III*

artist scribes bend their usually rigid register lines to show it in their pictures. Above the border of sand, in an alternative visualization of the same event, the beetle is shown pushing his way out of a mound of sand: the tomb and the night. The remaining hours of the *Amduat* become a triumphal progress as more and more of the underworld and its gods are revived and revealed. In the last hour we see the end of the Otherworld. The sun god's great bark, guided by the industrious scarab at its prow, is hauled along by a huge assembly of gods and goddesses. As the great borders that have surrounded the registers of the book join together in an elegant semi-circular motion, a graphic reminder of the architecture of the royal burial chamber itself, the scarab rolls the disc of the sun through the sand to dawn upon the surface of the Eastern Horizon. The abandoned mummy of the dead king is left in the Otherworld, propped against the curve of the sand and worshipped by a large number of the assembled gods.

The climactic Fifth Hour of the Amduat: *the moment when the power of the king bursts from the underworld in a series of dramatic images. The diagrammatic, almost Duchamp-like clarity of the* Amduat in the Tomb of Tuthmosis III *was greatly elaborated in the later royal tombs and the strange spacings and drawings in the tableaux gives the text and the rooms in which they were placed a mysterious, almost alien, quality*

Both of the tombs that Loret found had this long text and drawings upon the walls of the burial chambers but the version in the tomb of Tuthmosis III is infinitely finer, with warmer colours and better proportions. The text was painted after the burial of the king had taken place and the side chambers had been sealed up. Before the burial the tomb ceiling had been painted with rows of five-pointed stars and its *heker* frieze, which in size is exactly halfway between the

huge version of the well and the small version of the other room. Another tomb in the Valley, which was never used by its intended occupant, has been left exactly in this condition, with the great rounded walls decorated and smoothed, waiting for the burial and the attentions of the scribes who would paint the texts. Following the burial in the tomb of Tuthmosis III, three or four scribes skilled in such fast drawing, painted the texts upon the chamber walls. One of these men, however, made several mistakes and his work was erased and he did not, apparently, do any more. The drawing of the elegant figures and the marvellously fluid writing of the hieroglyphs owes much to its mixture of precision and speed of application. The scribes copied their text from a papyrus and occasionally they made mistakes such as recopying two or three words that they had already written because their eyes, flicking back and forth from the papyrus to the wall missed the right place in the text. Occasionally the papyrus itself was found to be damaged and some of the signs missing. Then, quickly, the words *Gem Ush* (found defective) were written in their place and the copying was continued.

The two tombs that had been uncovered by Loret were very different from the later monuments of the Valley with their seemingly endless books of ritual and religion carefully engraved upon the walls. These had taken years of careful workmanship —painting, carving, then repainting. Even this speedy process of decoration after the funeral was, perhaps, represented with token scenes or single figures in the later, more elaborate, tombs.

In Loret's two tombs are to be found the beginnings of architectural tradition in the Valley. Tuthmosis III's tomb already displays the main elements of the architecture of all the later tombs and in the order in which they were always used. However, the precise relationship and articulation of these units was left rather to expediency. Occasionally the precise direction of the corridor for example, was established by following a crack in the rock. The tomb of Tuthmosis III is a series of rooms and staircases joined haphazardly by tunnels. The son's tomb, that of Amenhotep II, is also made from these same elements, often only tentatively shaped and cut in the tomb of his father, the only addition being a single extra corridor added between the antechamber and the burial chamber. But all the units are greatly formalized and enlarged. Amenhotep II's architects took the somewhat random plan of Tuthmosis III's tomb and its wall paintings and, in a most typical Egyptian manner, formalized and refined them, adding geometrical exactness and

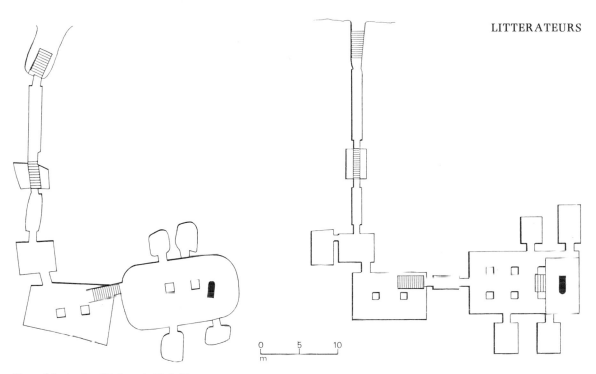

*Plans of the tombs of Tuthmosis III (left)
and Amenhotep II (right)*

symmetry. The vague bending back which occurs in the main axis of the father's tomb is formalized into an exact right angle in the son's. In a country where architects always used a straight line and symmetrical mirror-image design for their formal buildings this most radical right angle must have disorientated in the ancients—as it still does to us.

The greatest innovation in the tomb of Amenhotep II was the shape of its burial chamber. In his father's tomb the sarcophagus had been modestly tucked behind the second column of the burial chamber; in the son's it was placed in a large rectangular room at the end of the two rows of columns that gave the chamber great direction and strong symmetry. The sarcophagus itself was placed in a crypt, cut into the floor of the chamber. The cutting of this crypt was a change of plan, made after the original flat floor had been carefully finished and it left two of the side chambers with their doorways some five feet in the air. The large deep pit-crypt greatly intruded into the original design of the burial chamber and diminished the architectural effect. The two end columns in their rows teeter uncomfortably on the edge of this crypt and the sarcophagus seems to be strangely low in the hole. The successive tombs solve these problems of architecture by making the crypt larger and drawing the columns away from the edge. However, the exca-

vation of this crypt would have allowed for a set of shrines, like those plated in gold found surrounding the sarcophagus of Tutankhamen, to have been erected over Amenhotep's sarcophagus. The powerful shape of this gleaming outer shrine, would have restored the royal burial to a position of prominence in the room. All traces of these shrines have disappeared as have all Loret's records of his work.

It is possible that both the tombs of Tuthmosis III and Amenhotep II followed directly in a tradition of tomb design that was also used by their immediate ancestors, for none of these earlier tombs has yet been uncovered. Until that time it is these two tombs that represent the beginning of the tradition of royal tomb design in the Valley. In the later tombs this basic design was streamlined, modified and greatly enlarged, transformed almost beyond recognition. Frequently these monuments were of far less charm and true magnificence. Even in these secretive early tombs, which were shut off from the world by a rough stone wall and plaster, there is something of that element of walk-through theatricality that was present in the mortuary arrangements of the Old Kingdom kings and which returned in the later royal tombs of the Valley. These two tombs were designed for a moving eye, as an experience flowing in space, a processional: the path of the sun.

17

The Scene Changes

(1889–1902)

Although Loret had returned to Cairo without his royal mummies, the excavations in the Valley had obviously excited the new Director, and the following year he was back, giving orders for more *sondages*. Loret's system, which had been popularly employed in Egypt for more than fifty years, was the equivalent of sticking a pin in the map of the Valley hoping to strike a tomb. Upon reaching bedrock the *sondages* were simply refilled. Although one might lament the fact that Loret destroyed the ancient archeological strata through which he dug, it is somewhat academic because the areas he peppered were subsequently dug over twice again, and each time the ground was completely turned over down to the bedrock.

For this second season of excavation Loret chose to explore the end of the gully in which the tomb of Ramesses XI was situated. There he had a row of *sondages* dug and today it is interesting to compare the later maps of the Valley that show the tombs of this area, then unknown, and see how close Loret came to them. This comparison points to the basic inefficiency of the method, a process even further weakened by his workmen who simply did not tell him of some of their discoveries and, presumably, after taking some saleable items from the tombs for themselves, reclosed the burials. Close to the tomb numbered 21, Loret noted two other small tombs on his plan of the Valley, which he numbered 27 and 28, but apparently he made no attempt to have them dug out of the flood debris and chippings which largely filled them.

Loret now turned his attention to the area of the Valley between the tombs of Tuthmosis III and Amenhotep II. At the foot of the cliffs underneath the tomb of Tuthmosis III he ordered the ground to be peppered with more *sondages* but, his foreman told him, nothing was found. He then put the gang to work in the next rock bay, between the tombs of Seti II and Tausert, which had always stood open to view and here he was luckier. His men cleaned down a chiselled cliff face and discovered, much as he had found at the tomb of Amenhotep II, the top of a doorway. This they cleared out in early March 1899 and once again

Loret slithered over the debris into the tomb. This he found had originally been smaller and rougher than any previously discovered royal tomb in the Valley. The cartouche-shaped burial chamber had been flooded, the plaster had warped and peeled from the walls and quantities of flood debris covered the floor. But in all this destruction Loret found, upon a plinth of alabaster, a magnificent sarcophagus, similar to that which he had discovered in the tomb of Tuthmosis III. Next to this sarcophagus stood a cubic box, cut from the same stone and with the same fineness as the sarcophagus itself. This was a king's canopic chest, so called by egyptologists because some such chests had contained vases similar in shape to a peculiar image of Osiris, a vase surmounted with a human head, which was worshipped in the town of Canopus in the Delta. This container, however, held no pots but it did contain four stoppers covering compartments in which, mummified and set in resins, the viscera of the embalmed king had been placed. Loret had found fragments of a similar finely made alabaster chest in the tomb of Amenhotep II. On the sarcophagus Loret read the name of the king: Tuthmosis I, grandfather of Tuthmosis III. True, the sarcophagus had been made for him by Tuthmosis III, but it seemed to Loret that the primitive and ill-shaped tomb, which held many of the features of the royal tombs in its rough detail, was the first-made tomb of the Valley. Only a few years previously, a colleague of Loret's at the Archeological Institute had translated a stela in a private tomb chapel on Gurna, in which a court official named Ineni claimed to have excavated the tomb of Tuthmosis I, 'no one seeing, no one hearing'; it seemed that Loret had found that tomb.

Apart from the sarcophagus and the chest there was little else in the tomb. A pile of broken pottery shards, mainly from large food-storage jars of the Eighteenth Dynasty, lay in the single side room. In the debris on the floor Loret's men found a carved head from one of the compartments of the canopic chest, two small fragments of glass and a fragment of an alabaster jar which bore the name of the king. Apart from these there were two small pieces of limestone which bore a part of the *Amduat*. Although the tomb had not been filled with treasure or kings, Loret was pleased with his discovery for it seemed to him that he had found the first tomb to have been made in the Valley.

Next, Loret ordered *sondages* to be made in the low ground between his newly discovered tomb, which he numbered 38, and that of Amenhotep II. Parts of this site were covered in a heavy deposit of flood debris that Loret thought may well have obscured a tomb. He was not to be disappointed. Late in March his men brought him to a small shaft some six feet deep at the bottom of which a small chamber was cut into one side. Loret's men had found an intact burial, the first ever seen in the Valley of the Kings since the days of the ancient tomb robbers. Although someone had pushed the lid of the great black cedar wood coffin aside and rifled the jewellery of the mummy, most objects in the small chamber were exactly in the places that the ancient burial party had left them. It was the first indication that not all the mummies of the Valley had been taken off to the royal caches.

From the lines of golden hieroglyphs set into the black resin-covered sarcophagus Loret read the owner's name: Mahirpra 'The Lion on the Battlefields'. He had been a warrior companion of a king, perhaps also a relative or close friend, and as the objects were taken out of the tiny tomb all the possessions of just such a hard-living fighter came to light. Arrows of reed and wood, some tipped with flint, filled two leather quivers and there were also two dog collars, one inscribed for his pet, Tantanuet. Some coarse bread and pottery containing long-desiccated oils and fats were for the dead man's sustenance. Also buried with Mahirpra was a draughtboard that he had used while he was alive, a precious glass perfume jar, still stoppered and not opened to this day, and some bright dress jewellery and bracelets. A fine blue-glazed bowl, ornamented with fishes, gazelles and flowers, probably performed a ritual purpose related to the hunt as a symbol for the combating and defeat of Mahirpra's enemies in the next world. There was nothing in the tomb that would date it to the reign of any king but it was obvious that the burial was of the earlier Eighteenth Dynasty and—despite the name of Queen Hatshepsut on a piece of linen in the tomb which could well have been old when it was buried with the warrior—it is tempting to see Mahirpra as a companion of Amenhotep II whose tomb was close by. Most of the early royal tombs in the Valley had such subsidiary tombs cut below their entrances and many of the nobles of

the land were buried in these simple tombs and not under their elaborate personal monuments in the nobles' cemetery on Gurna. Amenhotep II had spent his life fighting, as had Tuthmosis III before him, and it was the bellicose deeds of these kings and their companions at arms which had secured the wealth of the New Kingdom and financed the state which later made the huge lavish tombs in the Valley.

Inside Mahirpra's great black sarcophagus, which had figures of gods covered in gold foil set into the outside, were two fine mummiform coffins, also covered in gold foil, but both were empty. Mahirpra's mummy was in a second set of coffins that was left in the tiny tomb by the side of the sarcophagus. This second set was exquisitely made, and painted with black shiny resin with beautifully made inlaid eyes set into the faces on the coffin lids—funereal works, but of great beauty and simplicity. By the side of the coffins stood two low rush bedsteads and on one of these, on top of a piece of linen, some wheat had been sewn at the time of the funeral which, in the darkness and warmth of the closed tomb had sprouted, had looked vainly for the light and then died. It was the heart of the mystery of Osiris, the sprouting grain, brought into the darkness of the tomb, a part of the magical process of rebirth. Loret had found fragments of similar seedlings in the two royal tombs he had opened the year before and these had been made into the shape of the silhouette of a standing Osiris wearing a tall crown with his arms folded across his chest. Loret had the tomb speedily emptied, so quickly that some of the fine pottery was left behind, loaded his treasure on the Museum boat and shipped them to Cairo.

In the Museum, a papyrus that they had taken from the tomb of Mahirpra was unwrapped and found to contain the most beautifully illustrated portions of the Book of the Dead that were yet known. In the purist early Eighteenth Dynasty style, which was one of the finest periods of Egyptian draughtsmanship, Mahirpra was shown making offerings to the gods and entering the Underworld. One aspect particularly engaged the attentions of the delighted egyptologists: although Mahirpra had been drawn with the normal profile of men of the period, his skin had been painted dark brown and his hair was drawn, untypically, short, thick and curly. At this time, the racial origins of the ancient Egyptians were exciting a great deal of interest and the many claims made for one group or another were based upon the flimsiest of evidence. This papyrus clearly showed that had the entire race been black, Mahirpra's con-

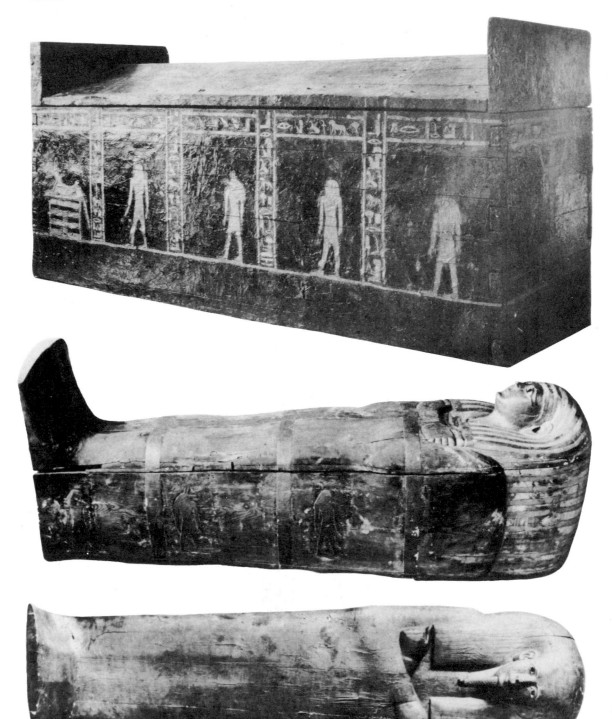

The great wooden sarcophagus, coffins and mummy of
Mahirpra, a Nubian soldier, probably a friend of Amenhotep II

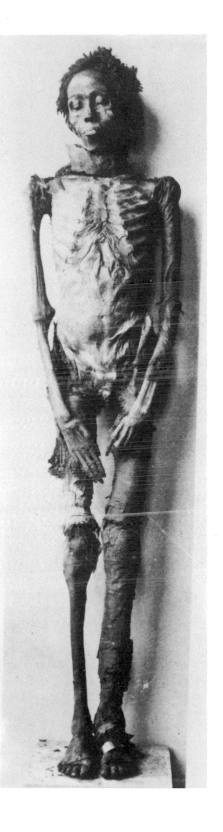

temporaries would have been drawn in a different manner. Two years later, Mahirpra's mummy was unwrapped at the Museum and, under a conventionally coloured mummy mask, the well preserved mummy of a black man was revealed with a short Nubian haircut.

Like Grébaut before him, Loret was no archeologist. The detailed records that he had compiled of his work in the Valley were never published and they are now lost. No plan or photographs were made of the objects as they had been anciently laid in the tomb of Mahirpra and with the workmen at liberty to open and close tombs without Loret's knowledge, there is no way of knowing what else may have been in the tombs when they were found. Many fine objects from these tombs, often in better condition than those Loret retrieved, are now in many different museums in Europe and the United States. Most of them had been bought from Luxor dealers by egyptologists and collectors, and this continual traffic in antiquities helped to create an abrasive relationship between Loret's *Service* and his colleagues who annually came to work in Egypt. Another problem was the way in which the work was carried out; for some of the German and English excavators had long employed methods of conducting and recording excavations that made Loret's system half a century out of date. Sir William Garstin, who had already intervened in the *Service's* affairs over the removal of the royal mummies from the Valley, was hearing loud complaints about the department, as was Lord Cromer, the British Consul-General and virtual ruler of the land.

Due mainly to the fact that the budget of the *Service* had been greatly reduced as a part of Cromer's economies to enable Egypt to discharge the Khedival debt, the ancient monuments were suffering from great neglect. At the same time several of the finest temples in the land were on the verge of partial collapse and the lucrative tourist trade, already enormous in its volume, was rising yearly. Because the monuments urgently required basic restoration work as well as extra facilities such as protective barriers and electric lights, the *Service* was to be reorganized and provided with a greatly increased budget for a programme of expansion and renewal. Loret, prickly and essentially impractical, was hardly the man to head this new *Service*, modelled in part as an arm of the national tourist industry. Furthermore, if new large expenditures were to be made, Cromer wanted British administrators to have an active hand in the work. So, in the year that Loret took Mahirpra

Sir Gaston Maspero. K.C.M.G.

Maspero at his desk in the Cairo Museum

from his tomb in the Valley, he was replaced in the directorship by Maspero, now fifty-three years old, who had been personally invited by Cromer to return to his old post at a greatly increased salary. A group of young archeologists were appointed under Maspero to supervize the work of the five administrative districts into which the sites of ancient Egypt had been divided. Two of these men, James Quibell and Howard Carter, were English and both had archeological experience in Egypt under the redoubtable Flinders Petrie.

In this new régime, Howard Carter, aged twenty-five, was appointed Inspector General of the Monuments of Upper Egypt. Carter was the sixth son of a well known Norfolk painter of animals and at the time of his appointment he had worked in Egypt for seven years, for the most part drawing the reliefs in the Temple of

Hatshepsut at Deir el Bahari, on the other side of the cliffs of the Valley of the Kings. He knew Thebes well and already had a special affection for the Valley. There was much work to be done in the new Inspectorate and Carter spent months visiting the temples and tombs that were under his charge. During his three-year tenure he supervized many major restoration works in the temples of Upper Egypt but it was in the Valley of the Kings that he expended the greater part of his time and energies.

In the autumn of 1900 two local residents of Luxor applied to Carter for a permit to excavate in the Valley, saying that they knew where a tomb was to be found. Suspecting that they had received this knowledge from Loret's workmen, Carter gave them a permit that entitled them to work under the supervision of the head guardian of the tombs, the *Reis* of the *gaffirs* (guardians), Ahmed Girigar. Carter had already made a good friend of him and it was to be an important relationship that lasted through all the trials and tribulations of the clearance of Tutankhamen's tomb some twenty years later. A few days later, supervised by the *Reis*, the workmen had uncovered the doorway of a tomb at the head of the Valley, up under the cliffs which held the tomb of Tuthmosis III. The entrance to the tomb was at the bottom of a fine flight of steps, steep but broad and well made. The workmen had dug some twenty feet down to reach the doorway and Carter walked to the bottom of the steps and climbed over the broken-down remnants of the original sealings of the tomb. He could already see that the tomb had been robbed and flooded and that it had been entered some short time before, probably by Loret's workmen. The tomb was very well made with straight tall corridors and a precise right angle bend on its main axis. After turning this corner and walking through a short corridor he found himself in the burial chamber, a great long oval chamber, like that of Tuthmosis III. But this tomb had never received its proper burial. The sarcophagus, unfinished, lay crooked and out of position at the end of the room and the walls, although painted with the *heker* and a starred ceiling, had never received the text of the *Amduat*. When the tomb was cleaned of the detritus carried into it by the flood waters the men found a collection of objects and fragments of canopic jars that had all been swept about in the tomb. They came from the burials of three people: Sennefer, the Mayor of Thebes in the reign of Amenhotep II, his wife, Sentnay, and another woman of no known affiliation to them, Beketre. Carter first believed that the tomb had been made for Sennefer in the style of the day. This was a shrewd deduction because the plan of the tomb was certainly a further development of that of Tuthmosis III's tomb yet it was lacking in certain essential elements of the royal tomb series, especially the crypt that was first introduced in the tomb of Amenhotep II. Thus, the tomb appeared to be a non-regal tomb of the period of Tuthmosis III to Amenhotep II. Many authorities disagreed with him, however, for the tomb of Tuthmosis II had not been found and this monument, they argued, was, judging from the size and opulence of the burial chamber with its walls prepared for the *Amduat*, obviously built for a king. But some twenty years later Carter retrieved evidence from outside the tomb that would enable a third conclusion to be drawn as to the ownership of the tomb: that it was in all probability made for a favoured prince or a queen of the reign of Tuthmosis III.

Carter's account of this tomb in the newly established *Annales des Service* is not a great report but it is,

The unfinished sarcophagus lying in tomb number 42. This is the only known photograph of the interior of the tomb, which has been blocked for many years

A fine stone head, the lid of a canopic jar, and ancient pieces of wood by one of the door jambs in tomb 42. This photograph, the only record of the location of the objects found in the tomb, suggests that it is not impossible that the burial of Sennefer and his family may have been swept down into the tomb by floodwaters—perhaps the same floods that devastated a part of the Valley during the Nineteenth Dynasty

175

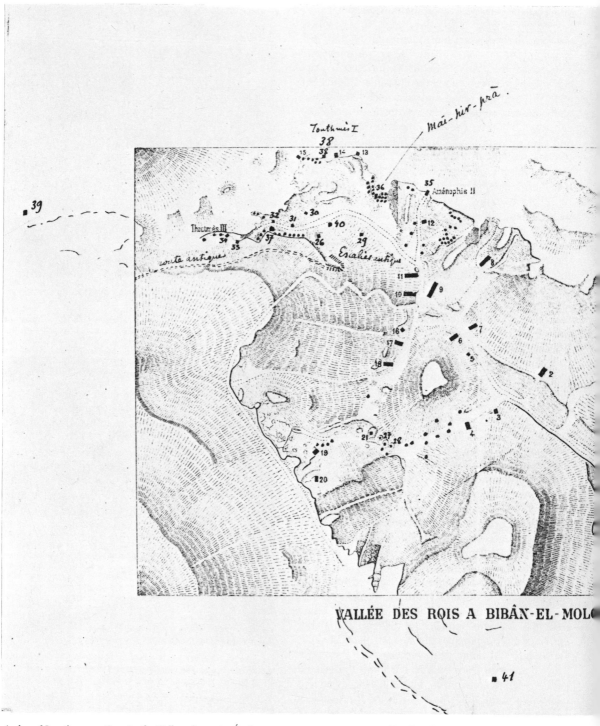

VALLÉE DES ROIS A BIBÂN-EL-MOL

A plan of Loret's excavations in the Valley, drawn by Émile Baraize—the Service architect. Loret never published a scientific account of his work in the Valley; his preliminary report—a narrative of his first descent into the two great royal tombs that he excavated—still survives. Valuable evidence of the extent and location of the excavations may be gained from

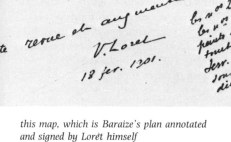

PI. 1

Echelle de $\frac{1}{3635}$

0 60 80 100 120 140 160 180 200

N.M.

Légende

Entrée de tombeau ∎

Sondage •

Chemin ∿

Torrent

Rocher à pic

this map, which is Baraize's plan annotated and signed by Loret himself

nevertheless, an archeological report. Such Valley tombs, damaged and without inscriptions, had never been noticed in publications before. Loret, for example, did not record the work in either the tomb of Tuthmosis I or of Mahirpra, believing that a catalogue of the objects in the Cairo Museum was sufficient. With the first year of Carter's work in the Valley we can see the beginnings of its archeological record.

During his work there Loret had asked Baraize to make a map of the Valley and on a copy of this, drawn after the first season, Loret later drew all the other pits and tombs, many of which had long been opened but never acknowledged. These he numbered from 26, where the record of Lefébure had stopped, through to 41. Three of these were the tombs of kings, one was Mahirpra's tiny tomb, the remaining eleven, small open shafts and small corridor tombs, lay in a group around the gully which leads up to the tomb of Tuthmosis III and which also contained the tomb that Carter had just excavated. This tomb was numbered 42.

A month later, *Reis* Ahmed told Carter of another tomb that he had seen during Loret's excavations. The *Reis* led Carter up the small gully which held the tomb of Ramesses XI where, two years before, Loret had made *sondages*, apparently with no success and showed him a depression in the dust and chippings that covered the area. Carter set a gang of men to dig into the depression and, after they had cleared a hole some fifteen feet deep through the debris and finally down into a shaft, they uncovered a doorway that was sealed and still intact. Carter had this scaled wall taken down and found, to his disappointment, that the tomb, later numbered 44, had been taken over for two fresh burials which had been deposited long after the New Kingdom. The original contents had been completely cleared out. On the ceiling were many mud wasps' nests, a common sight in open tombs at Thebes, and these Carter realized, must have been made between the Eighteenth Dynasty (which, from its general type, was the probable date of the tomb) and its re-use which had taken place during the Twenty-Second Dynasty. Two of the coffins, rough wooden boxes covered with black resin, bore the names of their occupants. The third, blank and with no inscriptions, contained a beautiful inner coffin, inside which was a mummy decorated with red leather straps similar to those that Wilbour had seen on Gurna some twenty years before. These mummies were refugees from the large cache at Deir el Bahari which Mohammed Abd er Rassul had presented to Grébaut. They were three singers from the

Great Temple of Amun at Karnak across the river, and around their mummy wrappings were marvellous wreaths of sacred persea leaves, mimosa and the blue flowers of water lilies. Working with him as Carter cleared the tomb was Percy Newberry, the man who had introduced him to egyptology when he had employed Carter to ink some tracings from Egyptian tombs in the offices of the British Museum. Newberry, a botanist, identified the flowers in the tomb for his protégé. He was to be a kindly eminence throughout much of Carter's stormy career.

During this two-day operation Carter had found, lying in the dirt of the gully, a fragmentary ushabti of the king Tuthmosis IV whose mummy had been found by Loret in the tomb of Amenhotep II two years earlier. Now, with the Valley yielding new tombs at every turn, it seemed very likely that the unknown tomb of this king could be found·close by and Carter and Newberry must have started looking carefully around the area for tell-tale depressions or clefts in the rock that might hide it. No one knew what such a monument might reveal; perhaps the smashed and flooded burial furniture; perhaps a group of kings; even, despite Loret's last experiences in the Valley, another intact burial. And they could imagine the wealth that such a tomb would hold. During his first excavation in the Valley, when he entered and cleared the unfinished tomb (number 42), Carter had found an exquisite rosette, part of a pendant made of gold and inlaid with semi-precious stones. No one at that time had seen much jewellery of the New Kingdom monarchs, but Carter had spent years at Deir el Bahari drawing, in part, the consumer goods of that day and could well imagine the extraordinary riches with which these kings and queens had been surrounded.

It was now apparent that the tombs that had been found during the past few years had been hidden since ancient times; no tourists of the Greek and Roman world, no travellers of the last two centuries had ever seen them. These were of a design different from the huge open tombs and of a different, earlier, age. And, as well as the possibility of discovering the remains of the court furnishings and other treasures of the days, there was really no telling what else might lie in these tombs; another papyrus containing a king list like that of Turin? A whole library of texts? Anything might come from the ground of the Valley. But the real fascination which had gripped Carter was to do with the work in the Valley itself. For the area he was exploring, though rocky and precipitous, was very small; one may walk in two

minutes from the small tomb that contained the three singers across the Valley to the tomb of Amenhotep II. Yet in this brief walk there is a variety of forms in the landscape which, in part, is covered, sometimes to a depth of twenty or thirty feet, with a mixture of flat, limestone chippings that had been taken from the huge open tombs during the work on them and dumped outside their doors, and the sand, rough flints and boulders brought down in the floods from the mountainsides above. This flood-borne material had set almost rock hard over the piles of ancient chippings and in some places created the appearance of natural slopes. But in reality, as Carter was rapidly learning, there was little in the Valley that was natural, apart from the cliffs that ringed it and the limestone hillocks into which the tombs had been cut.

The Valley was like a huge stone quarry, with the chippings of the workings still lying before the tombs. Since Belzoni's time, gangs of workmen had moved great heaps of these chippings all around the Valley floor as the whims of the different excavators had taken them. Both Loret and Carter had realized that, due to the actions of the floods, even the most natural-looking slopes might be just a few years old, cemented hard by the flood waters. Alternatively, some of the Eighteenth Dynasty tombs, such as Mahirpra's, had their shafts actually excavated in such hard flood debris, and the flood strata that the ancient masons exposed showed four successive floods across the Valley, even before that early date. Carter now recognized that any further work of excavation would properly be performed by cleaning out the debris and the ancient quarryings from entire sections of the gullies in the Valley down to the bedbedrock. It would require large gangs of men and constant supervision of the work; a hot, dusty and largely unrewarding occupation. But at this time there were other urgent problems that faced Carter in the Valley and which had prior claims upon the funds of the *Service*.

On 11 February 1901, a column and a part of the ceiling of the burial chamber in the tomb of Seti I collapsed. For several years small pieces of the tomb had fallen at odd intervals, but this latest collapse was of large slabs, some of which weighed several tons. This had left adjacent areas in the ceiling showing fresh cracks and blocks wedged only against each other, hanging dangerously. Carter had wooden beams moved into the tomb to prop up the ceiling slabs and made a report on the tomb for Maspero, who was at that time sailing upriver in the *Miriam*, a fine old *dahabiya* (Nile passenger boat), which had replaced the *Nimrud Hadachera* of his previous directorship. The tomb of Seti I, Carter wrote, apart from defacement by tourists and egyptologists, was blackened by the smoke of candles and torches brought in by the visitors and their guides. More than two thousand people a year were visiting the tomb. Luxor, as Maspero himself observed, was now a resort 'colonised from December to the beginning of April by scholars, idle folk and invalids. They chatter, intrigue, exchange cards, invite each other from hotel to hotel, or from boat to boat; they play tennis and bridge, plan picnics in the Valley of the Kings . . .' The bright brash town now boasted two hospitals, built by Thomas Cook, a race track and regular theatrical performances. 'Indeed,' Maspero continued, 'the native population is quite contaminated by European elements now established there, Greek hakals, Maltese tavern-keepers, subordinate railway employees, Italian photographers.'

Maspero brought with him on the *Miriam* the funds and equipment to instal electrical lighting in six of the royal tombs, to be powered by a generator that would be installed in the Valley. Carter and Maspero together selected the five most popular tombs for illumination and added to this list the recently discovered tomb of Amenhotep II. A great deal of work needed to be done in the Valley itself, Carter proposed. It was essential to build walls around the entrances of the tombs to stop boulders from rolling down into them. Gangways and hand railing were required for visitors and, most important of all, a system of paths, and walls should be built to prevent further flooding. Carter also proposed that the long cracks in the hills that formed such a distinctive part of the Valley landscape, should be cemented over as they were excellent channels for the flood water to drain into. This had resulted in some of the tombs being flooded from cracks in their roofs. Unknowingly, it was a suggestion that the engineers and geologists of our expedition to the Valley would propose again in the summer of 1979.

Maspero recognized the value of these suggestions and was very concerned about the rock falls in the tomb of Seti I which indeed had probably been caused by water entering the burial chamber through a crack in its roof. Despite the damage in this tomb it was not nearly as severe as that which had occurred in some of the other tombs. The tomb of Ramesses III, Bruce's Tomb, had its burial chamber filled with water from a similar source and although the upper sections which contained the six small chambers so

beloved of Wilkinson and his contemporaries had not been damaged by it, the lower parts of the tomb had been completely wrecked, smashed quite beyond repair, and were still partly filled with water and fine wet mud. These sections were blocked off and tourists have never visited them again. Today, although the mud has dried out completely the desiccation of the rock has left vast slabs of stone loose, and they hang over the huge corridors and ceiling vaults threatening to fall at the slightest vibrations. The early copies of the texts that this huge tomb once contained, and the work of Wilbour and Lefébure, are all that remain.

Maspero had also come from Cairo with the intention of removing the royal mummies from the tomb of Amenhotep II. According to Maspero it was decided in Cairo that the six kings who had been cached in the tomb had been there only 'by accident' and they would be moved 'to a comfortable glass case in Cairo' but that the king Amenhotep would be replaced in his sarcophagus and the three mummies found stripped and lying in a room on their own and the prince that had been stuck to a model boat, would all stay in the tomb. It was still believed that these four unknown figures were probably connected with the burial of the king being 'victims of human sacrifice or the like' though such visions of violence are completely at odds with what we now know about the Valley and the royal dead. This concept was perhaps a survival of the biblical vision of violent Egyptian society, one eagerly seized upon by Cecil B. de Mille and his Hollywood contemporaries but one which has very little basis in fact.

In truth, Maspero's concern about the royal mummies and his desire to get them all to the Museum was based, at least in part, on his instinct for collecting. He argued that ancient Egyptians themselves had been unable to guarantee security in these tombs and that 'An authentic king in the antiquity market has an incalculable value' and that all the excavators in the land—the Abd er Rassuls and their like—would soon enter upon a campaign, each to try to unearth his piece of the Dynasty. 'It would be necessary,' concluded Maspero, 'to recommence the old sentry rounds, only to arrive at a similar result after more or less delay'. Sadly, the truths of Maspero's observations are still relevant today. It is recognized that not even the museums of the world can provide a really secure home for the past. In truth, as Flinders Petrie had remarked, just the year before Maspero's comments: 'The printed description distributed in all the libraries of the world will last far longer than most

Workmen waiting outside the tomb of Amenhotep II before carrying the royal cache from his tomb to the Nile. The pile of debris by the path, at the top left, is in the position now occupied by the modern Rest House. This photograph by Maspero has long been incorrectly identified as showing the removal of the mummies from the Deir el Bahari cache in 1881

of the objects themselves.' Still, Maspero would leave these mummies in their tomb, and certainly it would be an experience that the visitors of those days never forgot. The three mummies were returned to the floor of the side chamber, the prince upon his boat to the pillared hall above, this time with chicken wire

The air was thick, warm, motionless, heavy with fine dust, and impregnated with an imperceptible odour of musty aromatics; a gradually increasing sensation of oppression in breathing and heavyness of head was felt, there was an overwhelming silence, and at the same time that sort of almost religious awe which makes us dislike speaking or, if speech is necessary, makes us talk in whispers. A few pieces of candle placed in a corner vaguely lighted the ante-chamber while the workmen were taking the pharaoh out of his modern case. With their bare feet and legs, the upper part of the body naked, a soft linen cloth round their loins, the head boxed in their tawny takieh [woollen skullcap], like the figures whose silhouettes adorn the walls of the Theban tombs, the Egyptians of today seem to be the Egyptians of long ago, resuscitated in order to recommence their funeral duties. The royal coffin, lifted without a sound, passed into their hands, and moved off into the darkness of the staircase; it slowly traversed the vault, descended the steps, slipped into the sarcophagus, fitted into it with a dry cracking sound, and for an instant I thought that time had suddenly gone backwards, and that at one swoop I had travelled back thirty four centuries to be present at the burial of Amenôthes [Amenhotep II].

Unfortunately the king did not remain undisturbed for very long. While Carter was working upon the reconstruction of a temple south of Thebes, just a few months later, he was summoned back to the Valley by a telegram and he returned to find that the tomb of Amenhotep II had been broken into, that the boat which had held the mummy had been stolen, and the mummy of Amenhotep II had been stripped of the fine linens in which the burial commission of the priest-kings had wrapped him. The king, broken and opened to view by the assault, was a melancholy sight; happily the robbers had ignored the three naked mummies that lay in the side chamber.

Carter set about finding and prosecuting the culprits with all the care and attention one would expect of an archeologist. He applied his attention to the Holmesian details of the raid; on the instrument used to break open the door, and the manner in which its lock had been camouflaged to appear as if it was shut tight. He took plaster casts of footprints by the tomb door and employed a spoor tracker, a desert Arab skilled in such work, to trace their origins. These led him directly to . . . the White House of the Abd er Rassuls. In a determined, if convoluted account of these proceedings, Carter shows his close knowledge

around him to prevent visitors from touching him. The king was replaced in his sarcophagus. Carter and Maspero found that if the coffin was laid in the bottom of the sarcophagus it would not be visible, and so two trestles were made to support the coffin high in the box.

of the *Gurnawis* and also the effects that such a small claustrophobic society had had upon this young Englishman who had spent a great part of his adult life amongst them. Despite a great understanding of the convolutions employed by the villagers during such enquiries Carter still possessed the European impatience with such conduct—hence the almost obsessional attention to the detail of the crime. He *would* beat the villagers at their own game. The stories of the *Service* guards were obviously lies, the denial of everything by the Abd er Rassuls, the same. And the other helpers, the blacksmith who had furnished the jemmies were all in collusion. Carter with his careful gathering of evidence would win the day. The White House was searched once again, as Maspero had done before, and enough incriminating evidence was found from robberies in other tombs to have some members of the family, including Mohammed, put on trial. However, in a Luxor courtroom, Carter's evidence was ignored and the Abd er Rassuls were all freed.

Today, the descendants of the three brothers, who exploited the royal cache during the 1870s, two of whom were implicated by Carter in the stripping of the mummy of Amenhotep II, still live on Gurna where they are a vital part of the village. The present head of the family, Sheik Ali Abd er Rassul, who himself excavated in the tomb of Seti I during the early fifties, is a hotel proprietor of extraordinary charm which compensates somewhat for the unusual condition of his accommodations. The White House is still the hub of the family life and all the family ceremonies of life and death are conducted there. When I began my work in the Valley, visiting and measuring the royal tombs, I was always accompanied by one Abd er Rassul, Abdelahi, who greatly delighted in wandering with me through the desert and speculating upon the possibilities of tombs and treasures that might lie under the sand or rock. Later, several members of the family worked for our expedition in the Valley and they have an habitual ease and patience with foreigners, gained by long experience, which is not shared by all the villagers. When the Abd er Rassuls are questioned about their predecessors, the names of Mohammed, Ahmed and Hussein are soon remembered as fine strong men, a credit to the family. Their tomb robbing exploits, however, seem to have been forgotten in any of its detail and, despite their claims to the contrary, none of the family now knows the Theban hills as well as did those three brothers back in the 1870s.

Maspero sympathized with his young Inspector on the outcome of the Luxor trial when he visited him during the following month but in reality it was but a storm in a village teacup, a village with the unusual habit of plundering kings.

After the robbery, Maspero and Carter replaced the king in the sarcophagus and left him exposed to the waist and in full view of the visitors who stood above the crypt in the space between the columns. Shortly after, Amenhotep II was illuminated with a small desk light placed over his head so that the king's face was directly lit. However, there was still a great deal of disquiet about the way the royal mummies were displayed, both in Amenhotep II's tomb and in the Cairo Museum. In 1931 the Government of Egypt decided to take them out of the Museum and the tomb of Amenhotep II, and place the ancient kings in a mausoleum. In the company of the then young Inspector, now Dr Labib Habashi, the celebrated scholar who was later to become the advisor and father-figure of so many expeditions in Egypt, including our own in the Valley, Amenhotep II was brought to Cairo in a steam train, in a first class sleeping car and given the priority of the top bunk. Despite their celebrity, the royal mummies were originally something of an embarrassment to the authorities. No one quite understood their roles; were they antiquities or long dead kings of Egypt? They had first been placed in a chamber at the Museum where only 'the mighty of the modern day might gaze upon their countenances'; then they were opened to public view. Joined by Amenhotep II they entered a huge mausoleum, originally intended for Saad Zaghlul, the great nationalist, but were later returned to the Museum where, today, they lie in rows in simple boxes—a strange, spare display.

18

Theodore M. Davis

(1902–03; 1903–04)

It was apparent to both Carter and Maspero that with the burden of the work of restoration and refurbishing in the Valley falling upon the *Service*, they would have to find funds from elsewhere if the excavations were to continue. This would not be difficult. Many amateur archeologists worked in Egypt at this time under the supervision of the *Service* and its Inspectors, and the Valley of the Kings was obviously a plum site. Archeology in Egypt was, in fact, a most enjoyable method of spending a winter. At Thebes one might live upon the river in a *dahabiya* or at one of the large hotels and, every day visit the excavations where a professional archeologist and a gang of workmen dug up antiquities on your behalf. Indeed, outside of specially controlled areas, such as the Valley of the Kings, these excavations might even be turned to profit as the antiquities found were divided between the Cairo Museum and the excavator. It was a system that in the past had honourably supported the work of many expeditions such as Flinders Petrie's, but it was one soon to be exploited by the lavish patrons that appeared in Egypt during the first decade of the new century.

Percy Newberry had often acted as an intermediary between the amateurs and the professional archeologists, and on occasions, he had himself joined forces with the patrons and excavated on their behalf. At Thebes, he had dug in temples, palaces and tombs with several wealthy amateurs whom he also advised in their purchases of antiquities. Some years before, he had found Carter his first employer in archeology, Lord Amherst of Hackney, and it was with funds given by Amherst to Petrie's excavations at Amarna that Carter had first dug under the eye of that great archeologist. Newberry must have been fully aware of the potential in the Valley for excavation and also of its attractiveness as a site for amateur archeologists. Consequently, he introduced Carter to Theodore M. Davis, a well-connected and wealthy New York lawyer who, at sixty-five, had recently retired and with the help of Newberry, had already excavated in a small way in Egypt. Davis was no scholar but a successful self-made business man, short, thin and

tough whose brusque and pushing manner made him few friends in archeology. Carter and Maspero between them aroused his interest in the Valley and while Davis admired and trusted their judgement he also felt strongly enough about the work in the Valley to identify the ancient kings and queens of the Valley as personalities—even as friends. It was agreed at the beginning of these excavations that Davis would excavate solely upon the behalf of the *Service*. He contributed funds, which were never in fact very large sums, and for this he received the pleasure and honour of directing the archeologists' excavations.

The first joint efforts of Carter and Davis were modest enough. When Maspero had been in Thebes during January 1902, he had walked the Valley with Carter examining areas that would give the new patron some chance of success. Obviously Davis would wish to see some tangible results from his donation but they also wanted to link the work of these new excavations with the other activities of the *Service* in the Valley. As Davis left for a month's trip to Aswan in his *dahabiya*, Carter started the work by clearing either side of the access road to the Valley which needed enlargement to accommodate the ever-increasing numbers of tourists. First they dug the area between the tombs of Ramesses II and Ramesses IV—a hundred-yard stretch to the north of the road. Carter used a gang of sixty men, who slowly cleared away great heaps of heavily patinated ancient tomb chippings. Then he crossed the road with his men and proceeded to clear the doorway of KV 5, the strange ruined tomb with a great pillared hall that Burton had planned some eighty years before. It was the last occasion that anyone had entered this tomb, but although Carter had found a few painted *ostraca* he still had little to show the new patron.

Carter now directed the gang to more promising archeological territory, close to where he had found the tomb of the three chantresses of Amun in the previous season. Slowly the gang worked up the gully towards the encircling cliffs, cleaning it down to bedrock, dumping the debris behind them. It was as if a trench was moved slowly across the Valley floor but,

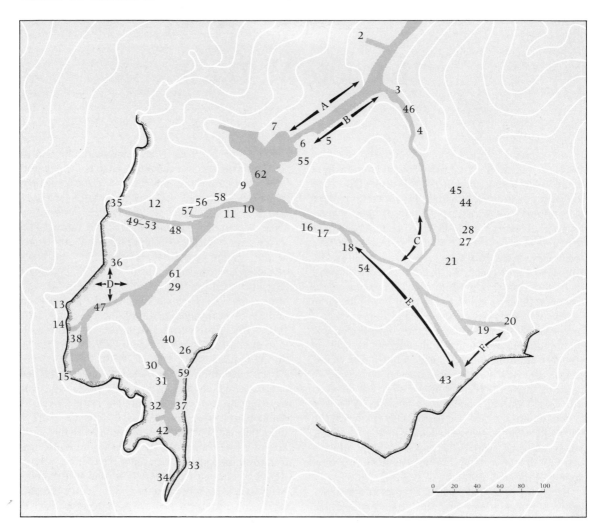

Map of the Davis excavations 1902 to 1904. The alphabetic order of the letters is the sequence in which the sites were excavated

of course, in the backfilling all traces of the ancient inhabitants of the Valley were disturbed and all the strata destroyed. After about a hundred feet they found the doorway of a sealed pit tomb which they carefully refilled to await Davis' return from Aswan. Carter and his men continued moving the trench up the gully and backfilled as before. They once more found the name of Tuthmosis IV, this time upon a fragment of alabaster. By now it seemed likely to Carter that the tomb of this king was in the area but, like the tomb of Amenhotep II, it had been plundered and its antiquities scattered far outside its

entrance. After increasing his workforce to one hundred men, Carter was forced to stop the work at the tip of the steep triangular hill that forms the centre of the Valley. The debris had become so deep —nearly forty feet of it—that the face had become unstable and presented too many problems for such a short enterprise.

On Davis' return from Aswan, at the end of February, he went with Carter to the sealed pit tomb, which had been especially cleared for its opening. Once inside they found to their disappointment that the burials of a man and his wife that it had once contained, had been largely destroyed by water. However, the man's name was found upon his heart scarab; Merenkhons, who had been another priestly official during much the same time as the three chantresses whose tomb Carter had found close by. When, in 1979, our expedition cleared the tomb of Ramesses XI we found another burial of the same age, though badly burnt and smashed by ancient robbers and this burial too had been placed in a pit taken over from an earlier age. Similarly, Carter also discovered that under the destroyed coffins was nearly two feet of ancient debris and chippings and, in this, he found the fragments of a set of canopic jars that had belonged to the original occupant of the tomb, Userhet, an Overseer of Temple Estates, who had lived during the Eighteenth Dynasty. The tomb is now number 45.

With the remainder of Davis' funds Carter now turned his men back towards Loret's old haunts and set a small gang to clear the entire area around the tomb of Mahirpra, which had been so badly peppered with *sondages*. He did not find another tomb but he did discover, under a rock next to Mahirpra's tomb, a yellow painted box with this warrior's titles written upon it. Inside were two nets of leather which, wrapped between his legs and tied around his waist, Marhirpra had used as his wrestling kit. It was a remarkable small discovery and in fine condition, the leather still soft and supple. Examples of similar wrestling kits were known from paintings, but had never actually been seen.

The workmanship was superb. Two gazelle skins had been cut with great care into fine strips, some of which had been removed to leave the skin like an open net, closed by a band of solid leather along its edges. The elasticity of this net had allowed it to fit exactly to the contours of Mahirpra's body. Carter was thrilled by the small discoveries, and his appreciative notes and comments upon the material found in the Valley during these early months shows that he was becoming aware of the fact that the climate and remoteness of the Valley were remarkable preservatives, probably superior to the sites nearer the cultivated land with its excess moisture and small animals, including insects, which ate the antiquities. Also he now appreciated that the objects, though damaged, were usually of the finest quality that the Egyptian Empire had been able to make.

Maspero presented Davis with the two leather loin cloths and their box, and also the canopic jars of Userhet, and Davis in turn gave them to museums in the United States. It was the beginning of a stream of excavated material from the Valley which Davis donated to the museums of his country, primarily the Boston and Metropolitan Museums and it advertised the results of excavation in a most dramatic manner.

Although the results of the month of excavation had been modest enough, they had shown that there were still things to be found in the Valley, even in areas that had apparently been recently cleared. No one had ever cleaned whole sections of the Valley down to bedrock before and there were still large tracts filled with chippings and detritus that had not been touched. Davis had also seen the broken ushabti and the alabaster vase fragment with the name of Tuthmosis IV upon them and examined the end of the Valley, as yet unexcavated, that lay above the end of Carter's deep trench. This area was obviously the next that should be cleared, and the work would start around the tomb of Ramesses X, where the diesel-electric generator was to be installed. Davis' excavations, controlled by Maspero and Carter, would continue to be of benefit to the *Service* and fascinating for him.

After a summer in England, Carter returned to his work in the Valley in the early autumn. The popularly visited tombs were now wired for electricity and Carter had encouraged further donations to help with the conservation of the Valley. One visitor, a Mrs Goff, had provided him with funds which he had used to restore the tomb of Seti II, and the industrialist Sir Robert Mond, appalled at the damage in the tomb of Seti I, had not only provided money for its restoration but helped Carter formulate a programme of work for the complicated tasks in the tomb. Davis planned to arrive at Luxor in December to start a full season of work in the Valley. Carter had the rest of Upper Egypt to inspect and control; meanwhile he also supervised the installation of electricity in the temple at Abu Simbel and was engaged in several other projects of restoration in temples and tombs.

When Davis arrived Carter started the workmen digging in the manner of the year before, up the Valley from the tomb of Seti I, past the new generator in the tomb of Ramesses X. By mid-January the men had progressed nearly one hundred and fifty yards up the gully and were close under the cliff face. On their way they had opened another small tomb containing the mummies of two old ladies, both lying in plain coffins. Newberry and Carter removed some mummified ducks that were in the tomb and, after copying the inscriptions on the coffins, reclosed it. The tomb has not been seen again to this day. Maps place its entrance, now numbered 60, in the courtyard of the tomb of Prince Montu-hir-kopesh-ef and it may well have been the workmen making this tomb who opened the burial, at that time some four hundred years old, and plundered it.

In the shadow of the cliff many more broken objects with the name of Tuthmosis IV, the son of Amenhotep II, were found and the workers felt sure that they were hot on the track of that king's tomb, which they now expected to have been robbed. As the men worked closer to the foot of the cliff, the bedrock rose to form a ledge that appeared to have been artificially levelled. As the men swept across the freshly cleared bedrock, which at this point on the Valley floor was cracked into small pieces and white as fresh cut stone, they came across some flat flakes of limestone covering two holes, each about three feet square. Between these two covered holes and the cliff, about twenty feet away, the platform of rock started to drop down towards the base of the cliff. After a little more excavation Carter saw that they stood at the top of a staircase that ran downwards against the face of the cliff.

The two covered holes proved to be about two and a half feet deep and filled with sand. Mixed in this sand were model tools, axes, adzes, chisels and plasterers' tools, as well as small pots and alabaster dishes. They were the typical contents of foundation deposits, assemblages of models and tools that were placed in holes outside the doors of many of the tombs in the Valley. All the little objects bore inscriptions, some carved and some quickly written in black ink: 'Good God, Menkeperure, Beloved of Osiris'. Menkeperure was the first name of Tuthmosis IV; Carter had found the king's tomb for Davis. The men cleared the steps, which were broad and steep, and burrowed deep into the cliff in the manner of the other Eighteenth Dynasty tombs in the Valley. By 18 January 1903 the door was sufficiently clear

Carter's photograph taken a few hours before the discovery of the tomb of Tuthmosis IV. The workmen are digging above the steps of the tomb, at the foot of the Valley cliff. The two pits behind the workmen held the foundation deposits of the tomb. As he climbed the nearby hill to take this photograph Carter must have known that he was probably on the brink of discovering a royal tomb. Behind the foundation deposit pits may be seen the beginnings of a drainage trench, cut in the Valley floor to carry floodwaters away from the mouth of the tomb

to allow entry, but Davis, who had left for Aswan, was out of communication on his *dahabiya*. Carter and another American archeological patron, the young Robb Tytus, with whom Newberry had been digging a palace at Thebes, made a rapid tour of the interior of the tomb.

There were broken antiquities scattered throughout the first corridors of the tomb then, at the well, the inevitable robbers' rope, this one a finely-made treble-twisted affair more than two inches thick. Painted on the walls around the top of the well were scenes of the king being greeted in his tomb by a number of gods, and as they waited for the men to bring them a ladder for crossing the well they read Tuthmosis IV's name in the simple inscriptions above the scenes. The tomb was large and well made, the well paintings small and elegant—auguring well for the quality of the interior sections of the tomb.

After they had crossed the well they passed first through another decorated chamber and then down into the burial chamber. Evidence of the devastation caused by the tomb robbers lay everywhere, yet it was obvious that the broken objects, of which there were thousands of fragments, were of the very highest quality, the faience, especially, being a light glassy blue with the finest of drawn decorations. And there was the possibility that many objects could be repaired. The burial chamber, disappointingly, had not been painted, but the contrast between the sharp smooth limestone of its walls and pillars, and the hard shiny stone sarcophagus that, like Amenhotep II's lay before them in the crypt of the tomb, was heightened. The king's mummy had already been found among the group in the side chamber of Amenhotep II's tomb and the people who had opened the great lid of the sarcophagus to take the king away had done so with care, resting it gently on piles of stone and, at one corner, a fine wooden sculpture of a cow's head, painted bright yellow. The two men peeped quickly into the side chambers which contained, among the usual piles of objects, the mummy of a boy, probably the Prince Amenemhet, which had been slit open from belly to chest in the search for jewellery and amulets, and who now leaned nonchalantly, his diaphragm flapping in front of him, against a chamber wall.

Sixteen days later came the official opening. Davis, Maspero and a group of egyptologists solemnly walked through the tomb as Carter's workmen, stationed every six feet or so through the tomb, held a rope for the visitors to grasp while others held cable and light bulbs brought especially to the tomb for

Although quite desiccated by 3,500 years in the tomb of Tuthmosis IV, a wooden statue of a cow's head—commonly found in many of the royal tombs—still supported the huge quartzite sarcophagus lid when Carter first entered the burial chamber. The care with which the lid had been laid down when the sarcophagus was opened suggests that it was the work of the ancient commissions who gathered up the royal mummies for reburial in other tombs

The little prince propped up against a side-chamber wall as Carter found him in the tomb of Tuthmosis IV, where he still is. Smashed royal burial equipment litters the floor

187

the occasion. Carter had laid a series of planks over the loose antiquities in the burial chamber and, one by one, the party walked down them to peer into the sarcophagus. Maspero thoroughly enjoyed such theatrics:

The electric light does not penetrate the dusty, heavy air very well, and from the corner where I stood my companions looked like vague silhouettes. The dread of the tomb, so lately shut up, and whence the visits of tourists has not banished the impression of death, has invaded them without their knowledge. They speak in whispers, moderate their gestures, walk or rather glide along as noiselessly as possible. Occasionally they stoop to pick up an object, or group themselves round a pillar, remaining motionless for a moment, then they resume their silent rounds, cross each other, join each other, and then separate again. Very rarely does some abrupt movement of one of them break the rhythm of their evolutions, or do they let fall some brief remark that sounds like a trumpet above their discreet whispers. The persons employed in the funeral and the priests must have so moved and spoken the evening of the ceremony when, the mummy sealed up in its sarcophagus, they hastened to perform the last rites by which the Pharoah was shut into his mysterious chamber.

Later Newberry helped Carter clear the tomb and write an account of the work for a large volume on the tomb underwritten by Davis. For this publication Maspero contributed an essay on the king's life and monuments, and Elliot Smith, the anatomist, wrote about the royal mummy. All in all, it was a splendid publication and proved to be the first of a series of similar volumes.

The tomb that Davis had found was magnificent, even in an era that would be filled with the discoveries of such royal monuments. Architecturally it was the fruition of the first type of royal tomb in the Valley that had been initiated by Tuthmosis III. The proportions of the tomb were the same as its predecessors though its size was greater and, with that extraordinary eye for tiny architectural detail shown by the Valley architects, every single element in the tomb, every wall, corner, corridor and door jamb was carefully designed, accurately planned and steeped in tradition and scholarship. All the uncertainties of the rough straggling corridors of Tuthmosis III's tomb had here been straightened out, rationalized and welded into one cohesive design. It was one of the great

talents of the Egyptian designers to take a complex design and transform it into a simple shape that belied its great subtlety. Indeed, a great part of the present attraction to ancient Egyptian objects may be because of this process of simplification which seems curiously to parallel the work of many modern artists and designers. The paintings in the tomb were a real triumph, set like jewels in two of the smaller rooms, the well and the antechamber. Apparently simple compositions, the multiple, almost identical figures of the king are interspaced between different gods who each face him as he enters the Otherworld. The different attributes of these gods, Osiris' white crown, Hathor's red head-dress of the sun framed by two cows' horns, and Anubis' two pointed ears on his black dog's head, create a wonderful series of those simple rhythms so beloved of Egyptian artists and which run through their paintings like a melody. The simplicity of this composition allowed the painters to concentrate on the colour which must be among the most successful examples of a unified colour scheme in all Egyptian painting. The walls sing with this light like a painting by Monet or Bonnard and, like a good Bonnard, they tell in their rich warmth, of an easy, happy life.

Other paintings from the period of the reign of Tuthmosis IV also make use of a hot yellow background which allows the rich red skin colour of the men in the paintings to glow upon the surface of the wall. But the large size of the paintings in the royal tomb give the colours there a special quality; they expand across the wall's surfaces in a magical way and the shapes of the figures and the ground against which they were painted throb with life. Understandably, this was a colour scheme that was much used later in the Dynasty during the Heresy Period and one that with lighter, less saturated hues, would survive right through the later New Kingdom. These figures in the tomb of Tuthmosis IV are the first in any of the royal tombs of the Valley that were painted in the normal Egyptian manner and it is interesting to see that the patterns in the clothes worn by Hathor and the other gods are only found in other pictures painted by the same artists in the tombs above their own ancient village.

The multitude of ritual objects in the tomb reflected the increasing artistic refinement of the New Kingdom court that reached its first culmination during the reign of Tuthmosis IV's son, Amenhotep III. Although the personal possessions of the king and the rich trappings of the royal office that had been placed in the tomb suffered especially badly at the

Carter's drawing of a fine relief cut into the side of a parade chariot found in the tomb of Tuthmosis IV. The king rides into battle magnificently equipped with the finest weapons of his day

hands of the ancient thieves, many fragments were found which especially evoked the richness of the original burial. There were fine woven tapestries—some of them heirlooms about fifty years old when they were first placed in the tomb—gaming boards, ostrich feather fans, chairs, footstools and thrones. The surviving fragments of weapons also produce an equally suggestive list: quivers, bows, archers' gauntlets and armlets, scabbards for the short bronze Egyptian swords, whips and, most magnificent of all, the remains of a superb parade chariot, both the elegantly decorated wooden body and its leather harnesses, all minutely decorated in grey and red appliqué. Such objects, most of which only survive in small fragments, are the only records of the everyday productions of the court craftsmen; objects not made for eternity like the great statues or the temple reliefs, but goods that reflect, far more than the large-scale official arts, the free use of flowing designs

that had originated in countries to the north of Egypt with which, through the growth of its Empire, Egypt had come into increasing contact.

Apart from these objects from the king's life, made for and used by the living man, there were huge amounts of supplies and ritual equipment to aid the royal progress in the Otherworld, and these had been made with unusual care and artistry. Some of these strange, intrinsically worthless objects—and thus left by the ransackers of the tombs—were blue faience and were in the shape of some of the hieroglyphic signs, such as the *ankh* or the 'life' sign, or they were models of papyrus scrolls. The ritual combats in the next world were fought with fragile throwsticks of a type which, when made of wood and not beautiful glassy faience, the kings and nobles used to bring down wildfowl in the marshes by the Nile. Other faiences included large numbers of vases and pots, sometimes elaborately made with complex techniques that entailed joining several differently manufactured segments to form one complete pot. The numerous ushabtis that were inevitably present in the tomb are among the finest in any burial in the Valley.

Such ritual objects, as well as many inscribed pots

made of various types of decorative stones, that were found in fragments, were identical to others that have occasionally been excavated from Egyptian temple sites. Indeed, some are so similar that occasionally the same designs drawn by the same hand, have been found on identical objects both in royal tombs and at remote temple sites hundreds of miles from Thebes. This strongly suggests that these ritual objects buried in the royal tombs were the same as those commonly used for the temple rituals. In some cases, such as the so-called *hes* vases, this is demonstrably true because pictures of the same jars that are found in the royal tombs are frequently shown in the king's hands in the paintings of offering scenes on the temple walls. Presumably these ritual objects were placed in the royal tomb so that the kings could continue these essential rituals even after death in the Otherworld.

With the evidence from these three tombs of the Eighteenth Dynasty—Tuthmosis III, Amenhotep II, and Tuthmosis IV, excavated by Loret and Carter, compared with the finds in other tombs of earlier and later periods, it is possible to reconstruct partly the original places occupied in the tombs by this smashed and scattered equipment, and to gain some idea of the original appearance and purpose of the completed royal burials. In the four small side chambers that always run off the burial chambers it appears that the two that were closer to the king contained food and provisions, perhaps the meat in the chamber at the head of the sarcophagus, the wheat, bread, oils and other provisions, at the foot end. The two chambers further away from the sarcophagus contained the glazed ritual objects—the vases, temple equipment and the ushabtis. The open area of the pillared hall probably contained the dead king's belongings, which may well have overflowed into the smaller antechambers above. The

Plan of the tomb of Tuthmosis IV

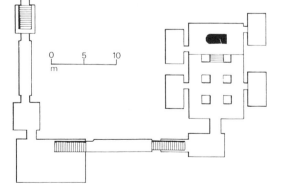

statues of the king and the gods stood around the sarcophagus, each in their separate shrines. Other statues may have been placed at particular points in the tomb, the pairs of life-sized statues of the king, for example, may have stood by the steps leading to the crypt, or even before the sealed doors of the burial chamber, as they were found in the tomb of Tutankhamen. Before the discovery of this intact tomb, which was unfortunately jumbled in both its layout and its contents, these wooden statues, painted with the resin that had been found in so many of the royal tombs, were so broken and had been so thrown around in the tombs, probably to render them into small portable pieces, that they were little understood or regarded. Wood was a precious commodity in a country where trees are not common; and those that do grow do not yield good strong planks or bulks suitable for carving. All the timbers of the tomb doors and the tomb equipment, and the heavier pieces of tomb furniture had generally been removed in distant antiquity for it is certainly true that all the tombs that have been discovered in the Valley during the present century had not been open since dynastic times.

On a blank plastered wall in one of the painted chambers in Tuthmosis IV's tomb, Carter found a fine large graffito of inspection:

> *The Year 8, the third month of the summer season under the Majesty of the King of Upper and Lower Egypt . . . Horemheb, beloved of Amun. His Majesty, Life Prosperity, Health, ordered that it should be recommended to the fanbearer on the left of the King, the Royal Scribe, the Superintendent of the Treasury, the Superintendent of the Works in the Place of Eternity . . . [i.e. the Valley] Maya . . . to renew the burial of Tuthmosis IV, justified in the Precious Habitation in Western Thebes.*

And, smaller, by the side of this inscription:

> *His Assistant, the Steward of Thebes, Tuthmosis . . .*

This proved to be the earliest of all the known graffiti that record renewals of the royal burials and records a re-wrapping of the royal mummy that took place within eighty years of the original burial, a period when the Valley was well guarded and filled with tomb workers and their supervisors. This may, therefore, have been a special circumstance—perhaps a robbery discovered which caused Maya and his assistant Tuthmosis to re-open the tomb. The possibility that the disturbance of the original burial may have occurred during the Heresy Period is distinct, but there is no evidence at present to support such a

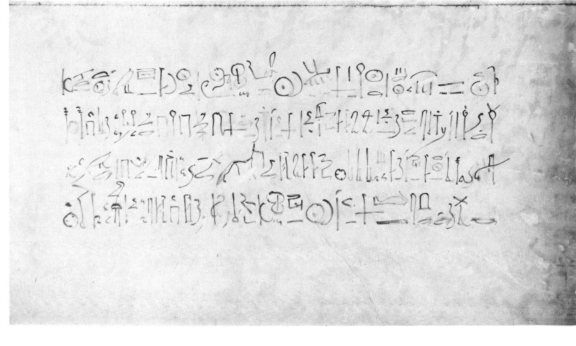

The splendid graffiti of Inspector Maya in the tomb of Tuthmosis IV, written about 1356 BC

view. Horemheb's seals, stamped with blue paint into the mud of the plaster covering of the rebuilt dry stone walls can still be seen across the edges of the once blocked doorways. These are similar in technique to the earlier examples of the necropolis seal that are in the tomb of Amenhotep II.

Today, this tomb is one of the greatest treasures of the Valley, for it still retains something of the quality of those first days of discovery. The robbers' rope, thick, heavy and as brittle as spun sugar, is still in place, tied around a column in the antechamber and running down towards the well. The prince—a naked little boy—still lies in the tomb as does a slaughtered bull and many huge coarse jars of oils and grains that still lie broken upon the floor of the sidechambers. Occasionally, a small fragment of blue faience, shattered three millennia ago, glistens on the floor. The sarcophagus, a smooth dull red, painted with the yellow figures of gods, stands magnificent in the crypt, and there are small untranslated graffiti still to be seen, scratched into the plain plaster patches on the burial chamber walls. The tomb is seldom visited,

A procession of workmen carrying the thousands of fragmented antiquities away from the tomb of Tuthmosis IV

being far from the guardians and the centre of the Valley, but if it were these fragile pleasures would disintegrate under the hands of curious visitors. The royal tombs were never meant to be visited by thousands of people. However, now the fine old tomb is changing. For reasons that are still obscure, although we are working hard on solutions, parts of the cliff into which the tomb was cut, are moving. Old cracks in the limestone cliffs, which the ancient masons had cut through as they quarried the tombs' chambers, are moving again; tiny heaps of splintered stone lie at the bottom of these cracks as the pressure of the rock movement once again pushes one surface against the other. And the surface of walls, which were plastered and painted, has been loosened and is cracked. These effects of the moving cliffs can be countered, but it will take much time and effort.

Despite the great elegance of the paintings in the tomb of Tuthmosis IV careful inspection reveals that they were painted at great speed and often with little care in the smaller details. This picture shows a carelessly drawn enlargement of the borders and edge of a painted wall in the room before the burial chamber. Such haste reinforces the impression gained in other tombs of the period: that the paintings in the Eighteenth Dynasty royal tombs were done during the funeral ceremonies, the walls being prepared previously by the necropolis workmen

Davis was delighted with the discovery—his first royal tomb. It was quickly pointed out to him that there was a good chance that an undiscovered one lay close by for, in the foundation deposits outside the tomb, some of the objects had been taken from another deposit and re-used by Tuthmosis IV's priests. Moreover, in the debris outside the tomb, cleared while Carter's men worked their way up to the end of the gully, the names of two pharaohs had been found: Tuthmosis I, whose flooded tomb Loret had uncovered some years before, and Queen Hatshepsut, whose name it was that had also been written upon a saucer found in one of the king's foundation deposits.

While the tomb of Tuthmosis IV was still being cleared by Carter and Newberry, a gang of workmen started clearing along the edge of the cliffs, working along the rock bay, down and around the tomb of Prince Montu-hir-kopesh-ef and up into the next bay which, at its narrow head, held the small door to the open but flooded tomb that had been planned and visited by almost all the early expeditions to the Valley. Here James Burton had tried to excavate, but was forced to 'abandon his researches owing to the danger of the mephitic air', and here, just in front of the rough and steeply cut entrance to the tunnel-like tomb, Carter's men found another foundation deposit, this one naming Queen Hatshepsut. In a small hole was another range of model tools, some made of bronze, more alabaster vases, cloth, loaves of bread and some magical wooden symbols. The deposit was not as lavish as those Carter had seen when he had drawn the reliefs in this queen's temple at Deir el Bahari, just the other side of the cliff into which this strange ill-shaped tomb was cut. There the Swiss archeologist Naville, who had excavated the site while Carter had drawn the reliefs in the temple had found magnificent deposits containing hundreds of fine scarabs, whole joints of meat and great quantities of model tools and other religious objects. But this more modest deposit was enough to show that the smoke blackened blocked tomb which lay behind it had been built for that queen or, at least, during her reign. Davis, who had witnessed the uncovering of the deposit, had a weakness for the ancient queens and now he willingly undertook to have the tomb cleared for the *Service*.

Eventually, the tomb turned out to be the longest and the deepest in Egypt. It took Carter's gangs two seasons: from February 1903, following the opening of the tomb of Tuthmosis IV until mid-April of the same year, when they were forced to stop the work because of the dust and the bad hot air deep in the ground; and from the following October until March of the next year, 1904. It was so hot in the tomb that the candles set up along the corridors melted and the dusty air was so bad that Davis had to have an air pump brought in, its pipe eventually running down more than 630 feet into the rock. Progress was very slow, not only because of the terrible conditions in the tomb, but also because the face of the flood debris that filled the corridor, at which the workmen hacked with their *fas* (the standard Egyptian peasant tool—a broad heavy adze for working soil and sand), would not permit more than two or three men to work at one time. Every load cut from the face of the flood debris had to be carried nearly seven hundred feet to the door of the tomb, which was nearly three hundred and thirty feet higher than the workface. Today it is a hard twenty-minute walk from the bottom and it is good to see the daylight creeping around the last corner of the tomb's curving corridor. With a basket-load of dirt upon their shoulders and the coarse palm-frond weave of the basket cutting into their flesh, the task must have been truly awesome for the workers. The men, all local villagers who usually worked in the fields by the Nile, cut their way through three successive chambers. Then, in the corner of the third—almost square—chamber, they found a staircase much smaller than those in the preceding passages. On its steps they found broken stone vases that bore the names of Ahmose Nefertari, Tuthmosis I and Queen Hatshepsut. Again, Carter realized, the tomb had been robbed—even before it had been flooded. On reaching the chamber at the bottom of the stairs, they found it too was filled with debris from the ceiling which had collapsed. The ancient masons had quarried down so far that they had cut through the creamy-white Theban limestone of the Valley into the soft grey clay-like shale that lies underneath. This produced a surface that could never be decorated, but had the tomb builders known, they need only have quarried for another fifteen feet to have hit the next stratum of soft chalk that underlies the shale, in which many of the famous private tomb chapels of Thebes were cut. However, the ancient workmen went no further than this chamber, and Carter's prize and his workmen's pride were two stone coffins, as intractable as the rock and the tomb itself. Of the burials that had once been placed in this deep tomb chamber very little remained: a fragment of a life-sized wooden statue and a stick or two of furniture. Fifteen fine limestone blocks bore the text of the *Amduat* drawn in a manner that was very reminiscent

Carter's watercolour of the devastated burial chamber in Hatshepsut's tomb

of the Middle Kingdom prototypes in the tombs on the same cliff's other face, at Deir el Bahari.

The sarcophagi were, however, remarkably interesting objects, as well as being superbly made; they were so accurate that no error was detectable using normal measuring equipment, and of such hard stone that on a slight hand smack they rang with a clear note. The stone is—as one authority has said, 'the hardest ever worked by any ancient people'— yellow quartzite, a glistening smooth variegated stone of silicified quartz sand. The inscriptions on the two sarcophagi identified them as being made for Hatshepsut and her father Tuthmosis I. They were the first in the long series of royal sarcophagi that stretched from the beginning of the Valley's history right through the New Kingdom until the last example in the tomb of Ramesses VII.

The basic pattern of these sarcophagi had been taken from private Middle Kingdom examples. It had been Queen Hatshepsut who first had a sarcophagus made in this old style, but in the hard yellow quartzite instead of the cedar planks of the older examples. This first sarcophagus, made for Hatshepsut when she was a wife of Tuthmosis II was left empty in a tomb that was abandoned when she became Pharaoh. The two sarcophagi that Carter had found in this long tomb were designed in the same manner as this earlier one. One of them was originally decorated with the name of Hatshepsut in her position as ruler of Egypt but later her names had been changed to those of her father, Tuthmosis I, and the inside of the sarcophagus had been cut away at the foot-end, probably to make room for the king's coffins which were found in the great cache. The second sarcophagus, made for Hatshepsut as a replacement of the one that was changed to hold her father, had for the first time, the cartouche form that became the normal shape of the later royal sarcophagi.

In this extraordinary tomb Hatshepsut had accommodated her father's burial in her own burial chamber and, given the time that elapsed between his death and her assumption of the throne, this implies that she must have taken his mummy from a previous burial in another tomb. An obvious claimant for Tuthmosis I's original tomb was one that Loret had found during his second season in the Valley. In that tomb another sarcophagus made for Tuthmosis I by his grandson Tuthmosis III had been found. Everybody, it seems, wanted to make sarcophagi for the old king!

Hatshepsut had assumed control of Egypt at the death of her husband, Tuthmosis II, who had died while still a young man. Although officially she was co-regent with her young nephew, Tuthmosis III, he was in reality largely powerless during her twenty-one year rule which ended only with her death. The queen, who took the royal titles of kingship, was surrounded with a group of loyal administrators who all fell swiftly from official grace after her death. One of her officials, Senmut, had built the great temple of Deir el Bahari for his queen and, most unusually, had representations of himself carved inside some of its shrines. One of his two tombs also suggests an unusual relationship with the queen, for its design is similar to her tomb in the Valley of the Kings. It is situated at the bottom of the quarries that supplied the great temple with its hardcore, its long corridors cut through the shale to its burial chamber, which is excavated from the chalk that underlies the great temple. When he came to power, Tuthmosis III seems to have conducted a limited, if public, attack upon the monuments of his aunt, breaking her statues and mutilating her reliefs in the temples. However, many of the advances in royal tomb design that were made during her reign were accepted into the pattern of future tombs, though later her very name was struck from the official lists of kings. In her elegant temple at Deir el Bahari, Hatshepsut is shown in reliefs in the company of her father, Tuthmosis I, as if by emphasizing her royal descent she was underlining her claim to the throne. In ancient Egypt, the legitimacy of the king was assured by his marriage to the daughter of the previous ruler; Hatshepsut may be seen as a queen who attempted to take this royal prerogative one step further and take the throne itself for the queens of Egypt. Like the later priest-kings who were also buried surrounded by the illustrious royal dead, she moved the burial of her father Tuthmosis I into her own sepulchre. When she died it seems that Tuthmosis III had another sarcophagus made for his grandfather, whom he probably had never known, and had him reburied again, this time in the tomb that Loret had rediscovered.

The tomb of Hatshepsut is the most individual and extraordinary tomb in the Valley—like no other in its design or in its truly fantastic dimensions. Its design is similar to an earlier group of royal monuments found at Abydos, north of Thebes, where Seti I had his cenotaph behind his great white temple. Obviously the long tomb was in use during Hatshepsut's reign as the inscriptions on the coffins and the foundation deposit show. But there is no evidence that the tomb itself was not built during an earlier period and its design is certainly in the manner of an older tomb style. Other tombs in the Valley also have foundations deposits by their doors that name kings other than the tomb owner and this example by Hatshepsut's tomb must have been put in place after most of the original work upon the tomb had been completed. This shallow deposit, lightly covered with sand would have been under the feet of every man who carried the quarried stone from the great excavation—several thousand cubic feet of rock—yet the contents of the deposit were in perfect condition.

The other tomb for Tuthmosis I—the one found by Loret—is also insecure in its date. Apart from the fine sarcophagus, which names the king and states clearly that it was made during a later reign, there was only one small fragment, of an inscribed alabaster jar, that had come from the original burial of the king. but this may easily have been placed in the tomb at the time of the reburial along with the two stray blocks of the *Amduat* which were also found in the tomb and which could have no possible function in the plastered burial chamber of the tomb. Carter had found fifteen similar blocks in the great long tomb of

Hatshepsut and quite possibly the objects found in Loret's little tomb had also been taken from there. Thus, there is no evidence that this little tomb is earlier in date than its sarcophagus. Indeed, like that sarcophagus, the tomb was probably made for Tuthmosis I by his grandson Tuthmosis III.

It is likely, therefore, that the great long tomb of Hatshepsut, excavated by Carter, was originally the tomb of Tuthmosis I (the one that Ineni supervised 'no one seeing, no one hearing'), and that only the burial chamber itself was added by the great queen, for the small flight of steps that leads to the burial chamber at the bottom of the tomb is quite different from the rest of the architecture. This may well represent a second stage of working in the tomb, made during the reign of Hatshepsut to accommodate the joint burial. Unlike the rest of the tomb, this burial chamber was planned using the same metrical systems employed in Hatshepsut's great temple at Deir el Bahari. It is likely that Tuthmosis I was originally buried in the larger room that lies above Hatshepsut's burial chamber in the tomb. The fragments of a large wooden box found by Carter in the tomb could be the remains of the original sarcophagus of the king.

Davis, absolutely delighted with the vast tomb that Carter and his men had cleared for him, despite the fact that the burial chamber had been filled with rubble, which had frustrated his hopes of another formal entry by a party of egyptologists, felt that the work had really accomplished something important for egyptology. Another great book of the excavations, with a description of the two sarcophagi, was prepared, Carter writing about the archeology and Naville, the director of his earlier work in the temple of Hatshepsut, writing about the queen's life and monuments. Davis himself contributed a preface describing the work and greatly praising the endurance of Carter and his men. Carter removed the sarcophagi from the tomb and also took the one out of the little tomb of Tuthmosis I, and Maspero presented Davis with Hatshepsut's sarcophagus that had been altered for her father's use. Davis was also given a very handsome share of the grave goods from the tomb of Tuthmosis IV excavated the previous year, and this magnificent collection of objects crossed the Atlantic to the museums of Boston and New York with the great royal sarcophagus being donated to the former.

In Cairo Davis' excavations were becoming well known. Carter, who had visited the city shortly after his discovery of the tomb of Tuthmosis IV was asked

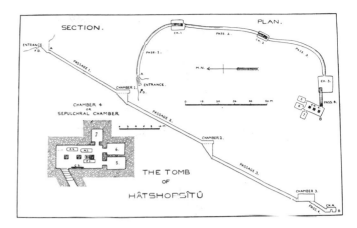

Plan and section of Hatshepsut's tomb drawn by Carter for Davis' publication

at a dinner party if he knew of the great treasures that had just been found at Thebes. When he professed his ignorance, he was told of a tomb that had been found in the Valley of the Theban Kings from which three white camels had been seen to emerge carrying the treasures of Pharaoh upon their swaying backs. Carter, who could probably still taste the salt and grit of the Valley in his mouth, made a wry reply; such conversations, like Belzoni's description of Mohammed Aga looking for his golden cockerel in the tomb of Seti I, did not endear the non-specialist public to him.

During that year, 1904, Carter had climbed to the top of his profession from the lowly post of assistant archeological artist taken to Egypt to draw hieroglyphs some twelve years before. As well as the work in the tomb of Hatshepsut, he had in that same season's work cleared out the large tomb of Merneptah, son of Ramesses II, which was also filled with hard flood debris. This was probably as much a task as the work in the long deep tomb of the queen although less celebrated because no one paid for a volume to commemorate the event. In the cemented dirt of the burial chamber Carter found the lid of a royal sarcophagus which, in his first enthusiasm, he described as 'one of the finest monuments that we have of the ancient pharaohs'. It still lies deep in the burial chamber. Carter fitted electric lights in the tomb, a splendid and, later, much visited monument famed at that time because the king, whose salty mummy had been found in the tomb of Amenhotep II, was believed to have been the pharaoh drowned in the Red Sea in pursuit of the Israelites!

195

As well as these fearsome excavations, as much feats of engineering enterprise as of archeology, Carter had also found time to restore the tomb of Seti I which, since the collapse of a part of the roof in 1901, had seen further damage. A new collapse had, unfortunately, brought down a part of the vaulted ceiling in the burial chamber; a section of the astronomical painting of the constellations had smashed on to the chamber floor in such small pieces that it could not be restored. The continuing deterioration of the tunnel underlying the burial chamber had caused the subsidence of the entire rear wall of the vaulted chamber and this in its turn had triggered the partial collapse of the ceiling. The long white room behind this chamber, where Belzoni had found a slaughtered bull, was completely ruined; the great long horizontal cracks that ran along its walls also appeared through the decorations of the vaulted burial chamber.

After the ceiling collapses, Carter had, as a temporary measure, propped up the loose and subsiding sections with pit props and timbers. With a dozen screw jacks placed in the tunnel that undercut the subsided wall, Carter and his men slowly raised the entire slab of rock to its previous position. While the wall of the great chamber was held by these jacks, bricklayers built vaults in the tunnel and underpinned the walls. The operation was a great success. The columns in the tomb that had been removed by Lepsius were rebuilt in brick to form a supporting pillar and the loose section of the roof, which had threatened collapse just two years before, were held with rolled-steel joists. Sensitive to the environment of the tomb, Carter then had these additions overpainted in colours that resembled the original. The extraordinary underground restoration was so successful that for almost sixty years it held the weak chambers perfectly. Since that time new movements in the rocks have once again opened the cracks in the walls and gaps have appeared between the bricklayers' concrete and the walls that they underpinned.

After his exhausting winter season of 1903–04 Carter visited Cairo on his way to England, to find that Maspero had decided to move him from Thebes to the post of Chief Inspector at Sakkara, a post that included the majority of the pyramids and many renowned private tombs of the Old Kingdom. Another inspector of the *Service*—James Quibell—would be sent to Thebes in Carter's place.

It is probable that Maspero believed that Carter, with his enormous energy and his ability to attract funds for excavation and conservation, was just the man for the site of Sakkara which, like Thebes, was suffering under the waves of mass tourism. In the following November Carter was duly installed in the house of the Inspectorate at Sakkara, with its superb desert views of the Pyramids and, back towards the Nile the magnificent palm groves of Memphis. However, within six weeks he had resigned from the department—the result of a rowdy incident concerning his workers at the Inspectorate and some highly connected French visitors. The mêlée, in which one of Carter's men had knocked a Frenchman to the ground, became inflated into a part of the Anglo-Gallic rivalry that was always present in Cairo and in the offices of the *Service*, but with which Maspero himself seldom acquiesced. The incident was quickly taken out of Maspero's hands by Cromer himself who demanded of Carter that he either apologize to the Frenchman or resign. Despite Maspero's protests, Carter chose the latter. It was a bitter end to his career in the *Service* but not with his connections with either Egyptian antiquities or the Valley of the Kings.

The magnificent quartzite sarcophagus of Tuthmosis IV lying in its funerary crypt (above), and some of the paintings in the antechamber of the tomb

19

Yuya and Tuya

(1904–05; 1905–06)

James Quibell, who had taken over Carter's position at Thebes, had also begun his career in archeology by working with Flinders Petrie but, unlike Carter, he had graduated from Christ Church, Oxford before coming to Egypt. His career had been brilliant; he had discovered many of the most famous objects of early antiquity during his excavations, contributed greatly to the study of Egyptian prehistory and already had a string of scholarly publications to his name. Quibell was certainly the most distinguished archeologist ever to be in a position to excavate in the Valley and it represented a real opportunity to investigate and record those apparently small details of the Valley's history that would certainly be uncovered by the forthcoming large-scale works that Davis intended to finance.

Quibell arrived in Luxor in mid-November 1904 and started to complete the tasks that Carter had left, putting lights into the tomb of Merneptah and shipping the three quartzite sarcophagi by barge to Cairo. Davis, eager to start his new season's work, wrote to Quibell on his arrival in Cairo in December and by the time he arrived in Luxor the following month the workmen had already started. First they continued the investigation of the gully that led up to the tomb of Hatshepsut, working slowly down the slope until they arrived at the trench that Carter had dug when he discovered the pit tombs for Davis two years previously. Next, a small side valley, hitherto overlooked, was completely cleared by Quibell who even had his men turning over the flints that lay on the rocky slopes above. But he found nothing and Davis, impatient for more discoveries, asked him to move the gangs further down towards the centre of the Valley where, Quibell had told him, there were vast deposits of untouched ancient chippings that might conceal earlier tombs.

One can well imagine that for a methodical archeologist of Quibell's calibre the prospect of working with such an obvious treasure seeker as Davis was

Objects from the burials of Yuya and Tuya, from paintings by Carter. Top left, chair and cushion; right, coffer bearing the names of Amenhotep III; bottom, dummy vases of wood

galling and it is quite likely that the two men disliked each other from the very beginning. Maspero was in Luxor on the *dahabiya* of the *Service*, and it was probably at that time that Quibell, feeling compromised by Davis, asked for and was granted a transfer to another Inspectorate. Another Englishman already in Luxor and a former assistant of Petrie's, Arthur Weigall, was appointed to take over from Quibell as soon as his appointment was confirmed. Meanwhile, Quibell had his workmen clear the southern lower side of the gully, again with no results; then his men attacked the area between the two open tombs of Ramesses XI and number 3—that of a prince of Ramesses III. The tone of Davis' continuing arguments with Quibell at this time are best explained by his own account of what happened:

The site was most unpromising, lying as it did between the Ramses tombs [Ramesses III and XI], which had required many men for many years [and thus, he reasoned, the surrounding area would have been plundered]; therefore it did not seem possible that a tomb could have existed in so narrow a space without being discovered. As an original proposition I would not have explored it, and certainly no egyptologist, exploring with another person's money would have thought of risking the time and expense. But I knew every yard of the lateral valley, except the space described and I decided that good exploration justified its investigation and that it would be a satisfaction to know the entire valley, even if the space yielded nothing.

The workmen started cutting away at the huge bank of chippings some thirty feet high, that lay on the side of the hill between the two tombs. They dug a trench through the sharp loose stones, clearing away the inevitable slides of chippings as they occurred. On many of the white stones the marks of a copper chisel could still be seen gleaming metallically; after some 3,000 years the metal had still not oxidized (or turned green). This bank was one of a pair either side of the doorway to the tomb of Ramesses XI, which had walls built out from its entrance to

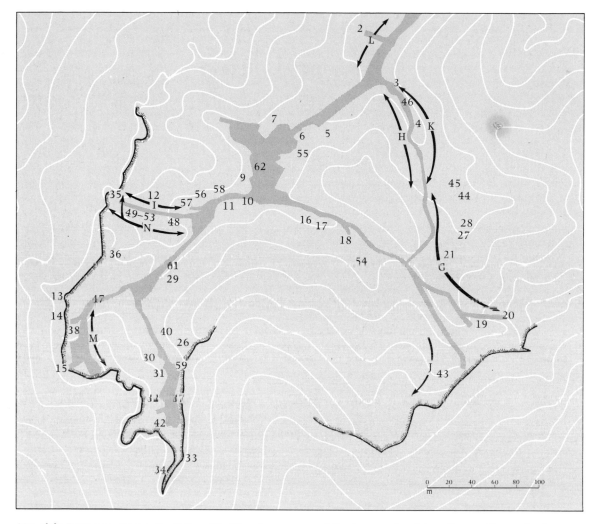

Map of the Davis excavations in the Valley of the Kings from 1904 to 1907. The sites were excavated in the order indicated alphabetically on the plan

prevent the chippings from dropping into it. Doubtless the products of the excavation of that tomb, the chippings had been carried along small paths to the top of the dumps—roughly level with the top of the tomb door—by the ancient workmen who then pitched them down towards the gully. This had been arranged with some care; the massive quantities of chips forming two heaps that with their tops levelled off must, before they turned the fine amber yellow of the desert patination, have looked like the great white pylons of a temple standing either side of the tomb's door. This was a typical arrangement of the larger Rameside tombs, adding another dimension to the tomb's

architecture and solving the problem of where to dump the vast quantity of tomb chippings.

Slowly the workmen cut away at the foot of the chippings and, after ten day's work, they came across a rectangular corner of a flight of steps that ran down into the bedrock and under the chippings. Several days were taken in clearing more of the chippings from the top of the excavation, each stone being checked carefully for inscriptions or pictures; a fruitless task because none of the flakes cut in the tomb of Ramesses XI seem to have been inscribed, a fact of which our expedition was made painfully aware while clearing that tomb!

By 11 February, some seventeen days after they had started to cut into the mound of chippings, the workmen exposed the top of a sealed door that protruded from the filling of limestone and sand that

The bank of chippings between the tombs of a prince of Ramesses III (left) and the huge doorway of the tomb of Ramesses XI. The position of the tomb that Quibell discovered for Davis in the centre of the bank is indicated by a small acute triangle of shadow

blocked the stairwell. By this time Quibell had left the Valley to act as the official guide to a tour of Egypt by the Duke of Connaught, the King's brother, and Weigall, his delegated successor was supervising the work. The men were excited at the appearance of this door sealing but it was late in the evening and, wisely, Weigall now sent them home. The *Reis*, however, remained behind with his small son and slowly Weigall and the *Reis* broke through the sealing at the top of the doorway, watched by Davis and the Valley guards. The workmen had not yet cleared away suffi-

cient of the filling to allow any of the men to pass through the hole, but through the break they could see a steeply sloping corridor dropping down into the gloom. The *Reis* then picked up his small son and, removing from his head the distinctive turban that all Upper Egyptians proudly wear, he passed the long scarf-like *shash* under the boy's arms and lowered him down gently through the small hole.

At first the little boy cried with fear as he hung in the air, but slowly his curiosity got the better of him and when he reached the tomb floor, he ran to a small group of objects which the men could see lying a few feet in front of him. The boy was told to pick up the objects, and he was hoisted back by his father and quickly relieved of his treasures. And treasures they were: a gold-covered yoke from a chariot, a magnificent staff of office and a scarab which, at first glance, appeared to be of solid gold but upon closer examination was found to be stone covered with a gold sheet. Because it was now dark it was obvious to the little group that they should stop their explorations. Davis gathered up his treasures and mounted a donkey for the trip back to the river while Weigall seated himself by the tomb with a guard to spend the night watching over the discovery. Weigall's caution, founded upon years of experience, was soon proved to have been necessary, for as Davis rode through the village on the way to his *dahabiya*, several of the villagers congratulated him upon his discovery and even speculated as to what he had hidden under his coat!

At the tomb Weigall had been disturbed by the approach of visitors who came up the path from the entrance of the Valley long after dark. At Weigall's command the Government guard levelled his gun and a sentry call rang out. The visitors were a young American artist, Joseph Lindon Smith and his wife Corinna, who had come to the tomb after Davis had told them the story and the three of them spent a hard, cold and nervous night. Davis, meanwhile, had sent a note from his boat to Maspero's, which was moored close by, asking him to 'come over and see something worth looking at'. Shortly after, the patient Maspero arrived, bringing an old mutual friend, Professor Sayce, a kindly scholar who had spent many years slowly sailing the length of Egypt. The two egyptologists examined the objects which, although quite magnificent and of fine craftsmanship, gave not a clue to the ownership of the tomb. It would be a fine thing, Maspero suggested, if the tomb could be opened during the following day so that an official opening might take place in the presence of the Duke of Connaught on the day after.

Early next morning the three foreigners at the tomb had been pleased to be awakened by the guards and given coffee and some of the fine local bread. Soon after sunrise the workmen returned for another day's digging and they quickly emptied the rest of the stairwell of its filling and bared the doorway. Shortly after Maspero arrived at the tomb with Davis, the sealed door was taken down and the small party of men advanced into the tomb. The corridor in which they stood was so steep that they had to hold their hands against the walls to avoid slipping. Slowly they walked into the darkness, each carrying a candle. In a wall niche lay a wreath of flowers and a huge wig, made of flax and dyed dark brown. As they walked further down the corridor they picked up a rolled papyrus and a parcel of onions, perhaps left behind in the tomb by robbers who had also broken through a hole in the top of the second sealed doorway that now confronted them. At the foot of this white door, which was covered with the stamps of the necropolis seal, lay the two pottery bowls in which the ancient craftsmen had mixed the final coat of white plaster. Maspero and Davis took down some of the top stones of this wall and on tiptoe peered through the hole.

We found that the opening which the robbers had made was too high and too small to allow of Monsieur Maspero getting through without injury. Though we had nothing but our bare hands, we managed to take down the upper layers of stones, then Monsieur Maspero and I put our head and candles into the chamber, which enabled us to get a glimpse of shining gold covering some kind of furniture, though we could not identify it. This stimulated us to make the entry without further enlarging the opening. I managed to get over the wall and found myself in the sepulchral chamber. With considerable difficulty we helped Monsieur Maspero safely to scale the obstruction, and then Mr. Weigall made his entry.

Maspero writes:

There is no slit behind which an archeologist suspects he may find something new or unknown too small for him to get through. He undergoes much discomfort, but he manages to squeeze through, and once he has set foot in the chamber he seems to have left behind him all the centuries that have elapsed since the dead man was alive.

One can feel sympathy for the young Inspector Weigall upon whose shoulders, doubtless, the shoes of Davis and the ever enthusiastic, if now rather portly figure of Maspero had trodden in their efforts to pass through the small opening. It was, one of them later explained, only accomplished so that the official visit of the Duke of Connaught, planned for the following day, should not disappoint him.

Each of the three visitors noticed different things in the tomb. Weigall compared it to a town house, closed for the summer, incredibly hot and just waiting to have the windows thrown open to light up the gloomy interior. Davis, groping in the darkness, moved his torch dangerously near the tinder-dry wood and resin and had to be restrained by Maspero. The Director saw the name of the owner of the tomb, Yuya, then his wife, Tuya. They had found the parents of the great Queen Tiy, the much beloved wife of Amenhotep III and mother of the heretic King Akhenaten!

Both their sarcophagi had been opened, their lids pushed aside and the coffins in them thrown off the mummies to get at the jewellery they were wearing. The elderly couple looked quietly up at the intruders in their tomb; they were so well preserved that it seemed as if they might open their eyes and speak. Everybody was impressed by them: Yuya, broad-boned and yellow-haired, with his hands crossed protectively under his neck; Tuya, thin-faced, also blonde, her ears pierced for the elaborate jewellery of the splendid court of which she had been an honoured member.

The tiny chamber was so packed with objects that they could not reach its far end. But at their side stood the finest ancient chair that had ever been seen, and canopic vases with elaborate rich decoration. And to their right stood another fabulous piece of furniture; a chair of richly polished red wood decorated with gilded figures of musicians and, on its back, the figures of a princess. This superb example of ancient craftsmanship had belonged to Amenhotep III's daughter and wife Sitamun, a sister of Tutankhamen, who had left the chair in the tomb of her grand-parents. On its back the relief figures of the princess in a double image, are being presented with golden collars by the Syrian princesses of Amenhotep's harem. The three men stood among the objects of the finest burial ever seen from antiquity made during one of the finest periods of New Kingdom history.

The following day, 13 February 1904, the tomb was visited by the Duke and his party; Maspero showed them what he could by the light of electric lamps held up by the door over the crowded objects in the tomb.

When Quibell eventually arrived on the following day, freed from his official duties, he was shocked to discover that Davis had already removed some of the

The heads of Yuya (left) and Tuya

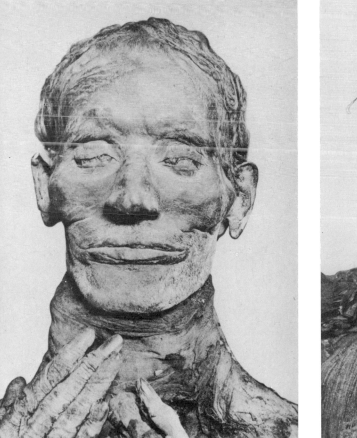
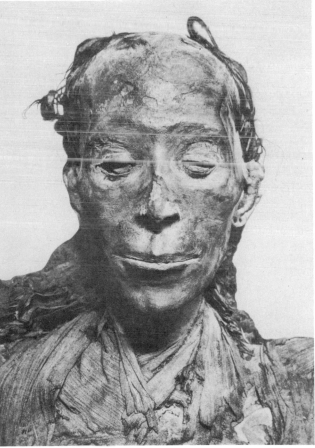

The outer coffin of Yuya standing in the gully in front of the tomb waiting to be packed for shipment to Cairo

objects to his boat without any check or record being made of them. Nevertheless, he now set about emptying the tomb which Maspero insisted should be done as quickly as possible for fear of thieves and robbery. For the packing and cataloguing Quibell enlisted the help of the staff from other excavations at Thebes, each member spending nights by the tomb door as well. From the Italian excavations in the ancient village of the royal tomb workers the Conte Malvezzi di Medici lent a hand, and Naville, working still at Deir el Bahari sent a young archeologist, Edward Ayrton, who had trained under Flinders Petrie. Smith, the American artist, made drawings of the heads of the two mummies and Davis subsequently hired Carter, now a freelance archeological artist, to make drawings of some of the finest pieces.

In three weeks all the objects had been removed but it was not until near the end of this operation that they were able to reach the magnificent jewel caskets of Amenhotep III that they could see lying among other objects at the end of the tomb. Although it was found to contain only two model hoes, digging equipment for the lavish ushabtis of the tomb, the chest itself is among the finest pieces of ancient furniture to have survived. At the back of the small chamber, lying on top of some fifty large jars filled with natron and other embalming relics, was a little chariot, not suitable, perhaps, for going to war, but a small light elegant model more fitted for being slowly driven around the sandy roads of Amenhotep III's great royal town, to the south of Thebes. At that time it was the second chariot known to have survived from ancient Egypt, and in excellent condition. As a commander of the royal chariots and Master of the Horse, the chariot was a most appropriate possession for Yuya to have taken with him to the grave. The floor of the tomb had been sprinkled with fine yellow sand, a traditional act according to the ancient texts where the dead are frequently called 'those that lay upon their sand'; but this had never before been seen in modern times.

Apart from the three pieces of lavish furniture that have become a central modern image of the brilliant court of Amenhotep III, the tomb was similar in its grave goods to that of Mahirpra, the coffins all in their splendid gilded sets. The wooden outer sarcophagi were so large, Quibell noticed, that they would not have been able to pass through the door in one piece. They were, he discovered, assembled in the chamber, even the black resin coating and the gilding of the gods having been accomplished in the limited space. The clumsy nature of the painting of

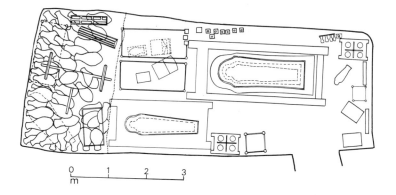

The tomb of Yuya and Tuya as excavated by Quibell. The distance from the burial chamber door, up two flights of stairs to the entrance of the tomb is about seventeen metres

much of this resin would certainly bear out this observation; in one tomb the paintings upon the wall of the burial chamber have been smeared with this resin, obviously at a later stage in the funeral ceremonies and in another, that of Tuthmosis IV, streaks of resin remain on the burial chamber walls. Quibell must have been very pleased to return to Cairo with his treasures for the Museum. Soon after he took the post that Carter had resigned at Sakkara and there he passed the rest of his distinguished career among the massive monuments of earlier times and far away from the vulgar glare of gold and the pressures of capricious sponsorship.

In future years Quibell would tell one amusing tale concerning his clearance of the tomb. He was visited one afternoon by an old lady plainly dressed with a mushroom hat and an old drab cloak. She was accompanied by a harried-looking Frenchman who addressed the old lady as 'Your Highness' and Quibell, not knowing the identity of his visitor, deferred to the title and welcomed her into the tomb. He apologized to the couple for the fact that nearly all the objects had been packed away and that there was nothing for them to sit on but the old lady, seeing the gilded chair of Sitamun said that it would do her very well and sat down. Remarkably the ancient stringing of the seat held up and, in their embarrassment the archeologists were loath to tell 'her Highness' to get up. Later they discovered that their visitor had been the Empress Eugenie of France, revisiting Egypt some thirty years after she had been the guest of honour of the Khedive Ismail at the grand ceremonial opening of the Suez Canal. So the last person to sit upon that ancient chair was another queen

and now, with all the rest of the tomb, it is displayed in the Cairo Museum.

Such intrusion into the past as the entering of those tombs is seldom captured by the dry archeological reports, and then, inadvertently, as an accidental detail suddenly pushes home the fact that it really was some three and a half thousand years since the ancient objects had seen the light of day. Yuya and Tuya had laid in their tomb nearly fifteen hundred years when Christ was preaching in Palestine and more than two thousand when the armies of Mohammed came out of the Arabian Peninsula. Maspero had a fine eye for the details of such extraordinary events. Here, despite the fact that the subject of his story eventually was found, under analysis, to have been not honey but ritual natron, is perhaps the most telling image of the opening of the tomb:

One of the vases we uncorked contained thick oil, another almost liquid honey, which still preserved its scent. If it had been left without its cover on one of the steps of the staircase, near the entrance of the corridor, a marauding wasp, having strayed into the Valley of the Kings, would have hovered gluttonously round the jar. We should have had to send it away by flapping a handkerchief to prevent it taking a portion of the honey gathered by ancient bees from the flowers of the Theban meadows more than three thousand years ago.

Davis was given four fine ushabti figures, 'as keepsakes' from the tomb. Quibell somewhat sourly announced in his brief report on the tomb that the season's excavation had cost Davis £E 80.00; the cost of packing and transporting the tomb's contents to the Museum in Cairo, borne by the *Service*, was £E 132.00. Davis was indeed getting very good value for his money but it had especially annoyed him that Quibell had announced the uncovering of the tomb in *The Times* as a discovery of the *Service*, which indeed, under the terms of Davis' agreement, it was. If he were to continue in the Valley, Davis told Maspero, then he must be allowed to conduct his own excavations. Of course, Maspero responded soothingly: he completely agreed, adding that under these circumstances Davis would not be allowed to work in the Valley of the Kings without a full time archeologist, employed by him, in constant attendance. Furthermore, suggested Maspero, the excavations should now be concentrated on one area of the Valley at a time, leaving nothing unexcavated before proceeding to the next area. Davis enthusiastically agreed and, in his next publication announced that his 'policy' had changed from 'exploring hither and thither' to 'exhausting every mountain and foot hill'. Maspero observed to Davis that this would require money, perseverance and patience and that he was not sure about the latter; a catalogue to which Davis cheerfully added 'hope'.

Thus Edward Ayrton, the young English archeologist then twenty-three, who had been working with Naville, came to work in the Valley for Davis,

being paid about £250 per year. It was Ayrton who established Davis' excavations in the Valley as a proper working expedition, rather than simply a gang of men supervised by the inspectors and visited by Davis. These arrangements had proved woefully inadequate during the clearance of the tomb of Yuya and Tuya; there was no storeroom available in the Valley, no workshops or laboratories for equipment and no facilities for accommodation. With Ayrton organizing the day-to-day excavations and so releasing the inspectors for their other duties, he would need accommodation close to the site and after searching for a suitable location, Ayrton and Davis built a small house of stone and mud at the entrance to the West Valley.

Theodore Davis standing in front of the house that he built in the West Valley. These fragments of glass negative were recovered from loose mud plaster in the ruined Davis House during its rebuilding by our expedition in 1978. The dryness of the Valley's climate has preserved the photographic emulsion perfectly for nearly seventy years

It was an excellent choice. Invisible from the track that took visitors to the Valley, yet only a five minute walk from the excavations, the house was cleverly situated in the shade of a cliff and sited so that the breezes that run down the desert valleys blew alongside it. The roof, slightly pitched and built of timber, was double skinned to keep the ceilings of the house cool during the long baking summers when temperatures stay over $100°$F for months on end. At first Ayrton designed a modest affair of four bedrooms, each ten feet square, in a row like monks' cells with one small window and a reception room in front of them with Arab-style divans surrounding a central table. A kitchen and guards' room was later added to one side and the house was subsequently further enlarged as more facilities were needed. Though lacking water and electricity, the house was clean and very dry.

Ayrton would leave the house for the excavations in the Valley around six o'clock every morning and there he would find the gangs of workmen waiting for the order to start the excavation. The expedition usually employed about forty men and sixty boys who had walked over the cliffs from Gurna and the surrounding villages where they lived. Most of the men would bring their own *fas* with them and would spend their days bent over in the dust scraping the chippings and debris into large baskets which, when filled, would be lifted on to the shoulder of a boy by another man who stood next to the excavator. It was difficult to decide where these tons of excavation debris should be dumped but labour was very cheap and Davis often had it moved from site to site with few problems. The workmen were overseen by a *Reis* who stood back from the face at which the men worked, holding a switch in his hands with which he would exhort the basket boys to hurry in their long procession from the trench to the dump and back again. It was easy to see if the work was going well, for with the correct ratio of excavators to attendent workmen, the pace of the excavation would be monotonously constant.

As the men worked a water carrier with a goatskin of water slung across his shoulders would move from group to group. The men took simple meals sitting in circles while they talked and ate the food that they had brought in little bundles tied to the end of long thick staffs, *naboots*, which most male rural Egyptians still carry with them. Usually their meals consisted of raw onions, tomatoes and brown homemade bread, all salted and heavily spiced. At a call from the *Reis* they would start again. They worked for six days and on Fridays they stayed in their village and dressed in their fine long robes. They visited the local mosque where a famous holy man and mystic Sheik Taib (Sheik 'Good') led the prayers and kept an eye upon the villagers. The Sheik, in common with some of the richer villagers, had made the pilgrimage to Holy Mecca, some four hundred miles away to the east.

The heat in the Valley, and the dust of excavation, was terrific but the noise of chanting and talking men provided an accompaniment to the whole proceedings which is remembered with great affection by all who have worked in such a way. Though wearing their elegant *gallabiyas*, the especially long flowing robes of the Upper Egyptians, to travel to the Valley, at work they would strip down to their simpler undergarments which looked remarkably like the short Roman *peplum*. They would work barefoot among the large, unstable rocks and the sharp flints; injuries, though rare, were sometimes severe and, with the primitive medical treatment available, were cause for real alarm. They worked for a few pennies a day, enough perhaps to buy six eggs or enough basic food to feed themselves and their families. The infant mortality rate in the villages was alarming. Bilharzia, that terrible debilitative disease, was endemic and epidemics of influenza or German measles killed large numbers of people. Many people died in their forties

Lines of men and boys carrying away the dirt from a site are still a familiar feature at any Egyptian excavation. This small fragment of a lost photograph, also found in the Davis House, is of an unidentified basket boy

and most had only eaten meat on a few feast days in their lives. The years of terrible taxation and famine had welded the villagers into closed communities that looked upon foreigners and the outside world with well-warranted suspicion. Yet, like the gold in hidden tombs in the hills around them, the foreigners from Cairo and beyond held enormous wealth and quite capriciously they might sometimes be made to part with a little. They also held great power and could arrange to send the villagers to prison. Seventy years earlier, a complaint to the local governor by a foreigner could have had them hung.

Understandably, if the workmen saw a small antiquity lying before them in the dirt they would often palm it with great skill, in the hope of selling it to the Luxor antiquities merchants. The excavations were a constant battle of wits between the hapless excavator standing by the dusty trench and the sweating workers, eyes alight for antiquities. Yet so casually conducted were many excavations at this period that there could often be quite lengthy periods when none of the archeologists were present at the work, which would then be entirely supervised by the *Reis*. It was the *Reis* who hired the men, for which he extracted a part of each man's tiny wages, and who kept the work running smoothly. It was, as Carter had well understood, a crucial post; obviously Loret's *Reis* had not told him of several of the tombs that the workmen had discovered and had also lightly plundered the royal tombs they had opened for him. Carter's *Reis* stayed with him, on and off, for more than twenty years and Carter often paid tribute to him in his accounts of the work. Indeed, an experienced *Reis* frequently understood more of the work of archeology than the foreigners who employed him. Both the *Reis* and his best workers had their own terms for the various strata typical of Theban excavations. The *nashu*, untouched debris of ancient Egyptian date which could hold literally anything, was the filling that they most liked to work into and this knowledge was also useful for their own covert excavations. The *Reis* was also the spokesman for the men, speaking upon their behalf if there were complaints or suggestions about the work. He would also protect the interests of the excavators. It was a difficult job that demanded abilities that were sometimes spontaneously recognized by the men in one of their number who could then become a respected and wealthy member of the village.

After the hectic month that surrounded the discovery and clearance of the tomb of Yuya and Tuya, Davis had dug for a short while around the northern slopes of the gully that led to the tomb of Amenhotep II and it was here that Ayrton started his work in the Valley. His men quickly cleared the area to bedrock without finding a tomb, and Ayrton shifted his men to work in the gully by the tomb of Tuthmosis IV to finish the clearance that had stopped when that tomb had been discovered. Here it seems that Davis' policy of 'exhausting every mountain' led to a certain amount of hither and thithering, as Ayrton skipped about the Valley, clearing areas around the tombs of Tuthmosis IV and finding nothing but an unfinished doorway. Ayrton and his men worked around the tomb of Yuya and Tuya, cutting trenches down towards the tomb of the prince of Ramesses III, next door, and across the gully up its other slope. But again they found nothing, and Ayrton shifted his men to the other side of the main path where they excavated in the ancient quarryman's dumps in front of the tomb of Ramesses IV.

Here the apparently natural hillside was discovered to have been partly man-made (as they had found by the tomb of Yuya and Tuya); and the surface had again been partially landscaped with loose flints scattered over it to resemble the natural hillsides. The great heaps of ancient debris held the remnants of the equipment used by the artists who had decorated the tombs; dishes of pigment, lamps and bowls with the remains of hard plaster set in them. Ayrton commented that many of the *ostraca* found in this area had the name of Ramesses II upon them and that 'it is probable that all this rubbish is from that tomb'. Unfortunately, this fascinating evidence of the craftsmen's tools and belongings passed largely unrecorded. Doubtless some of the finer antiquities, labelled 'Kings Valley Season 1905–6' with their significance and interest largely lost, are stored almost anonymously in Cairo or America. As the men worked closer to the tomb of Ramesses IV, they cleared away two levels of occupation in the area; traces of houses that Ayrton labelled Coptic and, underneath, Roman. These stood on some three feet of ancient masons' chippings, in which they found 'dozens of broken ushabtis' from the tomb of Ramesses IV.

The sad short record of the work is tantalizing, for it contains hints of entire lost chapters of the history of the Valley. However, it is probable that Ayrton kept some kind of expedition record and, indeed, a tattered map discovered in the ruins of the Davis House might be a part of it but Davis was only interested in *tombs* and Ayrton was scarcely allowed a few pages in Davis' lavish volumes to report on the archeology.

Ayrton next shifted the excavations to the southern head of the Valley in the bay adjacent to that which held the tomb of Tuthmosis III. Here was a row of royal tombs of the Nineteenth Dynasty, excavated into the rock at the base of the cliff, that had been open since ancient times. But opposite this cliff on the other side of the rock bay, the steep-sloped hill that separated this area from the gully beneath the tomb of Tuthmosis III, had never been excavated. Large amounts of chippings from the quarrying of the nearby royal tombs had been thrown against the hillside and had been penetrated by flood waters and their debris which had cemented the entire bank into a solid feature that might just have covered an earlier tomb beneath. Ayrton had several long trenches dug into this bank at two- and three-feet intervals and as they successively hit bedrock, trench after trench he discovered the real profile of the hillside as it lay under the debris. Then, at the northern end of one of the trenches they hit upon a flight of steps.

The cartouche of Siptah carved on the doorway of his tomb

At once every available workman was set to work, and after a day's hard labour we were able to catch a glimpse of the door lintel, and to read the cartouches of Siptah.

It was the last tomb of the Nineteenth and Twentieth Dynasty kings to be discovered in the Valley and as the workmen dug through the fine chippings that completely filled the outer corridors of the tomb its excavators could immediately see that it was a large monument of real size and grace. The king's names were written in thinly elegant and brightly coloured hieroglyphs upon the doorjambs. Near these names and titles were two fine reliefs of the goddess Isis and Nepthys sitting upon huge brightly coloured woven baskets (the *neb* hieroglyph) holding up their arms and wings as if beckoning the king to enter his tomb. The ceiling was beautifully painted with a procession of vultures whose wings spread across the corridor's width, and displayed above them, once again, the cartouches and titles of the king. Unbesmirched by soot and smoke they remain one of the finest examples of such ceilings in the Valley. In all, the tomb was decorated in a light, airy and elegant style that was predominantly green and filmy in its colour scheme. It contained the beginnings of the gracefulness of the later larger Ramesside tombs but it still had the same simplicity of design that was to be found in the earlier tombs of Seti I and the others of that period.

However, in the chippings in the first corridor of the tomb the workmen found a large fragment of an alabaster coffin, somewhat similar in style to the great coffin that Belzoni had taken from the tomb of Seti I. They also uncovered many other broken objects: pots, vases and the like, as well as some inscribed fragments that suggest a queen had also been buried in the tomb. Beyond the first two corridors, which beneath the loose filling and chippings were beautifully preserved, the tomb was half filled with hard flooded debris and the decorations were heavily damaged. All the lower sections were dangerously loose and heavily flooded right into the burial chamber. Ayrton immediately had part of the roof buttressed but the tomb was still far from secure. Believing that they would be little rewarded in continuing to excavate this solid dry flood debris—the king's mummy already on view in Cairo and his alabaster coffin smashed to fragments—the expedition abandoned the tomb for fresh pastures.

Ayrton and Davis now returned to the same gully by the tomb of Amenhotep II in which they had

207

begun their work at the start of the season some eight weeks earlier. Although its northern slopes had been completely explored, the southern side of the gully had been but only scratched by Loret's *sondages* that had created a series of small deep holes over the higher parts of the hill. Ayrton and Davis proposed to clear the entire area despite the considerable deposits of chippings, in some places about twelve feet thick. It was heavy work even for the large gang of men and, as always with the threat of debris studded with large rocks and boulders sliding down on them. Ayrton started by digging two *sondages* himself at the bottom of the gully to find the depth at which the bedrock lay, and from these two control points he and his team moved up the gully clearing towards the cliff face. Soon they found a tomb cut low down in the gully, a small affair like a miniature royal tomb. The original work on this tomb, later numbered 49, had never been finished and to make a chamber to hold the burial, loose chippings had been dumped into the unfinished stair well at the bottom of the excavation to make a flat floor. From the evidence of a single small wooden label with scribbled hieratic writing upon it, it would seem that a burial had taken place during the Eighteenth Dynasty and, to further corroborate this slender paleographic evidence, there were many fragments of yard-high storage jars of that same period in the burial chamber; some with stoppers, nearly five inches across were made of papyrus and sealed with Nile mud; others with sharply rounded bottoms had been made to rest either in a pottery stand or in a hollow in the sand. The entrance to this makeshift room had been sealed in the usual way, with a dry stone wall covered with gritty white plaster. Some of the stones—still plastered into place —hold between them a curved stone pillow that had, presumably, been made and used by one of the workmen in the Valley. The pillow, a rectangular block of soft limestone curved on its top surface like the pottery pillows of China, is engraved with the wings of a falcon, in the hope, perhaps, that this image of flight would have helped the workman to feel that his head rested softly on the grey chalky stone.

There was no record remaining of who had been buried in the tomb; it had probably been an official of the mid-Eighteenth Dynasty. Whoever it was may well have been collected with the royal mummies for reburial by one of the reburial commissions, for a fine red-painted, carefully written graffito over the entrance to the tomb records such a trip. There was nothing in the tomb, however, that Davis would have wanted to show his numerous guests and visitors, so Ayrton and his men pressed on further up the gully.

After some twenty yards or so they uncovered the mouths of three pits, each of which had a chamber at its bottom. Davis was lowered down into one of them

and entered the chamber, which proved to be extremely hot and too low for comfort. I was startled by seeing very near me a yellow dog of ordinary size standing on his feet, his short tail curved over his back, and his eyes open. Within a few inches of his nose sat a monkey in quite perfect condition; for an instant I thought they were alive, but I soon saw that they had been mummified, and that they had been unwrapped in ancient times by robbers. The attitude of the animals suggested that the monkey was saying, 'It's all over with me', and the dog, with his bright eyes and manner seemed to reply, 'Have courage, it will end all right'. I am quite sure the robbers arranged the group for their amusement. However this may be, it can be said to be a joke 3000 years old.

The other two pit tombs close by also contained mummified animals, one being completely filled with animals: ducks, apes (not monkeys), dogs, ibises and many types of unspecified birds were crammed into the little tomb. The other tomb contained two monkey burials, each with their own shrine-like coffin and, even, sets of canopic chests for their viscera. Some distance from the two monkey burials lay a small human-faced mummy mask of a type sometimes placed on top of the mummified contents of canopic jars. The style of this mask was Eighteenth Dynasty and so they dated the three tombs to that time and because of their closeness to the tomb of Amenhotep II, to his reign. But, in fact, another as yet unknown Eighteenth Dynasty royal tomb, that of Horemheb, lay much closer. All the animals had been embalmed and decorated with jewellery—one of the monkeys still wore a necklace of fine blue faience beads. Once again Ayrton's report is scanty and there is no way of knowing whether humans had also been buried in these tombs, the first one, which Davis had entered, being the largest with a room nearly twenty feet long and eight feet wide. The shafts, too, around twelve feet deep, were considerable but they would have presented no trouble to the Egyptian workmen —today they can still walk down the sides of a shaft using the opposite walls like two opposing ladders. That this excruciating exercise was the normal way of entering such shafts is shown by the footholds

Some of the monkey mummies found in the pit tombs nearby the tomb of Amenhotep II

that are frequently found cut into the sides of shafts; it is a truly hair-raising way of descending into tombs, hanging wedged in the shaft with a great drop beneath ones legs—ladders are a much better alternative for tomb tripping.

Two French biologists who later examined some of the animals at the Cairo Museum reported that they were of the very finest breeds, well fed and had led a life of ease. Animals such as ibis, apes and ducks were all kept as sacred animals in the temples, and it may well have been that this small animal cemetery was not the private zoo of a king, as some people have imagined, but a collection of sacred beasts laid by the side of the king's grave.

Although there was no funerary equipment discovered that could be identified as being from a human burial in these tombs, another shaft close by, now numbered 48, still contained its owner, lying stripped and broken on a layer of chippings that covered the chamber floor. The coffin too had been smashed and a tantalizing clay seal broken from a papyrus roll was also found in the chippings. Three mud bricks and some ushabtis gave the name of the owner of this humble tomb: none other than a Vizier of Egypt and Governor of Thebes, Amenemopet. He came from a distinguished family of civil servants who must have been the effective rulers of Egypt while the warrior kings were fighting for their empire in foreign lands, an activity which occupied much royal time during this period. Amenemopet was the brother of Sennefer, whose funerary equipment Carter had found in tomb 42. These two men, both powerful officials in the civil administration, had more than a passing interest in the Valley. In another of his tombs on the hill of Gurna, Sennefer had employed the same artist who decorated the columns in the tomb of his king, Amenhotep II, and Amenemopet's predecessor in his high office, User, had also employed the royal artists to decorate the burial chamber of his tomb on the same hill. Both these private tombs, decorated by the royal artists, are unusual in that it was the burial chamber, and not only the tomb chapel, as was usual, that had been decorated. In the case of User's tomb, his burial chamber, at the bottom of a deep shaft, imitates to some extent the royal tomb plan and even has the *Amduat* painted upon its walls, a quite unique occurrence at that time.

One of these brothers seems to have held the direct responsibility of being the overseer of the artists and craftsmen of the royal tombs. Other connections with the chief of the craftsmen of the royal tombs also appear in the titles of their father. Certainly, during the Eighteenth Dynasty, the 'rules' for burial in the Valley of the Kings were very different from later dynasties when it was virtually reserved solely for kings and, occasionally, queens. But during the early Eighteenth Dynasty a wide variety of people were certainly buried there and the positions of their tombs show clearly that with the tombs of Tuthmosis III, Amenhotep II and Tuthmosis IV being situated at the head of small gullies in the Valley, the tombs of their family members and special nobles were often buried in subsidiary cemeteries further down the gullies.

This particular gully still had one more surprise for Ayrton and Davis:

Whilst digging near the foot of a high hill in the Valley of the Tombs of the Kings, my attention was attracted to a large rock tilted to one side, and for some mysterious reason I felt interested in it, and on being carefully examined and dug about by my assistant, Mr Ayrton, with the hands, the beautiful blue cup . . . was found.

In fact, this cup had been buried some twelve feet down in the chippings and had been carefully placed under that rock for its protection. Painted on to its dark blue glaze were the names of Tutankhamen; the first notice of that king to be found in the Valley.

The little blue cup, of a type that was used to hold the balls of natron during the 'Opening of the Mouth' ritual, had been well buried even in ancient times for, some nine feet above it, Ayrton had found a miniature cachette of fourteen ushabtis of Ramesses IV. Possibly the cup had been used at the funeral of Tutankhamen and had later been hidden in the Valley but, as the excavators commented, 'Why or from what cause it made such a perilous journey is, of course, unknown'; this is still true today. But then, Tutankhamen's tomb is a most unusual monument in so many different ways.

20

The Sere and Yellow Leaf

(1906–07)

Ayrton returned to his work in the Valley in October 1906, one month before Davis returned to Egypt. At the end of the previous season Davis had asked him to clear the tomb of Montu-hir-kopesh-ef of the boulders that partly filled it, thus completing the exploration in that section of the Valley. The work of the expedition was now becoming increasingly confined in its scope, Davis' policy of 'exhausting every mountain and foot hill in the Valley' being just that: only the hill and gully sides were excavated by Ayrton, Davis being of the opinion that the ancient masons had not cut tombs in the flat floor of the Valley as they knew it to be a watercourse and vulnerable to flooding. By the end of Ayrton's second season virtually all the sides of the hills and gullies had been excavated, with the exception of the central arena around the tomb of Ramesses IX and the higher slopes above the tomb of Seti I, where Belzoni had excavated ninety years before.

Davis and Ayrton began their third season's excavations on the first day of 1907 by working into the debris that lay on the rocks to the south of the tomb of Ramesses IX—the central area of the Valley now occupied by the Rest House. Here the rock face was almost vertical and the trenches that were cut through the debris of the slope where the hillside joined the flat bedrock of the Valley floor were nearly twenty feet deep. The first trenches had been cut close to the door of the tomb of Ramesses IX, and the two men were moving southwards along the hillside. About thirty feet from the tomb of Ramesses IX they uncovered a group of pots that had been carefully buried in the debris, probably, Ayrton thought, of Twentieth Dynasty date. Underneath this little cache the men uncovered the square corners of a flight of steps to the doorway of a tomb. Ayrton kept a gang of men working straight down into the stairwell, clearing out the chippings and debris. Disappointingly they had seen that the upper levels of this debris were cemented together by flood water, but underneath, the workmen exposed the lintel of the tomb's door that was buried in clean loose chippings that had never been soaked. Lower down in the loose chippings

they uncovered a generous, well-made staircase of nineteen steps that ran down under the slope of the hill. At the foot of the steps they found a roughly built dry stone wall of limestone chips. It was reminiscent of the tomb of Yuya and Tuya, but in that tomb the sealed wall, through which the *Reis* had sent his young son, had been well made and sealed with plaster. In this new tomb it was not sealed and they found, to their surprise, it rested not on the bedrock of the door sill, but on a slide of chippings that ran from under the stairwell of the tomb down into a sloping corridor beyond. Behind the rough wall lay another one, carefully plastered over and bearing the seal so often found in the New Kingdom royal tombs, an impression of a seated jackal, Anubis upon his shrine, over the crouching figures of nine bound captives.

At this point in the work, just one week after the excavations had begun, Weigall, still the Chief Inspector and nominally in charge of Davis' excavations, was informed of the discovery and was now on hand to see what the new tomb would contain. Both blocking walls were taken down and the filling that lay around them was removed. It was clear that the outer wall had been built to reseal the tomb after the older inner one had been anciently penetrated. Now the three men looked down into a well-made sloping corridor about six feet wide and filled to within three feet of its ceiling with chippings, which Ayrton thought had never been exposed to the elements for any length of time because they appeared to be freshly cut and not mixed with sand or other detritus. Lying on the top of this fill and almost touching the ceiling above the right-hand wall of the corridor was a huge wooden panel covered in relief and inscriptions and completely gilded in fine gold leaf. Above it lay a smaller door, similarly gilded and decorated. The ceiling had a long crack running down its centre and during the Valley's floods this had leaked water that had dripped on to the golden panel and the door. Their condition was pitiable and the gentle breeze from the Valley that for the first time in some three thousand years blew down the shaft

The entrance corridor of tomb 55 (below). This photograph, by a certain R. Paul of Cairo, was made for Davis' publication and shows the corridor filled with debris and partly blocked by fragile gold shrines. The wooden plank that the Reis put down to enable the archeologists to penetrate the burial chamber is on the right-hand side

The modest entrance of Davis' tomb of 1907, later numbered 55, during its excavation. The mouth of the large tomb to its left is that of Ramesses IX. In more recent times a modern Rest House has been built close to the entrance of tomb 55 — on the right of this contemporary photograph

caused the loose gold leaf to shimmer and flash in the intrusive sunlight. It was obviously a desperate situation. The panels needed urgent and expert care if they were to be saved; parts of the woodwork were as soft yet as firmly shaped as cigar ash, and it was these intangible forms that still supported the gold leaf. There were archeologists and restorers in Egypt with skill and experience enough who could, perhaps, have saved these golden panels but unfortunately none of them was working in the Valley of the Kings.

Weigall and Ayrton quickly realized that the fragile panels should not be touched and the *Reis* was requested to make a way around them so that the archeologists could see what lay beyond. A small bridge consisting of a plank and a pit prop was set up on the left side of the corridor about a foot above the panels, and led by Davis, the three men inched one by one along the timbers and down into a relatively unencumbered passage that lay beyond. On his way past the panels Weigall paused to read their hieroglyphs; they had been made for Queen Tiy, wife of Amenhotep III, mother of Akhenaten, daughter of Yuya and Tuya. Davis, with his especial love of the great queens of Egypt was thrilled, eager to see the rest of the tomb. The group then collected electric lights, tapped from the main supply in the Valley, and walked down the remainder of the sloping corridor, again similar in shape to the tomb of Yuya and Tuya. At the end of the corridor a spill of chippings ran down from the corridor into a large high undecorated room around which further panels and other objects were lying, all apparently in complete confusion. Many of them were as fragile as the panels in the corridor and on some the gold leaf had already gently detached itself and floated weightlessly down to the ground and lay in frothy piles, unmoving in the still air of the room.

Stepping gingerly through the mixture of rock chippings and small antiquities the three men entered the chamber and found a golden coffin half-collapsed on the floor. It was completely covered with bright inlays of glass and semi-precious stones and had a royal serpent on its forehead. This too had been attacked by the dripping floodwaters and its small wooden bier had collapsed and set the coffin on the floor. The fall had jarred the lid off and the archeologists were able to look down at the head of a royal mummy, crowned by a vulture of gold sheet which had been jammed down hard upon its brow by the fall. Davis was delighted; he was, he thought, looking at the remains of the great Queen Tiy herself, a famous Egyptian beauty and a leading character in the Heresy period, the most romantic age, perhaps, of ancient Egypt's long history. It was a belief, Weigall later observed, 'that Davis held until his mind finally descended into infirmity'.

In a small unfinished niche in the chamber wall were four large alabaster pots and a stick of wood. The pots were canopic vases but the inscriptions that had originally named their owner had been very carefully obliterated by a gentle hammering of the stone. The jars, though elegant, were not exceptional but their strange, ill-fitting lids were capped with four small portrait heads that equal the finest surviving sculptures of the Amarna period. The close-grained alabaster of the heads, each about four inches high, had been carefully polished to create a texture close to human skin, a texture typical of much of the finer

The burial chamber of tomb 55 in the first weeks of its discovery. The niche containing the canopic vases is the large door-shaped opening in the end wall; in front lies the shattered coffin. The gold leaf from the shrines lies in heaps at the bottom of the panels leaning against the right-hand wall. A notebook, which unfortunately has not been preserved, rests on the sill of the niche.

sculpture of that period. The natural luminosity of the stone, which held the light within it like marble or flesh, aided this superb naturalistic effect yet the strong instincts towards abstraction shared by most Egyptian sculptors kept the forms of the four heads simple and distinct. In short, they were true masterpieces.

Wisely, the three men then left the tomb and stopped the work for several days to await the arrival from Cairo of a photographer who would take photographs of the tomb and its objects as they lay. Already tales of the glittering golden room had excited the imaginations of the local tomb-robbing fraternity. According to gossip the treasure was tremendous and 'news that Ayrton was knee deep in gold and precious stones, feverishly filling empty petroleum tins, pickle pots and cans from Chicago, with the spoil,' was widespread. It is at this point that the comedy of errors really began. Like the housewife who cleans away the marks of the burglary so that her domain will appear well-kept to the investigating detective, somebody 'cleared up' the burial chamber for the benefit of the photographer.

At the same time that Ayrton had sent off requests to Cairo for a photographer and an artist to draw the panel reliefs which, it was now clear, fitted together to form one large golden shrine, Weigall had also telegrammed Maspero the good news. Extra guards were put in the Valley and the entrance to the newly discovered tomb was surrounded by low walls to keep the corridors free of loose debris. At the end of the first day's work in the tomb, after Weigall and Davis had left the Valley, Ayrton visited his friends who were still living and working at the Deir el Bahari temples, which he had quit to dig in the Valley.

His face bore the expression of a gentle angler who, having landed a big fish, joins his companions who have done no more than lose their tackle.

He told them that he had found the tomb of Queen Tiy, but that it had been disturbed since her burial not, apparently, by robbers for her gold was still with her in the tomb. He had noticed that the figures of her heretic son, Akhenaten, had been hacked out of the reliefs on the golden panels leaving great shadow-like gashes where his image had been. The objects in the tomb were so fragile, Ayrton told his friends, that it was possible that the change of air in the tomb might well cause them to disintegrate.

Two of the four superb canopic vases that were found in tomb 55

While the expedition awaited the arrival of an artist and photographer, Lindon Smith the painter, who had kept Weigall company in the Valley as he guarded the tomb of Yuya and Tuya, was making drawings of the interior of the chamber. Visitors were barred from the fragile environment. Lindon Smith drew everything in the tomb: the row of panels lying at angles against the rear wall of the burial chamber and another that lay in front of them on the floor, the coffin and the collapsed bier crushed beneath it, and the small niche with its four alabaster jars and their magnificent portrait heads. There were other boxes laying about the chamber. One of these held the implements for the Opening of the Mouth ritual, another held small pots, faience wands and some small blue glazed vases. In addition to these pretty museum pieces, there were more prosaic objects: inscribed mud bricks, and a multitude of clay sealings broken from boxes and bundles. The ancient workmen, too, had left some of their tools behind: some chisels and a mallet head, perhaps used during the dismantling or for the intended re-erection of the panels of the golden shrine.

After a few days the photographer, a certain R. Paul, had taken his pictures and Lindon Smith had completed his drawings. By late January another artist, a Welshman Harold Jones, had started to copy the inscriptions and reliefs of the wooden shrines. But three days later, probably on the orders of Maspero who was always loath to leave objects in the Valley for long periods of time, the tomb was almost completely cleared out. Thus, by the end of the month everything but the surviving portions of the shrine and the pathetic bones of the mummy had been taken from the tomb and lay on board Davis' boat, moored off Luxor. Jones, who had been installed upon Davis' *dahabiya*, sometimes travelled to the Valley to continue copying the shrine but he found that his work was continually interrupted by visitors and acquaintances who wanted to see the tomb. At the same time he was drawing the smaller objects when on board the boat.

Maspero himself had arrived for the stripping of the royal mummy, a somewhat theatrical event, and had also inspected the gossamer-like panels. But even with the personal presence of the Inspector General the tomb's clearance was poorly done—in the most part due to the mixture of the personalities that were involved. The conservation of the shrines, if it were ever possible, would have been a laborious and skilful, not to say expensive, task and although Davis paid for the excavations, the *Service* had previously paid

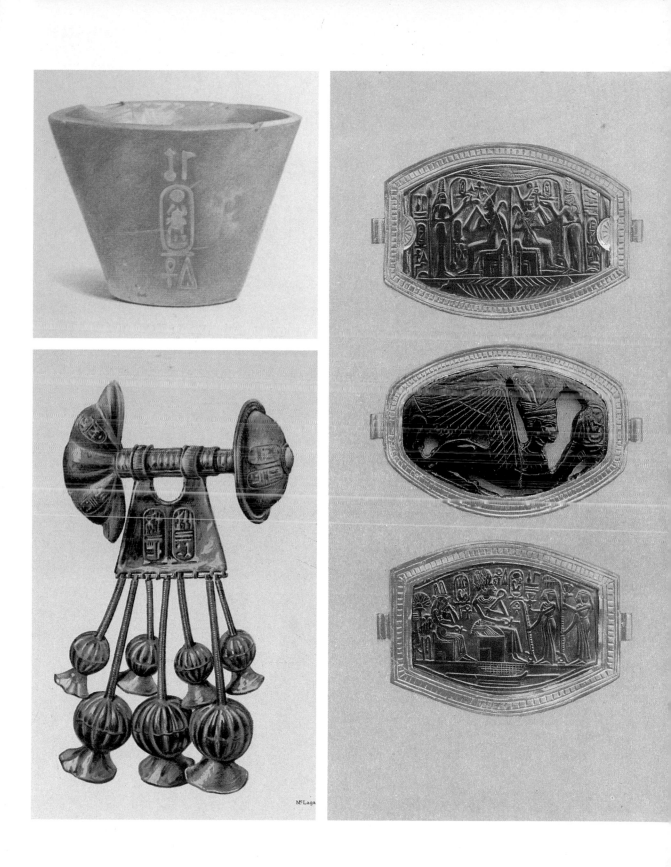

about the identity of the mummy in the tomb. The richly decorated coffin bore the titles of Akhenaten himself, though the ovals of gold that had once held the royal names in hieroglyphs of glass and precious stones had been cut out. The sheets of gold that had laid upon the mummy had also borne the name of the heretic king, but the great golden shrine and several small objects from the tomb had been made for the burial of Queen Tiy. All the archeologists had observed that the tomb had been entered several times and that the burial equipment was greatly disturbed and not a unity in itself. Davis, eager to preserve Queen Tiy's name for the title of his book of the tomb discovered a holidaying American obstetrician in Luxor and, in the company of a local doctor, an examination was made of the mummy bones. These were duly pronounced as feminine and Davis later published his *The Tomb of Queen Tiyi* to which Maspero added an outline of the life of the great lady. Later Maspero gave some of the mummy's jewellery and one of the four alabaster jars and portrait heads to Davis, who kept the masterpiece upon his desk as a memento of the tomb and the ancient queen.

Another section of Davis' book was written by Elliot Smith, the anatomist who had examined the royal mummies for Maspero in Cairo, and in it he declared the skeleton from the tomb to be that of a man, aged between twenty and thirty. Although he subsequently wrote to *The Times* upon the matter, medical speculation continued, due perhaps to Elliot Smith's somewhat scanty publication of the material. Unfortunately, some gold bands that had been 'mixed' with the mummy wrappings and which had reportedly borne the name of Akhenaten were pilfered from Elliot Smith's laboratory before they could be properly examined or catalogued. These may well have fallen on to the mummy from the interior of the lid of the coffin as did some of the other gold sheets that were found near the mummy. Some years later other experts worked on the bones that remained, One, Douglas Derry, restored the skull which had broken into fragments. Others looked for the skeletal effects of endocrine disorders in an attempt to identify the mummy as Akhenaten, who had been a much older man at his death than the skeleton from the tomb had first appeared. This was an essential investigation, for several pieces of inscriptional evidence in the tomb pointed to Akhenaten as being the occupant of the

The face on the coffin from tomb 55. Presumably the gold mask was ripped off the wooden coffin to destroy the likeness of its original owner

The golden coffin as it lay in the tomb. It had been left on a low bier that had collapsed under its weight, spilling the coffin on the floor and jarring off its lid. Subsequently, a rock falling from the roof hit the lid and split it down its centre. The delicate shapes on the wooden form which underlies the golden mask, but long since ripped away, are still plainly visible and display features quite different from any of the sculptures of the central figures of the heresy. The mummy's head can be seen lying just above the damaged left shoulder of the lid. The 'crown' that Lyndon Smith 'lifted from the brow of the queen' is also visible, still curled around its head

coffin. The four mud bricks, for example, that had been placed in the burial chamber, as in most Eighteenth Dynasty royal tombs, where they served as protective amulets for the kings, had been made for Akhenaten but they employed a form of his name that was abandoned in his later years and had probably been made eight or ten years before his death.

Recent research has shown the basic truth of Elliot Smith's statements and added something more to them. Although embalmed in the pose normally associated with queens of the period, the mummy was of a young man about twenty years old. Highly refined blood analysis techniques have demonstrated that he was a close relative, probably a brother, of Tutankhamen. The only candidate who survives this process of elimination is the king Smenkare, the ephemeral co-regent of Akhenaten whose mummy had not been found previously and who would also fulfil both these biological requirements.

Upon detailed examination the coffin too proved to be a curiously inconsistent object. When first lifted it had collapsed and Ayrton had to collect up many of the hundreds of inlays that were later fitted back into their cloisonné-like mountings during extensive restoration at the Cairo Museum. In the course of this work it is possible that parts of the coffin were wrongly fitted together or, a more drastic alternative, that the coffin had originally been made from two separate parts in the first place. Following this restoration, the royal neck on the coffin lid sits far below the shoulder line and the hands are more prominent than the wig, a unique condition when compared with other coffins. The inlaid decoration too, appears to be curiously inconsistent in its design. Far more of the floral collar that runs across the chest of the coffin may be seen upon its right side than its left. The wig itself, made of small plaques of black wood, probably ebony, appears to have been roughly sawn off along its bottom—the carefully carved ringlets of hair that terminate in small neatly drilled holes to simulate the inside of curls appear only in the upper portions of the wig. At the line where they meet the chest they are roughly cut, their jagged edges only roughly touching the crooked angle of the shoulders. In short, the coffin lid itself appears to be as mixed as the other contents of the tomb; in this case the head of one coffin, with the golden mask that covered its face ripped off to disguise its original identity, joined to an amorphous golden coffin with a clumsy crooked joint.

The coffin was adapted for the burial by the addition of a beard and the royal snake on the forehead, the latter so inaccurately catalogued that there must be some doubt about the inscription that it supposedly bore, as it subsequently became confused with another similar example that was found lying loose in the tomb. The coffin had originally been made for a young woman, as is proven by its measurements and its design, but its inscriptions had been carefully altered from feminine to masculine genders. These inscriptions, a royal puzzle in themselves, have been subjected to many interpretations, but on balance they seem to have been made for a queen of Akhenaten's, probably either his daughter Meryaten or a shadowy lesser figure, Ki'a. The king's names would normally have been more prominent than the coffin's owner, as was usual on burial equipment and the tombs of other members of the royal family.

The inscriptional evidence in the tomb, however, mentioned neither Meryaten, Ki'a nor Smenkare, but Akhenaten and Queen Tiy. Her great golden shrine may now be seen as similar in type to the middle shrine of the set of three that was found in the tomb of Tutankhamen, similar examples of which had doubtless surrounded the sarcophagus of every New Kingdom monarch. This shrine had been expressly made for the queen by her son, Akhenaten, and showed scenes of that king before his own god, the Aten, the Living Disk of the Sun. Like the coffin, the shrine had Akhenaten's names excised from its inscriptions and his father, Amenhotep III's name had been added in red ink. Probably the greatest single disaster in the clearance of the tomb was the treatment of the shrine. Not only were no measurements taken, but no drawings of its separate parts were made so that it could have one day been reconstructed—if only upon paper—and no serious attempt was made either to record or preserve the marvellous reliefs of gilded stucco work. Jones drew but one panel, and that with no scale upon it; approximate measurements may be guessed only from the photographs of the tomb. Undoubtedly, the shrine was a major work of Amarna art and would have become known as a major example of the craftsmanship of that most extraordinary period. Unfortunately, it seems as if the people who visited the panels in the tomb saw the pitiable and ever worsening condition of the panels and decided that nothing could be done for them. The shrine *could* have been restored; instead of which it was virtually destroyed.

Several other objects inscribed with the names of Queen Tiy, contained in two small boxes, were found in the tomb and sealings that bore the cartouches of Tutankhamen were scattered about the chamber. This odd collection of damaged and altered burial equipment that accompanied Smenkare therefore dates from periods both before and after that king's death: from the reign of Amenhotep III, Queen Tiy's husband, through three different phases of Akhenaten's reign and latterly, the reign of Tutankhamen who followed Smenkare to the throne in 1361 BC, making the burial a nest of ambiguities and contradictions. Many different historians have argued long and hard for different scenarios to fit this evidence. These usually concern the removal of one or two original burials—normally named as Queen Tiy's and Akhenaten's—and the substitution of a third; perforce, Smenkare's. But such a disparate assemblage might just as easily represent the caching of a collection of unwanted grave goods along with an embarrassing heretical monarch in an empty, or previously cleared-out tomb. Indeed, if there is ever to be a successful interpretation of this extraordinary collection, the strange burial of Smenkare and his antiquated and ill-used burial equipment, now known as the Amarna Cache, more external evidence must be utilized, especially from the nearby contemporary tomb of Tutankhamen. This was similar in design to the Amarna Cache tomb situated some forty feet across the valley floor, and was elaborately stocked with a variety of grave goods including several fine pieces that had belonged to Smenkare.

The continuing interest in and debate on this tomb reflects the differing attitudes and opinions of scholars on the ancient society. After years of study, many historians obtain an understanding of their subject, the ancient Egyptians, as a living entity, a live culture, and it is this personal vision of that society that they bring to bear on fresh problems. Because these are such personal visions, they will often be fought for with surprising acrimony in what appear, at first glance, to be insignificant issues. Although there is general agreement today about many major aspects of ancient Egyptian culture, when the evidence is as ambiguous as the Amarna Cache, these slightly differing visions of this same society can easily produce very different interpretations of the evidence, as is still true of the Heresy period that preceded this rude burial of Smenkare. Once again, one is suddenly made aware of the elusiveness of the ancient Egyptians as they slip easily in and out of the historical record, and once again ancient Egypt is seen as a mirror of our own society, from the vacuous and inept pomposities of the first reports to modern theories that would have Akhenaten a homosexual partner of Smenkare or transmute the beautiful Nefertiti, Akhenaten's great queen, into Smenkare and late in her life, change her to a man.

After drawing some of the objects from the Amarna Cache, Harold Jones accepted a full-time job offered by Davis, who presented him with £160 to give up his other archeological work in order to stay in the Valley and work with Ayrton. A studio with huge windows and a fine north light was added to the house and Jones moved in before the end of the season. Initially Davis employed him to copy the reliefs and paintings from the tombs that had been discovered during the previous seasons. Soon, however, he was supervizing another gang of workmen digging in the Valley and while clearing the bottom end of the gully that led up to the tomb of Amenhotep II, low down on the site where it joined the centre of the Valley, Jones' workmen found another tomb. It was a simple enough affair that lay some twenty-five feet down under the chippings of the Valley, a great wide shaft that, from the mud which they found dried hard in hexagonal patterns over the floor of the single chamber at its bottom, had been repeatedly flooded since ancient times.

In the tomb and probably stuck in the hard mud, were the remains of at least one box. In it they found several pieces of gold foil bearing the names of Tutankhamen and his queen, and Ay. The scenes represented the usual war scenes of Egyptian art: Ay mounted in a chariot loosing off arrows at Asiatics, and Tutankhamen clubbing a Lybian supported by Ay and his queen. The fragments, of unusual shapes, had probably come from chariot harnesses, horse blinkers and the like. Scattered about in the tomb were more pieces of gold foil that had been screwed up into small balls but when these were flattened out and some even rejoined, it was apparent that these too formed some kind of continuous pattern which may also have overlaid the leather straps of a fancy parade harness from a chariot.

Other objects from this simple room included a variety of furniture, fitments, knobs, decorative friezes and so on, some of which bore the name of Ay. There may even have been the remains of a burial stuck fast in the mud of the tomb but the unskilful methods of Ayrton and Jones simply in retrieving the unperishable objects and not recording the subtle stains that the rotton wood would have left in the mud as it decayed, destroyed its slender existence. They also found a fine statue of a late Eighteenth Dynasty noble, hands folded across his chest in the manner of an Osiris statue. It is possible that this beautiful alabaster statue, some nine inches high, was once inscribed with its owner's name in ink, perhaps even with the texts common to such ushabtis. Now numbered 58 in the register, it is another of the Valley's puzzling tombs that date from that period which follows the return of the court from Amarna to Thebes, and the kings from heresy to orthodoxy. At the very end of the season Jones made a colour drawing of the alabaster statue, published by Davis in one of his large green books. In fact it was the second season running in which the expedition had completed their work with a find from the reign of Tutankhamen and now, unknowingly they were digging within some fifty feet of that king's tomb.

21

Horemheb and Tutankhamen's Feast

(1907–08)

Ayrton and Jones started their next season in the Valley in December 1907, as Davis arrived back in Cairo. By January the workmen were digging again, close by the spot where they had found tomb 58 and its pieces of gold foil engraved with the names of Tutankhamen and Ay, and after a few days the men struck the mouth of another pit of somewhat similar size. This turned out to be a large shaft, again more than twenty feet deep and this with a tall, odd-shaped room at its bottom, whose floor was covered by more than three feet of hard dried mud. In the mud they could see the embedded outlines of alabaster and pottery vases, and other less regularly shaped objects. Now, at the best of times, excavating such flooded tombs is slow, skilled time-consuming work but with Davis, who had now arrived at Thebes, maintaining a constant pressure to extend the work, Ayrton had little time, even if he possessed the inclination and experience, for such delicate operations. So, in the large room, lit by a fine yellow light from the doorway to the shaft and with its walls stained amber by the clay of the flood waters, Ayrton set to work with a carving knife. On his second day of slicing away he found a small piece of gold, stuck hard in the mud. Davis came to see the glittering fragment and it was decided to soak the area around it to enable them to release the object without further damage. Soon they had washed two fine gold earrings from the dissolved mud.

The earrings bore the cartouches of Seti II whose tomb was higher up the Valley at its southern end. They were large and somewhat ungainly, hammered out of sheet gold with all the finesse of a good tinsmith. From a large cylindrical spacer which once had fitted through a pierced ear lobe, seven golden poppy-seed cases hung from a triangular plate on which the name of the king had been embossed. Very pleased with their discovery they went to the house for lunch, then returned to the tomb in the afternoon armed with more water. In the next few hours they flooded a much larger area of the filling and released more jewellery and a quantity of fragments of stucco and gold leaf. Some

of the jewellery continued the poppy motif of the morning's earrings, and a simple circlet of sixteen poppy flowers on a thin gold band was made with the same somewhat crude technique. Some of the poppy flowers on the circlet had been stained red by a gold plating process using a microscopic coating of iron oxides. This technique, which has something of the appearance of anodizing, had probably been introduced into Egypt from countries to the north. Other examples of foreign techniques were also apparent in the large numbers of superb filigree beads, some of which were cylindrical while others were once again shaped in the form of a poppy-seed head. This has remained the earliest example of filigree work yet discovered in Egypt, a technique still much beloved of the craftsmen in the jewellery souks of modern Cairo.

From the filling, now loose and muddy again with the water they retrieved two small gloves made of silver. Back in the house, Davis, after soaking them in water, poured out eight fine gold finger rings, which bore the cartouches of Ramesses II and Seti II, from their fingers. Unknowingly he had also poured away the remains of two small rotted hands, a part of the burial that they had unwittingly destroyed. It was not until some fifty-five years later that the mystery of this jewellery, scattered through the mud of this large chamber, was solved by a careful comparison with other similar archeological situations. From the evidence that remained it was probable that a little girl of five or six years had been buried in the tall room, inside a gilded coffin. Her parents, perhaps Seti II and Queen Tausert, whose names occur on her jewellery, made the burial for her and had some of the jewellery—the poppy-pattern pieces—especially manufactured for the occasion. The ring of Ramesses II was an heirloom of a particularly illustrious ancestor.

Soon after the burial, the tomb had been entered and the hole that was left in the sealing of the chamber doorway allowed floodwaters to enter. The shaft of the tomb had been cut so low and was situated so centrally in the Valley that water would have passed over it, even after quite light falls of rain. Until the wide shaft had become resealed by flood debris cemented into a hard mass by the flood waters, the chamber would have been regularly flooded. Thus the little coffin would have been sent floating around inside its burial chamber until, perhaps centuries later, the water eventually evaporated and left the rotted burial embedded in the deep flood sediments.

By this time Davis had nearly exhausted the locations in the Valley in which he felt it would be worthwhile to excavate for tombs, but a few areas above Belzoni's old workings and a small area close to the little princess's tomb, or the Gold Tomb as number 56 became known, remained for Ayrton and his gangs. Jones, meanwhile, was drawing both the freshly discovered objects and some of the great quantities of antiquities that were stored in the magazine of the excavation house. During the work of the previous two seasons Ayrton had found literally hundreds of small objects in the Valley but, apart from attaching a small label to them which recorded the season of their discovery and a reference to their find spot (indicated by a simple code), none had been catalogued or studied. Although the finest objects had already been sent to museums in Cairo and the United States, there was still a considerable collection of fragments of royal tomb furniture, hundreds of inscribed and painted *ostraca* and even pieces of the tombs themselves—great slabs of texts and decoration—lying in the magazine of the expedition house. And outside, in a row by the side of the front door, lay the capitals from the small Coptic church in the tomb of a prince of Ramesses III that Ayrton had dismantled when he had cleared the tomb.

The excavations were now shifted to points above the gully that held the tombs of Ramesses X and Seti I, which had been Belzoni's old stamping ground, where Ayrton dug into the deep piles of large limestone chippings that covered the area. He worked eastwards up the Valley towards the tomb of Tuthmosis IV and as his men worked by the tomb of Ramesses X they uncovered a rectangular pit in the rock about four feet deep. 'It was', says Davis, 'filled with large earthen pots containing what would seem to be the debris from a tomb, such as dried wreaths of leaves and flowers, and small bags containing a powdered substance. The cover of one of these jars had been broken and wrapped about it was a cloth on which was inscribed the name of Toutankhamanou [Tutankhamen]'. He concluded that, with the inscribed gold foil that bore Tutankhamen's name which he had found the previous season, he had found the tomb of that king, the pots representing

the cleaned up mess left behind by the plunderers who had also left the blue cup under the rock. The tomb itself (number 58) had been found the season before, robbed but still recognizable from the small pieces of inscribed gold foil that named both Ay and Tutankhamen. Davis' next publication—his last book of the excavations—included an account of the discovery of the tomb and a life of Tutankhamen by Maspero who, at the Cairo Museum, had now named one of the upstairs rooms the 'Salle Theodore Davis', filled, as it was, with objects from the excavations in the Valley. In Cairene society Davis was known as the archeologist who found a king a year and his work in the Valley was celebrated and reported around the world. Even the British Consul-General in Egypt, Lord Cromer's successor, Sir Eldon Gorst, recognized the American's work and was, in fact, intending to visit the house in the Valley, eat lunch there and attend, if possible, the opening of the tomb in the early afternoon.

Davis was delighted with the prospect of their visit but he had little to show Gorst apart from the jewellery from the Gold Tomb, which was not considered spectacular enough, and the collection of large pots from the pit. These rough storage jars were not thought to be of any value or significance until Davis casually opened one that had been brought back to the house. In it he had found a fine, small yellow mummy mask, similar to those placed around the intestines when they were put inside their canopic vases. Immediately, the other pots, their wide mouths all securely sealed with dried mud and papyrus stoppers, became of greater interest. Gorst, Davis planned, could witness his archeological amusements outside the expedition house as, one by one, the pots were opened in his presence. But as archeological luck would have it, the little mask proved to be the only object of its type in all the numerous pots they opened and after Gorst's departure in the late afternoon, a disappointed Davis turned upon Ayrton, blaming him for the poor show the ancient Egyptians had given the Consul-General. Davis, who had expected from the very beginning of his work in the Valley to discover great tombs and noble antiquities, had never really suffered a disappointment and saw no reason to excuse Ayrton on this occasion.

The hapless pots were now all gathered together and put into the storeroom of the house—a dark, airless room, plastered with mud and lined with shelves filled with fine fragments of broken objects excavated from the Valley. The next year Jones persuaded Davis to present them to the expedition of the Metropolitan Museum of New York, which had taken over the site of Deir el Bahari and the surrounding areas from the British expedition. A young egyptologist, on the staff of the American expedition, Herbert Winlock from Washington, D.C., had seen the aftermath of the cermonial unsealing of the pots for Gorst and, although he knew there was nothing of intrinsic value in them, his expedition needed some objects to send back to New York after a lean season's work. Like Ayrton, Winlock's expedition had to produce tangible results; Davis had no use for his latest discovery, other than as party pieces when he would grab one of the necklaces of papyrus and threaded flowers that some of the pots had contained and tear them up to show his guests just how strong they still were after thirty undisturbed centuries, and he agreed to donate the entire find to the Metropolitan Museum.

On their arrival at the Metropolitan Museum, the pots were examined, emptied and their contents carefully catalogued. However, it was not until some fifteen years later, after his expedition had found similar, if somewhat smaller deposits in their own excavations, that Winlock realized what it was he had begged from Davis. It was no less than the materials used during royal embalming procedures and the inscriptional evidence from the find —broken clay seals and hieratic inscriptions upon pieces of cloth—named the king as Tutankhamen! One of the inscriptions on a linen head scarf had already received some small scholarly fame as recording the highest date of the king's reign—year six—and on re-examining the rest of the material, Winlock now recognized the other scraps of material and the odd fragments of bandages as the left-overs from the wrapping of Tutankhamen's mummy, all carefully gathered for burial. In addition to the cloth there were the rags that had been used for wiping both the king's corpse and the grease of the embalming area. Winlock also remembered that he had left a number of square limestone blocks at Davis' house and these he now recognized as the slabs in which Tutankhamen's body had lain during the long slow mummification processes. Winlock had also seen great amounts of the natron used in the mummification, but the twenty or so ancient bags of the naturally occurring crystalline compound that he sent to the museum only represented about half the entire quantity that had been found. Natron, a compound of sodium carbonate and bicarbonate, which in Egypt in its natural state contained a large quantity of salt mixed in with it, was used to desiccate the corpse. This is the essential process of mummification aided, usually, by the removal of the body organs and, sometimes, the dissolving of muscle tissue and fats by immersion in natron baths. The perfumes of the rare, precious oils killed off any offensive smells that remained after these preservative processes but, rather than perform any chemically useful functions, in Tutankhamen's case they actually helped destroy the mummy during the long processes of their own decay and carbonization. Every small portion of the material connected with the royal mummification including, it would seem, the headscarf of one of the participants, was gathered up for burial close to the royal tomb.

Some of the largest jars, which were nearly three feet high with their necks around eighteen inches wide, had been filled with broken pottery. Ayrton, not even bothering to bring all this material back to the house, had broken many of them as they lay in the pit and these had not been collected or examined by Winlock. But when the restorers started to repair the New York ceramics, Winlock saw that they were a hoard of small dishes, an elegant wine decanter, and further large jars of a type that had been used for the fermentation and storage of wine and beer. Careful records of wines were kept by the ancient vintners. The best grew in the vineyards of the Delta where the long straggling plants, their leaves burnt brown and yellow by the fierce Egyptian sun, were left to grow into huge vines that little resemble the products of modern viticulture. Differences between sweet and dry wines and their year of manufacture was sometimes noted upon the ceramic jars in hieratic inscriptions.

As well as these fragmentary wine jars—none in this case labelled with precise information as to their contents—there were the small dishes that the ancient Egyptians had used while eating and from which they had picked up food with their fingers. Even the remains of the meals that had been eaten from these broken plates were found in the jars: beef, rather carelessly butchered, lamb chops and a whole heap of game birds' bones, including ducks, teal and geese, the latter being of several species but not the modern domesticated varieties. There was no evidence as to how this feast had been prepared, but other examples from ancient Egypt indicate that roasting was common, sometimes with a glaze of honey, as well as stewing, stuffing, probably with a soft wheat, pickling and salting.

Along with the remains of the feast, Winlock had also taken three magnificent floral collars to New

York, these being fine examples of those shown in practically every painted tomb chapel at Thebes as being worn by guests at feasts and banquets. Sharing the same designs and proportions as the faience necklaces that were largely inspired by the passing splendours of real flowers, the three necklaces were made from olive branches and cornflowers with real berries and blue beads added here and there into the garlands—all carefully hemmed in red cloth to make a most handsome ephemereal decoration. Davis had pulled most of the other examples apart during his shows of strength and only a few fragments still remained. But originally everything from this ancient feast had been cleared up and carefully placed in these jars, even the reed brooms that had been used to sweep up after the banqueters had finished the meal.

The feast had probably been shared by eight people. Winlock suggests that it was accompanied by bread, cakes, beer and water as well as wine. It may have taken place inside the tomb of the king itself, the brooms being used to sweep the footprints of the guests from the limestone dust on the tomb's floor. The ritual of the funerary feast is widely illustrated in private tomb chapels where it is portrayed as a communion with the dead person who is himself present. These scenes are not to be found, however, on the walls of the royal tombs and no other examples of such elaborate remains of feasts have ever been found in the Valley of the Kings. In the reign of Tutankhamen, however, like the belongings of the dead king and the remains of his embalming, everything was buried in the course of the royal funeral. The remains of the feast were all carefully gathered together and, after the larger pieces were broken to fit them into the large storage jars, it was all buried in a pit alongside the natron and rags of the royal embalmers. Found by Ayrton, brutally exploited by Davis, the feast was preserved for our interest and study by Winlock.

After the social fiasco of the luncheon with Gorst, Ayrton was once again back in the Valley with his men 'exhausting every mountain and foothill' and by the end of February, at a spot within fifteen feet of the shaft that had contained the fragments of furniture and gold foil inscribed for Tutankhamen and Ay, they uncovered the mouth of another tomb. It was to be the last monument that Davis' expedition would find in the Valley and it was certainly a real climax to its rampageous career. The tomb's entrance, as deep as the others had been in that area, was cut

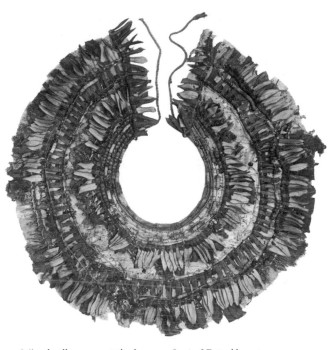

A floral collar worn at the funerary feast of Tutankhamen. It is one of three that escaped the attentions of Davis' after-dinner tricks

low in the gully's side but this time a large stairway ran down from the rectangle quarried from the limestone. Ayrton crawled over the blocking of sand and limestone chippings that nearly filled the wide corridor at the bottom of the steps and, just as he could proceed no further, he saw the name of Horemheb in a small hieratic inscription written, once again, by one of the tomb inspection and reburial commissions. He was surprised to find this name in the Valley because Horemheb, the general who had succeeded Ay to rule over Egypt, was long since known to have had a tomb in the desert above Memphis. But there it was, and Weigall, still Chief Inspector, was advised of the discovery so that he might be present at the opening of the new tomb.

It took them three days to make the journey to the lowest sections of the tomb, two to clear the upper corridors of the obstructing dirt and another to bridge the well and dig out the staircase in the room beyond which, like the almost identical staircase in the tomb of Seti I, had originally been sealed over. Even while they stood on the edge of the well, the archeologists could see the pillared chamber beyond, through a hole in the brightly painted reliefs, and after crossing the well they were able to penetrate the chamber

The interior of the tomb as it was discovered, showing the fine paintings half buried in the masons' chippings from the continuation of their work in the lower sections of the tomb

and the small rooms beyond—cut, perhaps, for other members of Horemheb's family.

The tomb was the first full-sized royal tomb to be made in the Valley since that of Amenhotep III's in the Western Valley and that, initiated during the reign of Tuthmosis IV, had been a hundred years before. Horemheb's tomb was, however, the same design as the earlier royal tombs but the right angle in the plan of the earlier monuments was eliminated,

the tomb virtually turned into a straight line that ran down into the rock. It was the missing link between the huge tombs of the later dynasties and the more secret and smaller monuments of the Eighteenth Dynasty.

The condition of the interior of this splendid fresh tomb was an extraordinary mixture of natural preservation and the destructive hand of its ancient visitors. Although it was situated low down in the main water course and, indeed, on the very floor of a bank that took the main brunt of the floods from the head of the Valley, the tomb had never been badly flooded and the walls and their decorations were perfect, as bright as new. Some movements in the

A small chamber in the tomb had a remarkable painting of Osiris on its walls. Smashed tomb figures had been anciently thrown around the empty chamber and were found scattered on the floor

limestone rock of the hillside had, however, shattered some of the columns and several of the walls were cracked and loose. The sculptors and quarrymen, interrupted in their tasks by the royal burial, had left the tomb half filled with chippings that lay throughout the tomb like drifts of coarse sand against walls, columns and staircases. They found a scramble of human bones in the tomb; the opulent sarcophagus held some, others were thrown into different rooms;

but Davis' report is vague and there is really little to be understood from it. Horemheb and his famous queen, Mutnejmet, had not been recovered with the other royal mummies in the two caches of kings, so it is perhaps possible that some of these broken, stripped and ultimately unrecorded fragments may have belonged to them, though the presence of the inspection graffiti upon the door jamb of the tomb makes this less than certain. Possibly, a long report that Ayrton wrote about the tomb and its contents would have solved such problems but Davis would not publish it in his book on the tomb and it has since been lost.

Horemheb's burial equipment had been shattered and plundered, as in the majority of the other Eighteenth Dynasty tombs, and lay strewn throughout the tomb. Apparently the king had not been buried with great quantities of faience, amulets or ritual equipment, but there had been a very fine assemblage of gods and it is the earliest tomb in which some of the more bizarre conglomerations of animal and human forms have been found. Probably these had all originally stood in the crypt which in this innovatory tomb was greatly enlarged and had gained considerably in architectural significance, foreshadowing the fine vault which was cut above this section of the burial chamber in the tomb of Seti I—the next finished monument to be made in the Valley. In one of the small rooms that ran from the burial chamber a strange vivid picture of Osiris had been painted life-size on the rough finished limestone of the chamber wall. This white wall dramatically reflected the vivid green paint that had been used for the background to the figure. It is a unique painting, probably made hurriedly in the last stages of the funeral ceremonies. Representations of this figure of Osiris are sometimes found in similar positions in other royal tombs and perhaps these verdant greens in Horemheb's tomb accompanied the 'Osiris beds' of wheat seed, a good example of which was also discovered in the tomb.

Another major interest in the tomb is its relationship to the previous royal tomb, that of the heretic at Amarna. Akhenaten's tomb, excavated in a desolate valley that is similar in many ways to the Valley of the Kings is, with the exception of a special suite of rooms excavated to hold the burial of a predeceased daughter, a faithful rendering of its Theban predecessors. The size of this monument was, however, truly gigantic, being nearly twice as large in the measurements of its rooms and corridors as the largest of the royal tombs in the Valley. Had it been

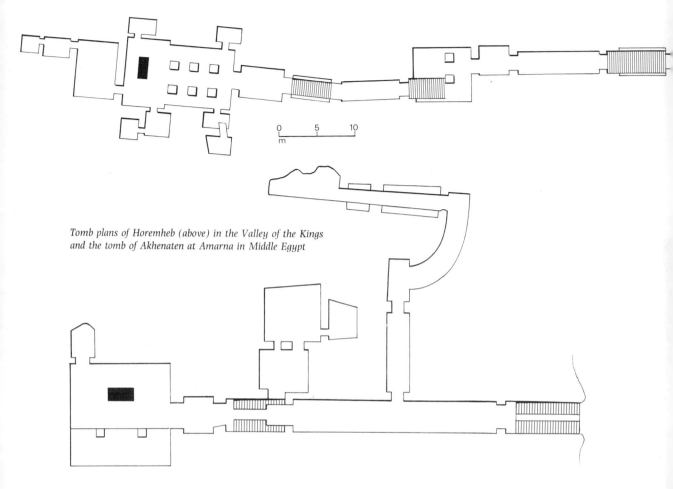

Tomb plans of Horemheb (above) in the Valley of the Kings and the tomb of Akhenaten at Amarna in Middle Egypt

completed, the descent to the burial chamber, running down through gigantic corridors and halls, would have continued for more than three hundred and fifty feet. But despite its vast size the proportions of the rooms and corridors remained the same as the Theban royal tombs and it fits easily into the overall progression of the royal tomb design.

However, Akhenaten's tomb was not completed and, like King Ay, he was buried in the pillared hall that lay beyond the well. This room was enlarged upon its right hand side, where two columns were taken down and a crypt was excavated to hold the royal sarcophagus and the golden shrines that presumably covered it. The height of the room was also raised. The decorations in this chamber, quickly made in plaster relief, a favourite technique employed in Akhenaten's new town close by, are the first examples of relief in the royal tombs of the New Kingdom, though incised hieroglyphs were common in the royal

tombs of earlier Kingdoms. In keeping with the values of the new religion, the subject matter of these reliefs, as far as it is possible to discern in the mutilated and smoke-blackened tomb, were very different from any Theban tombs.

Paradoxically, the heretic's tomb had a great effect upon those of his orthodox successors at Thebes. The text that had been traditionally painted in the burial chambers of the earlier pharaohs, the *Amduat*, was discarded and the Book of Gates, severe and loaded with the implication that the actions of even the king himself were subject to abstract moral laws, was drawn upon the walls of the burial chamber. Immediately above the sarcophagus of Horemheb a huge judgement scene was drawn showing Osiris officiating at the weighing of the soul—the heart of man balanced against the feather of truth—and awful punishments were awaiting those who failed the test. Some authorities have seen this introduction

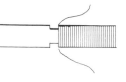

Despite its gigantic size and the heretical ideas of the monarch who was to inhabit it, the royal tomb in a lonely desert wadi behind the ancient town of Amarna owes its inspiration to its Theban predecessors in the Valley of the Kings. Even its situation in the side of a small wadi off the main water course is similar to the Theban tombs of Akhenaten's two predecessors

of the Book of Gates into the royal tomb as a direct reaction to the rule of Akhenaten who, although the king of Egypt, was judged by the orthodox priests to have fallen outside the pale of good order and moral responsibility. Akenaten, descended from a bloodline of kings, apparently believed in his own godhead; Horemheb, who succeeded to the throne by political success, had been born a mere mortal and may have had fewer reservations about the fixed concepts of moral responsibility of the ruler of Egypt.

However, Horemheb's tomb continued Akhenaten's innovation of decorating the royal tomb in relief which, at Thebes, was cut into the fine even-grained limestone of the tombs. But the timetable that this imposed upon the workforce was a novel one and they did not complete the decoration in time for the king's funeral. All over the tomb there are examples of this half-finished work, left as the gangs stopped one evening more than three thousand years ago. Some of the scenes are merely sketched in by the first outline draughtsmen but with an ease and beauty that still seems fresh; other areas, having been drawn, bear the marks of a careful checking and correction while further sections of the scenes show various stages of the carving, the initial outlining of the figures, the cutting down of the backgrounds, the modelling of the forms upon the elements in the scenes, and all the rest of the laborious process right through to the final finished and painted reliefs. Only the great figures of the gods and the king in the well scenes were actually completed in the tomb and they, as Maspero was quick to observe in an early visit to the tomb, bear a distinct resemblance to similarly positioned figures in the tomb of Seti I. There is, of course, only some twenty-five years separating these two monuments; long enough for the hot colours of Horemheb's tomb, still present in the hasty paintings in the intervening tomb of Ramesses I, to have been tempered by the purity of antique revivalism; but close enough to have actually employed some of the same artists in the two monuments.

Like Horemheb's tomb, Seti I's was also carved, but unlike Horemheb's, the work for the most part was completed. In apparent recognition of this new and much heavier demand upon the workforce imposed by this new programme of work on carving the tomb, the village of the community that made the royal tombs was enlarged and drastically re-organized. The careful bureaucratic control and constant monitoring of the work in the royal tombs is henceforth evidenced by thousands of small documents preserved from this community which begin to appear at

The grand figure of Osiris, the judge, and an assistant weighing the hearts of the dead; from the superb line drawing on the burial chamber wall by the sarcophagus of Horemheb

exactly this time, following the royal return to Thebes. Similar administrative documents from before the heresy are not common and are of a different type. Thus in many different ways, the tomb of Horemheb is the vital link in the Valley tombs between the simpler earlier monuments and the grandiose tombs of the later period.

The tomb itself is grand and austere. Though large and well-made, it lacks most of its decoration, having pure white walls over most of its corridors. The judgement scene from the Book of Gates, painted large on the magnificent royal sarcophagus, is an elegant drawing in black line, a tour de force of sheer craftsmanship, splendid on a carefully plastered creamy wall. The sarcophagus was in the new style, in the manner of Ay's, Tutankhamen's and Akhenaten's. In this design the old plain forms of the earlier kings' sarcophagi were abandoned for a lavish rectangular

The burial chamber of the tomb of Horemheb (right) photographed by Harry Burton. Note the judgement scene drawn on the wall behind the king's florid sarcophagus

affair with goddesses supporting the corners of an architecturally conceived box crowned with a cavetto cornice and a taurus moulding, like a temple pylon. This late Eighteenth Dynasty luxuriance was not continued by their successors, who opted for a return to the old cartouche form, albeit in ever enlarging dimensions.

Weigall's impressions of the first entry into the depths of this unknown tomb still holds a little of such marvellous events. In the tomb he found nothing as impressive as the view across the well, through the hole in the paintings that was the entrance to the lower sections of the tomb. At their feet lay the dark pit of the well, around them gleamed the gaudy paintings, and through that window-like aperture before them a dim suggestion could be obtained of the white four-columned pillared hall.

> *The intense eagerness to know what was beyond, and, at the same time, the feeling that it was almost desecration to climb into those halls which have stood silent for thousands of years, cast a spell over the scene and made it unforgettable . . . There is something peculiarly sensational in the examining of a tomb which has not been entered for such thousands of years, but it must be left to the imaginative reader to infuse a touch of that feeling of the dramatic into these words . . . one cannot describe the silence, the echoing steps, the dark shadows, the hot, breathless air; nor tell of the sense of vast Time and the penetrating of it . . .*
>
> *As we passed out of this hot, dark tomb into the brilliant sunlight and the bracing north wind, the gloomy wreck of the place was brought before the imagination with renewed force. The scattered bones, the broken statues, the dead flowers, grouped themselves in the mind into a picture of utter decay. In some of the tombs which have been opened the freshness of the objects has caused one to exclaim at the inaction of the years; but here, the vivid and well preserved wall paintings looked down upon a jumbled collection of smashed fragments of wood and bones, one felt how hardly the Powers deal with the dead. How far away seemed the great fight between Amon and Aten . . .*

Watched by Davis' workmen and snapped by a visitor to the Valley, Weigall emerges from the first trip to the bottom of the tomb of Horemheb made in modern times

It was now necessary that without further delay Davis should arrange to have the positions of the objects in the tomb recorded along with the condition of the interiors, with the drafts of chippings and shattered columns that would soon have to be restored. Davis engaged a photographer for the work, a twenty-nine year old Englishman, Henry Burton. Called Harry by his friends and known by that name in most of his publications and photographic credits, Burton was a real perfectionist who had already developed extra-ordinary photographic techniques with large plate cameras and in printing negatives, in which he obtained extraordinary tonal range and clarity. His complete mastery of artificial light photography, and all with simple mirrors and the most elementary of lighting systems, was already apparent in the very first work he did for Davis His landscape photography too was no less accomplished, being both accurate and sensitive, retaining the uncanny tactile realism of the early photographers. Burton was the second of his name to work in the Valley and he would serve it as well as his namesake James. Some thirty years later this slight, neat Norfolk man with the small, modestly smiling face was still at work making photographic records of the Theban monuments that are not only superb archeological documents, but truly lyrical photographs of the ancient buildings and the landscape that held them.

Davis also asked Burton to photograph other loca-

Edward Ayrton

tions in the Valley, as well as Ayrton's house and some interesting features of the arid desert landscape. Burton moved into the expedition house with Ayrton and Jones and, on and off, he lived there for several years. Behind the studio and almost under the cliffs, he built a photographic darkroom that even boasted a set of double doors with a light trap between them so that visitors would not spoil his film processing, all made in massive walls of stone and mud some two feet thick.

Ayrton's upright British figure with two dogs at his heels was a familiar sight around Thebes and many tourists remarked upon this young man who knew the Valley and the ancient monuments so well and lived in the solitary house in the desert. One visitor described him, athletic and beflannelled and quite alone in the midday desert sun, playing 'diabolo'—a popular game of that period, which involves the balancing of a spinning turning of wood upon a string held up by two sticks. Ayrton frequently entertained interested visitors and guided them around the monuments; he and his colleagues became minor heroes to the tourists, upholding the Flag of Empire in what seemed to them to be a lonely and desolate place. One evening in every week, however, the little group of archeologists left their desert house attired in evening dress, bound for the hotels of Luxor where they would join the holiday makers in their entertainments, and dance the fashionable waltzes and polkas of the day.

But after three years of this life Ayrton, then twenty-six, had had enough of Davis and his desert house. His old friends had left the work at the temples of Deir el Bahari for other archeological sites and now he could no longer escape from the lonely valley to join them for an evening's conversation. He had also lost his taste for high speed archeology in the pursuit of bigger and better discoveries and, swapping the relatively well-paid but highly pressured life of working for the erratic and parsimonious Davis, Ayrton rejoined the British expedition, now working at Abydos, and undertook the excavation of a small pre-dynastic cemetery while living rough in a tent pitched on the flat desert sand. After only one season's work, however, Ayrton was offered an appointment with the Archeological Survey of India and, after a year's study at Oxford, he set off for that country. In a short time he was appointed the Director of Archeology in Ceylon but after only a few months at his new work, in the spring of 1914, he was drowned while hunting, at the age of thirty-one.

22

'No More Tombs'

(1908–17)

In 1906 a small private excavation financed and directed by Lord Carnarvon started excavating at the eastern end of the great flat plain in front of the temples of Deir el Bahari. Carnarvon was an invalid who had wintered in Egypt for some years and, like Davis, had taken up egyptology with a great enthusiasm. He had dug unsupervised for his first season but for his future work Maspero had suggested he engage the assistance of an archeologist and had introduced him to Howard Carter who, at that time, was earning a modest living in Luxor painting watercolours or making drawings of the monuments for friends and patrons and, in common with most of the antiquarians of the day, keeping an expert eye on the antiquities trade. From his position of government archeologist and conservator of the monuments, Carter had entered another world of dealing and private patronage and it was an area to which, with his fine eye for antiquities and his ability to associate happily with the wealthy patrons of archeology, he was very well suited.

At that time the antiquities trade inhabited a sort of no man's land, officially frowned upon by the *Service*. It was so heavily patronized by the wealthy residents and visitors to Egypt that Maspero could only apply pressure at the local end of the trade, attacking the villagers and the dealers which whom they dealt. Many archeological sites in Egypt were being unmercifully plundered and there was a call from many archeologists for stricter controls but the necessity for such surveillance was not really appreciated by Maspero and his assistants. The Cairo Museum already had huge collections and, provided the illicit antiquities sold by the dealers were not considered to be unique or, like the royal mummies, of particular importance to the national heritage, the exportation of antiquities purchased from the illegal markets but which were bound for display in the museums and drawing rooms of Europe and America was not the subject of great alarm. The robbery of paintings and reliefs from the walls of standing monuments was, however, considered in quite a different light and this traffic had generally been mercilessly

attacked since the days of Mariette.

Despite his prodigious reputation as a scholar, Maspero was never truly involved in archeology as a science in its own right, but more as a method of retrieving valuable antiquities and ancient texts that were buried and lost. Thus he would happily and sometimes capriciously grant licences with the most generous of terms for the excavators who were allowed to keep large amounts of their findings. It was a policy that inevitably led to excavations being made principally for the collection of antiquities; the Metropolitan Museum's excavations at Deir el Bahari were, for example, principally financed from funds donated specifically for the acquisition of objects. The presence of such teams of excavators in Egypt with previously unheard of sums of money donated by such financiers as Rockefeller and J. P. Morgan, was rapidly transforming both the scale of the archeological work and the state of the antiquities market. British officials of the administration considered that these large injections of money into the poorer sections of the country such as Upper Egypt were making significant contributions to the national economy. Briefly, ancient Egypt and its uncovering became a national resource. Davis' small excavations in the Valley, which had shown to many the practicability of investment in legitimate direct archeology to obtain a collection of antiquities, were now passé; on the other side of the cliffs at Deir el Bahari, Winlock and his colleagues were employing hundreds upon hundreds of workmen and cutting huge swathes through the Theban landscape, albeit in excellent scholarly order, and coming up with enormous quantities of antiquities. It was obviously a situation that could not last if the monuments of Egypt were to be properly protected. Further, the distortion of the traditional steady trade in antiquities by the injection of huge and quite unprecedented sums of money placed further pressure upon the monuments and archeological sites as the rewards of illicit excavation rapidly rose.

With the help and advice of Carter, Carnarvon was already beginning to build up a collection of Egyptian antiquities that later became one of the finest private collections of the century. Carnarvon enjoyed excavation and loved his visits to Egypt but, from the beginning, his hobby was expected to make money for him or at least pay its way. In 1907 it became obvious to Carter that, once again, an unknown royal tomb in the Theban necropolis was being plundered by the villagers. A short time before, a fragment of a funerary papyrus, possibly belonging to a king and of early Eighteenth Dynasty date, had surfaced on the Paris antiquity market and Carter himself had bought fragments of alabaster and hard stone vases with the names of Amenhotep I and Ahmose Nefertari upon them. Both these royal mummies had been found by Brugsch in the great cache, but their tombs had never been located. Newberry, however, had discovered the mortuary temple of this royal pair, mother and son, at the edge of the cultivated plain on the west bank and not far from the mouth of the *wadi* that leads to the Valley of the Kings. Carter had walked widely in the hills behind this temple, the foothills through which the *Wadyein* runs, in search of this tomb, but without success. He had been encouraged on these walks by the local gossip which told of a great tomb being behind a rocky ridge in this area called the Dra Abu el Naga and he had discovered a graffito that recorded a trip of an ancient tomb inspection commission that was also recorded upon a papyrus—the Abbott Papyrus. Other graffiti close by included cartouches of the Queen Nefertari and the hieroglyphic sign that is sometimes interpreted as signifying 'tomb' or 'tomb-chamber'.

At this time Carter was directing Carnarvon's excavations near Deir el Bahari and had started to build a house for himself in Western Thebes. He chose a beautiful site upon a platform above a royal tomb of the early Middle Kingdom that rises gently above the huge low area washed by the outflow of floods from the Valley. It is still one of the few modern buildings pointed out to visitors to Western Thebes, standing just above a road junction known as the *Sitt Zeinab*, after the tomb of a local holy woman of that name close by. The house was only a twenty-minute ride to the Valley and its verandah looked down the length of Dra Abu el Naga along the lines of the amazing ruins of the mortuary temples that lay at the edge of the brilliant green mile-wide cultivations. It is a unique setting which, unusually upon the west bank at Thebes, perfectly frames the wildly theatrical sunsets that are one of the most unforgettable features of Upper Egypt. The house, like his restoration work for the *Service*, was built of dull-red baked brick and was square, with a high domed chamber in the centre.

Lord Carnarvon standing in the doorway of Carter's House

The dome was the only real decorative concession to the orient in the building, which had English cottage doors, each with a Suffolk latch, and rooms that, though tall and red-tiled in deference to the heat, were modestly proportioned.

Carter had frequently visited Ayrton's excavations in the Valley and seen many of the tombs, including the Smenkare burial, shortly after their discovery. Before his earlier experiences in the Valley some nine years earlier he had seen the royal necropolis being turned slowly upside down by Davis and his men. Huge amounts of debris had been shuffled and shifted round the Valley and, while they had maintained a successful list of discoveries, the excavations had for the most part been capriciously conducted. In his belief that tombs were only to be found along the edges of cliffs and the sides of gullies, Davis had ignored the flood courses of the Valley. In some places great cliffs of anciently cemented debris stood some fifteen or twenty feet high in the lower areas, separated from the cliffs and gully slopes by Davis' excavations. With the new hints of early Eighteenth Dynasty royal tombs lying undiscovered at Thebes, Carter must have realized the possibilities of further discoveries in the royal Valley but in the light of his long experience he knew that it would be foolish to expect great treasures to be found.

For his season in the Valley of 1909–10, Davis appointed Harold Jones to take over from Ayrton as excavator. Another artist, Lancelot Crane, son of the illustrator Walter Crane, was employed to draw the reliefs in the tomb of Horemheb, and Burton continued his photographic work. Davis shifted the site of the excavations to areas outside the main Valley. Following in the footsteps of a small French excavation that had cleared around a small tomb close by the tomb of Amenhotep III, Davis started to clear the sides of the gullies and cliffs that lined the West Valley. This was a truly mammoth undertaking which took the form of digging hundreds of trenches, each spaced about a yard apart, for a distance of well over a mile on both sides of the rugged valley. Poor Jones and his gangs of men were unlucky and despite the presence of the ruins of an ancient workmen's village in the valley and even the re-excavation of areas buried deep under earlier excavators' dumps, they found very little. Crossing the path that led visitors to the tombs in the main East Valley, he started his men digging in a similar fashion in other, smaller, valleys but again the hard unremitting labour met with no success. For his next season, 1910–11, Davis turned his attention to some well trodden areas in the hope of finding something of value. While Jones completed the trenching of the *wadis* around the mouth of the main Valley, Burton dug the area around the mouth of the tomb of Amenhotep III in the West Valley where, just five years earlier, the French expedition had not even been rewarded with the name of the owner of the small tomb that they had cleared. Apparently Burton's search had been equally unrewarding but a short time later Carter bought three fine engraved gems in Luxor which, the

dealer told him, had come from the excavations in the West Valley.

With two others purchased separately, these remarkable plaques are now in the Metropolitan Museum in New York. Just over two inches long and cut in oval shapes with truncated ends, the stones, carnelian and sard, are engraved with scenes of Amenhotep III celebrating his jubilee, or show Queen Tiy in the form of a winged sphinx holding the cartouche of her husband in her hands. The engravings on the fine rich stones have been claimed as fake by some and as masterpieces by others. Carnarvon was very pleased with his purchase, however, and he supplied funds to Carter for more antiquities of this type—small, courtly and of fine workmanship, they became his abiding interest in egyptology. It was also certainly his main impulse for excavation.

As the Chief Inspector of Upper Egypt and based at Thebes, Weigall too had heard the rumour of the Eighteenth Dynasty royal tomb behind the Dra Abu el Naga and although tempted to look for it himself, he told Davis about it, probably hoping to encourage him to continue the work at Thebes despite his current lack of success. Consequently, when Burton had finished his work around the tomb of Amenhotep III Davis sent him down to the long desert valley of the *Wadyein* to search for the other tomb. Burton would have needed the eyes of a hawk to find it. A few years earlier Flinders Petrie had spent some considerable time on the same mission, following a tip from Carter. Although the great archeologist had not discovered the royal tomb, his careful search had located a fine lonely burial of the rare Seventeenth Dynasty. Once again Burton was unlucky in his explorations and, once again, at the end of the season Davis had nothing to show for his efforts.

Before he left Thebes, Davis looked around for other sites to excavate in the coming season and decided to leave the hunt for royal tombs and excavate some particularly fruitful-looking mounds that lay beside one of the mortuary temples. He knew that Carnarvon, at Carter's instigation, was after the concession to excavate in the Valley but Davis did not want to let it go and he decided to work again in some of the tombs that he had already discovered but not completely excavated. Then, quite suddenly at the end of March, Harold Jones died in the excavation house after only a short illness. At this time Davis had already left Egypt and it was Burton and Crane who arranged for the Welshman's body to be taken to Luxor and buried in the little walled Christian cemetery that lies upon the side of the small, dusty

avenue of sphinxes that ran between the Temple of Luxor and the Temples of Karnak. Jones had excavated widely in Egypt, and drawn many tombs but he did not find a tomb in the Valley; neither did he write about his work there. Today he is best remembered, perhaps, for the drawing of the panel of the golden shrine of Queen Tiy that he made during the three hectic days while that tomb was being emptied.

Davis, now seventy-five years old and ailing, came to Thebes for his last season late in January of the following year, 1912. Accompanied by Burton he squeezed into the rear chambers of the tomb of Siptah, which Ayrton had found seven years before. Now they saw that the tomb had not sustained further damage since that time and Davis decided to clear it out. It proved to be a bigger job than they had anticipated and it took the photographer the remainder of the season merely to clear the corridor as far as the final descent to the burial chamber, which was not completely cleared of its flood debris until January of the following year.

In the flood debris they found a fine collection of alabaster ushabtis and enough of the king's fragmented tomb equipment to indicate that he had been buried in the tomb. Some of these fragments of faience jars and vases of a type that had been common in such tombs as Tuthmosis IV are the last known examples of their type in the history of the Valley. In the centre of the burial chamber they dug out a fine sarcophagus of rose granite which bore upon its lid an effigy of the king. Some six feet high and ten feet long, its discovery was to be Davis' last donation to the Valley, for although his expedition continued for another season's work, Davis' active involvement was at an end.

Described by Weigall as 'a very charming American gentleman who in his old age, used to spend his winters on a *dahabiya* at Luxor and there became interested in egyptology', Davis had displayed the same tenacity in his hobby as he had in his career as a lawyer. He was most certainly not, as he has been described, a Croesus of archeology and he was often rude and overbearing to his staff. But he was good company with those he considered to be his equals and he was quite willing to be led into new archeological methods by the likes of Maspero and Sayce whenever they were proposed to him. One memoir pictures Davis as a slight, sharp figure in a dusty black suit, chain-smoking and nervously pacing up and down outside a tomb as Ayrton scrambled about in the darkness below searching for the name of its owner. The problems that have since arisen from the poor recording and publication of his work in the Valley must be properly laid at the door of the scholars who supervised and encouraged the work. The last lines that Davis wrote upon the Valley, the site that had occupied so much of his time and energies were: 'I fear that the Valley of the Kings is now exhausted', but, as the world must surely know, it was only Davis that had grown tired and other secrets still lay beneath the chippings and limestone dust.

The burial chamber in the tomb of Ramesses II half filled with flood debris and partially cleared by Harry Burton's men while it was still wet from flooding

In the spring of 1914 Burton was still working at the expedition house in the West Valley, engaged upon the final photographic work and Lancelot Crane too was busy drawing the sarcophagus of Siptah. From his home at Newport, Long Island, Davis had sent word that Burton should excavate the area between the tomb of Merneptah and Ramesses VI, a large bay that was filled with tremendous piles of chippings moved there from Davis' earlier excavations. Burton scratched the sides and top of the mounds and made soundings in other parts of the area but could not begin its clearance because he had neither the funds nor the resources for such a task. In March there was a terrible flood that ran down through the Valley and entered several tombs. Once again the tomb of Ramesses III was flooded and that of Ramesses II, long since freed by Salt and Lepsius of the worst of its encumbering filling, was blocked again. Burton took his gang of men into the tombs in an attempt to clear them. The tomb of Ramesses III had sustained such damage following the expansion of the rock that Burton felt that it was too dangerous to work there. In the tomb of Ramesses II, however, the ceilings and

Fragments of a glass negative found in the ruins of Davis House showing Burton's men clearing the upper passages in the tomb of Ramesses II. The floodwaters tended to drop the coarser material in the upper parts of the tomb, the lower sections being choked with fine sand which, on drying, set as hard as icing sugar

walls had held and Davis had his men cut the wet mud from the tomb and take it up to the surface of the Valley. Conditions in the tomb during the first few days after the flood were appalling. Soaked with water and filled with wet mud, Burton recorded a temperature of over 90°F in the burial chamber, and this in a room which in normal circumstances hardly varied at around 70°F.

In the West Valley Burton had turned the house into a home. In one of the small bedrooms he pinned pictures on the walls; photographs he had taken of the Great Sphinx by the Giza pyramids, which had appeared in the *Illustrated London News*, and others of country houses set in the green English landscape. Burton ordered his clothes from British tailors with branches in Cairo, having them sent down, on approval, to 'H.H. Burton Esq., Tombs of the Kings, Luxor'. Small framed mottoes were hung in the house, fine archeological advice such as 'The fellow who does a lot of running around isn't the one who gets ahead'. He also had food and photographic equipment sent by rail from Cairo, all the requirements of expedition life and quite luxurious. Tinned meats and Oxford sausages from England, French mineral water, German beers, even, it seems, Sanatogen and bicarbonate of soda. Yet the newspapers that they received, the *Daily Mail* and the *Westminster Gazette*, were filled with ominous reports of the political situation in Europe—the tensions and alliances that led to the First World War. Burton's calendar at the house, which he marked off each day, stopped in the middle of the year. The expedition was over; Crane returned to Europe and to the war and Burton joined the Metropolitan Museum's expedition at Deir el Bahari.

The opulent era of pre-war archeology had ended before the death of Davis in Florida in 1915 when, in the late summer of the previous year, Maspero, at this time knighted for his services in Egypt, left for France in an attempt to regain his failing health. In the fourteen years of his second term as Director of the *Service*, Maspero had created a masterly organization for the care of the monuments, reorganized the vast Museum in its new palatial buildings in Cairo; his scholarly achievements were enormous. He remains the greatest of historians and egyptologists, world renowned with more than twelve hundred publications to his name. With considerable tact and diplomacy he had bridged the traditional hostility between the French and the British interests in Egypt at a most delicate political period and he had also been instrumental, by his successful popularizing of

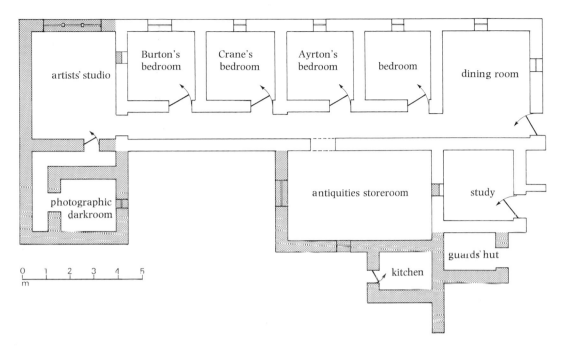

Plan of the Davis House during the last phase of its occupation before World War I. The untinted walls are those of the original house, designed by Ayrton. In 1978–79 it was enlarged and altered for use as our expedition headquarters

ancient Egypt, in bringing about a change of public attitude towards the subject of his life's work. As well as the study of ancient texts and a library full of books, egyptology had now been enlarged to include the recovery and conservation of all the relics of the ancient civilization.

Before he resigned his post in Cairo, Maspero had seen to the drawing up of a contract between the *Service* and Lord Carnarvon, which allowed Carnarvon, under Carter's daily direction, the rights of excavation in the Valley of the Kings for a period of ten years. Untypically, the contract did include a paragraph upon the division of the objects that the excavators might discover; intact royal burials, for example, were the property of the Government of Egypt, but it also stipulated that Carnarvon should receive a share of the results of the work that was equal to his efforts and to the expenses he had incurred. The contract was a simple document, a gentlemen's agreement written on paper and it was never imagined by either party that it would eventually be tested in a court of law. However, the three men who made the agreement, Carter—the professional archeologist whose entire career had been

built in Egypt, Carnarvon—a wealthy amateur like Belmore and Dufferin before him, and Maspero the benign overseer of ancient Egypt for so many years, were already acting in the past. The popular interest that had been generated in ancient Egypt and the large sums of money that were now available for its exploitation, had distorted their gentlemanly occupation beyond their imaginings. But of the three parties named in the contract, only one of them, Lord Carnarvon, would later come to realize this fact and attempt to exploit it.

Carter and Carnarvon now planned a long and expensive first season in the Valley, employing some three hundred men to remove the huge dumps of chippings that Davis had piled up over some of the unexcavated portions of the Valley. A site which particularly attracted their attention was the gully that contained the tomb of Merneptah, the triangle between the doors of the tombs of Ramesses II, Merneptah and Ramesses VI in the central area of the Valley where Davis had set Burton working during his last season. In this area heaps of chippings, some thirty feet high, rolled along in great mounds that covered the unexcavated stratum of flood debris beneath. Both men well knew that there were many kings of the New Kingdom, at least five of the Eighteenth Dynasty as well as several monarchs of the Ramesside and post-Ramesside period that had

237

not yet been found but that, if they should find another royal tomb in the Valley, it would probably have been robbed. They also knew, however, that small intact Valley tombs such as those of Mahirpra, Yuya and Tuya had been discovered low in the Valley under the debris of New Kingdom floods and that there were, therefore, two chances in their work: the slender one of discovering a royal tomb and the probability of the discovery of a noble's tomb. But they also knew full well that there had been nearly a hundred years of sporadic excavations in the Valley and that the chances of finding another tomb must be low. The continuing tragedy for modern archeology in all this was that none of these archeologists seriously imagined that the chippings themselves held the story of the ancient community in the Valley.

In England, now at war, Carnarvon was persuaded by Kitchener to turn the family seat, Highclere, into a military hospital. As a semi-invalid himself, Carnarvon could not join the army but neither would he dig in Egypt during the hostilities and so the plans for the winter's excavations were scrapped. Carter, with his long experience in Egypt, spent his time working on several different government tasks and from the first, that of King's Messenger, acting as a courier for the Foreign Office in the Middle East, he was dismissed for a breach of discipline, once described as 'trivial yet distinct'. It was the second time that the establishment of the Empire had brusquely dismissed him.

The declaration of war made by Turkey upon the Allies had encouraged Britain to declare Egypt, which had been nominally still a part of the Ottoman Empire, a protectorate. In 1915 Turkey threatened to invade Egypt where it would have controlled the Suez Canal, blocking efficient contact with the Empire in the Far East. Several military campaigns were mounted from Egypt, notably by Allenby, who eventually rode into Jerusalem at the head of his army on a white horse, and by T. E. Lawrence, an archeologist and another of Petrie's pupils, who encouraged and helped to lead a revolt against the Turks in Arabia. Cairo became a huge wartime base and the peasantry and the Egyptian harvests were ruthlessly exploited for the war effort. Nationalistic sentiment, always a strongly present force in the land since the days of the British invasion of 1882, began to grow and in 1916 the country was placed under martial law.

Shortly before the war had started, Carter had been relaxing one evening on the verandah of his house by the Valley road when he was approached by a villager. Mohammed Abd el Gaffer who had a basketful of alabaster jar fragments that he wanted to sell. Some of them had Eighteenth Dynasty cartouches upon them. Carter could see that Mohammed had come from the tomb which so many archeologists had searched for in vain and he asked Mohammed what the tomb was like. Mohammed told of a large tomb with a deep pit in its centre and, to his delight, Carter recognized in this a description of the well shaft, only found in royal tombs. After some bargaining Carter not only bought the alabaster from Mohammed but paid him to lead him to the tomb. As Carter was led up a steep gully behind the Dra Abu el Naga he suddenly realized that the cunning villagers who, years before, had so confidentially told him of the location of the tomb had deliberately misled him! Now, however, with the tomb quite robbed, the information of its whereabouts was surrendered; it turned out to be not a thousand yards from Carter's own verandah.

After a quick inspection, an awkward descent into a deep shaft whose entrance was completely hidden under a group of huge overhanging boulders in a desolate shallow valley, Carter found that the smoke-blackened burnt-out tomb held little of obvious value, but it was apparent that it was of great importance in the history of the royal tomb. If it was indeed the tomb of Amenhotep I it was the earliest royal tomb yet discovered and had belonged to the king whom the ancient workers themselves had worshipped as the patron and probably the founder of their colony of quarriers and craftsmen. So as Burton was finishing his work in the Valley, Carter received permission to clear the tomb and by the summer of 1914 he had finished the work. He found little of intrinsic value among the thousands of small fragments of broken vessels of both ceramic and alabaster, many of which dated from a later period, when apparently the burials in the tomb had been replaced by others. There were some fragments of mummy jewellery from a later period of re-use as well as pieces of burnt coffin.

Fragments of inscriptions upon the vases named both Amenhotep I and his mother Nefertari and there was also a great deal of pottery of that same early period. Carter always believed that he had found the tomb of that king. On a papyrus that described the inspection tour of a number of the royal tombs, which included that of Amenhotep I, a description of the location of his tomb was given, using ancient place names that were not accurately understood but Carter believed by a process of deduction that the ancient description of Amenhotep's tomb fitted perfectly with the one that he had just discovered.

*The royal tomb on the Dra Abu el Naga. This Carter
photograph was marked by him to indicate the tomb's position.
Its entrance shaft was hidden under a large boulder and is only
visible from a distance of a few feet*

Indeed, it has many of the traits that would be expected of a royal tomb of that early period but Carter's
method for tallying the measurements in the tomb
with cubit measurements given in the papyrus are
not very convincing. As for the inscriptional evidence,
it was too confusing, and so much had already been
taken from the tomb that a simple tally of names
which actually brought Nefertari out in front as the
chief claimant, proved very little.

Nevertheless, Carter's explanations were widely
accepted; obviously the tomb was a royal one and
the early pottery and inscriptions dated it to that
particular period. He sent a long article on the tomb

to Carnarvon; it was, he described in his published
account, 'discovered by the Earl of Carnarvon' who
had 'the good fortune to reveal its hiding place'. At
every turn Carter gave full credit to his sponsor, who
already had in his collection at Highclere a royal
head that Carter had bought and further fragments
of which were found in the tomb. Though Carter
described this head as being 'bought from a dealer
in Cairo' this was, in fact, a well-used euphemism at
the time for articles purchased on the illicit antiquities
market, and Carter had probably bought it at Luxor,
perhaps even from Abd el Gaffer. Carter, like Ayrton
before him, had to supply his patron with results.

Most of the archeological activity in Egypt was
stopped for the duration of the war and many of the
young archeologists, of many nations, were sadly
wasted in bloody battles. Carter managed to return

to Thebes from time to time, as his war duties permitted, and he used these brief trips to make small sallies into the landscape of the Valley to solve some of its smaller mysteries, which required the use of but a few workers.

February 1915 saw Carter working by the tomb of Amenhotep III for although Burton and others before him had dug in the small bay that held the tomb, none of them had cleared out the tomb itself or excavated around its entrance. Remembering his experiences in front of the tombs of Hatshepsut and Tuthmosis IV, Carter set about looking for foundation deposits in front of the tomb door. To his surprise, he found broken antiquities even before his men were down into ancient levels, a ushabti of Queen Tiy and many fragments of glass and faience. Knowing that the fine engraved gems had probably come from this area Carter kept a close eye on his men.

Carter found five deposits in front of the tomb, and all of them were intact. There were hundreds of small objects and models of tools, all placed in pits cut into the limestone rock and mixed with the whitish sand of the valley floor, and covered with small pieces of rubble. Although there was no discernible order in the placing of the objects in the deposits, in the three larger, more central ones, there were the three heads of young calves that had been placed on top of the other objects. Most surprising of all was that the inscriptions in the deposits named not Amenhotep III, whose tomb they stood in front of, but Tuthmosis IV, his father. Carter therefore concluded that the tomb had been initiated for the crown prince during the reign of Tuthmosis IV and that he had retained the tomb after he came to the throne. A comparison of the two tombs certainly bears this out for, although Amenhotep III's tomb has more elaborate rooms and side chambers than his father's, the burial chamber is of small dimensions and of quite a different proportion from the standard 1.72:1 that had been used in the previous royal tombs including that of his father's. Thus the tomb of Amenhotep III had not been made originally for a king but, like tomb number 42, was designed to be virtually identical to the true royal tomb but with subtle differences of measurement and proportion which, along with the foundation deposits, indicate that it was contemporary with the tomb of Tuthmosis IV and not its successor.

Nine days later Carter was excavating in the well inside the tomb which, despite visits by virtually every expedition to the Valley since Napoleon's day, had never been excavated. It was part filled with stone, fragments of wood and dead animals which had collected in it over the years and the clearance, along with that of the small room that was discovered at its bottom, brought interesting results. Carter well knew that the reign of this king was the period of probably the finest ancient Egyptian faiences and also some of the other classes of small objects. In the well he found plentiful evidence of this superb craftsmanship but sadly most of it was broken and partly burnt. From the original burial equipment of the king there remained fragments of two different statues, a snake and the goddess Sekhmet. There was also a mass of fragments of fine faience amulets and many parts of a full-sized chariot with its harnesses, further pieces of which had already been found by both Carter and Burton outside the tomb.

There were also pieces of at least seventeen of the royal ushabtis in the well, all sadly broken examples of figures that were already represented in several major museums by others already taken from the tomb. These were of the highest quality, of ebony with hieroglyphs inlaid with ivory and bone, of alabaster and hard stone and faiences of many different colours. There were *kohl* tubes—small cylinders which held the black eye make-up used both at court and when hunting in the desert—typical of the small objects of the king often found in the excavations of his huge palace at Thebes. There were also amulets, pectorals and pendants in fragments of magnificent faience all bearing the royal cartouche, but so damaged that it took all Carter's long experience to identify them. The remains of two later burials in the tomb from another much later period were also found, but their coffins had been smashed and partly burnt along with the mummies.

Most interesting were the pathetic remnants from the burial of Queen Tiy, of which two alabaster ushabtis, a fragmentary wooden box painted with resin and the torso of a fine, nearly lifesized wooden statue remained. Certainly they were part of the burial equipment of the queen, and it was difficult to imagine that they had been put into the tomb at any other time than her funeral. But, as Carter knew well, Akhenaten had also provided Queen Tiy with a great golden shrine decorated in the faith of his new religion and Davis had died believing that *he* had found the tomb of the queen. Another fragment from the well inscribed with the name of another queen, Sitamon, indicated to Carter that she, too, very probably had been buried in the tomb.

The royal tombs were beginning to present many such small mysteries and historical problems to

Carter and he was becoming increasingly interested in them. During the next few years, Carter spent as much time as he could in the Valley studying and making plans of the tombs, especially of the Eighteenth Dynasty, in which he was particularly interested. He corresponded with the curators of the egyptological collections that held objects from the royal burials and asked for lists of their holdings. When he was in England during the summer months he spent much time in egyptological libraries researching the history of the Valley and its excavation. He was the first person to look deeply into the history of the Valley; he studied the early maps and records, looking for evidence of tombs that might have since been lost, and for new ideas about the site. The Valley had completely absorbed him and his research was directed towards a better understanding of the royal tombs, especially the earlier ones. In the process he compiled the first catalogue of the Valley and its tombs. He also surveyed and drew a large scale map of the Valley that showed the relative positions of the tombs as they lay, deep in the rock.

The following year, 1916, saw Carter back at Thebes, where extraordinary rumours of illicit treasures from a robbed tomb were going around the villagers, the archeologists and the antiquities dealers of Luxor. There had certainly been another major tomb discovered and from odd inscribed canopic vases shown to several archeologists by the Luxor dealers, it had held several princesses from the period of the early Eighteenth Dynasty. The location of the empty plundered tomb was common knowledge after a few months, and it greatly interested Carter. It was situated in a remote desert valley behind the Valley of the Kings, high in a cleft at the end of the valley floor, a position in the landscape that greatly resembled the tomb of Tuthmosis III in the Valley. When Carter visited the tomb he was struck by the number of ancient paths and graffiti in the area, also by the fact that the villagers had obviously been digging in other spots in the area. For the next months, Carter walked in many of the valleys that were situated on the western side of the peak that overlooked the Valley of the Kings.

During these walks he found two more tombs, one from the evidence of a small graffito upon a rock by its entrance, he called that of Princess Neferu, the daughter of Hatshepsut and this too was situated high in the face of a cliff and difficult of access. The other was cut more than one hundred feet above an ancient path that ran at its base and which, in its turn, ran along a ledge some one hundred and thirty feet above

the valley floor. It was an extraordinary tomb in a beautiful remote valley of two sheer cliffs of limestone nearly 400 feet high, narrow and dramatic. Carter discovered the tomb in an unusually unnerving manner: he surprised a gang of tomb robbers who were burrowing deep into the flooded tomb during the night after some villagers had told him of the tomb following disagreements among themselves.

It took Carter's men twenty days to clear away the flooded debris, but he could see that it was a royal tomb type and well worth the effort and danger of excavating in such an extraordinary location—in the centre of a sheer cliff! Eventually his men dug out a fine sarcophagus inscribed for Hatshepsut, the third example discovered by Carter that had been made for this great queen. This one, however, was earlier than the other two; the very monument, in fact, from which the design of all the royal sarcophagi of the Eighteenth Dynasty had been derived. It had been made for Hatshepsut before she ruled over Egypt, when she was but a wife of Tuthmosis II. When she became queen in her own right this sarcophagus was left in the remote tomb, unused, at the top of a small flight of steps which led to the tiny square burial chamber. The queen's artists later used the design for her new sarcophagus, slightly altered and improved, as was the usual Egyptian way, and thus initiated the design used by the kings of the New Kingdom.

Plan of the tomb on Dra Abu el Naga (above) and of the cliff tomb of Queen Hatshepsut. The two tombs are different in shape but identical in many of their measurements. The ancient Egyptian designers consistently re-employed measurements from monuments separated by great distances of both time and space

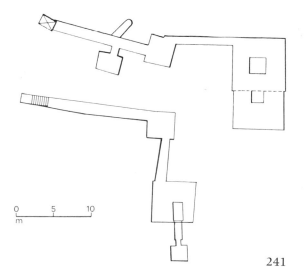

0   5   10
m

Four tombs, two of them discovered by Carter, which have locations similar to the tomb of Tuthmosis III in the Valley of the Kings. They are older than Tuthmosis III's tomb and situated in remote desert valleys at Thebes. Top left, Bab el-Maaleg [the doorway of the king?] is the local name for this extraordinary tomb cut in the sheer cliff face nearly 150 feet from the ground. Top right, the tomb of Queen Hatshepsut, more than 100 feet from the ground. Below left, the tomb of Princess Neferu, daughter of Queen Hatshepsut. Below right, the tomb of the three princesses, which contained the treasure that Carter purchased for the Metropolitan Museum. The entrance to this tomb, like that of Tuthmosis III, is a short distance down the cleft in the rock face

This lonely tomb also had a profound effect upon the design of the royal tombs at Thebes. Previous to Hatshepsut's reign, such tombs had been long straggling affairs, like the earlier ones at Abydos, or the tomb in the Valley that Hatshepsut had used for her burial with her father, Tuthmosis I. While she was still wife of Tuthmosis II, Hatshepsut's architects had designed her lonely cliff tomb as a smaller version of the tomb—probably that of Queen Nefertari, which Carter had cleared some two years before in the hills behind Dra Abu el Naga. With almost archeological care that tomb had been studied and copied by Queen Hatshepsut's architects and it was this adaptation that so influenced the architects of the next royal tomb in the Valley, that of Tuthmosis III. Although that great king may well have destroyed much of the sculptures of Hatshepsut and had her name cut from her buildings, his architects nevertheless copied the design of her tomb, which became a standard for the next three kings and remained as a nucleus for the designs of the subsequent royal tombs in the Valley. In the clearing and planning of these two tombs—the extraordinary cliff tomb of Hatshepsut and the huge smoke-blackened tomb behind Dra Abu el Naga—Carter had supplied egyptology with the information required to reconstruct the entire history of the beginnings of the royal tombs in the Valley of the Kings.

The following year Carter was back in the Valley, working in the tomb of Ramesses IV as a part of a project of the great philologist Sir Alan Gardiner, who had been studying a papyrus in the Museo Egizio, Turin which bore a fragmentary plan of a royal tomb. The ancient cartographers had not made a scale plan of their tomb, however, for such things were not drawn by the ancient designers. But the dimensions of the tomb were on the papyrus and Gardiner wanted to discover just how accurately the ancient architects had described the actual tomb. It was work

close to Carter's heart and he set out to measure the tomb using the system of cubits and digits that had been employed on the ancient plan. After his survey Carter sent Gardiner a new plan of the tomb and a careful line by line commentary on the physical state of the tomb compared with the original comments on the papyrus. This close study of the design, following every measurement and comment, was obviously a pleasure for Carter and he discovered that his ancient counterparts had been far more accurate within the limits of their measuring system than had previously been supposed. Carter also believed that some of the errors in the papyrus indicated that it had been prepared away from the Valley with the aid of some notes, for the inaccuracies were so obvious when standing in the tomb that they

A contemporary plan of the burial chamber of Ramesses IV, from a papyrus now in the Museo Egizio, Turin. The close-packed group of rectangles in the middle of the plan represent the great wooden shrines and the funeral canopy that surrounded the granite sarcophagus. Cartouche-shaped, it is shown with its lid decorated with the king, Isis and Nepthys. Gardiner translated the hieratic text: 'The House of Gold wherein one rests, 16 cubits by 16 cubits by 10 cubits [a cubit usually measured about 0,52 metres] being drawn with outline, graven with chisels, filled with colour and completed [a condition report upon the state of the wall decorations] and being provided with the [burial] equipment of his majesty on every side of it together with the divine Ennead [statues of the gods?] which is in the Other world'; and the small text by the entrance door, drawn on the right of the burial chamber: 'Its door is fastened'

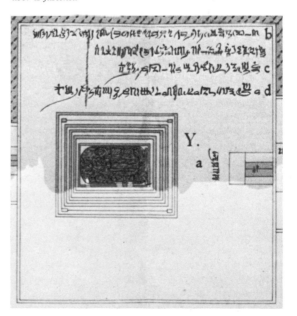

would never have been made if a direct comparison had been possible. The papyrus also showed the interesting difference between modern and ancient attitudes to the planning of architecture. In common with other ancient tomb plans that have survived, the Turin papyrus shows clearly that the ancient quarrymen were very careful to achieve the precise measurements required for the tomb rooms, but were not so concerned about the rooms' exact inter-relationships. If a convenient crack in the rock helped in the quarry work, the axis of the tomb might well be shifted slightly, especially in the Eighteenth Dynasty tombs. This is a very important factor to take into account when studying the relationships of tombs. It means that two tombs with very different plans on paper can share many resemblances, for the ancient architects did not work with set squares and pencils on a drawing board, but with stakes and string in the limestone cliffs, knowing that some of the rooms they would have to make had to be cut exactly to the correct dimensions. Such a non-mechanical attitude to planning tombs would make abstract computerized surveys of the plans and measurements virtually meaningless without careful archeological controls. It is a splendid example of ancient methods not readily responding to modern analysis, and shows that an understanding of the ancients and their very human technologies requires great time and patience.

Carter had greatly enjoyed the work in the tomb of Ramesses IV and he prepared once again to dig in the Valley. Throughout most of the war archeological activity in Egypt had come to a standstill, but slowly during the later years of the war it had started again, though sadly without many of the younger archeologists. Britain, Germany and France all lost scholars and archeologists of great promise; the death of one of Maspero's sons on the Western Front so grieved the old man that he never really recovered from the shock and he died some months later as he rose from his chair to address a meeting of the French Academy in 1916. The Egyptians too had been greatly affected by the war. There was tremendous inflation in the country and levies on both labour and produce by Britain had a particularly bad effect upon the economy of the countryside. During 1918, more people died in Egypt than were born; truly an incredible statistic for a country of traditionally large families. While not paying close attention to the situation inside Egypt after the war, the British Government slowly relaxed its tight grip on the land. Half-hearted attempts at withdrawal were attended, however, by many repressive measures which greatly inflamed public opinion and caused rioting and campaigns of civil disobedience throughout the land. Old European residents of Egypt had their own methods of dealing with such 'disturbances', but they quickly discovered that times had changed and their simple-minded colonialism was not automatically supported by the politicians in Westminster who had other, more immediate, problems to face. Along with thousands of other foreigners, Howard Carter collided with these strong new forces of nationalism which were present, even in the Valley of the Kings.

The Ayrton-Carter excavation map of the Valley. It is not difficult to see two hands at work on this sheet: Carter's neat drawings of the tombs as they lay under the ground and his characteristic handwriting, in pencil, contrasting with the carelessly delineated cliffs, paths and excavation areas. Ayrton's contribution was the detailed information concerning Davis' excavations and discoveries. Nowhere else is such information recorded and because this work was performed in the 1904–05 season by Ayrton and his men such information could only have come from him. It is probable, therefore, that this map was drawn by Ayrton and later amended by Carter. It was found in the magazine of the Davis House during its re-building

Lord Carnarvon's Excavations

(1917–22)

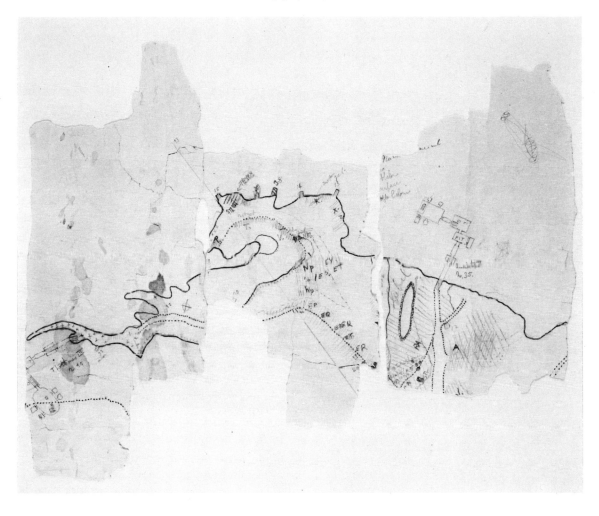

When Carter took over from Davis' expedition he converted their desert house into a store and continued to live in his own elegant dwelling overlooking the Nile Valley. In the desert house he found a roughly drawn excavation map on thick cartridge paper on which Ayrton had drawn the sites that he had excavated for Davis. It was the last link in the long chain of research that Carter had conducted on the Valley and its excavation. From these written sources and his own intimate knowledge of the Valley landscape he drew up a continuing plan of operations, and when Lord Carnarvon's excavations in the Valley began in December 1917, Carter chose the same location that Burton had probed during the last season of Davis' excavations: between the tombs of Merneptah and Ramesses VI—the tomb of Memnon.

It took a large gang of workmen a month to clear away the heaps of chippings and excavation debris

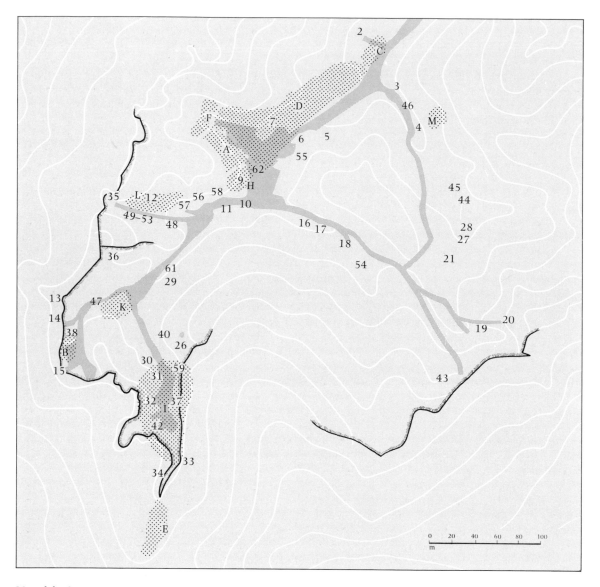

Map of the Carter-Carnarvon excavations in the Valley of the Kings. The alphabetic notation is Carter's own

thrown across this area by earlier archeologists. Even in this 'rubbish', as the loose debris of the Valley was usually called, fragmentary antiquities were discovered and although these may have originated from almost anywhere in the Valley, Carter listed and catalogued them all. This laborious large-scale work was generally dirty and unrewarding. From the officers of the *Service* Carter borrowed a 'Decauville' system, a prefabricated railway with tipping trucks that were pushed along the rails by manpower. The

small robust track and carts are still in use in excavations at Thebes today and the long tongues of debris that marked the progress of the track as it was extended further and further away from the site of excavation may still be seen in parts of the Valley, as it can in the areas surrounding the sites of most of the large-scale excavations at Thebes. With the help of the Decauville, Carter's gangs were able to move the vast heaps of excavation debris out of the work area with reasonable speed, taking hundreds of cartloads further down the Valley where the floor was wider and had already been excavated. By the beginning of January they had exposed a flat stratum which covered older, untouched levels.

Despite the war, there were still tourists at Luxor, and Carter had to ensure that the edge of his excavation was walled up and well supported so that the tourist paths to the tombs would not subside into it. At the eastern end of the work, by the tomb of Ramesses VI, the excavation was very deep and visitors looked down some thirty feet into the bottom of the trench, where Carter's men, here close to bedrock, were working. In common with several other of the large Ramesside tombs, the door of the tomb of Ramesses VI had been cut into the limestone hillside at a point some fifteen feet above the floor of the Valley, presumably to raise it above the floods. Some twelve feet beneath the door lay the remains of a group of ancient workmens' huts. Carter had already seen another section of this settlement when Davis and Ayrton had cut right through them to expose the tomb that had held the Amarna Cache. Now, at a similar height on the Valley floor Carter carefully cleaned another part of this group, at the northern side of the door.

In the ancient houses, made of simple slabs of stone up-ended and originally roofed with branches and rush, he found the desiccated corpse of a snake in a pot; perhaps the pet of some ancient workman or the star of a long-forgotten snake charmer's act. He also found an *ostracon* written by the scribe Djehuti-mes dated to the reign of Ramesses II, which gave him some idea of the age of the village. Carter knew, of course, that just forty feet south of where his men were working Davis and Ayrton had cut through the undisturbed flood debris on which these ancient huts had been built, to expose the unplundered tomb of the Amarna Cache of late Eighteenth Dynasty date beneath. By the tomb of Ramesses VI Carter found that the huts stood upon an artificially built-up level of flints, boulders and sand. His men cut a small section through the floor of one hut and found bedrock just three feet beneath. Apart from some *ostraca* from the workmen's village they found little of intrinsic value in this artificial stratum but a few small pieces of gold foil and fine glass beads that must have greatly interested Carter. Obviously no one over the past centuries had dug in the area—a large portion of the centre of the Valley that lay under the huts of the Nineteenth Dynasty village.

During World War I there were relatively small numbers of tourists in Egypt and certainly in the period 1918 to 1920, riots and other civil commotions throughout the country kept tourism well below the pre-war levels. To continue the dig in the centre of the Valley, Carter would have had to disrupt the normal passage of the tourist visits to the tombs and this slack period would have been the perfect time for the operation. Such a plum site, so large and obviously untouched since Eighteenth Dynasty times, was a real find. Most of the Valley now resembled the fields of Flanders in the confusions of its earlier excavations, and Ayrton's map could hardly have filled Carter with much hope of discovering further large and hitherto untouched sites in the Valley. Carter did not continue across the centre of the Valley that season—he saved it for a time when his patron's enthusiasm for excavation had flagged. Then he was able to produce for Carnarvon the prospect of a season's excavations at a very promising location; the huge area of Eighteenth Dynasty date that lay undisturbed under the workmen's huts in the centre of the Valley. A site that had already produced the extraordinary golden shrines and coffin of the Amarna Cache at one of its edges could well hold more material of a similar date and quality. By this time Carter had already realized that the tomb claimed to be that of Tutankhamon by Davis in his last publication was but a cache of grave goods which, while related to the actual burial, certainly had not contained the king. That tomb, at least, had not yet come to light and judging by the evidence was almost certainly somewhere in the Valley.

On 2 February 1918, Carter shut down the excavation and did not start work again until the February of the following year. Then he excavated for five days in front of tomb number 38 in which Loret had found a sarcophagus of Tuthmosis I, made for his reburial by his grandson Tuthmosis III. Carter too thought that this tomb was the oldest in the Valley and he was looking for foundation deposits that might have given him an exact idea as to its origins. Such work was certainly not that of a treasure seeker or someone doggedly searching for a 'lost tomb' and indeed most of Carter's activities in the Valley were of this type, designed to settle scholarly questions on the dating and origin of the tombs. He found a foundation deposit during his brief excavation but the severe floods in that area had moved the objects from their original positions and, washing through them, had erased any ink inscriptions that may originally have been on them. However, the small copper chisels and pottery vessels that he found strongly resembled early Eighteenth Dynasty examples from other similar deposits.

At this period Carter was deeply involved in the purchase of some of the treasures from the remote

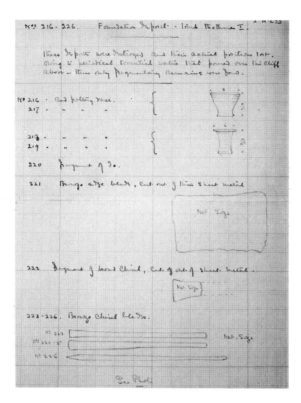

Carter's records of the disturbed foundation deposits discovered by the tomb made for Tuthmosis I (number 38). The pottery (above) is of a type made during the first half of the Eighteenth Dynasty but lack of inscriptions preclude a more accurate dating

bought some of the less precious grave goods from the tomb for his museum but, apart from any ethical considerations, he had little experience in dealing with the wily Luxor merchants who were now asking for previously unheard of sums of money for the richer grave goods from the tomb. Through Carter, who had many years of experience in such dealings, Carnarvon had already started to negotiate for the treasures and the officers of the Metropolitan had been approached so that a joint buying policy might be established in order that they would not be played off one against the other, as was the normal ploy of the Luxor dealers. Eventually Carnarvon found the arrangement with the Metropolitan Museum so profitable that he sold his part of the treasure through Carter to the Museum which, with Carter's assistance, obtained the lion's share of the treasure. For his role in these negotiations Carter received a large sum of money that assured him of never again being in the desperate straits that had resulted from his resignation from the *Service* some fourteen years before.

Thus, during the lean war years, although Carter did not dig for his patron, Carnarvon, he was engaged in all manner of business for him in Egypt. Carter had always understood that the patrons of that day were not usually interested in scholarship for its own sake but required a tangible return for their outlay and thus he organized a whole programme of excavations and discoveries in the Valley around Carnarvon's annual visits to Egypt. It was a style of working that he had derived from Maspero and his contemporaries, one considered quite appropriate for a professional excavator who socially, perhaps, stood somewhere between an estate manager and a gentleman. All Carter's work was performed in his patron's name, everything was discovered 'by the researches of Lord Carnarvon' whether the Earl was in Egypt or not. When they had first worked together in front of Deir el Bahari Carter had painted Carnarvon's baronial crest above the door of every tomb they discovered. The extraordinary thing about Carter was, however, that he employed this patronage so wisely, satisfying as best he could the needs of scholarship and also the expectations of a patron who, as well as running a string of race horses and marrying with a vast dowry the illegitimate daughter of a Rothschild, was as his son described, a man who 'always had an eye to the main chance'. Though Carnarvon adored Egypt and his extraordinarily fine collection of antiquities, he was always aware of their investment potential. Obviously the prospect of excavation in the Valley of the Kings, though a truly lordly extrava-

cliff tomb which he had surveyed some years before. After a suitable period the Luxor dealers had produced the rich grave goods and had offered them to the agents of the British Museum, the Metropolitan Museum and Lord Carnarvon, at that time the three biggest purchasers of antiquities in the market. The British Museum, however, could not properly deal in such treasures during a world war. The Governors had already seen a superb Middle Kingdom treasure, legally excavated and awarded in a division to the archeologists by Maspero, sold to the Metropolitan and now they would have to watch while the bulk of another travelled the same path.

In 1917 the Metropolitan's archeologist at Thebes, Ambrose Lansing, was digging in the very same cemeteries, the widely spaced tombs of the queens and princesses of the Eighteenth Dynasty, as those from which these magnificent treasures had been stolen and he could have been easily compromised by purchasing such illicit prizes. In fact, Lansing had already

gance, fitted well into the scheme of things.

It was not until the following year, 1920, that Carter continued the excavations in the Valley. His first task was to find another site to dump the debris from the excavation by the tomb of Merneptah. The Decauville railway was laid down the slopes of the Valley, as it had been during the 1917 excavations, and now extended close to the mouth of the tomb of Ramesses IV, and to ensure that he was not dumping his debris onto hidden tombs, Carter first sounded the area of his tip. Typically, before he started this work of trenching the Valley side he made a small exploratory excavation directly in front of the mouth

5 January 1920. Carter excavating at site C. The woman with a parasol standing next to Carter is not, apparently, Lady Evelyn Herbert, Carnarvon's daughter—neither she nor her father arrived in the Valley until later in the month

of the tomb of Ramesses IV. There he found five fine foundation deposits, each bearing a variety of goods with the king's name upon them: tools, faience plaques, beads, and even models of the parts of animals that Carter had discovered in their reality in other deposits in the Valley. Although not of great intrinsic value, this collection of little objects, all in fine condition and with the glassy Ramesside faience shining in a particularly brilliant blue, would certainly impress Carnarvon when he arrived.

Carter had decided to look for these deposits because Ayrton had found only one deposit during his excavations, which had been his first work in the Valley, close to the site of the houses of the Classical period. Carter, however, with his deep knowledge of the Valley, knew that there should be more and, in fact, he not only found five intact deposits but also four other ancient closed pits that had, mysteriously, been left empty. Carter found no trace of the pit that Ayrton had described and it would appear that it had held merely a few loose objects from the royal tomb that had been displaced and was not a foundation deposit at all; it is an indication of how carelessly the earlier excavations in the Valley had been conducted. Although there were probably no great sealed tombs left undetected by Ayrton and his workmen, the archeology of the Valley had been widely disturbed and passed over unrecorded. A brave patron was required to finance excavations in the Valley, not with the aim of discovering sensational new tombs but simply to recover such small traces of the archeology of the sites as still remained. This is, quite possibly, a thankless task and certainly not one for which Carnarvon was suited; to this day it is waiting to be performed.

After this small probing excavation Carter again started his large gangs working in the rock bay of the tomb of Merneptah, particularly in that area by the side of the tomb of Ramesses II. By the time the Earl and Lady Evelyn arrived in late February, the entire area had been cleared down to a stratum of cemented flood debris that had not been disturbed since New Kingdom times and Carter could now show his patron an area of the Valley which held the promise of fresh discoveries. In fact, Carter had finished the preliminary work in this area some weeks before Carnarvon's arrival and, delaying this final clearance, he skipped across the Valley with his workmen for a brief excavation above the tomb of Tuthmosis III. This fresh site bore obvious signs of being greatly disturbed and had also been dug about in ancient times. Loret before him had made *sondages* in the area

24 January 1920. Carter's gangs finishing the preliminary excavations at site A before Carnarvon's arrival. They are digging southwards, away from the mouth of the tomb of Ramesses II, indicated by the pit almost at the centre of the photograph, which faces north east. The Decauville track has been extended down the main path to the Valley, which is filled by Carter debris to a depth of four or five feet. This system of tipping debris has buried the entrance to the mysterious tomb 5 (see Chapter 11) which, since the laying of asphalt road on top of Carter's dump has never been seen again

and Carter further cleared a large section of the cleft that held the royal tomb, but did not find anything. On reflection he later realized that much of the debris through which he had dug had been thrown into this cleft to obscure the tips of chippings from the excavation of another tomb, number 39, which was high above the main Valley. In the early Eighteenth Dynasty the quarrymen had often covered their tracks by hiding the chippings at some distance from the tombs and, as Carter realized, these small chippings, so unlike the large long creamy flakes of the Rames-side period, were certainly of this early date.

Carnarvon appeared in Thebes at the end of February and, almost to order, Carter found in the course of the excavation of the undisturbed strata a cache of thirteen alabaster vases of Ramesses II and his son Merneptah, buried in the debris on the hillside a little above the mouth of Merneptah's tomb. These splendid vessels were probably the most beautiful things that Carnarvon had so far found in all his fifteen years' experience of excavation and Lady Evelyn insisted on digging them out from the flood debris that held them, with her own hands. Carter planned the pots in their relative positions, photographed them and catalogued each in a card index that he maintained for all his work in the Valley. After this first excitement, Carter trenched in front of Merneptah's tomb but there they found nothing but a few broken tools and the foundations of another ancient hut. The season was concluded in the middle of March, and the thirteen alabaster jars were taken to Cairo for division with the Museum.

Pierre Lacau, the French Jesuit who had suc-ceeded Maspero as the Director of the *Service*, took the majority of the vases for the Museum but gave some of the finest to Carnarvon. Several had been damaged by the action of the waterfall that ran off the rocks above the tomb of Merneptah, others had been slightly crushed by the loose stones that had surrounded them. Six sturdy jars, some decorated with ibex heads, whose horns formed the elegant handles, went to Highclere and into Carnarvon's private museum. Before the division Carter had ex-tracted some of the contents of these pots and taken the substances to his friend Arthur Lucas for a scientific analysis. Lucas was the Director of the Government Analytical Laboratory in Cairo and before that appointment he had for a brief time been the analytical chemist for the *Service*. He was a fine chemist and was deeply interested in antiquities and their preservation. In a field dominated by philolo-gists and archeologists his scientific precision brought a much-needed clarity to discussions of ancient tech-nology. Today his text books on the subject remain the standard works and are the envy of scholars in other related fields. When Carter returned to Cairo in the autumn of 1920 Lucas told him the results of his analysis: the alabaster jars contained not natron or the other substances used in embalming, but mainly mixtures of quartz and limestone, with some sodium sulphate added. Other substances included wood pitch and resin. The analysis corresponded in

26 February 1920. The alabaster pots emerging from the debris of the ancient stone masons at Carter's site F—an extension of his site A. Though damaged, these fine vessels were easily restored. They were probably a cache of objects used during the mummification of Merneptah, similar to Tutankhamen's cache found by Ayrton and Davis some years before

The certificate of the division of the cache of alabaster pots, signed by Laucau for the Service, Carter for Carnarvon, and by Quibell on behalf of the Museum. This document shows that the Service and Carnarvon were both operating inside the normal arrangements for foreign expeditions

10 March 1920. Site F. Carter's men clearing debris from a deep trench, anciently cut down the middle of the gully that holds the tomb of Merneptah. Several of the royal tombs in the Valley were anciently protected by similar trenches and dykes. This trench, which (at the time) Carter may have thought led to the door of a buried tomb, was apparently designed to carry flood water away from Merneptah's tomb. Behind the cutting, at the face of the excavations, are the strata typical of the lower sections of the Valley. The top, darker layer was composed of hard cemented natural debris brought down by flooding from higher points in the Valley often forming an apparently 'natural' slope. Underneath was a lighter coloured stratum, nearly two metres thick, of loose chippings anciently deposited by the gangs of workmen. Carter's notebooks show that this particular deposit was laid down when the lower sections of the tomb of Merneptah were quarried. Beneath these chippings was a deposit, some fifty centimetres deep, of fine sand which would have either been blown by wind into the drainage gully or deposited by light rains. Steep slopes such as this appear to be quite stable but, given a heavy soaking they can slide into the centre of the Valley in one terrifying mass, destroying and burying the centrally located tombs

part to the hieratic inscriptions that were written on some of the jars. During the summer months Carter's friend Gardiner, to whom he had sent copies of the inscriptions, had translated some of these as 'best quality holy oil'; 'best quality Libyan oil' and the like. Carter had also consulted archeological publications to compare the jars with other similar discoveries. All this information was entered on his card index and accompanied his accomplished drawings and precise descriptions. He planned to publish a complete account of this discovery in a scientific journal within a year or so.

Back in the Valley in early December of the same year Carter determined to finish the work in the bay by the tomb of Merneptah. As soon as his workmen started this task, he took a small group of men to another area of the Valley in an attempt to solve an old archeological puzzle: the ownership of tomb 12, which James Burton had planned so carefully but which, with its complete absence of inscriptions, remained anonymous. Carter cleared all around the mouth of the tomb, but found nothing that would fix the date, the whole area having already been swept clean by Ayrton and Davis. Next, Carter cleaned out the upper sections of the tomb of Ramesses XI so that it could be used as a store and dining room. Crates of French wines and other imported luxuries were stored in the central sections of the tomb, and the first corridor was set with a long table and chairs for the use of Carnarvon and his guests during their visits. Carter took dirt from his excavations to level off the first corridor which, with its drop of over a yard in nearly thirty feet, would have made luncheon a somewhat clumsy affair. However, Carter's normally sharp-eyed men missed one antiquity in this operation: when our expedition removed Carter's floor to make a plan of the tomb we found a part of a small ushabti of Ramesses VII buried in it. Much of the debris of the Valley is studded with such antiquities.

Up at the tomb of Merneptah there remained only the small area in front of the tomb and this was quickly cleared to bedrock, the only discoveries being heaps of chippings of coloured hieroglyphic relief that had been cut from the decorated door jambs of the tomb when they had anciently been shaved down to allow the king's three gigantic sarcophagi lids to pass through to the burial chamber. The largest pieces of these demolished door jambs were taken to the old Davis expedition house for storage where, some sixty years later, our expedition unexpectedly rediscovered them, lying under wind blown sand.

By Christmas Eve Carter was once again digging close to the workmen's huts that he had exposed underneath the entrance to the tomb of Ramesses VI. He cleared out some more of the ancient ruins and found more small belongings of the craftsmen who had lived there while they decorated the tomb of Ramesses VI above. At this point the excavation was very close to the door of the tomb of Ramesses VI and as the Sultan Hussein, the ruler of Egypt, was due shortly to make an official visit to the tomb, Carter stopped the work of clearing out the huts and began a fresh excavation in a southern section of the Valley, the gully that led up to the tomb of Tuthmosis III. Once again Carter had to clear away deep mounds of Davis' dumps to reveal the undisturbed levels of flood debris that covered the Eighteenth and early Nineteenth Dynasty deposits and once these dumps were cleared away Carter immediately began to find traces of these earlier periods. Several fresh fragments of inscribed canopic vases from the burial of Sennefer in tomb 42 were uncovered. Twenty years before, when he had been a young Government Inspector, this tomb had been Carter's first excavation in the Valley. Slowly the entire gully was cleared down to bedrock as Carter and his men worked up the little valley, planning as they proceeded the numerous private tombs, probably of the courtiers of Tuthmosis III who had been buried in the rock cleft above them.

In four neat holes cut in front of tomb 42 Carter found four intact foundation deposits inscribed in the name of Queen Meryt-re Hatshepsut, wife of Tuthmosis III and the mother of Amenhotep II. The holes that held these deposits were accurately planned by Carter and, a few years ago, I was able to uncover one of them that had once again been buried in loose debris. These had clearly been a part of the work of excavation of tomb 42 and the deposits in them proved that this tomb had indeed been excavated during one of the two reigns in which that queen had flourished. The objects are now in the Metropolitan Museum and have been catalogued as being bought from 'a dealer in Cairo'. However, this label has recently been identified as being used to cover the origins of 'sensitive' purchases and the objects have long been identified as coming from the Valley. Carter himself was invariably accurate in his descriptions of his own discoveries, even sometimes to his posthumous detriment.

Close by these deposits Carter found, under a huge scree of debris that had been washed by the floods from the top of the terrace, four more foundation deposits made in a very similar style and inscribed

for Tuthmosis III. Apparently these were related to the tomb of that king above. The similarity of these deposits to those of Queen Meryt-re Hatshepsut beside them makes their relative positions seem like the parts of one overall ancient plan.

Back at his house, Carter pondered over these discoveries. He was particularly interested in the history of the early phases of the royal tombs, and he drew a careful map of this entire area showing all the Eighteenth Dynasty tombs and their foundation deposits. On the same map he also drew the plans of the three tombs that have cartouche-shaped burial chambers so that it showed the entire great cemetery that had been excavated in the Valley during the reign of Tuthmosis III. With the rearrangement of the earlier royal burials of his dynasty by Tuthmosis III the entire royal necropolis of Thebes had been reorganized and properly established in the Valley of the Kings. By following the basic design of his predecessors' tombs in his own monument, while at the same time creating a masterpiece of tomb architecture from this basic plan, Tuthmosis III's architects established the designs of all the succeeding royal tombs in the Valley. Tuthmosis III was truly the father of the Valley of the Kings and its royal tombs.

The clear distinction between royal and non-royal tombs that exists in later monuments in the Valley was not clearly maintained during this early period, several of the earlier private tombs being shaped like the royal tomb design in miniature. The huge tomb, number 42, which includes several of the features of Tuthmosis III's own tomb plan in its design, was evidently not considered to be of an exclusively royal type for, within a few years of its excavation, it was apparently occupied by Sennefer, the Mayor of Thebes and his wife. Originally, tomb 42 was probably excavated either for the queen or perhaps a crown prince; lying open and unused it had been employed for the burial of the Mayor of Thebes because there was no room in the nobles' cemetery that surrounded the tomb of Amenhotep II.

With his men completing the work in the gully below the tomb of Tuthmosis III, Carter still had found nothing to show Carnarvon for the season's work and so he quickly put a gang of workers back in the central area of the Valley where they dug out the space between the tomb of the Amarna Cache and the fine decorated tomb of Ramesses IX. Cutting straight through the floors of more of the ruined houses of the ancient workmen's village, Carter soon struck bedrock but found little on the way down except a fragment of a canopic vase of Queen Takha't, a wife of Seti II who had been perhaps, buried in the tomb of that king. Obviously this area had been disturbed since Eighteenth Dynasty times, unlike the other sections of the workmen's village that Carter had exposed. Still hoping for some small success to show his patron, Carter put his men to work on the other side of the entrance to the tomb of the Amarna Cache and again his men cut down through the ancient floor levels to the bedrock. Again they found very little, uncovering only a small crack in the rock by the side of the tomb, in which they found a small cache of objects that had been taken from the tomb and apparently hidden there in ancient times. Among this little cache of objects there were some bronze rosettes that had originally been sewn on to a funerary shroud, and a smooth red jasper stone shaped for burnishing papyri allowing a scribe to write upon the smoothed surface. Around the mouth of the tomb Carter's men found further evidence of an ancient spoilation, many fragments of faience, glass and bronze lying in the debris. But by the end of the season they still had very little to show for the hard, expensive work. At the head of the Valley around the tomb of Tuthmosis III, Carter's gangs had literally moved mountains of debris with the little Decauville railway system, clearing hundreds of square feet of undisturbed Valley floor. Yet they had not found a new tomb. Perhaps, after all, Davis' statement that the ancients had never excavated tombs in the Valley floor, as they knew it to be a watercourse which flooded regularly, was proving to be true.

It was not, then, with any sense of urgency that Carter thought of returning to work in the Valley. During the following year, 1922, the secret deals with the Metropolitan Museum concerning the treasures of the plundered tomb of the princesses were completed and, doubtless, Carter was assigned a large role in procuring the objects and transferring funds for the Museum. Such profits must have enabled Carnarvon to view his continuing Egyptian enterprises with a degree of optimism. Nonetheless, he must have started to look at his concession in the Valley of the Kings, now six years old, with some doubt, for it had produced little more than those six alabaster pots.

Carter began work in the Valley again in February 1922; a brief campaign of one month's duration. He started at the east side of the tomb of Siptah, an area of the hillside not excavated by Davis and one which proved, once he had cleared away the dumps of earlier excavations, to have been untouched since ancient times. It was like excavating in glue. For two weeks of excavation in the untouched strata of the Valley, Carter had first to shift huge tips of debris which he moved around the corner into the gully of Tuthmosis III's tomb, then clean to bedrock. The work took forty men and one hundred-and-twenty boys ten long days, but when Carnarvon appeared in the Valley the ancient levels were revealed and he was able to watch its excavation. The gangs found hundreds of *ostraca* inscribed and drawn on by the ancient scribes and even an ancient water pot, set up for the convenience of the workmen and never removed afterwards. But they found no tombs.

When Carter returned to England in the summer of 1922, having completed the dealings with the Metropolitan Museum for the treasure, he had little idea what Carnarvon wanted to do next. Obviously there was not much territory remaining for original excavation in the Valley and his two largest programmes of work, the three- and four-month affairs in 1920 and 1921, had produced very little for the Highclere collections. The Valley was now littered with piles of freshly shifted white chippings and pock-marked with great holes dug by Davis and his excavators. Carnarvon was not keen to continue the work but Carter still thought it worthwhile to investigate the central area of the Valley where he had touched on both sides of the ancient village that had flourished during the early Nineteenth Dynasty. In reality this was probably more a feeling of finishing the work in the Valley rather than a 'last ditch hope of finding treasure', as it is frequently portrayed.

Carter was now forty-eight, his career built entirely in a country whose inhabitants were in a state of near rebellion, and there was little hope of immediate change. From the evidence of his notebooks and file indexes, it would seem likely that he now intended to retire from excavation and to publish a great volume upon the New Kingdom royal tombs at Thebes. He had personally surveyed many of the royal tombs in the Valley and elsewhere; his notes and plans now awaited plotting and drawing up. He had also made a great map of the Valley showing the underground locations of the tombs and their relationships to each other. In the gully below the tomb of Tuthmosis III he had surveyed the Eighteenth Dynasty levels of the Valley, with the huts and small workings connected with the tombs. At that time very little was known about the workers who had built the tombs, the vocabulary of the inscriptions upon the *ostraca* in the Valley was not properly understood and the extensive ancient workmen's village, outside the Valley, which was only fully excavated during the 1930s, was not yet recognized as the extraordinary source of information on this ancient community that it would prove to be. Obviously, the village that Carter knew lay under the filling in the centre of the Valley could be a major source of information about these craftsmen and Carter, always intensely interested in the simple mechanics of the procedures of these ancient artists, determined to clear it out. Carter had also reserved this plum site, right in the centre of the Valley, close to the tomb of the Amarna Cache, for just such a moment as this, when Carnarvon's budget and energies were low. For Carnarvon, at fifty-six an invalid for some twenty years, was tired of excavation and had lost his zest and stamina for the work. Egypt, unwelcoming since World War I, was probably not his first choice for a restful holiday. Determinedly Carter persuaded him to invest in one more season and, set on clearing the very central area, he returned to Thebes early in the autumn.

This time Carter had arrived in the Valley to excavate in earnest with none of the delays and theatricalities of waiting for Carnarvon before cutting into the lower, more ancient levels. Intending to cut the access across the tomb of Ramesses VI right at the beginning of the work so as to cause the minimum of inconvenience to tourists at the height of the tourist season, two months later, Carter put his men back to clear away the section that he had left on 2 January of the previous year, 1921. The men were working at the bottom of a great trench again and the removal of yet another area of dumped debris took them four days before they were able to reach the floor level of the ancient huts and work through the thin levels of undisturbed rock and sand that lay beneath. Almost as soon as they started to uncover more of the bedrock that lay beneath this filling they exposed the corner of a rectangular pit cut in the rock. For an entire day the gang worked all around this cutting, completely exposing it to view and building a wall behind it to stop the loose debris above from falling into the work. Carter had no idea whether or not he had found a finished or unfinished tomb, 'a commencement' as the latter were known, and these were fairly common in the Valley. Further, most of the other tombs that were in such low locations in the Valley had been well flooded and not for many years had someone found a tomb in the Valley containing the sort of valuables that Carnarvon was after. Carter, therefore, though obviously very intrigued, could

hardly have been very optimistic. However, on the next day—5 November—it became clear to Carter that he had found a tomb, and one with an entrance very similar to that of the tombs of the Amarna Cache or Yuya and Tuya. Finally, at the bottom of a stairway of sixteen steep and well-cut steps, Carter's men uncovered a doorway that was still blocked and had its plaster covering intact. It bore the stamp of the royal necropolis seal, that of Anubis above nine bound captives. Over the years Carter had seen that sealing in almost every Eighteenth Dynasty tomb in the Valley. Now he knew that he had truly found another tomb.

By the end of the day's work, Carter was able to stand in front of the sealed doorway and shine a torch into a small crack which had opened between the sealed wall and the wooden lintel of the doorway above. Then, after taking down some of the small stones from the top of the sealed wall he could see further into a passage beyond that was almost completely filled with debris. This passage ran right under the tomb of Ramesses VI and Carter could clearly see that it had not been disturbed since ancient times. Setting his Reis as guard over the tomb, Carter rode back in the moonlight down the long Valley to his house, and the next day he sent Carnarvon a telegram: 'At last have made a wonderful discovery in Valley; a magnificent tomb with seals intact; recovered same for your arrival; congratulations'. Ever the showman for his patron, Carter had decided that he was as well hung for a sheep as for a lamb and, on calling Carnarvon to Egypt months before his annual trip was due, had adopted an heroic pose in his communications! Awaiting Carnarvon's arrival, Carter had his men replace more of the debris back over the tomb and asked his old friend Arthur Callender, a retired engineer and a manager of the Egyptian Railways who lived at Armant some fifteen miles south of Luxor, if he would guard the tomb while he went to Cairo to meet Carnarvon. Callender turned up quickly, obviously eager to help his friend in such exciting work. From his own experiences, Carter knew that it would be unwise to trust the local villagers to guard the tomb, subject as they were to strong local pressures inside their own community, so he had soldiers brought to the Valley and stationed them around the buried entrance. Finally, on top of the debris that covered the stairway of the tomb, Carter placed a large stone with the Carnarvon crest upon it. It had been nine years since Carter had inscribed the simple two entwined letter 'C's under the Earl's coronet, over an Egyptian tomb.

Like the other photographs in this chapter these two, probably taken by Carter or a friend while the entrance of Tutankhamen's tomb was being uncovered, have never before been published. The left-hand picture shows the first sealed doorway of the tomb. The wooden beam and the stone beneath it that Carter removed in order to shine his torch into the passageway beyond may be clearly seen on the right. The two lumps that stick out from the lower left section of the wall are the result of careless plastering during two ancient resealings. Impressions of the sealing stamps used by the necropolis guards may also be seen in the plaster. The filling of the corridor that lay beyond the first sealed wall, photographed from the same position, is shown in the right-hand picture. Several interesting objects were discovered in this filling and the hole dug by the robbers through it can be seen at the top left-hand side of the photograph

Carnarvon arrived in Luxor on 23 November. Carter having previously met him in Cairo had travelled down to Luxor in advance to re-open the doorway of the tomb for Carnarvon's personal inspection. By the following day the staircase was once again revealed and, at the bottom part of the plastered door which Carter had not before uncovered they found a different sealing that bore the cartouche of a king. It was, of course, Tutankhamen's. As well as these cartouches there was evidence on the lower half of the doorway that it had been twice broken through and twice plastered over: a circumstance that would not have surprised Carter or Carnarvon because no royal tombs had ever been found in the pristine condition

that the priests had left them in at the conclusion of the funeral. At least, Carter realized, both of these robber holes had been subsequently sealed and, almost certainly, the tomb had been undisturbed ever since the ancient village had been built over it, probably early in the Nineteenth Dynasty.

In the chippings that had lain over the bottom half of the doorway they found a collection of broken objects that was of considerable interest. Apart from a large quantity of pottery fragments and pieces of other materials such as glass and resin there were several objects that bore the names of different kings. There was, for example, a scarab of Tuthmosis III, who had died centuries before Tutankhamen's day, as well as another of Amenhotep III, who was probably Tutankhamen's grandfather. Most interesting were the inscriptions on fragmentary wooden boxes, one of which described its contents as having once consisted of a silver chain and seal and 'three silver jugs for milk'. This bore the cartouches of Tutankhamen but another inscribed fragment, a piece of a white-painted, badly smashed wooden box, bore the cartouches of Akhenaten and Smenkare, and presumably dated from the brief period of their co-regency during the last two years of Akhenaten's life. The list of contents on this box fragment named garments made of the very finest royal linen, which is of a type still regarded as an extraordinary technical achievement by modern weavers. The box was described in the ancient inscription as 'belonging to the house-of-repelling-the-bowmen', an alternative name for the first pillared hall that traditionally followed the well in the plan of a royal tomb. This is the earliest known text which names this room and, probably this box had been removed from another royal tomb.

These inscribed objects were certainly suggestive more of another royal cache than a grand tomb and obviously bore close similarities to the objects in the tomb of the Amarna Cache, which lay only thirty feet or so from the doorway that they had just uncovered and it was a similarity not only in the date and names of the kings they had found but also of the architecture of the doorway itself. While Callender supervised the construction of a massive grille to take the place of the sealed doorway that they would demolish, Carter and Rex Engelbach, the successor to Weigall as Chief Inspector, examined the discoveries so far. Engelbach was so unimpressed with these that he went off on a tour of inspection, only returning to Thebes some days later. Meanwhile, Carter drew and photographed the doorway with its seal impressions, and then had it taken down.

He now stood at the top of a descending passage nearly filled to its ceiling with dirt and debris. It was just about seven feet square and twenty-eight feet long and took them two days to clear. During the work large quantities of the broken fragments of ancient tomb furniture were found. On the second day of this operation the men uncovered several broken antiquities, one of which proved to be, upon its restoration, a fine Amarna-style painted wooden head of a young king, coming out of a half-open lotus flower, appearing as if it were being reborn. Later in the afternoon, the workmen uncovered a second sealed door which was almost an exact replica of the first and by now Carter was convinced that he had found another cache.

Carter and Carnarvon now took down a small section of the right-hand corner of the second sealed doorway but, in the blackness of the tomb beyond, they could see nothing. Then they inserted an iron rod into the hole, using it as a probe, but this too touched upon nothing. Now they knew that they were beyond the filling of the upper corridors of the tomb and were standing at the entrance to its inner sections. Carter enlarged the small hole in the stone wall and, after testing the air inside for its purity with the flame of his candle, peered again into the tomb. For a moment the rush of the hot ancient air out of the darkness disturbed the light of his candle's flame and his eyes struggled to focus. When he

eventually did see the glitter of the treasures that were laid out just a few feet in front of his candle, he was amazed. Carnarvon, standing close by Carter in the company of his daughter, Lady Evelyn Herbert, could only see his archeologist's back and hear his exclamation. After waiting impatiently for a while he asked Carter if he could see anything in the darkness beyond the doorway. 'Yes,' said Carter, 'Wonderful things'. Later Carter described his first view of the treasure in more detail:

As my eyes grew accustomed to the light, details of the room within emerged slowly from the mist, strange animals, statues, and gold—everywhere the glint of gold.

Carnarvon next allowed his daughter to look through the hole at the treasure and when, at last, it was his turn he too was completely amazed. In the dim light he thought that the room they could see was filled with bars of gold. The vision heralded the end of excavations in the Valley of the Kings and the beginning of the strange story of the clearance of the treasures of Tutankhamen from his tomb.

During the next few months Carter and Carnarvon's lives spun away from scholarship and the esoteric pursuits of connoisseurship into a gross new dimension. Carter's records of his excavations for Carnarvon in the Valley end in mid-sentence:

Nov. 1. 1922 Season 1922–23 begins: Excavations before the tomb of Ramesses VI (ridge L.M. 16) in bedrock flow of water course discovered 4th Nov 1922 Entrance to the tomb of . . .

When most of the other royal tombs of the Valley had first been opened they had set their discoverers pondering as they felt time itself shrink into the darkest corners. Now, by the sheer blaze of its gold, Tutankhamen's tomb turned the Valley into a bedlam, archeology into a commodity for deals, rights and diplomatic coups. It is to Howard Carter's everlasting credit, that he enabled the tomb and its treasures to survive these outrageous pressures. It took ten long seasons of wrangling, recording, packing and shipping to transfer the contents of the tomb to the Cairo Museum. However, at the end of it all, both Carter and the Director of the *Service*, Pierre Lacau, could look back and see that the obligations and responsibilities of both parties had been honoured to the letter and spirit of the simple agreement that had been signed some sixteen years earlier by Maspero and Carnarvon, both then long dead.

24

The Fortunes of Tutankhamen

Carter's initial reaction to the fantastic discovery was 'one of congratulations that my faith in the Valley had not been unjustified'. He loved the Valley and its monuments and in part he saw the tomb as an affirmation of the beauty and significance of the site in which, at the end of his career in Egypt, he had worked over a period of more than thirty years. But the gold glinting in the darkness of the tomb would transform his modest private studies into a public nightmare. The first chamber of the tomb was an overwhelming experience for its visitors. The now famous view of the row of three great gilded bizarre animal couches piled with heaps of objects and packed underneath with furniture, vases, boxes and thrones appeared before Carter's amazed guests as a tangible vision of the almost mythical wealth and beauty of ancient Egypt. When James Breasted first saw the treasures in the antechamber, just a few days after Carter and Carnarvon's initial sally into the tomb, the great egyptologist was moved to tears, as were several of their companions. Words failed them; their first reports on their experiences in the tomb compared its contents to the greatest treasures and works of art of the world's civilizations. In beauty, age and frailty, the ancient court itself was heaped up before them. The ancient courtly objects that the early egyptologists had so much admired in the little paintings had been found in their reality; from stone vases of fantastic shapes and decoration to ostrich feather fans bound on to golden handles—all the tastes of an ancient civilization, the elegant delights that Wilkinson, Maspero and Breasted had so long proclaimed in their writings. It was an egyptological apotheosis and it broke the bounds of their studies and their profession.

After the wall that blocked the end of the descending corridor had been taken down, Carter had a huge heavy iron grille, designed by Callender and made in Cairo, fitted in its place. It would never prove possible to exhibit this treasure-packed room that Carter had named the Antechamber, for the objects were all stacked closely together and spilled almost right across the floor. A careless footstep could topple the pile of treasure heaped as it was pell-mell around the room. Breasted, whom Carter had enlisted to record the hieroglyphic texts in the room a month after the discovery, was forced to stand upon ancient reeds, which had been scattered over the floor, while he studied the seal impressions of a second sealed door which ran off the Antechamber. As he worked, surrounded on all sides by the stacks of ancient objects, he became aware of 'strange rustling, murmuring, whispering sounds which rose and fell and sometimes wholly died away'. These erratic fluttering sounds were caused by the slow physical changes that were taking place in the objects. Taking down the plaster-covered wall to the chamber had broken the hermetic sealing of the tomb. The stable, sterile environment had, after thousands of years of slow physical change and chemical interaction with the atmosphere of the tomb, reached a balance that had been completely tipped up by the intrusion of the archeologists.

All the objects in the tomb were desiccated. The wood, leather, jars of wine and beer, meat, fruits and flowers, all had lost their water to the dry salty limestone of the tomb. In some cases, small amounts of flood water had seeped through cracks in the tomb's walls causing some of the objects touched by it to rot and decay. The profound effects of such isolation over such vast spans of time, more than three millennia, is not readily comprehensible. Many of the materials used by the ancient craftsmen were quite transformed. Carter imagined that 'There must have been periods when, due to condensation, a moist vapour steamed from every article comprising the equipment, and those chambers were like some infernal chemist's shop'. Every object in the tomb was covered with a fine pink film from one such imponderable process. Carter and his helpers were able to remove this by using hot water but, and this was obvious to all those early visitors to the tomb, the problems of conservation were immense and would devour large quantities of time and money. It was work that demanded knowledge, patience, skill and, in no small measure, great courage. The responsi-

One of the great guardian statues standing in the Valley laboratory in the tomb of Seti II. The statue still bears, quite literally, the dust of ages. Years of patient work by Carter's conservationists ensured that these fragile objects would be strong enough to withstand the journey to the Museum at Cairo

bility weighed hard on the shoulders of the archeologists. The treasure, glinting beguilingly in the electric lights at the scholars, represented a tremendous burden. Carter later recounted moving a particularly large and fragile object:

Everything may be going well until suddenly, in the crisis of the process, you hear a crack — little pieces of surface ornament fall. Your nerves are at an almost painful tension. What is happening? All available room in the narrow space is crowded by your men. What action is needed to avert a catastrophe?

Such reactions can only be engendered in those who are sensitive to the beauty and quality of the objects they are handling and it is exactly such people, with this level of near-painful sensitivity to the work who should properly handle such objects. It is a task of truly tremendous strain—one that Carter endured for ten long seasons at the tomb.

Confronted by this veritable jackpot of treasure the archeologists took time to gather their wits. Carter and Carnarvon tried to photograph the chamber as it stood, but the results obtained with their magnesium flash equipment, which as well as being somewhat erratic also created a fire risk, were not a success. It was now obvious to Carter that the Antechamber should be emptied of its treasure with all reasonable speed for, as it lay, it was extremely vulnerable and the pressure to admit more and more visitors must inevitably result in damage. A week after their first glimpse of the Antechamber Carnarvon organized a discreet 'public opening' of the room. The guests included Lord Allenby, then Gorst's successor and High Commissioner in Egypt, a handful of local officials and a single reporter from *The Times* of London. By the end of November that paper's scoop had become world-wide news and Carter was inundated with requests to see the tomb.

Carnarvon decided to hold a ceremonial opening of the sealed doorway in the Antechamber after Carter had emptied the chamber of its antiquities and he fixed a date in the middle of the following February. The two men travelled back to Cairo together; Carnarvon to go on to London while Carter bought equipment for the work ahead. On the advice of Lucas, whom he met in Cairo, Carter purchased large quantities of conservationists' chemicals and equipment, enormous amounts of packing materials and even a motor car to run upon the west bank at Thebes. However, before he could even begin to clear the Antechamber, Carter also needed a skilled photographer to work in the tomb. Doubtless upon the advice of Winlock, he cabled officials of the Metropolitan Museum who were then in London, asking for the loan of Harry Burton who was working with Winlock and Lansing at the Museum's excavations around Deir el Bahari. Burton was immediately released and his pictures were the first of a nine-year association with Carter working in the tomb. They are a marvellous legacy in themselves as well as fine records of the discovery.

Many of the eminent egyptologists of that day were interviewed about the sensational find. In London, Flinders Petrie offered the view that Carter's skills would ensure the preservation of the objects from the tomb and Sir E. A. Wallis Budge, Curator of the British Museum Egyptian collections, observed that Carnarvon had dug for many years and should be entitled to a division of the objects. Budge could perhaps see a glint of Tutankhamen's gold in the British Museum. While in London, Carnarvon gave a public lecture about the tomb and reported the discovery in an audience with the King. Despite worldwide interest in the excavation, Carnarvon was now in something of a quandary. It was obvious that the clearance of the tomb would be an extremely slow and costly affair but if the task was handed over to the *Service* he would surrender his rights to any of the objects and have to rely, as Davis had done before him, upon the generosity of the Director of the *Service*. But Lacau was certainly no Maspero. He had often openly stated his dislike of the British and American system of privately sponsored excavations that continued only by obtaining large portions of the previous season's discoveries. Indeed, there had been extreme concern about his attitudes in the Anglo-American archeological community even before the discovery of Tutankhamen's tomb, and the irascible Flinders Petrie had organized a meeting in Cairo in which he had tried to gather together all the excavators concerned in an attempt to foil new regulations that would effectively stop this traditional system of archeological finance. Carnarvon wanted and expected to obtain a share of the antiquities from Tutankhamen's tomb but it was obvious that he could only uphold his claim by maintaining control of the work in the Valley. To offset the high expense of clearing the tomb and restoring the objects he asked the Metropolitan Museum for the continuing loan of Burton whose photographs, Carter had telegraphed, were a great success. In return Carnarvon offered the Metropolitan Museum a share of his portion of the objects from the tomb. The Museum officials were so delighted at this proposal that they offered not only Burton but three more of their archeological staff, two draughtsmen and Arthur Mace, a nephew of Flinders Petrie and a fine archeologist of great experience.

Carter, meanwhile, was gathering around him the best people that he knew for the work ahead. Lucas, on final leave before retiring from government service in Egypt, had already offered his services and, as the greatest living authority on ancient Egyptian artefacts, he was the best choice. With the philologists Breasted and Gardiner, the latter an old friend of Carter's, and Burton the photographer, Carter had

picked the world's best to serve the tomb. Mace, the same age as Carter, was another enormous asset to the team, quietly organizing the restoration and packing of objects and never crossing swords with Carter though he was an experienced director of excavations in his own right.

Carnarvon returned to the Valley in late January 1923 and found this team of workers barely managing to cope with the stream of antiquities that Carter was lifting, one by one, from the Antechamber. They had taken over the tomb of Seti II, at the end of the Valley and easily guarded, as a laboratory and store. Burton was using the empty tomb of the Amarna Cache as his darkroom. The old storeroom in the tomb of Ramesses XI was now serving only as a dining room and the fragments of the plaster doors covered with seal impressions and the antiquities that had been found in the filling of the staircase and corridors, were taken to the rear of the tomb behind the dining area. As fresh objects were taken out from the tomb and carried in trays up to the laboratory the large crowds in the Valley would applaud and take photographs. It was a grand spectacle for the tourists and the journalists; the Valley now resembled a fairground. While he had been in England, Carnarvon had signed an exclusive agreement with *The Times* to report the progress of the clearance of the tomb and this had quickly excited the rest of the media to eloquent anger. Subsequently, a hard eye was fixed upon Carnarvon, Carter and his colleagues.

For the grand opening of the sealed wall in the Antechamber on 17 February 1923 both Carnarvon and Carter maintained the polite fiction that no one had yet seen beyond it. In fact, this sealed doorway, like that of the small annex that also lay off the Antechamber, had been penetrated anciently by robbers who had made small holes at the bottom of the wall. Several members of the team working in the tomb knew that, as Lucas later confirmed, Carter and Carnarvon had crawled through this break in the wall and seen some of the contents of the rooms that lay beyond, shortly after they had opened the tomb.

The entrance to Tutankhamen's tomb photographed within a year of its discovery before the Valley floor was remodelled to accommodate the huge influx of visitors. The tomb is at the foot of the entrance to the tomb of Ramesses VI which, like the other large Ramesside tombs, had its doorway situated three to four metres above the Valley floor and the buried Eighteenth Dynasty tombs. The excavations of November 1922, seen here, were a direct continuation of the work at site D during late January 1920 (see p. 249)

However, Carter's account of the proceedings, that the official opening of the next rooms of the tomb was the first modern view of the treasures beyond the sealed wall, was the etiquette for all such events in the Valley and has subsequently misled many people. It was hardly likely, however, that Carnarvon would have invited both the King of Egypt and the British High Commissioner to an event in the remote Valley of the Kings with no known outcome—an archeological pig in a poke. After all, a similarly placed chamber in the almost identical tomb of the Amarna Cache had contained but four vases and a stick of wood.

When Breasted had first been told of the contents of the Antechamber by Carter shortly after the discovery, he had supposed, as Carter himself had done while he had supervised the clearing of the steps and corridor, that he had found another cache of miscellaneous objects, albeit a richer haul than that in the tomb of the Amarna Cache. Carter, who knew more about the design and contents of royal tombs than anyone else of his time, must have realized the instant he first saw the Antechamber, that the room was unique, certainly not of the orthodox royal tomb design and that the objects stacked in it were not placed as they would have been in an orthodox royal burial. Without a preliminary investigation of the other parts of the tomb he could not possibly have known what, if anything, lay beyond the Antechamber. Carnarvon's delighted comments as he entered the tomb for the ceremony of the official opening of the inner chambers of the tomb, 'We are going to have a concert, Carter's going to sing a song', and Carter's confident archeological performance as he took down the sealed wall in the presence of the assembled high dignitaries of Egypt, could never have occurred without some previous knowledge of the rooms that lay beyond and certainly no such gathering would have been organized if this had not already been tacitly understood by all those present. If the forty notables and archeologists had been disappointed at the ceremony Carnarvon would have been a laughing stock; Davis' embarrassing experience as the host of Sir Eldon Gorst repeated with a world-wide audience!

But, of course, Carnarvon's guests were not disappointed and the four-hour ordeal in the hot tomb was very moving. Slowly, as Carter and Carnarvon took down the stone wall, an extraordinary golden panel, inlaid with the finest of blue faiences, came into view. It was a part of the shrines that enclosed the sarcophagus of the king. Years before, while working

When Carter dismantled the stone wall that had been built between the burial chamber and the Antechamber—this being essential to remove the panels of the shrines—he had to cut this figure of the goddess Isis because it was painted on the back of the stone wall, from the south wall of the burial chamber. It formed part of a larger painting, the rest of which is still in the burial chamber, that showed Tutankhamen with two other gods. The painting is in the unusual style employed in both Tutankhamen's and Ay's burial chambers. It has been suggested that its curiously squat proportions are the result of the artists not being able to stand more than one or two feet away from their work because of the great golden shrines that filled the burial chamber. As is typical in the Eighteenth Dynasty royal tombs, these paintings were made during Tutankhamen's burial ceremonies

with Gardiner, Carter had seen an ancient plan drawn upon a papyrus of a similar set of shrines within the tomb of Ramesses IV. He knew that there would be smaller shrines inside this large one, each one standing inside the other. Beyond this shrine-filled burial chamber was a small open room that Carter named the Treasury. In it were many of the objects that in the orthodox royal tomb plan would have been placed in the burial chamber around the shrines which enclosed the sarcophagus. Here they were all packed tightly into a small room, crowded in with many other objects and, once again, the sprawling mass of fragile antiquities was quite unsuitable for exhibition to large numbers of visitors.

Carter and his team had finished clearing the Antechamber just two days before it was filled with guests for the ceremony of the opening of the burial chamber. Such a pressured timetable was very unfortunate; ancient objects can hardly be preserved to short order and Carter was under severe strain. The official opening had been followed by the visits of more dignitaries and nobility to the tomb, the long desert road to the Valley was now lined with dress regiments of the Egyptian Army standing daily at attention as the processions of notables continued. It was obvious that the treasures would not withstand even the visits of the elect in such large numbers indefinitely and it was fortunate that, nine days after the dismantling of the sealed door, the entire tomb was shut down for the summer. The great iron grille to the Antechamber was closed, locked and chained and the entrance corridors refilled with excavation debris. Work continued in the laboratory upon the conservation of dozens of small objects; necklaces, elaborate bejewelled robes and costumes, that had been packed into the numerous boxes that had lain in the Antechamber.

Carnarvon left for Cairo to negotiate with Lacau about the division of objects. It had been most carefully established by the egyptologists that the tomb had been anciently entered and robbed. Indeed, there was still evidence of this in the tomb itself and Lacau was necessarily conciliatory. Carnarvon, after all, had the world's ear at this time and both the Court of Egypt and Allenby were his friends and had been guests at the tomb. Lacau was now faced with the prospect of having the richest treasure ever found being cleared by agents of the two biggest collectors of Egyptian antiquities in the world: The Metropolitan Museum and Lord Carnarvon. The archeologists were among the best available for the work, but Lacau knew that a high toll would be exacted for their services and such a division of antiquities would seriously imperil his attempt to enforce his new policies. Moreover, it was becoming increasingly apparent that the British and American excavators had joined forces not only to clear the tomb of Tutankhamen, but to use the growing celebrity of the monument as a major aspect of their campaign to prevent the changing of expedition regulations upon which both their work and careers in Egypt depended.

Placed in a vulnerable position Lacau was unexpectedly rescued from yet further prevarication by the physical collapse of Carnarvon, who already in a weak condition, aggravated no doubt by the excitements of the last months, had come down with blood poisoning from an infected mosquito bite. Slowly and at the despair of his family, who joined him in Cairo, he died. Carnarvon's body was shipped back to England and during May he was buried in the park at Highclere in which, planted by his ancestors, there grew a grove of cedars brought back from the Middle East more than one hundred and fifty years earlier by Bishop Pococke. The funeral, a simple private ceremony, was disturbed by a small aeroplane carrying a photographer from the *Daily Express*. Carnarvon was, Beaverbrook said, 'hot news'.

When Carter arrived in Cairo to begin the next winter's work at the tomb he first re-applied for the concession to work in the Valley naming the Dowager Lady Carnarvon, the inheritor of Carnarvon's personal estate, as the excavator. Carter now bore the responsibility of the business affairs of the expedition as well as the work in the tomb; the communications with the press; the problems of the division of the objects; ever pressing matters of visits of official parties; and much much more. Unfortunately, Carter, a professional archeologist, had inherited the actions of a lord and he suffered for it. Carnarvon had dealt with Lacau and the *Service* high-handedly; he had easy access to their superiors and, doubtless, he would have complained loudly had Lacau obstructed the work on the tomb or attempted to take all its contents for the Cairo Museum. Carter alone, however, was highly vulnerable to the officers of the *Service*, who immediately began to assert their positions. On his return to Luxor, Carter discovered that the lighting arrangements for the tomb, promised by the *Service*, were not in place. Further, the *Service* now insisted upon issuing its own bulletin of the daily progress of the work in the tomb, thus undermining Carnarvon's exclusive contract with *The Times* that had so outraged public opinion in Egypt. The Nationalist Party holding office in the Egyptian Government had been deeply disturbed and insulted at the publicity that had attended the first stages of the clearing of the tomb. True, Carnarvon had consulted the Egyptian Court Chamberlain on the constituents of the guest list for the opening of the sealed wall of the burial chamber, but the whole process had been handled and controlled by Englishmen, the un-

A sequence of photographs by Harry Burton showing Carter and Mace on a plank above the shrines high up in the burial chamber rolling and packing the fabric of the fragile funerary canopy for shipment to Cairo

crowned rulers of Egypt. Carter's attitude, typical of his day, was unsympathetic, colonialist, and he greatly underestimated the importance of the issue. Although Egyptian public opinion was content to allow Carter and his foreigners to work in the tomb, the Egyptian press, which had been especially angered at Carnarvon's agreement with *The Times*, considered that the archeologists should properly display the attitude of people who were guests of the Egyptian nation, acknowledging that Tutankhamen had been a ruler of ancient Egypt. Lacau harnessed the political expression of this indignation to further his own plans for the treasure and Carter, intransigent and concerned more with other matters, did not appreciate this powerful alliance that now stood against his work in the tomb.

For the second season, 1923–24, Carter planned to work in the burial chamber, first clearing the objects between the golden shrines, then dismantling the shrines themselves. This was to become the most difficult and suspenseful operation of the entire clearance. The enormous outer shrine, for example, is some sixteen feet long and nearly nine feet high. It is made of wood and covered with gold foil and several hundred plates of blue faience. The shrine was built, like that of Queen Tiy's in the Amarna Cache, of separate panels, each of enormous weight. The panels of this outermost shrine fitted closely into the little burial chamber which had obviously been specially cut to accommodate the shrine. There was very little room for manoeuvre. The wood of the shrines had desiccated and, under the gold and faience was perhaps partly rotten. There was no way of knowing if these huge panels could stand their own weight while they were being moved from the chamber. Each panel, and there were twelve of them as well as the eight doors of the shrines, had to be dismantled and lifted up the yard-high step from the burial chamber to the Antechamber, then out of the tomb and into the laboratory. Each shrine also had elaborate roofs of similar materials. Between two of the shrines there hung a thin funerary canopy, already slightly damaged by the weight of numerous bronze rosettes that had dropped off the fine material and fallen onto the floor. In the heat of the tomb, despite the skilful help of the imperturbable Callender and the dexterous village workmen, it must have been a nightmare, a continuous tightrope of small decisions, double checks and finger crossing. At any moment, as they were swung out of position, the panels could have bent, crumpled and collapsed on to each other, rendering them all into heaps of glittering stucco and faience and wood fragments. Working with simple ropes and pulleys, wooden scaffolding and cotton packing, the men performed prodigious feats of conservation and, happily, the wood proved to be still strong enough to take all the strains that were asked of it.

While he worked at dismantling these great shrines, each held together with wedges and bronze tenons, Carter was also keeping an archeological record. He noted how the shrines had been erected, the marks of the ancient carpenters, the positions of the sealings, the knots on the ancient cord, a pile of wood shavings, all with a careful eye. On 12 February 1924, after removing the last of the four shrines from the burial chamber, Carter and his workmen lifted the lid off the sarcophagus that had nestled in the centre of the shrines. Weighing about two tons, this had been anciently broken across its centre. For the first time in three thousand years, albeit wrapped in black funerary shrouds and garlanded with ancient dried wreaths, the exterior coffin of the king was exposed to view. The little group of guests that had been invited to witness this moment, about twenty in all, were greatly moved by the experience. The next day Carter showed the coffin to a party of the press despite the vexatious problem of *The Times* exclusive contract, which continued to anger the rest of the press and other media. After this tour Carter planned to escort the wives of his team of helpers around the burial chamber and then adjourn to a Luxor hotel for a grand celebratory dinner. Certainly they all needed a diversion after the strains of the last months.

But the request to the Minister of Public Works to admit the wives of the expedition was not granted and for Carter this was the final petty straw that broke the camel's back. He closed down the tomb. Throughout the course of the season Lacau and his subordinates had so bound Carter with red tape that, inevitably, he finally tripped and fell. Carter had spent a third of the season so far on trips to Cairo, meeting Lacau and other officials. Abrupt and unyielding in his dealings at the best of times, he obviously had other concerns uppermost in his mind than ploys for coping with a hostile bureaucracy. Earlier in the season, already concerned at the effect that Lacau's campaign was having upon Carter's work at the tomb, four of the most eminent egyptologists, among them Gardiner and Breasted who were intermittently working in the tomb, had written Lacau a stern public letter strongly criticizing his personal handling of the affair. For at least one of the signatories of that letter, an official of the Metro-politan Museum, the letter also represented a further step in a general campaign to discredit Lacau, for other efforts were being made to have the French authorities remove or control him. It could hardly have endeared Carter to the embattled Frenchman who was also under increasing pressure from his Minister to control further the actions of the foreign archeologists. Now, Lacau had also to suffer the embarrassment of Carter's public expressions of anger and frustration as he vented it upon the officials who had so goaded him.

Carter had spent his adult life in Egypt and had lived at Thebes longer than anywhere else and although he was long used to the wily dealings of the villagers and the petty politics of archeology, he had little experience of diplomatic negotiation. It was typical that his impulse to publicly shame the *Service* and the Minister should have taken the form of a notice, which he dramatically pinned to the notice board of the Winter Palace Hotel at Luxor. The fine old hotel had long been the centre of Carter's social world, where he had planned to hold his celebratory dinner and where, in the past, matters of business had been settled over drinks on the terrace or dinner in the spacious dining room. His notice, which told of the withdrawal of his associates and the closing down of the tomb due, he claimed, to the restrictions and discourtesies imposed upon them by the authorities, was a violent blustering step well beyond the bounds of conduct that Lacau had imagined his continuous harassment would produce. Its effect was disastrous and the fact that the wording of the notice had been agreed by most of the members of Carter's team clearly shows the strains to which they had all been subjected. The pressures of the excavation were suddenly catapulted into the international news by Carter's action, and the media, already affronted by Carnarvon's exclusive agreement with *The Times*, were pleased to show him as a quick-tempered and imperious man. Foolishly, Carter had withdrawn from the tomb on an insignificant domestic issue and the whole problem of excavators' rights in Egypt, the real root of the problem was never mooted. Carter, who was only peripherally concerned with this issue, was seen as a fool.

Nine days later, with the express agreement of the government, Lacau broke into the tomb and released the sarcophagus lid which, almost symbolically, Carter had left suspended over the coffins held by pulleys and ropes. Carter who arrived later in the Valley was turned away from the tomb by government guards. Lacau now let thousands of visitors through the tomb and Carter, in desperation, appealed to the Prime Minister of Egypt to be allowed to return to work, but he was met by a dignified and cogently worded refusal. The Prime Minister, Saad Zaghlul, who was dedicated to an independent Egypt, had himself visited the tomb after Lacau had reopened it and his trip from Cairo had turned into another powerful demonstration of the high nationalist sentiments that were sweeping through the country. The following month Carter and Lady Carnarvon instituted legal proceedings against the Ministry in the Mixed Court at Cairo—the deeply distrusted relic of Ottoman domination which, with its foreign judges, symbolized outside interference in the affairs of Egypt. Carter could never really appreciate that matters other than the successful clearance of the tomb were involved in the dispute, matters which to other people were as important, even more important, than the treasure itself. Almost at the point of settlement, an insulting remark by the British legal counsel so angered the Minister that, once again, the situation was deadlocked. Carter, beaten and close to a breakdown, left Egypt not knowing whether he would ever be able to work there again.

Nobody enjoyed this situation. Lacau lacked both funds and the experienced staff to undertake the tomb clearance for the *Service*, and no other archeologist would take the task from Carter who, it was universally recognized, was a master of such difficult work and should be allowed to continue. At one bitter point in the continuing debate even Lacau came forward to defend Carter's reputation: it was obvious that eventually he would be allowed to return to his work in the tomb.

During this time Carter embarked on a tour of America, lecturing about the tomb and its contents. Privately he reviewed the events of the last years. Among other things, Carter saw that the tomb had been made into the spearhead of the campaign to discredit Lacau and his new policies concerning antiquities, and he and his team had become a gilded stick with which to beat the Frenchman. Even as he toured America the debates concerning these wider issues continued. Carter, unused to the subtleties of such diplomacies, quarrelled badly with his friends at the Metropolitan Museum.

On his return to England, and in agreement with Lady Carnarvon, Carter drafted a letter to Lacau renouncing all rights to the antiquities of the tomb. Carter now wanted above all to return to his work in the Valley and, following his successful lecture tour and the publication of a popular book on the

tomb, he was in a position to be freed from personally defending the contentious position of the Carnarvon estate which could independently pursue its claims to a share of the treasure. Under these circumstances it seemed likely that Carter would soon be working again in the tomb and in fresh negotiations in Cairo it was even proposed by the Minister that some duplicate pieces from the tomb would be presented to the excavators upon completion of the work.

With the Nationalist Government of Saad Zaghlul bullied from power following the assassination of the British Commander of the Egyptian Army, Carter's progress to the tomb was speeded, for the first time, by the co-operation of British Government officials in Cairo. At a meeting presided over by the new pro-British Prime Minister all the problems concerning the tomb were quickly resolved to the satisfaction of both Carter and the *Service*. Then, right at the end of the meeting, Lacau craftily insisted on the retention of every object from the tomb, for he knew that Carter, who could see himself working again after all the disputes and delays, would finally agree, which somewhat grudgingly, he did. A few days later, Carter was handed a set of the new keys to the tomb by Lacau who expressed his personal pleasure at his return to the work, and soon Carter headed for Luxor for a short season's work, packing objects for delivery to the Museum in Cairo. While on an earlier visit to the Museum, Carter had seen, to his dismay, the results of the hasty transference and assemblage of some of the objects from the tomb that had been removed by the officers of the *Service*. Chariots taken from the tomb had been wrongly remounted and the linen pall that had hung over the sarcophagus was completely destroyed. Obviously, Carter was desperately needed at the tomb. However, the battle with Lacau also resulted in a great victory for archeology: never again would excavations in Egypt be conducted with the aims and principles of a treasure hunt and always, in future, a ministry of the Egyptian Government would exercise ultimate control of the work.

The first season's work, which continued the clearance of the tomb, started in October of the same year, 1925, when Carter, now fifty-one, tackled the problems of raising the coffins out of the sarcophagus. With a few exceptions the same group was once again assembled for the work in the tomb and the laboratory. After the shut-down during the 1923–4 season, Arthur Mace, who had suffered from tuberculosis for some years, fell very ill and was never able to work in Egypt again. He had been a good friend to Carter and there is strong evidence that it was he who wrote the better part of the first volume of the popular book upon the tomb. Following the withdrawal of rights to objects from the tomb by Carter and Lady Carnarvon, the Metropolitan Museum was now represented at the tomb by Harry Burton only, whose magnificent photographs continued to record the work and the objects for the next five seasons. Breasted and Gardiner returned to transcribe and copy the inscriptions in the tomb and Callender and Lucas were once again full-time members of Carter's team. Newberry, too, Carter's oldest friend in Egypt who, some thirty-four years earlier had started him upon his career in egyptology, also lent a hand. Generally the work in the tomb now proceeded quietly and efficiently though the immense problems of conservation still kept the group on edge.

By common consent, the crushing pressures imposed by schedules of public 'openings' were not continued and the work was able to proceed at a steady pace. With Mace no longer in the laboratory, Carter spent more time on secondary conservation procedures, all the time maintaining his card indexes which listed each object, giving its dimensions, materials and a description with notes on the conservation treatments it had undergone—such as spraying with wax or celluloids or other more extreme measures. The coffins, which were the first objects to be removed from the tomb following Carter's return to the work, posed further extraordinary problems. When the granite of the sarcophagus lid had first been removed, and the black pall that covered the coffin rolled back, the great outer gilded coffin of the king had been revealed. This fitted tightly in the huge stone sarcophagus, which was a florid Amarnan design, somewhat resembling Horemheb's. Carter now decided to remove the lid of the coffin, leaving the rest of it and its contents still in position. First they extracted the ten silver plates from the lid which fixed it to its bottom. Then, by means of the handles on the lid with which the coffin had been lowered into the sarcophagus some three thousand years before, they attached fresh ropes to the lid. A complex system of pulleys had been set up on a scaffold over the sarcophagus and slowly the lid was raised, absolutely vertically, so that it would not scrape against the adjacent sides of the sarcophagus. When they had swung the lid away they found another shrouded coffin inside, wreathed in olive and willow leaves, lotuses and cornflowers. The gold hand of the image of the king on the coffin lid gleamed freshly through the centre of the black linen. Like the outer coffin, this too was a lavish affair of gilded wood, certainly the finest example of its type that had been preserved with a magnificent portrait of the king, in polished gold foil at its head.

With the large lid of the outer coffin removed it was now possible to obtain access to the sides of the outer coffin and Carter and his men were able to lift out the coffins from the sarcophagus and rest them on a platform of boards that had been placed across its rim. The silken-smooth operation of the complex pulley system, which had lifted accurately the enormous weight of the three coffins was due to the fact that Carter and Callender had spent a considerable time during the summer months designing a suitable system specifically for use in the tomb.

This second coffin, the lid of which was now revealed, nestled inside the outer one, was weak and in a bad condition. So precisely did it fit into the bottom of the outer coffin that nothing could be pushed down between them to enable them to be lifted and separated. It took Carter two days to work out the next stage of the operation. Unlike the outer coffin, the second coffin lid did not have handles but the silver pins that held it to its bottom could be pulled out halfway and copper wire was bound around them and attached to the scaffold above. Metal eyelets were screwed into the edge of the bottom of the outer coffin, and slowly, very slowly, after taking away the boards that had supported the coffin on the top of the sarcophagus, the outer coffin was lowered into it, leaving the second coffin disengaged and hanging by the copper wires and the ancient silver pins in mid air. Then, quickly, the boards were slipped back underneath the coffin across the rim of the sarcophagus. It was a difficult and delicate task, for the coffins, though fragile, were extraordinarily heavy—a combination that made control very difficult. The second coffin, now completely revealed, was beautifully decorated in thick bright gold foil and inlays, but it was an ungainly shape, being some seven feet long and nearly three feet deep. Once again, Carter looked carefully at the joint for a way in.

The silver nails were now completely extracted and more eyelets were screwed into strong parts of the lid that would be recovered with the gold foil when the operation was over. The coffin lid was then lifted from its bottom. Carter now found another black shroud which, after Burton's photography and careful measuring and note taking, was rolled off to reveal another smaller coffin. Then suddenly, they realized that this third coffin, which was over six

The bottom of Tutankhamen's outer coffin with the second coffin still nestling inside it supported by planks of wood lying on top of the sarcophagus. In the next operation the coffins were raised to allow the removal of the planks beneath; then the bottom of the outer coffin was lowered into the sarcophagus leaving the second coffin suspended. The thin wires that were attached to the silver nails of the second coffin and held it in place during this delicate manœuvre are clearly visible

feet long and, they later discovered, about an inch thick, was made of solid gold. It was this unimaginable circumstance that had accounted for the extraordinary weight of the combined coffins as they had been gingerly separated. Once again, the fairytale tomb had defied all the archeologists' imaginings.

An examination showed that the third gold coffin and the bottom of the second coffin that held it were stuck together in a gluey embrace of dried oils and resins, which had been poured lavishly over the burial by the priests and had set in a solid mass. Carter next decided to lift the lid of the gold coffin which, like the outermost coffin, was provided with handles. Notching the end of a screwdriver so that it would fasten on the shaft of the golden nails which held the tenons that connected the lid to its bottom, the nails were eased out into the narrow gap between the two coffins and, by cutting each of them into several small pieces, they were entirely removed. While Lucas worked in the laboratory making chemical analyses of the glassy black residue of the ceremonial unguents, which glued the bodies of the coffins together in an attempt to discover a solvent for the dried oils, Carter raised the lid of the gold coffin. Finally, he had exposed the mummy of the king, all wrapped in bandages studded with golden amulets and wearing the golden mask that has now been seen by millions of people all over the world. Now Carter discovered that the dried oils and unguents had cemented both the mummy and its mask to the inside of the golden coffin as the second outer coffin in its turn was cemented to the inner golden coffin. Carter decided to take the coffins and the mummy, still glued together, to the laboratory in the tomb of Seti II. This task required a gang of ten men.

Lucas had found that the black glue in the coffins could be softened only by heating and so the coffins and the royal mummy were exposed in the sun of the Valley for several hours in an attempt to separate them. There in the heat of midday, the king endured a temperature of 149°F, but still his two coffins would not be parted. Far higher temperatures were required and it was now apparent that the royal mummy

Carter at the moment of rolling back the black shroud that covered the third coffin

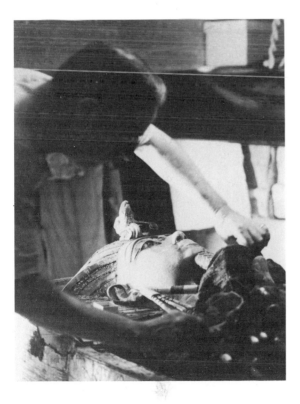

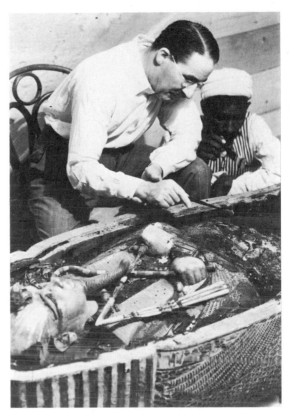

Carter carefully tapping the lid of the golden coffin with a small hammer to remove the heavy layer of resins. The gold coffin is still inside the second coffin

would have to be unwrapped and examined as it lay in its gold coffin, and that it could not be removed in one simple bundle like the other royal mummies. Lacau and several government dignitaries were informed that the mummy, now exposed, was about to be unwrapped and its jewellery removed, and so they all came to the Valley. Dr Douglas Derry, Elliot Smith's successor as Professor of Anatomy at Cairo University and Dr Salah Bey Hammdi were to perform the unwrapping and examination of the mummy, with Carter supervising the removal of the body jewellery, and the amulets that were expected to be discovered lying in the wrappings and on the mummy.

The mummy, still stuck inside its two coffins, now lay in the first corridor of the tomb of Seti II. While Burton was taking photographs of the assembly of dignitaries, and the coffins covered with white sheets, which left the mummy exposed like a patient on an operating table, the examination started. As they cut slowly down through the layers of the mummy wrappings, which they had first strengthened with

269

paraffin wax because the precious oils had almost completely carbonized them, hundreds of pieces of magnificent jewellery and amulets were uncovered. Ironically the body of Tutankhamen, the only king ever found undisturbed in his own tomb, proved to be in a worse condition than the robbed kings in the royal caches. Carter estimated that two bucketfuls of oils had been poured into the coffins, and the inner gold coffin had acted as an efficient seal preventing all but the slowest processes of drying. The gold mask that covered not only the head of the king but the upper parts of his chest was also stuck fast.

The body, in bad condition and already virtually separated in several pieces, was lifted, fragment by fragment, from the coffin. The doctors thought that the king had been about nineteen or twenty when

Tutankhamen's chest, having been cut from the lower part of his trunk, lies on a sheet of paper placed in the coffin. The broad collar and the amulets on golden wires had been placed around the king's neck. His head, hands and forearms have all been removed

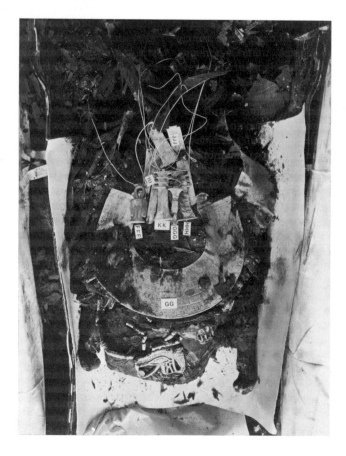

he died. The bandages that covered the face were removed by gentle movements of a sable hair brush which caused them to crumble into dust. The head, its fatty tissue entirely dissolved by the processes of mummification, had been transformed into that of a nervous thin-faced toothy young man with a flesh wound on his left cheek. To extract the torso and head from the golden coffin, Derry and Saleh Bey had to use heated knives to prise up pieces of the body from the black gluey mass.

Two pieces of iron were found on the mummy: a small amulet in the shape of a head rest, which had been placed under the neck of the king, and a superb dagger of pure iron encased in a gold sheath and mounted with a handle of gold and a pommel of rock crystal. Apart from a few small rust spots in the blade, the iron still gleamed brightly. The dagger remains one of the earliest examples of ironwork known in ancient Egypt and, in a country without the technology to produce or work this new hard metal, it was probably imported from western Asia, then the centre of the technological revolution that was taking place. The sad shrivelled remnants of the young king's arms, which lay, bent at the elbows, across his lower chest, were encased in lavish jewellery of gold, glittering glazes and polished stones. His fingers too, were covered in rings, more of which were found scattered through the mummy wrappings. His neck was hung with a variety of pendants—huge pectoral collars of gold and inlaid stones—overlaid one on another on the royal chest. The jewellery taken from the mummy defies the imagination, equalling if not surpassing the treasure chests of Solomon in the tales of Rider Haggard.

With the mummy removed from his coffin, Carter and Lucas were again faced with the problem of separating the two coffin bodies and the gold mask. They lined the gold coffin with sheets of zinc and stood the two coffins and the mask upside down on two trestles. The outer coffin was covered over with wet blankets, as was the face of the gold mask. Three primus stoves burning at full blast were set underneath the gold coffin. It took three hours before a movement was discernible, then the coffins slowly began to fall apart. Gingerly they lifted the body of the second coffin, leaving the gold coffin covered in a 'dripping mass of viscous pitch-like material' on the trestles. The golden mask was also freed but unfortunately some of the faience strips from the back had become detached and these now had to be carefully prized from the loosened oils in the gold coffin and stuck back into their positions on the

Carter escorting King Fuad and a party of government officials to the tomb

mask. Even acetone proved to be insufficient to remove this gluey mess from the gold and the back of the mask; the inside of the coffin was subsequently cleaned with a plumber's blow-lamp and constant wiping with a cloth. After more than two months of work Carter finally delivered the two inner coffins, the mask and the mummy's jewellery to Lacau in the Cairo Museum. It had been a triumph of conserva tion. During the rest of the season the team worked in the laboratory on the small objects that had earlier been removed from the burial chamber. There were, Carter reported, nearly thirteen thousand visitors to the tomb at this time.

During the following two seasons in the Valley, Carter cleared the small room that lay behind the burial chamber—the Treasury. Since the very first days after the discovery it was obvious that the little tomb was not of the royal tomb plan but simply a group of four chambers expediently designed to store the royal burial and the copious grave goods that normally would have been laid throughout the rooms and corridors of an orthodox royal tomb. Of all the rooms in the tomb, the Treasury, however, seemed to hold groups of objects that partly reflected the normal arrangements of an orthodox royal burial. The room was dominated by a tall square shrine of gilded wood, guarded by statues of golden goddesses, each marvellously sculpted in the purist Amarnan style. The shrine was topped with a cornice of royal cobras which decoratively guarded its contents—the canopic chest of the king. Similar in style to the chests that had been found by Loret and Davis, all smashed to pieces in the other royal tombs, Tutankhamen's was also made of white alabaster and decorated with

hieroglyphic texts and with a goddess on each of its corners. It was perfect, carefully sealed and draped with a fine black linen pall just as the ancient priests had left it. Each one of the royal tombs must once have contained such gilded shrines, the sad frag ments of the alabaster boxes being the only surviving remnants of the elaborate shrines, which had all been smashed up and taken from the tombs. These tall, architectural structures must have provided a major element of the groups of funerary goods that were placed in the burial chamber. In the orthodox royal tombs, as in the tomb of Tutankhamen, these shrines would have been placed at the foot-end of the royal sarcophagus.

After the golden canopy which enclosed the cano pic chest had been disassembled, the alabaster box was left standing alone upon the black resin-covered cedarwood sledge on which it had been carried in the funeral procession to the tomb. When Carter cut the ancient seals and removed the shrine-shaped ala baster lid of the chest, he revealed four alabaster heads of the king, which were facing each other in pairs, nose to nose. They were the elaborate sculp tural lids that, as in the other royal canopic chests, covered the rectangular compartments of the centre of the box which, Carter now discovered, held four exquisite miniature coffins, each of solid gold inlaid with faience, polished agates and carnelians. Origin ally they had been inscribed with the name of Tutan khamen's predecessor, the young king Smenkare. Inside these little coffins were some of the embalmed organs of the dead king removed during the mummi fication. Carter had already discovered several other objects made for the burial of Smenkare in the tomb including some of the most intimate mummy wrap pings and jewellery. It has even been suggested that the great gold mask that fitted over the royal mummy was originally made for Smenkare and that the car touches engraved upon it were altered to those of Tutankhamen.

By the sides of the canopic shrine were statues of the gods and the king, grouped in black resin-painted shrines that were stacked along the walls. These differed in both pose and size from the two guardian statues that Carter had found standing in the Ante-chamber. The enshrined figures, more than thirty in all, formed a most remarkable group of statuary. Mainly gilded with a fine bright yellow foil, sparsely decorated and inlaid with copper and the finest blue faiences, each separate figure could hold a central place in the finest of the world's collections of ancient Egyptian art. These figures in their shrines were a unique intact set of the statues of which many frag-ments had previously been recovered from the other, robbed royal tombs. Salt's first collection, which he sold to the British Museum, and which was partly gathered by Belzoni, from the tombs in the Valley, contains many such figures. In an orthodox royal tomb these figures would have been placed, each boxed in their black shrines, around the enshrined sarcophagus and the canopic chest of the king. The royal tomb was truly, as the *Amduat* proclaims, the 'place where the gods stand' and the figures, after the ritual of the Opening of the Mouth, were the gods themselves. The dead king was left, literally, in their presence.

Other enshrined statues represented the king and showed him in traditional ritual hunting postures as he combated the evil forces that challenged his nightly progress through the Underworld. In the other royal tombs most of the statues' shrines have disappeared and some of the statue fragments are of different poses and show different aspects of the dead king's journey, but still the underlying principle was the same: to know the gods, to have them present in the royal tomb and to represent at the tomb some of the crucial aspects of the metamorphosis of the dead king as he was slowly revived during his long night journey.

When these figures from Tutankhamen's tomb are compared, each of them standing side by side, many obvious physical differences between those that repre-sent the king become clear. It seems that the statues of at least two different monarchs were enshrined in the name of King Tutankhamen and placed in his tomb and that some of these were certainly taken, once again, from the burial equipment of Smenkare. Standing in the doorway of the Treasury and half blocking access to it, had stood a fine figure of a life-sized jackal, the matt-black figure of Anubis, sitting with his ears pricked up attentively, staring out of the Treasury towards the burial chamber. In front of this guardian figure lay a small and modest mud brick bearing an inscription to aid magically the protection of the tomb. A reed candle, which had been set in this brick and left alight in the dark tomb, had burnt down and harmlessly fallen among the objects in the tinderbox tomb without causing any damage. Later Carter found similar charms and amulets set into the walls of the burial chamber underneath the plaster that bore the strange hurried paintings. Many other tombs in the Valley had contained similar pro-tective amulets, some of which were also set into the walls of the burial chamber. Once again, the ex-amples from Tutankhamen's tomb became the yard-stick by which other surviving examples could be identified and explained.

Like the representation upon the necropolis seal, which showed Anubis triumphing over the Nine Enemies of Egypt, this great figure of the guardian dog was also sitting on a pylon-shaped shrine, a fine gilded box with sloping sides. Inside this box was another rich collection of ritual objects, each in their separate compartment. One of these sections held a series of precious pectorals which, Carter surmised, may have been worn by the officials of the procession who carried this sculpture by the two stout carrying poles that extended from the base of the shrine. If this was so, these men had worn jewels as fine as those that Carter had taken from the mummy of the king, splendidly designed heavy pendants of gold set with faience and precious stones. The figure of Anubis on his shrine had probably protected and housed the objects used in the burial ceremonials during the procession from the mortuary temple of the king to the tomb in the Valley of the Kings. The jackal would have formed a primary element in this procession of officials and priests who carried the collections of ritual objects to the tomb. The great Anubis is a fine example of processional sculpture with a crisp distinctive silhouette, a magnificent image of all the magical protectors of the burial. Behind Anubis stood the head of a great cow, an image of the matriarchal goddess Hathor, Horus' mother, the goddess of the western mountains of Thebes, to whose womb her children returned each evening to be born again every morning with the rising sun. Fragments of such animal sculptures had been found by earlier expeditions scattered through-out other royal tombs; Carter himself had discovered a similar Hathor head in the tomb of Tuthmosis IV some twenty years earlier. There, it had been used in ancient times to support the lid of the sarcophagus when it was removed to take out the coffins and the king. The excavators had found the yellow-painted cedar-wood sculpture still supporting the huge slab of quartzite.

Four large and beautiful boxes lay in a row beside the Anubis statue and each one contained a rare mixture of personal belongings and objects of court ceremonial including a small set of the sceptres of kingship. These fragile remainders of personal possessions and ceremonial equipment now prod the senses; they seem to bring the ancient court and its manners right into the modern world. It is the very centre of the mystery of ancient Egypt. One may hold an ancient staff worn smooth by an ancient hand yet know so little of its owner. The ancient culture about which we know so much is still, ultimately, elusive and that is its supreme fascination. These objects from the life of the king and his ceremonials, were central parts of a system built by people who inhabited an ancient, now unfelt, cosmos.

The Treasury also contained other objects made for the royal burial: ushabtis of the king, some presented by his General, Minakht, and 'The Overseer of the Treasury', Maya. This Maya was the same man who had inscribed the fine graffito in the tomb of Tuthmosis IV that Carter had discovered for Davis many years before. Maya had also dedicated a little wooden effigy of Tutankhamen lying upon a bier similar to the one that Carter had found underneath the coffins inside the sarcophagus. By the side of the little figure of the recumbent king were two birds, one with a human head, who spread their wings protectively over the royal mummy. They were aspects of the identity of the spirit of the dead king, released from the physical presence of his body by his death but dependent upon the body's continued well-being for their proper survival.

The inscription on Maya's effigy of the king, which was housed in a small black sarcophagus-shaped box, named him as the Superintendent of the Royal Necropolis and he it must have been who supervised the burial of Tutankhamen, an office that he also exercised in the reign of Horemheb, as the inspection graffito in the tomb of Tuthmosis IV inform us. Maya, it must also have been who organized and supervised the burial of Smenkare in the Amarna Cache and it is likely that he performed this same function for Ay, Tutankhamen's successor, whose tomb had been found by Belzoni in the West Valley. The strange paintings in Ay's tomb find their only parallels in the burial chamber in Tutankhamen's tomb—the only room that was decorated. These are indeed a strange series of paintings for a royal tomb: the beginning of the *Amduat*; pictures of the king meeting the gods, as was normal, on the columns and upper sections of earlier royal tombs; and, unique in the Valley, a representation of the royal funeral procession with twelve people pulling along a huge sledge with the sarcophagus on it. Equally unusual, and reflecting perhaps the political strains of the period, is the scene showing King Ay dressed as a priest 'Opening the Mouth' of the mummy of Tutankhamen. Tutankhamen was the last surviving king of the illustrious royal bloodline of the Eighteenth Dynasty and Ay, his successor, is here shown with the gods of the tomb performing a traditional act of filial devotion, legitimizing his claim to the throne.

There were also a great number of model boats in the Treasury, typical features of the other destroyed royal burials where the identities of the numerous fragments of miniature cabins and rigging often taxed the imaginations of the discoverers. In Tutankhamen's tomb the boats were all intact, perfect. Some of them were rigged for sailing up the Nile; others for drifting down it with the stream. There are the boats which took the king upon his ceremonial journeys through Egypt after his death, the bark that he would use to travel through the heavens with the sun, the little skiffs he would use for hunting in the celestial marshes. As well as providing an extension of earthly delights in the next world, the hunt was also an image of vanquishing foes and enemies as was portrayed in some of the enshrined statues and the paintings in the tomb of Ay. Many weapons, such as bows, throw sticks and swords were found throughout Tutankhamen's tomb, though some of them, like the six magnificent chariots, were undoubtedly used by the king during his lifetime. Objects of travel, from shoes and sticks to large Nile craft were also plentiful.

Carter started to clear the last room of the tomb, the Annex which ran off the Antechamber, during the season of 1927–8, and he finished this work two years later. The small room, only eight feet wide, was stacked high with more than four hundred objects, some fine, like a magnificent ivory box with scenes of Tutankhamen and his young queen exquisitely engraved on its faces, others as utilitarian as the vegetable supplies for the tomb: more than a hundred baskets of fruit, and a whole cellar full of wine; also domestic paraphernalia: beds, chairs, and many gaming boards and their pieces that had belonged to the king. A particularly obtrusive ornament was an alabaster boat, manned by figures of two dwarfs which, mounted upon a hollow plinth that could be filled with water, would appear to float in the little pool. The over-decoration of this elaborate ornament suggests, as one commentator has remarked, a childish taste, an object to delight the boy-king. Another alabaster piece made with a similar simple illusion is a thin-sided vase which has a scene painted on its inside which, when a light such as an oil wick was placed inside, appeared through the translucent alabaster. It may have been such vulgarities of Empire that prompted Osbert Lancaster to describe the tomb's furniture as resembling 'the sale of effects of some Second Empire coquette kept by a Jewish impresario of antiquarian tastes', and although we may not entirely sympathize with Mr Lancaster's prejudices, nevertheless, much of the design and decoration of the objects in the tomb is very overblown, having little of the reserve and fine elegance that typified so much of ancient Egyptian design. It is as well to remember, however, that most of these objects are unique, and that the examples which survived from other reigns are of a different type. These personal and ephemeral objects from the court, with their frequent overtones of foreign influence—Cretan, Asiatic and the like—may well represent the daily taste of a court of which we have virtually no other knowledge. Popular art, after all, is poorly represented in either Westminster Abbey or the throne room of Buckingham Palace.

Working carefully through this incredible mélange of objects, Carter eventually completed the clearing of the tomb in 1929 with much work still to be accomplished in the laboratory before everything could be sent to Cairo. The Antechamber, the first room that he had seen, in the company of Carnarvon and his daughter, could now be seen to contain, in its vast range of objects, pieces which should have been placed in all the different parts of the royal burial, each normally accorded their own distinct place in orthodox royal tombs, but here placed largely by the expedience of room-sizes. The three great couches which dominated the Antechamber and which so awed the early visitors to the tomb, were a part of the grave goods and must surely have been used in the ceremonies that accompanied the emplacement of the dead king in his coffins. Perhaps too, they played a role in the high ceremonial of the wrappings of the mummy, glimpses of which may be had in the 'Book of the Dead' which lists the rituals connected with, and the purposes of, many of the amulets that were laid upon the mummy. Other objects, the chariots,

the food offerings, the thrones, the costumes and the great boxes had formed major parts of the funeral procession and many contained objects relating to the king, his ritual roles on earth and his tomb furnishings. There was some confusion among the contents of the tomb which was caused in part by the thieves who disturbed many of the boxes in the tomb and stole some of the precious objects, principally the gold. Subsequently the tomb was tidied by a party of necropolis officials who replaced objects in boxes other than those that listed the intended contents on their lids and who also restacked many of the goods in the tomb. The thieves had penetrated every room of the tomb but, remarkably, did little apparent damage. Carter discovered their footprints on a bow case in the Annex, and a piece of cloth that contained some fine heavy gold rings, which the thieves had dropped as they were leaving the tomb.

Why the tomb was not emptied of its treasures like the other royal tombs is, ultimately, a mystery. In fact, none of the tombs in the low central area of the Valley were robbed and this would imply that, although their positions were known by Maya during the reign of Horemheb, knowledge of their existence was lost during the later New Kingdom.

Tutankhamen had been buried in a private tomb that originally had consisted of but the one room, the Antechamber. The other rooms, including the burial chamber, were specially cut to hold this royal burial. As a private monument, the tomb belongs to a group of three in the Valley, identifiable by their design and size and their unique drop of about a yard at the end of the first descending corridor. The other two in this group, the tombs of the Amarna Cache, and Yuya and Tuya, were not so extensively enlarged, although a start was made in the right wall of the Amarna Cache tomb which was never extended beyond its beginnings, and in Yuya and Tuya's tomb their burial chamber was enlarged at its left side. The enlargements, a second stage of quarrying, show up clearly on the ceiling of Tutankhamen's tomb between the Antechamber and the Burial Chamber, where the original edge of the room and the rougher chisel cuts of the second stage of quarrying may be clearly seen. Yuya and Tuya's tomb dates to the reign of Amenhotep III, so it would be reasonable to suppose that the other two of this group were also cut at that time and taken over for use for royal burials after the return of the court from Amarna, when the Valley, once again, was used as the burial ground of the kings. Amenhotep III's own tomb was in the West Valley and, as we have already seen, there was little room for further royal burials in the main Valley, in the locations preferred by the Eighteenth Dynasty kings. Temporarily deserted by the kings the old royal cemetery was used for other courtly burials, such as that of Yuya and Tuya, the parents of his queen, Tiy. It is impossible to speculate upon the original owners of the two other tombs in the group. Possibly the great range of names on the burial equipment found in the tomb of the Amarna Cache might suggest that some of this was cleared out of the tomb of Tutankhamen to allow for his burial in the little tomb.

Obviously the tomb of Tutankhamen and the Amarna Cache are two parts of the same puzzle. Like the odd mixture of burial equipment found in the Amarna Cache, the burial of Tutankhamen also shows many unusual features. The names of both Smenkare and Akhenaten occur frequently in Tutankhamen's tomb and not only on objects that may be classed as family belongings, 'heirlooms' or 'antiquities'. Some of the most intimate objects of the burial had been taken from Smenkare's own burial equipment and there is no way of knowing how many other pieces, then uninscribed, were simply used by Maya for the burial of the young king. Some of these adaptations had been very skilfully made, the hieroglyphs of the cartouches being carefully changed from one king's name to the other's. Many other objects, as yet undetected, may have also undergone this transformation.

This is a very different picture from that which may be obtained from the objects found with the burial of Smenkare in the Amarna Cache. There, none of the tomb's furniture had been adapted for Smenkare's burial, except perhaps the crudest of alterations to the gilded coffin, such as ripping off the gold portrait mask; moreover, his cartouche was not found once in the tomb. The Amarna Cache, then, probably represents the rejected unusable objects from the mass of burial equipment gathered for the burial of Tutankhamen, a house cleaning of the funeral equipment available to the royal burial following the return to Thebes. Smenkare was buried in a nameless tomb, his identity hidden from his contemporaries if not from modern science, and his rich funeral equipment was taken and used by his successor, Tutankhamen. That tomb contained a mass of all the objects of an orthodox royal burial with most of the necessary changes in the cartouches carefully made. But it was, nevertheless, a burial which far outstripped those of the other kings in its sheer wealth of precious materials, especially gold. Of this there can be very little

doubt. Several of the coffins of some of the most famous and long-lived kings that were buried in the Valley have survived, and none of them is of solid gold. The physical condition of the other royal mummies, too, shows that these wooden coffins allowed the moisture of the royal mummies and the embalming oils to evaporate and leave the immediate vicinity of the corpse, unlike the mummy of Tutankhamen, probably the worst preserved of all the New Kingdom pharaohs. Furthermore, a careful examination of some of the multitudes of fragments of the burial equipment of other kings that has survived clearly shows that they were not decorated nearly as lavishly with the heavy gold foil that is such a typical feature of Tutankhamen's tomb. The shiny smooth surface of the black resin-painted figures of the remnants of the royal furniture that Salt collected, or that from the tomb of Tuthmosis' III and IV had never been covered with gold leaf. The gold that has survived in other royal tombs, a tiny fragment in the tomb of Ramesses I and others upon the royal coffins or that discovered by our expedition in the tomb of Ramesses XI is usually very much thinner than the heavy foil used widely in Tutankhamen's tomb, resembling in most examples, the micro-thin gold leaf of modern times.

In its plan, its grave goods and its coffins, Tutankhamen's tomb was a golden exception in the Valley. But where did all this wealth come from, why was it laid in this tomb, and why, after the golden secret was kept by Maya for two succeeding reigns, was it so completely forgotten? The poor jumbled tomb of the Amarna Cache and the carefully handled, most lavish burial of Smenkare's successor, Tutankhamen, reflect two faces of the return to Thebes and orthodoxy and the abandonment of Amarna and the heresy. As well as containing many pieces made for Smenkare, Tutankhamen's burial almost certainly contained some made for Akhenaten himself, these perhaps dating from before the adoption of the most extreme forms of the heretic faith which would have outlawed such splendid examples of the old religion. At the least, Tutankhamen's tomb represents a housekeeping supervised by Maya of all the fragments of royal burial made before or during the heresy and not used by their owners. At the most, it represents a reworking of the gold brought from Amarna, the wealth of the burials of the heretic and his family, rendered down and returned to Thebes for re-use after the burials in the Royal Valley at Amarna and dismantled like those of the Valley at the end of the New Kingdom.

Apart from jewellery that may have belonged to some of the Amarnan coffins and reports which are somewhat fanciful about the coffins themselves in the hands of Arab grave robbers, not one small fragment of gold leaf was found by the excavators of the royal tombs there. Although the burial equipment that had been left in the tomb, mainly of stone and faience, was carefully smashed into small pieces, the gilded objects had been removed from the tomb and broken and stripped elsewhere. In this, the fate of the royal tomb of Amarna was similar to, if more severe than, that of most of the tombs in the Valley of the Kings.

It is difficult to study properly the contents of Tutankhamen's tomb because there is no detailed catalogue of its contents available other than Carter's original lists and records compiled while he worked in the tomb and in the laboratory. While many have criticized Carter for not scientifically publishing the contents of the tomb, no one has yet decided to take these remarkable records over and fulfil this task. However, a series of slim books on the contents of the tomb that heavily utilize Carter's material is steadily appearing. Carter himself, nearing sixty when he completed the clearance of the tomb, spent two more years in the Valley, first preparing the objects taken from the Annex for shipment, and in his final season, supervising the packing of the great golden shrines and their subsequent re-erection in the Cairo Museum.

Howard Carter received no honours from his own country for his work on the tomb. His indiscretion and abrupt manner, perhaps even his dealings in antiquities, especially the fact that he aided Lady Carnarvon in the disposal of her husband's collection to the Metropolitan Museum, plus the jealousies that his discovery aroused, all told against him. One obituary notice, by an English official of the Cairo Museum, unconsciously summed up much of the rancour that was felt against him and showed clearly the standing in which some of his colleagues wished to hold him. The obituary concluded, 'Had Carter enjoyed the discipline and rough and tumble of a big school [it] might have made him a really great man'. Even without this great advantage Carter's work in the Valley represents one of the great triumphs of egyptology.

The discovery of Tutankhamen's tomb and the quarrels that surrounded its clearance, marked the end of excavation in the Valley and a watershed in egyptological research. It was fortunate for the tomb that Carter, a man who spanned the two eras of private excavation for gain and government-supervised excavation for knowledge, remained in control of the clearance. His reputation in those changing times suffered but the treasures of Tutankhamen did not. Although he returned to Egypt several times after sending the great shrines from the Valley to Cairo in 1931, he never excavated again. Carter died in 1939 in London. Little has happened to the Valley since that time. Tutankhamen's tomb still lacks a proper archeological plan, and the tomb of Seti II still wears the huge fortress-like gate that Callender fitted when it was used as a laboratory. Boxes and packing cases used by Carter still lie around that tomb, now serving as blackboards that record the graffiti of modern visitors from all over the world. The sealings from the doors of Tutankhamen's tomb were taken from the tomb of Ramesses XI, the storeroom and dining room of Carter's expedition and were put into the empty Antechamber in 1979, at the same time as the 'Treasures' of the king proceeded around the world. Each one carefully floodlit and brilliantly displayed, looking completely unearthly, like Kodachromes or television pictures. Burton's photographs are still the only records that show the objects as tangible products of the hand of man with dust upon them and a real metallic shine. Still, the only place where one may see the true quality of the yellow gold, almost experience the weight of the metal, the sheen upon the statues, is in the Cairo Museum where they are lit by the Egyptian sun streaming in from one direction through the large old-fashioned glass windows. Now the 'Treasures' have entered the historical consciousness of the entire world. The ancient kings who were buried in the Valley live again, as was their intention. The paint brushes and the chisels of their masons, sculptors and artists, the blowpipes and the hammers of their goldsmiths have transmuted their simple raw materials into some of mankind's most precious memorials.

Postscript

There has been relatively little activity in the Valley since Carter closed down the laboratories in the tomb of Seti II in 1932. It is seldom that present-day archeologists can afford to maintain the huge field operations of the magnitude that were organized and overseen by Davis and Carter and, in any case, modern scientific aims and standards would seldom allow such work. Most archeologists who work in Egypt today represent learned institutions, usually museums or universities and they dig primarily for more knowledge. Fine antiquities are a bonus rather than the mainspring of the work. It is not really a problem to discover more of the ruins of ancient Egypt in excavation—the civilization once spanned the country and it still lies under the sand like a ruined and plundered city. The trick of selecting a worthwhile site for excavation is in finding one that will repay, in terms of knowledge gained, the expenses and hard labour of the work.

There has been no archeology outside in the Valley of the Kings since Carter's day and only the inside of one tomb, Ramesses XI's, has been scientifically cleared, and that by our expedition during its 1978-9 season. The most unwelcome glare of publicity and the frictions that surrounded Carter's work are still widely regarded with great distaste in egyptological circles and in the years that followed the discovery of the tomb of Tutankhamen there seemed to be little left in the Valley for science. The royal tombs, all covered in their lengthy esoteric texts, became the hunting ground of cranks, clairvoyants and expounders of the 'ancient curse'—a legend that was probably dreamed up by Arthur Weigall while he stood in the sun with his journalist colleagues waiting for Carter to appear from the tomb of Tutankhamen bearing another treasure. Orthodox egyptology shunned such publicity; the Valley and its tombs largely ceased to be of interest. Its historical information, it was imagined, had long been exhausted along with the archeological possibilities of the site. Apart from a few learned studies on the texts in the tombs by German egyptologists very little interest was shown in the tombs.

One exception to this rule was the brilliant work of William Hayes, then a young egyptologist working with the Metropolitan Museum's excavations at Deir el Bahari who, in 1935, published a remarkable analysis of the royal sarcophagi of the Eighteenth Dynasty placing them, for the first time, in their correct order and establishing their origins in earlier kingdoms. Only one man, the Russian, Alexander Piankoff, continued a detailed study of the texts in the royal tombs and, between the 1930s and his death in 1966 a steady stream of volumes on the royal tombs appeared, each with commentaries and translations. His work eventually inspired a fresh interest in these long and difficult compositions and many young egyptologists have taken up this work.

During the 1930s an expedition of the French Archeological Institute at Cairo completely excavated the remarkable village of the ancient workers who had made the royal tombs in the Valley. The huge volume of the records of the ancient community were studied in great detail by Jaroslav Černý, a Czech egyptologist, whose great insights, enthusiasm and generosity have prompted a whole school of egyptologists to continue this fascinating work. Presently, this village is probably the best documented and closest studied of any small group in the ancient world. There is a steadily growing library on the genealogy of the families, the life of the village, its letters, its politics— the entire orbit of their ancient world. The studies reveal an extraordinary community, a unique group of artists and craftsmen with a high percentage of literacy for its time and place, probably the first such group to be supported by the resources of the state.

Since World War II interest has been greatly revived in the study of the Valley by two people. In 1966, a remarkable volume was privately printed in New Jersey by an American egyptologist, Elizabeth Thomas, which for the first time gathered together all the known information concerning the archeology of the Valley and made the first detailed analysis of the vast range and scope of the ancient necropolis. It was largely through this work that I was able to pursue my own interests with such facility. At the same time, in Basle, Switzerland, another egyptologist, Eric Hornung, was engaged on a further study of the royal tombs, bringing to the study of their texts new levels of accuracy and the detailed attention that is necessary to obtain a better understanding of the subtleties of the ancient religion. At last accurate copies of many of the major texts in the Valley tombs are available and others are being produced.

Ever since the early 1950s the dedicated officials of the *Service* and the body that succeeded it, the Egyptian Organisation of Antiquities (EOA) have been responsible for the large amounts of restoration work and general improvements in the Valley. Its craftsmen have lavished great care and attention on the site, which is now considered to be one of the noblest and most renowned monuments of the nation. During the last decade, however, fresh dangers to the Valley have become apparent, dangers so potentially overwhelming that it will take the resources of many different specialist organizations to cope with them. There is now an urgent need for programmes of conservation and documentation in the Valley.

Memories of the last flood in the Valley, which occurred in 1916, have receded and the damage that it caused has largely been forgotten. Yet the work of our expedition, in co-operation with the officers of the EOA clearly established the reality of the threat to the Valley. Although the deserts of Upper Egypt are slowly desiccating, as they have been for several thousand years, the flash floods will come again and, like an awful Russian roulette running right across the landscape, they will pass from the high desert down to the plain by the valleys of which the Valley of the Kings is one. Then the great mounds of loose chippings built up by Davis and the other archeologists will come crashing down the mountainsides and Valley slopes like the slag heaps of Aberfan. The Rest House at the Valley's centre, acting as a baffle for the flood waters that will pour from the cleft at the head of the Valley, will deflect the main force of the flood waters into the tombs that are all around it. Carter's clearances around the mouths of many of the tombs have left their doors lying open to the floods like the mouths of gasping fishes. The construction of the path system in the Valley and the raising of its floor by ten feet or so has completely changed the ancient patterns of drainage. Carter, who had seen many floods in the Valley, was fearful of just such a catastrophe when he was clearing the tomb of Tutankhamen.

There are other threats, though none so dramatic, so instantly catastrophic. The tourist industry is constantly enlarging and the growth of package tours and more efficient systems of mass transportation will bring hundreds of thousands of visitors to the sites each year to pass through tombs, each covered in fine paintings and reliefs, that in many instances are no larger than a sitting room. New levels of protection for the tombs must be installed. There are fresh rock movements taking place in the Valley landscape that need further study and, if possible, control. In some of the tombs these movements, now no more than a few inches, have begun to push the plaster and paintings from the surface of the wall.

It has long been recognized that there is a great need for the complete documentation of the Valley, an essential record without which the effects of these continuing hazards cannot be accurately judged and without which the continuing study of the monuments is severely handicapped. And the Valley still has a considerable body of historical information to yield in its smallest and apparently insignificant details. Even during the simple clearing operation in the tomb of Ramesses XI our expedition recovered fresh information regarding the Royal Cache and its mummies, some aspects of which have already been mentioned. A full analysis of this important archeological material, the first to appear concerning the royal mummies and their fate for a very long time, still awaits further field work. Certainly there is much more information to be gleaned from the material which waits, lying in two hundred crates, at the bottom of the dark tomb. After specialists have examined the ancient plants, animals and the human remains, and after the fragments of the statues and ancient furniture have been restored, and the drawings of the work in the tomb have been prepared, a new chapter will be added to the Valley's history. And this will have been derived from a modest clearance operation designed principally so that an accurate plan of the tomb could be drawn and the geologists and engineers might study the rock deterioration and formations that are visible in the tomb.

One day, a careful investigation of the areas in the Valley that remain unexcavated—and a part of the central ancient village was not excavated by Carter—should be undertaken. These modest untouched sites hold all the future information on the life of the ancient community who made the tombs that we are ever likely to possess. There is no more; ancient Egypt is a finite commodity. Enough probably still remains in the Valley to make a significant additional contribution to the information contained in the thousands of written documents that have survived.

However, these sites, being buried deep under the debris of the old archeologists should not decay and, unlike the work of conservation, there is little urgency in the task.

The work of restoration and protection, both from the floods that will come and the visitors that stream through the tombs is expensive and time consuming. In a crisis-ridden world funds for such tasks are scarce but the fight to preserve one of the central images of world history is surely worth the effort and money. Documentation, however elaborate, leaves but an imperfect record of its subject. Only the tombs themselves remain the authentic touchstones of the past and in a world where many would distort man's own image of himself for their own ends, such relics of the Royal Tombs remain essential yardsticks of civilization and its achievements.

In 1979, with the help of a small group of friends, the Theban Foundation was established to 'preserve and record the Royal Tombs of Thebes'. We are promised the help of many leading scholars and are looking towards other foundations and industry for

support. During our first two years in the Valley we refurbished the old expedition house of Theodore Davis that Edward Ayrton built, and we walk to our work along the pathways of the Valley floor that the old archeologists cleared. Today we are not, perhaps, as self-confident as those earlier excavators and historians and our aims are less dramatic—more concerned with the care of the past than with collecting its remains. Nevertheless, the great Valley holds the members of our expedition in awe; its unearthly amber glow in the late evening when all the visitors have left is as old as the tombs themselves, and the warm nights with the moonlit hills and the sharp stars are as they have always been. When you climb the ancient track to the peak that stands above the Valley, or when you walk down the white Valley paths and down through the tombs into the underworld, you move in the steps of the ancient people and there is nowhere on earth, not in the libraries or galleries of the great museums where you may feel the ancient people so close to you.

The Ancient Names for the Parts of the Royal Tomb

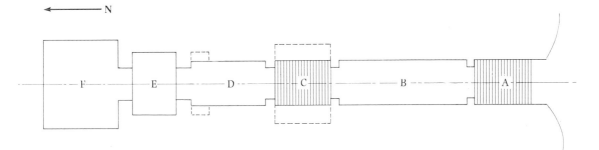

Research into the origin of the plan used for the royal tombs has shown that it had its beginnings in a type of queen's tomb cut at Thebes during the Middle and early New Kingdoms. The first royal tombs that were developed from these were of simple plan: a sequence of four corridors and two rooms. This basic pattern is always present in the plans of the later royal tombs. The later designs of royal tombs in the Valley consist

The basic plan of the royal tomb in the Valley. The various elements, each designated by a letter in the diagram, are described in the text

of this basic plan repeated twice, one after another, the king being buried in the last large room of the final sequence. Names for the different parts of this basic sequence of rooms and corridors have been preserved on a number of ancient *ostraca* and on a single papyrus. These documents were used by the men who were working on the tombs and, for the most part, were found in the debris that lay in the tombs and covered the central parts of the Valley until the early years of this century. The list of names has been greatly augmented by recent research, and although some of the translations of these terms may still be in some doubt, the basic titles of the rooms and corridors have been fully established.

The compass direction shown in the diagram is that employed by the ancient workmen and it was usually applied irrespective of the actual orientation of the tombs. The builders also used the terms 'left' (east) and 'right' (west), but always from a position looking *out* from the burial chamber (F). This emphasizes that they saw the order of the tomb as originating from the resting place of the dead king.

Slightly differing translations of the room and corridor titles have been rendered into a single acceptable form. For example, 'god's passage' has been variously named as 'the first god's passage' or even 'the first god's passage of the sun's path'.

The first four passages, A, B, C, D, beginning with the entrance stair (A) outside the tomb, were named in numerical order. In 'the god's third passage' (C) the niches that are found there (drawn as dotted lines) were called 'the sanctuaries in which the gods of the East/West repose', and this title would have referred to the statues of the gods in their shrines, such as the famous gold-covered statues seen in the Tutankhamen exhibitions. The small niches (again represented by dotted lines) off the fourth passage (D) are called, for reasons which are somewhat obscure, the 'two door keepers rooms'. This point in the tomb may well have been the last open place before the rooms that held the bulk of the grave goods, and thus held some guards during the king's interment. The hall of waiting (E) has also been called 'the hall of hindering', and this title would, perhaps, refer to the large pit that was dug in the floor of this room in many of the earlier tombs. Certainly this would be a great obstacle for any visitors to the lower sections of the tomb; in many tombs it has also caught the waters of desert flash floods and saved the lower sections of the tomb from grave damage. Religious motives have also been suggested for the name, and of course, it is hard to imagine any ancient Egyptian activity that did not combine utility and cult. This room is sometimes called the 'well' in archeological jargon. In the earliest royal tombs at Thebes the room (F) beyond the well was the burial chamber but after a few reigns had passed and more tombs were developed, a stairway was cut

down through its floor and the burial chamber put on a lower level. Eventually the mature plan called for the doubling of the simplest scheme drawn in the diagram. So eventually two basic tomb plans followed each other, one after the other, to the burial chamber called 'the house of gold' or 'the house in which one rests'—epithets that encourage the vision of sets of huge golden shrines standing around the sarcophagi, one inside the other like the magnificent examples found in the little tomb of Tutankhamen.

After the tomb was extended, the original burial hall (F) became known as the 'chariot hall'. This did not necessarily refer to the fact that the chariots of the king were placed in it, but probably denoted some warlike associations. One tomb has a frieze of beheaded enemies on the walls of this room. Frequently the room had four pillars in it, and one *ostracon* shows a sketch of its plan and unequivocally states it to be 'a hall of repelling rebels; what is in it; four pillars'.

There are few ancient references to the names of the repeated sections of the royal tombs, but the corridors that correspond to the first two in the upper parts of the plan (A and B) were designated 'another first corridor' and 'another second corridor' in three separate documents. This clearly underlines the deliberate choice of the architects to duplicate the original plan in their later designs. The second well-room of the tomb was sometimes designated 'the hall of truth', perhaps in reference to the judgement hall of the dead where the dead king was literally judged to be good or bad by his Lord Osiris. In a finished plan, the burial chamber followed this room. Various rooms running off the burial chamber have names that denote storerooms of different kinds and often these are of differing shapes. Variously they are sometimes called 'the treasury of the end', 'the ushabti place'—referring to the small figures left with the burial to act as workmen upon the king's behalf in the next world—'the resting place of the gods', another reference to the enshrined statues of the gods of Egypt that were frequently buried with the king. Other storerooms and small chambers in the tombs were labelled clearly with what one might expect to find in them; 'the house of food' or the 'treasury', for example. One small room in the tomb of Ramesses III which has a scene of two blind harpists on its walls is called 'the hall of the two' and may indeed have contained two harps, the music of which the king may have been fond.

Most of the tombs in the Valley are unfinished and have been hastily adapted for the royal burials. They are a compromise between what was planned and what was actually achieved in excavation. On the only papyrus of a tomb plan that has been preserved we can see the scribe dealing with this situation as he redesignates the chambers of the tomb to fit the royal burial into the room properly designated as the 'chariot hall'. The different titles employed for the same rooms listed on the front and the back of this papyrus shows the scribe actually involved in making these decisions of relocation although the state of the decoration in the tomb indicated in the text proves that the artists and scribes working on the walls of the tomb had already made the necessary provisions for the burial. The papyrus, therefore, probably represents a final official check on the condition of the hastily completed tomb prior to the burial, and was probably made away from the Valley from a verbal report.

Through the study of the names and sizes of the tomb corridors and rooms it becomes increasingly apparent that the ancient designers had firm ideas about the exact shape and functions of the different parts. It is a very great shame that the only intact royal burial ever discovered in the Valley, that of Tutankhamen, was not in a true royal tomb but in the adapted rooms of a noble's tomb, where the copious traditional grave goods were crammed into a few small rooms off the sarcophagus chamber and were not lying in their properly appointed places throughout the tomb. Nevertheless, it is still possible to reconstruct some of the normal arrangements of the royal burial, and the detailed research necessary for this work is presently under way.

This room and corridor sequence in the royal tombs was carefully controlled in size and proportion so that the original measurements of the early tombs were reflected in the designs of the later ones. Unfortunately, of the twenty-five royal tombs in the Valley less than half have been accurately planned and it is presently impossible to make a complete study of this fascinating subject. However, by using the available sources and supplementing them with my own measurements, a simple, accurate pattern of the transformation of the shape and size of the tombs' rooms and corridors has emerged. This is the mechanism by which the original shape of the royal tomb plan was precisely preserved from tomb to tomb over a five-hundred-year period. Observations upon the 'conservatism' of the ancient Egyptian designers are now commonplace, yet the actual mechanisms by which original designs were maintained over such a long period have hardly been examined at all in

the study of this ancient architecture. Here in the Valley we have proof that the ancient architects used numerical systems and that the records of their application were kept over long periods of time.

By comparing and analyzing the measurements and rooms of all the royal tombs in the Valley it is apparent that an overall enlargement from tomb to succeeding tomb is the common rule. The rate of enlargement, which is remarkably constant from one tomb to the next, is typically just under fifty per cent during the entire time-span of the Valley tombs. These increases are found in the length of the corridors and chambers, and the width and height of the corridors and doorways. Some parts of the tomb plans, however, were even further enlarged as new rooms or doors were introduced into the original tomb plan. The room E, originally the well, was not increased in size after the well shafts were no longer cut but, nevertheless, the chamber itself was always retained until the last tombs were made, a vestigial remnant of the original plan. Although the 'chariot hall' was eventually discarded as a separate room, by lengthening its dimensions it was turned into a part of the principal straight corridor of the later tombs with two niches (remnants of the original plan) running off its side. Such carefully controlled changes of size in the tomb plans enable the archeologists to state with some certainty the period in which the tomb was made—a most useful device in the case of the uninscribed tombs. However, these numerical systems only apply to the royal monuments and are not present in the fifty private tombs of the Valley.

This constant use of such precise methods points to an extraordinary level of refinement in the designs of the ancient architects. Research has recently shown, for the first time, particular problems faced by the architects. For example, the ever-increasing proportions of the tombs meant that the workmen were trapped in a situation where they had to quarry tombs of ever-enlarging size. Thus, although the workforce was considerably increased the later tombs in the Valley were hardly ever finished! Two different solutions were found for this problem. In one, a king continued the tomb of his predecessor and between them they nearly managed to finish an entire monument. The second solution, which is seen in the last tomb to be cut in the Valley, radically shortened the full design and although the enlargements of the upper sections of the tomb were kept to their proper proportions, the architecture of the lower parts was greatly attenuated.

Select Bibliography

The following abbreviations have been employed—

JEA: Journal of Egyptian Archeology
ASAE: Annales du Service des Antiquités de l'Egypte
MDAIK: Mitteilungen des Deutschen Archäologisches Instituts Abteilung Kairo

The chapter numbers in square brackets after the *op. cit.* entries direct the reader to that part of the bibliography where the full title of the work can be found.

GENERAL

Baedeker's Egypt and the Sudan. 8th edn. Leipzig, 1929
Baikie, James. *Egyptian Antiquities in the Nile Valley.* London, 1932
Burke, Sir Bernard. *A Dictionary of the Peerage and Baronetage.* London, 1888
Burke, Sir Bernard. *A History of the Landed Gentry of Great Britain.* London, 1906
Cambridge Ancient History. 2nd edn. Cambridge, 1964–71
Carter, Howard. The papers of Howard Carter at the Griffith Institute (MSS.), Ashmolean Museum, Oxford
Dawson, Warren, and Eric Uphill. *Who was Who in Egyptology.* London, 1972
Encyclopaedia Britannica, The. 14th edn. London, 1929
Gardiner, Sir Alan. *Egypt of the Pharaohs.* Oxford, 1961
Lefébure, Eugène. *Les Hypogées Royaux des Thèbes.* 2 vols. Paris 1885–9
Lucas, Arthur, rev. by J. R. Harris. *Ancient Egyptian Materials and Industries.* 4th edn. London, 1962
Porter, Rosalind and Bertha Moss. *Topographical Bibliography of Ancient Egyptian Hieroglyphic Texts, Reliefs and Paintings.* 7 vols. Oxford, 1927–
Thomas, Elizabeth. *The Royal Necropoleis of Thebes.* Princeton, 1966
Weigall, Arthur. *A Guide to the Antiquities of Upper Egypt.* London, 1910

CHAPTER 1

Černý, Jaroslav, *et al. Graffiti de la Montaigne Thébaine.* Cairo, 1969–
Herodotus Book II (trans. W. G. Waddell). London, 1939
Hume, W. F. *Geology of Egypt.* Cairo, 1925
Said, Rushti. *The Geology of Egypt.* New York, 1962

CHAPTER 2

Bennett, John. 'Pyramid names', *JEA* 52, 1966
Černý, Jaroslav *et al. op. cit.* 1969 [Chap. 1]
Edwards, I. E. S. *The Pyramids of Egypt.* London, 1961
Frankfurt, Henri. *Kingship and the Gods.* Chicago, 1948
Frankfurt, Henri. *Ancient Egyptian Religion.* New York, 1948
Giedion, Siegfried. *The Eternal Present: The Beginnings of Architecture.* London, 1964
Piankoff, Alexandre. 'The Theology of the New Kingdom', *Antiquity and Survival,* 6, 1956
Piankoff, Alexandre. *Egyptian Religion Texts and Representations.* 5 vols. Princeton, 1954–68
Schott, Siegfried. 'The Feasts of Thebes' in Nelson and Holscher. *Work in Western Thebes 1931–33.* Chicago, 1934
Spengler, Oswald. *The Decline of the West.* New York, 1926–28
Spiegel, Joachim. *Das Auferstehungsritual der Unas—Pyramide.* Wiesbaden, 1971

CHAPTER 3

Baillet, Jules. *Inscriptions Grèques et Latines des Tombeaux des Rois ou Syringes à Thèbe.* Cairo, 1926
Bell, Sir H. Idris. *Egypt.* Oxford 1948
Bierbrier, M. L. *The Late New Kingdom in Egypt.* Warminster, 1975
Browne, William. *Travels in Africa, Egypt and Syria.* 2nd edn. London, 1806
Bruce, James. *Travels to Discover the Source of the Nile.* Edinburgh, 1790
Carré, Jean-Marie. *Voyageurs et Écrivains Français en Égypte.* Cairo, 1931
Ciccarello, Mark and John Romer. 'A Preliminary Report of the Recent Work in the Tombs of Ramesses X and XI' in J. Romer *et al. Theban Royal Tomb Project. A Report of the First Two Seasons.* San Francisco, 1979
Diodorus Siculus
Greener, Leslie. *The Discovery of Egypt.* London, 1968
Hitti, Philip. *History of the Arabs.* London, 1943
Milne, Joseph Grafton. 'Greek and Roman Tourists in Egypt', *JEA,* III, 1916
Pococke, Richard. *A Description of the East.* London, 1743
Sicard, Claude, *Lettre à Mgr. le Comte de Toulouse.* Paris, 1716
Sicard, Claude. 'Relation d'un voyage aux cataractes et dans le Delta' in *Nouveaux Mémoires des Missions de la Comp. de Jesus.* Paris, 1717
Strabo's *Geography*
Winlock, Herbert. *The Monastery of Epiphanius at Thebes.* New York, 1926

CHAPTER 4

Barthélemy. Auguste and J. P. A. Méry. *Napoléon en Égypte.* Paris, 1828

Wallis Budge, Sir E. A. *The Mummy.* 2nd edn. Cambridge, 1925

Denon, Vivant (trans. Arthur Aikin). *Travels in Upper and Lower Egypt.* London, 1803

Description de l'Égypte. 24 vols. Paris, 1809–22

Elgood, P. G. *Bonaparte's Adventure in Egypt.* Oxford, 1931

Jollois, Prosper. *Journal d'un Ingénieur attaché à l'Expedition d'Égypte.* Paris, 1904

Legrain, G. and Jean de Metz. *Aux Pays de Napoléon l'Égypte.* Grenoble, 1913

de Villiers du Terrage, Marc. *Journal et Souvenirs sur l'Expédition d'Égypte.* Paris, 1899

CHAPTER 5

Budge, Sir E. A. Wallis. *The Rosetta Stone in the British Museum.* London, 1929

Hamilton, William. *Remarks on Several Parts of Turkey.* London, 1809

Legh, Thomas. *Narrative of a Journey in Egypt and the Country beyond the Cataracts.* London, 1816

Menglu, Felix. *Histoire de l'Égypte sous le gouvernement de Mohammed Aly.* Paris, 1823

Thackeray, William Makepeace. *Vanity Fair.* London, 1848

Wilson, Sir Robert. *History of the British Expedition to Egypt.* London, 1802

CHAPTER 6

Arundale, Francis and Joseph Bonomi. *Gallery of Antiquities selected from the British Museum.* London, 1841–43

Belzoni, Giovanni. *Narrative of the Operations and Recent Discoveries within the Pyramids, Temples, Tombs and Excavations in Egypt and Nubia.* London, 1822

Clair, Colin. *Strong Man Egyptologist.* London, n.d. (c. 1957)

Disher, Maurice Wilson. *Pharaoh's Fool.* London, 1957

Halls, J. J. *The Life and Correspondence of Henry Salt Esq. F.R.S.* London, 1834

Irby, The Hon. Charles and James Mangles. *Travels in Egypt and Nubia, Syria and the Holy Land.* London, 1868

Mayes, Stanley. *The Great Belzoni.* London, 1959

CHAPTER 7

Frankfurt, Henri. *The Cenotaph of Seti I at Abydos.* 2 vols. London, 1933

Romer, John. "Tuthmosis I and the Bibân el-Molûk', *JEA*, 60, 1974

Salt, Henry. *Egypt, a descriptive Poem, with notes.* Alexandria, 1824

Sharpe, Samuel and Joseph Bonomi. *The Alabaster Sarcophagus of Oimenepthah I.* London, 1864

CHAPTER 8

Forbin, Count de. *Travels in Egypt 1817–18.* London, 1819

Gentleman's Magazine, 1818

Hall, Henry Holland. 'Letters to Sir William Gell', *JEA*, II,
1915

Jowett, William. *Christian Researches.* London, 1822

Montifiore, Judith. *Private Journal of a Visit to Egypt and Palestine by way of Italy and the Mediterranean.* London, 1836

Romer, John and Rutherford & Chekene. *Damage in the Royal Tombs in the Valley of the Kings.* San Francisco, 1977

Richardson, Robert. *Travels Along the Mediterranean and Parts Adjacent in Company with the Earl of Belmore, during the years 1816–17–18.* 2 vols. London, 1822

St John James. *Egypt and Nubia, their Scenery and their people.* London, n.d.

CHAPTER 9

Budge, Sir E. A. Wallis. *op. cit.,* 1925 [Chap. 4]

Champollion, Jean François. *Lettre à M. Dacier rélative a l'Alphabet des Hiéroglyphes phonétiques.* Paris, 1822

Claydon, P. W. *Samuel Sharpe.* London, 1883

Hall, Henry Holland. *op. cit.,* 1915 [Chap. 8]

Iverson, Erik. *The Myth of Egypt and its Hieroglyphs in European Tradition.* Copenhagen 1961

Wilkinson, Sir John Gardner. *Topography of Thebes and General View of Egypt.* London, 1835

Wilkinson, Sir John Gardner. *The Manners and Customs of the Ancient Egyptians.* London, 1837–78 (various editions)

Young, Thomas. *Remarks on Egyptian Papyri.* London, 1815

Young, Thomas *Egypt* (Supplement to the fourth and fifth editions *Encyclopedia Britannica*). London, 1819

CHAPTER 10

Claydon, P. W. *op. cit.,* 1883 [Chap. 9]

Wilkinson, Sir John Gardner. *op. cit.,* 1835 [Chap. 9]

Wilkinson, Sir John Gardner. *op. cit.,* 1837 [Chap. 9]

Wilkinson, Sir John Gardner. *Hand Book for Travellers in Egypt.* London, 1847

CHAPTER 11

Bruce, James. *op. cit.,* 1790 [Chap. 3]

Burton, James. Add. MSS. 25613–75, British Library, London

Hall, Henry Holland. *op. cit.,* 1915 [Chap. 8]

Hoskins, G. A. *Visit to the Great Oasis of the Libyan Desert.* London, 1837

Lane, Edward. *The Manners and Customs of the Modern Egyptians.* London, 1836

Lane, Edward. Griffith Institute (MSS.), Ashmolean Museum, Oxford

Summerson, Sir John. *Georgian London.* London, 1978

Wilkinson, Sir John Gardner. *op. cit.,* 1835 [Chap. 9]

CHAPTER 12

Champollion, Jean François. *Monuments de l'Égypte et de la Nubie.* 4 vols. Paris, 1835–45

Claydon, P. W. *op. cit.,* 1883 [Chap. 7]

Gunnis, Rupert. *Dictionary of British Sculptors 1660–1851*. London, 1964

Hari, Robert. *Prefaces to Reprints of Champollion Monuments and Lepsius Denkmäler*. Geneva, n.d.

Lepsius, Richard. *Denkmäler aus Aegypten und Aethiopien*. 12 vols. Berlin, 1849–59

Lepsius, Richard. *Discoveries in Egypt*. London, 1852

Rosellini, Ippolito. *I Monumenti dell' Egitto e della Nubia*. 3 vols. Florence, 1832–44

Schäfer, Heinrich. *Das altägyptische Bildnis*. Glückstadt, 1936

Schäfer, Heinrich (trans. John Baines). *Principles of Egyptian Art*. Oxford, 1974

Toomer, G. J. *Mathematics and Astronomy in The Legacy of Egypt*. 2nd edn. Oxford, 1971

CHAPTER 13

Legrain, Georges. *Répertoire généalogique et onomastique du Musée du Caire*. Cairo, 1908

Mariette, Auguste. *The Monuments of Upper Egypt*. London, 1877

Marlowe, John. *Spoiling the Egyptians*. London, 1974

Maspero, Sir Gaston. *La Trouvaille de Deir el Bahari*. Cairo, 1881

Rhind, Henry. *Thebes, its Tombs and their Tenants*. London, 1862

Romer, Isabella. *A Pilgrimage to the Temples and Tombs of Egypt, Nubia and Palestine*. London, 1846

Russell, William Howard. *A Dairy in the East during the tour of the Prince and Princess of Wales*. London, 1869

Stanley, Arthur Penrhyn. *Sinai and Palestine*. London, 1856

CHAPTER 14

Budge, Sir E. A. Wallis. *The Greenfield Papyrus*. London, 1912

Dewachter, Michael. 'Contribution à l'histoire de la Cachette Royale de Deir el Bahari', *Bulletin de la Societé Française d'Égyptologie*, 74, 1976

Charmes, Gabriel. *L'Égypte*. Paris, 1891

Edwards, Amelia. 'Royal Mummies found near Thebes', *Illustrated London News*, 4 February, 1882

Edwards, Amelia. *A Thousand Miles up the Nile*. London, 1877

Gordon, Lady Duff. *Letters from Egypt* (ed. Gordon Waterfield). London, 1969

Loftie, William. *A Ride in Egypt from Sioot to Luxor*. London, 1879

Marlowe, John. *op. cit.*, 1974 [Chap. 13]

Maspero, Sir Gaston. *The Struggle of the Nations*. London, 1896

Maspero, Sir Gaston. *op. cit.*, 1881 [Chap. 13]

Maspero, Sir Gaston. *Guide du visiteur au Musée du Caire*. 4th edn. Cairo, 1915

Russell, William Howard. *op. cit.*, 1869 [Chap. 13]

Al-Sayid, Afaf Lutfi. *Egypt and Cromer*. London, 1968

Thomas, Elizabeth. 'The K'y of Queen Inhapy'. *JARCE*, XVI, 1979

Wilbour, Charles Edwin. *Travels in Egypt*. Brooklyn, 1936

Wilson, Edward. 'Finding Pharaoh', *The Century Magazine*, May, 1887

CHAPTER 15

Baikie, James. *A Century of Excavation in the Land of the Pharaohs*. London, 1924

Brugsch Bey, Émile. *La Tente Funéraire de la Princesse Isimkheb*. Cairo, 1889

Černý, Jaroslav. 'Studies in the Chronology of the Twenty First Dynasty, *JEA*, 32, 1946

Černý, Jaroslav. *A Community of Workmen at Thebes in the Ramesside Period*. Cairo, 1973

Daressy, Georges. *Cercueils des cachettes royales*. Cairo, 1909

Harrison, R. G. *et al*. 'Seriological evidence for the parentage of Tut'ankhamūn and Smenkhkare, *JEA*, 62, 1976

Hölscher, Uvo. *The Excavation of Medinet Habu*, Vol. I. Chicago, 1934

Lefébure, Eugène. 'Le Puits de Dier el Bahari', *Annales du Musée Guimet*, 4, 1882

Lynch, Jeremiah. *Egyptian Sketches*. New York, 1890

Manning, Samuel. *The Land of the Pharaohs*. London, 1887

Maspero, Gaston. *Les Momies Royales de Deir el Bahari*. Cairo, 1889

Maspero, Gaston. *op. cit.*, 1896 [Chap. 14]

Smith, Sir Grafton Elliot. *The Royal Mummies*. Cairo, 1912

Traill, H. D. *From Cairo to the Soudan Frontier*. London, 1896

CHAPTER 16

Baillet, Jules. *op. cit.*, 1926 [Chap. 3]

Bénedite, Georges. *Égypte*. Paris, 1900

Daressy, Georges. *Fouilles de la Vallée des Rois 1898–1899*. Cairo, 1902

Daressy, Georges. 'Déblaiement des tombes 6 et 9 de Biban el Molouk', *ASAE*, XVIII, 1919

Loret, Victor. 'Les Tombeaux de Thoutmés III et d'Amenophis II', *Bulletin de l'Institut Égyptien*. Cairo, 1899

Maspero, Gaston. *op. cit.*, 1896 [Chap. 14]

Petrie, Sir William Flinders. *A History of Egypt*, Vol. II. London, 1924

Petrie, Sir William Flinders. *Seventy Years in Archeology*. London, 1933

Piankoff, Alexandre. *The Tomb of Ramesses VI*. Princeton, 1954

'Queen Tiye Found!', *Oriental Institute News and Notes*, 30, 1976

Romer, John. 'The Tomb of Tuthmosis III', *MDAIK* 31, 2, 1975

Wilbour, Charles Edwin. *op. cit.*, 1936 [Chap. 14]

CHAPTER 17

Carter, Howard. 'Report upon the Tomb of Sen-nefer', *ASAE*, II, 1901

Carter, Howard. 'Report on a Tomb Pit', *ASAE*, II, 1901

Carter, Howard. 'Report on the robbery of the Tomb of Amenothes II', *ASAE*, III, 1902

Carter, Howard. 'Report on General Work', *ASAE*,IV, 1903
Carter, Howard, 'Report of work done in Upper Egypt', *ASAE*, VI, 1905
Daressy, Georges, *op. cit.*, 1902 [Chap. 16]
Loret, Victor. *op. cit.*, 1899 [Chap. 16]
Maspero, Sir Gaston. *Egypt: Ancient Sites and Modern Scenes*. London, 1910
Newberry, Percy. 'Howard Carter' (obituary), *JEA*, 25, 1939
Petrie, Sir William Flinders. *The Royal Tombs of the Earliest Dynasties*. Vol. II. London, 1901
Petrie, Sir William Flinders. *op. cit.*, 1933 [Chap. 16]
Romer, John. *op. cit.*, 1974 [Chap. 7]
Romer, John and Rutherford & Chekene. *op. cit.*, 1977 [Chap. 8]

CHAPTER 18

Carter, Howard. *op. cit.*, 1903 [Chap. 17]
Carter, Howard. 'Excavations at Biban el Moluk', *ASAE*, IV, 1903
Carter, Howard. *op. cit.*, 1905 [Chap. 17]
Davis, Theodore M. *et al. The Tomb of Thoutmôsis IV*. London, 1906
Davis, Theodore M. *et al. The Tomb of Hâtshopsitû*. London, 1906
Frankfort, Henri. *op. cit.*, 1933 [Chap. 7]
Hayes, William C. *Royal Sarcophagi of the XVIII Dynasty*. Princeton, 1935
Maspero, Sir Gaston. *op. cit.*, 1910 [Chap. 17]
Newberry, Percy. *op. cit.*, 1939 [Chap. 17]
Romer, John. *op. cit.*, 1974 [Chap. 7]
Weigall, Arthur. *Tutankhamen and other Essays*. New York, 1924
Winlock, Herbert. *Excavations at Deir el Bahari: 1911–1931*. New York, 1942

CHAPTER 19

Currelly, Charles. *I Brought the Ages Home*. Toronto, 1956
Davis, Theodore M. *et al. The Tomb of Iouiya and Touiyou*. London, 1907
Davis, Theodore M. *et al. The Tomb of Siptah*. London, 1908
Davis, Theodore M. *et al. The Tombs of Harmharbi and Touatânkhamanou*. London, 1912
Gaillard, Claude and Georges Daressy. *La Faune Momifiée de l'Antique Égypte*. Cairo, 1905
Hornung, Erik. 'Die Grabkammer des Vizirs User', *Nachrichten der Akademie der Wissenschaften in Göttingen*, 5, 1961
Lortet, Louis and Claude Gaillard. *La Faune Momifiée de l'Ancienne Égypte*. Lyon, 1903–9
Maspero, Gaston. *New Light on Ancient Egypt*. London, 1908
Myśliwiec, Karol. *Le Portrait Royal dans le Bas-Relief du Nouvel Empire*. Warsaw, 1976
Quibell, James. 'Report on work done in Upper Egypt', *ASAE*, VII, 1906
Quibell, James. *Tomb of Yuaa and Thuiu*. Cairo, 1908
Smith, Joseph Lindon. *Tombs, Temples and Ancient Art.*
Oklahoma, 1956
Weigall, Arthur. *The Treasury of Ancient Egypt*. London, 1911

CHAPTER 20

Aldred, Cyril. 'The Harold Jones Collection', *JEA*, 48, 1962
Aldred, Cyril. 'The Amarna Period and the End of the Eighteenth Dynasty', *Cambridge Ancient History*. 2nd edn. 1971
Bosse-Griffiths, Kate. 'Finds from the tomb of Queen Tiye', *JEA*, 47, 1961
Currelly, Charles. *op. cit.*, 1956 [Chap. 19]
Davis, Theodore M. *et al. The Tomb of Queen Tiyi*. London, 1910
Davis, Theodore M. *et al. op cit.*, 1912 [Chap. 19]
Derry, Douglas. 'Note on the skeleton hitherto believed to be that of King Akhenaten', *ASAE*, 31, 1931
Harrison, R. G. 'The Anatomical Examination of the Pharonic Remains Purported to be Akhenaten', *JEA*, 52, 1966
Maspero, Gaston. *op. cit.*, 1908 [Chap. 19]
Perepelkin, G. *The Secret of the Gold Coffin* Moscow, 1978
Smith, Joseph Lindon. *op. cit.*, 1956 [Chap. 19]
Tyndale, Walter. *Below the Cataracts*. London, 1907
Weigall, Arthur. *op. cit.*, 1911 [Chap. 19]

CHAPTER 21

Aldred, Cyril. 'Valley Tomb no. 56 at Thebes', *JEA*, 49, 1963
Aldred, Cyril. *Jewels of the Pharaohs*, London, 1971
Ayrton, Edward and William Loat. *The Pre-Dynastic Cemetery at el Mahasna*. London, 1911
Cone, Polly, ed. *The Discovery of Tutankhamun's Tomb*. New York, 1976
Darby, William *et al. Food: The Gift of Osiris*. London, 1977
Davis, Theodore M. *et al. op. cit.*, 1912 [Chap. 19]
Hall, Henry Holland. 'Edward Ayrton' (obituary), *JEA*, II, 1915
Lorimer, Norma. *By the Waters of Egypt*. London, 1909
Martin, Geoffrey T. *The Royal Tomb at El-Amarna*. London, 1974
Weigall, Arthur. *op. cit.*, 1911 [Chap. 19]
Winlock, Herbert. *Materials used at the Embalming of King Tūt-ankh-amūn*. New York, 1941

CHAPTER 22

Brackman, Arnold. *The Search for the Gold of Tutankhamen*. New York, 1976
Breasted, Charles. *Pioneer to the Past*. New York, 1943
Brunton, Guy. 'Howard Carter' (obituary), *ASAE*, XXXIX, 1939
Burton, Henry. 'The Late Theodore M. Davis Excavations at Thebes in 1912–13', *Bulletin of the Metropolitan Museum of Art*, XI, 1916
Carnarvon, The Earl of, and Howard Carter. *Five Years' Exploration at Thebes*. London, 1912
Carnarvon, The Earl of. *No Regrets*. London, 1976
Carter, Howard. 'Report on the Tomb of Zeser-ka-ra. Amenhotep I', *JEA*, III, 1916

Carter, Howard and Alan Gardiner. 'The Tomb of
    Ramesses IV and the Turin Plan', *JEA*, iv, 1917
Carter, Howard. 'A Tomb prepared for Queen Hatshepsut',
    JEA, iv, 1917
Carter, Howard and Arthur Mace. *The Tomb of
    Tutankhamen*. Vol. i. London, 1923
Davis, Theodore M. *op. cit.*, 1912 [Chap. 19]
Hayes, William. *The Sceptre of Egypt*. Part II. New York,
    1959
Hayes, William. *op. cit.*, 1935 [Chap. 18]
Hoving, Thomas. *Tutankhamun: the Untold Story*. New
    York, 1978
Lucas, Arthur. 'Note on the Temperature and Humidity of
    several Tombs in the Valley'. *ASAE*, xxiv, 1924
Milne, Joseph Grafton. 'Three Engraved Plaques in the
    Collection of the Earl of Carnarvon'. *JEA*, iii, 1916
Naville, Edouard. 'Sir Gaston Maspero KCMG' (obituary),
    JEA, iii, 1916
Newberry, Percy. *op. cit.*, 1939 [Chap. 17]
Petrie, Sir William Flinders. *Qurneh*. London, 1898
Romer, John, 'Royal Tombs of the Early Eighteenth
    Dynasty', *MDAIK*, 32, 1976
Weigall, Arthur. 'Excavations and Explorations in Egypt',
    Exploration Fund Report 1909–1910
Weigall, Arthur. *op. cit.*, 1911 [Chap. 19]
Winlock, Herbert. *op. cit.*, 1942 [Chap. 18]
Winlock, Herbert. *The Treasure of Three Egyptian Princesses*.
    New York, 1948

CHAPTER 23

Carnarvon, The Earl of. *op. cit.*, 1976 [Chap. 22]
Carter, Howard. *The Tomb of Tutankhamen*. Vol. ii and iii.
    London, 1927, 1933
Carter, Howard. 'Excavation Journal', Griffith Institute
    (MSS.), Ashmolean Museum, Oxford
Černý, Jaroslav. *Hieratic Inscriptions from the Tomb of
    Tut'ankhamūn*. Oxford, 1965
Ciccarello, Mark and John Romer. *op. cit.*, 1979 [Chap. 3]

Hoving, Thomas. *op. cit.*, 1978 [Chap. 22]
Weigall, Arthur. *op. cit.*, 1924 [Chap. 18]

CHAPTER 24

Brackman, Arnold. *op. cit.*, 1976 [Chap. 22]
Breasted, Charles. *op. cit.*, 1943 [Chap. 22]
Brunton, Paul. *op. cit.*, [Chap. 22]
Carnarvon, The Earl of. *op. cit.*, 1939 [Chap. 22]
Carter, Howard. *op. cit.*, 1927, 1933 [Chap. 23]
Cone, Polly, ed. *op. cit.*, 1976 [Chap. 21]
Davis, Theodore M. *et al. op. cit.*, 1910 [Chap. 20]
Hoving, Thomas. *op. cit.*, 1978 [Chap. 22]
Lancaster, Osbert. *Pillar to Post*. London, 1938
Leek, F. Filce. *The Human Remains from the Tomb of
    Tut'ankhamūn*. Oxford, 1972
McLeod, W. *Composite Bows from the Tomb of Tut'ankhamūn*.
    Oxford, 1970
Murray, Helen. *A Handlist to Howard Carter's Catalogue of
    Objects in Tut'ankhamūm's Tomb*. Oxford, 1963
Petrie, Sir William Flinders. *op. cit.*, 1933 [Chap. 16]
Weigall, Arthur. *op. cit.*, 1924 [Chap. 18]

POSTSCRIPT AND APPENDIX

Černý, Jaroslav. *op. cit.*, 1973 [Chap. 15]
Černý, Jaroslav. *The Valley of the Kings*. Cairo, 1973
Grapow, Herman. 'Studien zu den thebanischen
    Königsgräbern', *Zeitschrift für Ägyptische Sprache und
    Altertumskunde*, 72, 1936
Hayes, William. *op. cit.*, 1935 [Chap. 18]
Romer, John. *op. cit.*, 1976 [Chap. 22]
Romer, John, and Rutherford & Chekene. *op. cit.*, 1977
    [Chap. 8]
Romer, John *et al.* in Ciccarello, Mark and John Romer.
    op. cit., 1979 [Chap. 3]

Picture Credits

The chapter number at the end of some entries directs the reader to the chapter in the Select Bibliography where the full title of the work from which the illustration has been taken will be found

PLATES

facing 26 John Romer
between 26–7 John Romer
facing 27 above, John Romer; below, John G. Ross
facing 66 John Romer
between 66–7 Derrick Witty by courtesy of the Victoria and Albert Museum; left, Belzoni 1822 [Chap. 6]; right, Sharpe and Bonomi 1864 [Chap. 7]
facing 67 above, by kind permission of the British Library Board; below, Derrick Witty: Wilkinson 1837 [Chap. 9]
facing 96 John G. Ross
facing 97 by kind permission of the British Library Board
facing 116 John Romer
facing 117 John Romer
facing 196 John G. Ross
facing 197 Derrick Witty by courtesy of the Victoria and Albert Museum: Davis 1907 [Chap. 19]
facing 216 Derrick Witty; above left, Davis 1912 [Chap. 19]; below left, Davis 1908 [Chap. 19]; right, Milne 1916 [Chap. 22]

MONOCHROMES

Endpapers: a decoration made from part of the Litany of Re; original photo by John Romer
13, 14 drawn by Constance and Brian Dear
22–3, 29 Harry Burton, © The Griffith Institute, Ashmolean Museum, Oxford
31 John Romer
33 above, Derrick Witty; below, John Romer: Pococke 1743 [Chap. 3]
34 Derrick Witty by courtesy of the Victoria and Albert Museum: Bruce 1790 [Chap. 3]
35 Harry Burton (rephotographed John Romer), © The Griffith Institute, Ashmolean Museum, Oxford
36 Derrick Witty: Manning 1887 [Chap. 15]
38 Derrick Witty: Barthélemy and Méry 1828 [Chap. 4]
40 Derrick Witty; above, by courtesy of the Victorian and Albert Museum: Francis Frith *Photographs of Lower Egypt*, London 1860; below, Champollion 1835 [Chap. 12]
42, 43, 44 John Romer: *Description* 1809 [Chap. 4]
45 Derrick Witty

52 John Romer
53 by courtesy of the Fitzwilliam Museum, Cambridge
54, 58 John Romer
61 John G. Ross
62 Harry Burton (rephotographed John Romer): The Metropolitan Museum of Art, New York
64 drawn by Constance and Brian Dear
65 Derrick Witty: Arundale and Bonomi 1841 [Chap. 6]
68 John Romer
71 Harry Burton (rephotographed John Romer): The Metropolitan Museum of Art, New York
72 John Romer
73 Derrick Witty, by courtesy of the Victoria and Albert Museum: Sharpe and Bonomi 1864 [Chap. 7]
74 drawn by Constance and Brian Dear
77 John Romer
81 Derrick Witty, from an unknown Italian book published c. 1830
82 John Romer: Belzoni 1822 [Chap. 6]
85 John Romer
86 by kind permission of the British Library Board
91 Derrick Witty: Belzoni 1822 [Chap. 6]
92 Derrick Witty: Manning 1887 [Chap. 15]
95 John Romer, © The Griffith Institute, Ashmolean Museum, Oxford
97 John Romer
105 drawn by Constance and Brian Dear
108 by kind permission of the British Library Board
110 Derrick Witty: Manning 1887 [Chap. 15]
112 by kind permission of the British Library Board
115 John Romer
116, 118 Derrick Witty: Champollion 1835 [Chap. 12]
119 John Romer: Lepsius 1849 [Chap. 12]
120 John Romer
123 by kind permission of the British Library Board
125 Derrick Witty: Manning 1887 [Chap. 15]
127, 129 Derrick Witty: Maspero 1881 [Chap. 13]
131 Derrick Witty, by courtesy of the Brooklyn Museum, New York: Wilbour 1936 [Chap. 14]
133 Derrick Witty, from an old postcard
134 John Romer
136 above, drawn by Constance and Brian Dear; below, Derrick Witty: Maspero 1881 [Chap. 13]
137 Derrick Witty: Maspero 1881 [Chap. 13]
139 Derrick Witty: Wilson 1887 [Chap. 14]
140, 142 Derrick Witty: Wilson 1887 [Chap. 14]
143 Derrick Witty: Maspero 1881 [Chap. 13]
144 John Romer: left, Daressy 1909 [Chap. 15]; right, Smith 1912 [Chap. 15]

145, 146, 149 Derrick Witty: Maspero 1881 [Chap. 13]
150 Derrick Witty: Maspero 1915 [Chap. 14]
154 Derrick Witty: Lefébure 1882 [Chap. 15]
157 John Romer: Davies *et al.* 1912 [Chap. 19]
159 Harry Burton (rephotographed John Romer), The Metropolitan Museum of Art, New York
160 Derrick Witty: Loret 1899 [Chap. 16]
162 Derrick Witty, from a postcard
165, 167, 168 John Romer
169 drawn by Constance and Brian Dear
172, 173 John Romer: Daressy 1902 [Chap. 16]
174 Derrick Witty: Naville 1916 [Chap. 22]
175 John Romer: Carter ('Sen-nefer') 1901 [Chap. 17]
176 Derrick Witty: Loret 1899 [Chap. 16]; annotations by hand in Library of the Brooklyn Museum, New York, 1901
180 Henri Maspero, © Mme Henri Maspero
184 drawn by Constance and Brian Dear
186 John Romer: Carter MSS © The Griffith Institute, Ashmolean Museum, Oxford
187, 189 John Romer: Davis *et al.* (*Thoutmôsis*) 1906 [Chap. 18]
190 drawn by Constance and Brian Dear
191 John Romer: Davis *et al.* (*Thoutmôsis*) 1906 [Chap. 18]
192 John Romer
193, 195 John Romer: Davis *et al.* (*Hâtshopsitû*) 1906 [Chap. 18]
198 drawn by Constance and Brian Dear
199 John Romer
201 John Romer: Davis *et al.* 1907 [Chap. 19]
202 Derrick Witty: Maspero 1908 [Chap. 19]
203 drawn by Constance and Brian Dear
204, 205 unknown photographer—possibly Harry Burton
207 John Romer
209 Derrick Witty: Davis *et al.* 1908 [Chap. 19]
211, 213, 214, 215, 217 John Romer: Davis *et al.* 1910 [Chap. 20]

223 Harry Burton, The Metropolitan Museum of Art, New York
223, 225 Derrick Witty: Davis *et al.* 1912 [Chap. 19]
226 drawn by Constance and Brian Dear
227 John Romer
228 Harry Burton (rephotographed John Romer), The Metropolitan Museum of Art, New York
229 above, Harry Burton (rephotographed John Romer), The Metropolitan Museum of Art, New York; below, Derrick Witty: Weigall 1911 [Chap. 19]
230 Derrick Witty: Hall 1915 [Chap. 21]
232 John Romer: Carter MSS © The Griffith Institute, Ashmolean Museum, Oxford
234 above, John Romer: Davis *et al.* 1912 [Chap. 19]; below, John Romer
235 John Romer
236 unknown photographer—possibly Harry Burton
237 drawn by Constance and Brian Dear
239 John Romer: Carter MSS © The Griffith Institute, Ashmolean Museum, Oxford
241 drawn by Constance and Brian Dear
242 John Romer
243 John Romer: Carter and Gardiner 1917 [Chap. 22]
245 Derrick Witty
246 drawn by Constance and Brian Dear
248, 249, 250, 251, 252 John Romer: Carter MSS © The Griffith Institute, Ashmolean Museum, Oxford
256 John Romer (probably Carter photographs): Carter MSS © The Griffith Institute Ashmolean Museum, Oxford
259, 261, 262, 264, 268, 269, 270 Harry Burton, © The Griffith Institute, Ashmolean Museum, Oxford
271 John Romer: Carter MSS © The Griffith Institute, Ashmolean Museum, Oxford
279 drawn by Constance and Brian Dear

Index

Italic figures refer the reader to a caption on that page. Captions are
not so indicated when there is a textural reference on the same page.